Language in the Inner City

LANGUAGE
IN THE
INNER CITY

Studies in the Black English Vernacular

WILLIAM LABOV

University of Pennsylvania Press
Philadelphia

Library of Congress Catalog Number: 72-80377
ISBN: (clothbound edition): 0-8122-7658-2
ISBN: (paper bound edition): 0–8122–1051–6
Printed in the United States of America

*To the Jets, the Cobras, and the Thunderbirds
who took on all odds and were dealt all low cards*

CONTENTS

FIGURES

TABLES

INTRODUCTION

These explorations of the black English vernacular will consider the language, the culture, the social organization, and the political situation of black youth in the inner cities of the United States. They begin with problems of linguistic analysis—the concerns of a linguist who asks how dialect differences may cause reading failure—and they extend to broader areas because the problem cannot be solved by the study of grammar narrowly conceived. But the black English vernacular is at the heart of the matter: it defines and is defined by the social organization of peer groups in the inner city.

By the "black English vernacular" we mean the relatively uniform dialect spoken by the majority of black youth in most parts of the United States today, especially in the inner city areas of New York, Boston, Detroit, Philadelphia, Washington, Cleveland, Chicago, St. Louis, San Francisco, Los Angeles, and other urban centers. It is also spoken in most rural areas and used in the casual, intimate speech of many adults. The term "black English" is not suitable for this dialect, since that phrase implies a dichotomy between Standard English on the one hand and black English on the other. "Black English" might best be used for the whole range of language forms used by black people in the United States: a very large range indeed, extending from the Creole grammar of Gullah spoken in the Sea Islands of South Carolina to the most formal and accomplished literary style. A great deal of misunderstanding has been created by the use of this term, "black English," which replaced our original "Nonstandard Negro English" when the latter became less acceptable to many people.

Throughout this volume I will then refer to the black English vernacular (BEV) as that relatively uniform grammar found in its most consistent form in the speech of black youth from 8 to 19 years old who participate fully in the street culture of the inner cities. Even within that restricted scope, there are no doubt regional differences not yet charted, and we are continuing to discover new aspects of the grammar in our past records and in new observations.

The findings reported here are the work of four investigators: myself, Paul Cohen, Clarence Robins, and John Lewis. Our work focuses on certain aspects of BEV grammar which assumed importance for us because of our interest in reading problems as well as our theoretical concerns. The definitive work on the grammar of BEV has not yet been done and will no doubt be written by black linguists who fully participate in the vernacular culture.

In our own group competence is divided between white researchers (Labov and Cohen) who are primarily linguists and outsiders to the vernacular culture, and black researchers (Robins and Lewis) who know the culture of the inner city as full participants and share a deep understanding of it, but who remain relative outsiders to linguistic theory. There are advantages to that combination, especially when it is coupled with controlled sociolinguistic methods; but we are looking forward to the deeper penetration that can be achieved by linguists from the black community.

In 1965, we began research supported by the Office of Education into the differences between the vernacular language of south-central Harlem and the standard English of the classroom (Cooperative Research Projects 3091 and 3288). Our major concern was the reading failure that was painfully obvious in the New York City schools. Did dialect differences have anything to do with it? From the outset, we did not feel that the study of the internal structure of BEV—its grammar and sound system—would provide all the answers we needed. It was true enough that this vernacular provided a great challenge for linguistic theory; while we generally understood what people were saying—especially the two members of the group who were raised in the community—yet we did not know the grammar. But as we proceeded, it seemed ever clearer that the major reading problems did not stem from structural interference in any simple sense, and our concern with the uses of the vernacular increased. One major conclusion of our work as it emerges in this volume is that the major causes of reading failure are political and cultural conflicts in the classroom, and dialect differences are important because they are symbols of this conflict.

We must then understand the way in which the vernacular culture uses language and how verbal skills develop in this culture. The tests, trials, screens, and checks of the school system report failure for black youth in a regular and systematic way; but they do not explain that failure (chapter 5). We find no connection between linguistic skill in the vernacular culture and success in reading (chapter 6). A large part of our work involved the documentation of those verbal skills, and the analysis of vernacular speech events (chapters 8 and 9). Our research is outside of school or any other adult-dominated, institutional setting; but we did gain access to the school records of our subjects and gain some insight into why these verbal skills could not be used in school.

The organization of this book reflects this dual approach to the structure and function of language. Part I (chapters 1-4) deals with the grammar and the sound system of the black English vernacular, especially the area where the two systems intersect. Chapters 1 and 2 are written with both linguistic and educational problems in mind, in a relatively nontechnical style which I hope will be accessible to all interested readers. Chapter 1 focuses on reading problems which may in fact proceed from such structural differences, but also shows in some detail how we approach such problems as the variation in simplification of consonant clusters, its effects on the -ed suffix and the consequences for reading. Chapter 2 addresses the broader question of whether BEV is a separate system, or more exactly, to what extent it forms a separate system and must be treated as such by those teaching standard English grammar. The approach here is synchronic—concerned with what the dialect is now in the urban centers where it is most uniform; at the same time, I try to indicate where the hypothesis of a Creole origin has illuminated my own thinking and is supported in the data.

Chapters 3 and 4 are detailed studies of specific aspects of the vernacular structure. Chapter 3 deals with the contraction and deletion of the copula, and its location in a larger set of ordered phonological rules. Chapter 4 concerns negative concord, or multiple negation, a nonstandard feature which involves a great many other aspects of English grammar. These are both technical studies, written primarily for linguists, and many readers interested in broader questions may not find them accessible. The findings of Chapters 3 and 4 are summarized in the previous and following chapters, and the book is so designed that a reader may move from chapter 2 to chapter 5 without loss of continuity. On the other hand, many linguists will find that chapters 3 and 4, making up one third of this book, are the most important parts for them. Chapter 3 is a study of variability which provides the basis for the development of variable rules, including recent innovations in the formal interpretation of these rules following Cedergren and Sankoff's probability model. Chapter 4 is a companion study of invariance, contrasting the obligatory rule of negative attraction with the variable rule of negative concord; it explores in some detail the relation of quantifiers to negation and the underlying features of the indeterminate *any*. Chapters 3 and 4 therefore provide the detailed background for the overall view of a socially realistic linguistics set forth in chapters 8 and 9 of *Sociolinguistic Patterns* (1972).

Part II examines the vernacular in its social setting, looking directly at the relations between the social system and the vernacular culture. "The Logic of Nonstandard English" (chapter 5) is a polemic directed against the deficit theory of educational psychologists who see the language of black children as inadequate for learning and logical thinking. This chapter also aims to show the relevance of linguistic data to the position of Jensen and others who claim that black children are genetically deficient in the ability to form concepts and solve problems. I have attempted to capture here the extraordinary consensus of linguists on this matter. Since this statement first appeared in the Georgetown Monograph Series of 1969, it has been widely reprinted; see also "Academic Ignorance and Black Intelligence," a condensed version in the *Atlantic Monthly* of June, 1972. Further implications for experimental psychology are spelled out in Cole and Bruner 1972.

Chapter 6 presents the most important data to proceed from our research: the comparison of reading success and failure with participation in the vernacular culture. Here we document the claim that the major problem in reading failure is the political and cultural conflict within the classroom. Chapter 7 explores more deeply the relation of BEV to social structure. In this discussion of "the linguistic consequences of being a lame" I present in greater detail the data which justifies the distinction between the broader term "black English" and the more specific "black English vernacular."

Part III contains two studies of the vernacular culture itself. Chapter 8 deals with the institution of ritual insults and chapter 9 with personal narrative. In both chapters I have attempted to develop some of the fundamental rules of discourse which will eventually enable us to treat the uses of language as systematically as we treat grammar. But these chapters are self-contained in their technical terminology and should be immediately accessible to all readers.

Some chapters of this volume have appeared elsewhere and are modified and rewritten to fit in with the present overall perspective and organization of the book. Chapter 3 in particular contains a radically revised formal interpretation of variable rules quite different from the original version. Chapters 1, 6, and 8 have been considerably revised here from their original form. Chapters 2, 7, and 9 were written for this book and have not previously appeared in print.

Source material for much of this discussion is to be found in the following two technical reports on our research in south-central Harlem: W. Labov, P. Cohen, and C. Robins, Cooperative Research Report 3091, "A Preliminary Study of the Structure of English Used by Negro and Puerto Rican Speakers in New York City" (1965); and W. Labov, P. Cohen, C. Robins, and J. Lewis, Cooperative Research Report 3288, "A Study of the Nonstandard English of Negro and Puerto Rican Speakers in New York City." Volume I: Phonological and Grammatical Analysis. Volume II: The use of language in the speech community (1968). These reports are currently being reproduced by the U.S. Regional Survey, 204 No. 35th St., Philadelphia 19104.

Throughout this report, references will be made to the final report as "CRR 3288." (In other publications, this is referred to as Labov, Cohen, Robins, and Lewis 1968).

Detailed accounts of the methods used in our research are given in these reports. Individual interviews are discussed in 3091 and the group sessions and experimental methods in 3288. In the remaining pages of this introduction I would like to give the reader some idea of these methods, since to evaluate what we have done it is necessary to present first some information on how it was done.

The nine chapters that follow are about the structure and the use of the vernacular; they are not "expert opinion" or intuitive notions about black English elicited in a formal setting. To obtain that information, we had to solve the Observer's Paradox, described in some detail in chapter 8 of *Sociolinguistic Patterns* which sums up the experience of previous sociolinguistic research in Martha's Vineyard, New York City and elsewhere. To obtain data on the most systematic form of language (the vernacular), we must observe how people speak when they are not being observed. The warrant for the nine chapters to follow must depend on the various methods we used to solve that paradox—or rather to approximate a solution, since it can never be entirely solved in principle.

Given the current state of black-white relations in the United States, the reader should certainly want to know how any report on the black English vernacular was prepared: who did the talking and who did the listening, who were the investigators, where did they work, and how did they attack the methodological problem. It is an unfortunate fact that most papers, articles, and discussions on black English fail heavily in this respect. Many are essentially scholastic rather than secular studies, based upon interviews in offices, schools, playgrounds, homes, and other formal institutions which reflect the dominance of adult, middle-class culture. Some are even based on formal face-to-face elicitation in the linguist's office, with one lame nonmember of the street culture whose connection with the vernacular is one of wishful approximation. To the best of my knowledge, the only other research project in black English that has been carried out by members of the community is Mitchell-Kernan 1969.

Our first research in south-central Harlem consisted of exploratory interviews carried out by myself and Clarence Robins, with Robins gradually assuming the major role. We then began a series of individual interviews with adolescents 10 to 12 years old in a geographically random series of "Vacation Day Camps" throughout Harlem. (see chapter 7). These interviews used techniques first developed in the Lower East Side study for overcoming the formal constraints of the interview situation (*Sociolinguistic Patterns,* chapter 3), but as noted below, the selection was biased towards isolated members of the community and the interview settings did not favor the vernacular. Some subjects in this series were peer-group members who we met later in a more favorable setting.

We then began the most important phase of our work: long-term participant-observation with peer groups. We first worked with the preadolescent "Thunderbirds," who lived in a single low-income project on Fifth Avenue (chapter 7). Our model was one that we continued to use throughout our work with peer groups: individual interviews with leading members of the group, followed by a series of group outings and group sessions. In the group sessions, the speech of each member was recorded through a lavaliere microphone on a separate track, and in addition the group as a whole was recorded on a central mike. The setting was essentially that of a party rather than an interview, with card games, eating and drinking, singing and sounding. The effect of observation and recording was of course present, but the natural interaction of the group overrode all other effects. Here is an extract from the second group session with the Thunderbirds (Tapes 451–456).

C. R.	Who's tougher, Alvin or Larry?	
Boot		Larry.
Money		Larry.
David		
Rickey		
Roger		D-D-D-D-D-Dem nigger's wild!

C. R.		
Boot	No.	And Alvin the dumbest! Alvin don't.
Money	No.	Alvin.
David		
Rickey	Uh-uh.	Alvin is.
Roger		Larry an' Alvin, they ust—they didn't

C. R.		How come?
Boot	Aks him to spell	"hurricane" yesterday.
Money	Alvin don't! (L)	Alvin don't! (Screaming)
David		
Rickey		
Roger	—do—they didn't fight with us. They didn't fight with

C. R.	
Boot	
Money	
David	Why? Alviinnn!!!
Rickey	That's his.
Roger	us. I don't know why; they jus—they turned yellow.

C. R.	They did? Why?	
Boot	Hunh? I know.	Alvinn!
Money	Oh, damnn!	
David		
Rickey	That's his.	
Roger		Tsk—Sometime they don't

C. R.	
Boot	(Aks him to spell it out, Mr. Cohen.)
Money	Alvin!

David
Rickey
Roger   wanna fight. You know—and sometime—dat's why they

C. R.
Boot
Money   He can't spell it?
David   Everybo—   Everybody alw—
Rickey
Roger   don't come to c'ub meeting'. So I—I put 'em out.

Five leading members of the Thunderbirds are present, along with
Clarence Robins. This extract is to be read like a musical score;
whatever speech is found in any of the six rows is spoken simultaneously with the others. There is an extraordinary amount of overlap: in the second and third lines, four of the six people present are
talking at once. We can see how Boot, the verbal leader, dominates
the group. In one sequence after another Boot speaks up first, Money
repeats his answer a half-second later, and in some cases David or
Rickey join in a few seconds later. The other co-equal leader of the
group, Roger, is not dominated by Boot and answers independently
here. Note that in the sixth line Boot turns to Money and instructs
him under cover of the general commotion to ask Paul Cohen how
to spell *hurricane,* which he has just accused Alvin of not being able
to spell.

   We developed contacts with another preadolescent group in a
neighboring building, the "Aces," and also began a parallel series of
individual interviews and group sessions with an older group in the
Thunderbirds' building, the "Oscar Brothers." We then turned to our
major study of adolescent peer groups in the tenement area from
110th St. to 118th St. between Fifth and Seventh Avenues. At this
point, John Lewis ("K.C.") joined our research group. He was one
of the young adults that Clarence Robins had first interviewed in
our exploratory series, and it was immediately evident to us that
John Lewis had a great command of the vernacular (some of his own
stories are found in chapter 9) and was also an excellent field worker.
He was the participant-observer in our work with the "Jets" and the
"Cobras," the two named peer groups in the tenement area we were
considering. Lewis rented a "club-house" on 112th St. and associated
with the Jets daily through most of 1966. The Jets and Cobras were

then hostile to each other, and Lewis acted on his own concern as an intermediary and peace-maker between the groups. The Cobras were deeply involved in nationalist ideology; as members of "The Nation of Islam" headed by Clarence 37X Smith they became vegetarians, developed a deep knowledge of Islamic lore, and believed for a time that the world was coming to an end on July 4, 1966. (On the depth and seriousness of this belief, see CRR 3288: 4.2.5). They became "The Bohemian Brothers" and then simply "The Nation"; and they then temporarily broke off all relations with us. The Jets were hostile to Islam and all religious thinking, partly due to the climate of the area in which they lived. The Jets included 37 members when they expanded to include the neighboring block; some of the group sessions included nine or ten members and frequently broke up into several conversations. The following extract is from the second group session with the Jets (Tapes 572–578).

```
KC (to Grp)       Awright, man. Card game over. Okay, Brothers.
Rel           Hey, you like—Hey, look at dat—(to Reg) Hey, quit.
Stn
Reg
Lar
Stv
Tom
Jhn (to Tnk)                            Fat-man Tinkerrr! Blub-
Tnk
```
```
KC (to Grp)       Card game over. O.K. Brothers. Brothers put the
Rel (to Reg)
Stn
Reg (to Pch)
Lar (to Grp)      Card game over!!! (shouting)
Stv
Tom (to John)                              Say, Blackmaaan!
Jhn         berrrr!
Tnk
```
```
KC (to Grp)   cards away, Brothers, put the cards back, put the cards
Rel (to Pch)  Now (if) you d-      (if) you don't stop, man.
Stn
Reg (to Grp)                                              Let's
Lar (to Grp)       Card game over!!! (shouting)
Stv (to Tom) (singing)  Di-di-di-di-di-di-              Di-di-di-
```

Tom
Jhn
Tnk

KC (to Grp)   back (intoning)
Rel (to Reg)
Stn
Reg (to Grp)   get some more money, get five dollars and get a bag.
Lar
Stv (to Tom)   di-di-di-   black maaan! (singing)
Tom
Jhn
Tnk

We have more information on this Jet session than the Thunderbirds session since we used a videotape recorder for most of it. We know who was talking to whom, what the members were doing, and what gestures they used. This particular extract occurs just as K.C. is arguing with the group to stop the card playing in favor of something else; the Jets are showing their usual resistance to any suggestion. As K.C. intones "Card game over" there are three separate activities going on among the members. Among the older members of the group, Rel (prime minister) is arguing on one side with Reginald (vice-president) who is beginning to play solitaire and on the other side with Peaches who is trying to burn him with a cigarette. Larry makes an insincere show of putting the group in order, putting his hand to his mouth and calling out "Card game over!" in imitation of K.C. Reginald then makes another disruptive move, suggesting that they get a bag of reefer (marijuana). Completely apart from this activity, younger members of the Jets from the "200's block" are exchanging ritual insults (chapter 8). First Johnny insults Tinker by sounding on his ritualized attribute of "Blubber." Then Stevie insults Johnny in a complicated way, playing on two ritual attributes. He looks sideways at Johnny and rubs the top of his head with the flat of his hand, and at the same time sings the theme from the television show "Batman," ending with "Black maannn!" Johnny is the blackest member of the group. Furthermore, he had a curious bald spot on the top of his head several months ago, since grown over, and he is still sounded on regularly by reference to this bald spot throughout our sessions.

In this extract, we see how even the strong intervention of John

Lewis fails to dampen the peer-group interaction, which erupts continually in bursts of sounding, mock fighting, and other ritual activity. From the group sessions we obtain our best records of the vernacular grammar, as well as a wealth of information on the use of language.

John Lewis carried out in full the S-G-S paradigm, in which he interviewed some leaders of the group first, then after many outings and group sessions, completed the individual interviews with each member. Some of these later interviews were conducted with two Jets and rivaled the group sessions in naturalness and intensity of interaction. Chapter 6 quotes an argument between Junior and Ronald taken from one of these double interviews.

We also interviewed isolated individuals in the Thunderbirds building and in the Jet and Cobra areas to compare their use of black English to the basic vernacular of the peer groups (chapter 7). We then began a series of 100 interviews with adults, carried out by Clarence Robins. A random sample was constructed of 20 middle-class adults from the Lenox and Riverton apartment houses, 40 working-class adults from the Cobra area and 40 from the Jet area. These interviews followed the Lower East Side model, considerably developed in the light of the BEV value system: casual speech emerged from the main body of the interview (careful speech) at predictable points. This casual speech contrasts with careful speech in the same interview in roughly the same way as speech in the adolescent group sessions contrasts with speech in their individual interviews.

Finally, we carried out our S-G-S paradigm with two groups of white boys from the Inwood section of upper Manhattan: one pre-adolescent and the other adolescent. This area was as remote from direct black influence as one could find in Manhattan, although we did find some indirect influence of BEV in the speech of the Inwood groups (chapter 7). The interviewing and group sessions were carried out by Paul Cohen and Joshua Waletzky.

A more complete account of the methodology is given in CRR 3288, along with a description of a number of formal tests: repetition tests, subjective reaction tests, vernacular correction tests, and classroom correction tests. But the account just given of the group sessions should give the reader the basic orientation of our approach to the vernacular which warrants and justifies much of the discussion to follow.

It is obvious from what has just been said about our methods that I am heavily indebted to Clarence Robins, John Lewis, and Paul Cohen. The many contributions of Cohen are present in almost every chapter: he not only did most of the transcription and detailed analysis of the linguistic variables, but contributed a great deal to the solution of theoretical problems at each point. In addition, important contributions were made by Joshua Waletzky, especially in the formulation of variable rules; the work on narrative analysis in chapter 9 was carried out primarily by Waletzky. Benji Wald also made a number of valuable contributions to our work.

I am especially indebted to my wife Teresa, who did the analysis underlying chapter 7. The sociometric diagrams and the basic understanding of Jet peer-group structure are her work, and many other suggestions and insights which greatly increased our understanding of the social structures we encountered.

The formulation of variable rules in chapter 3 has been revised in the light of the important contributions of Henrietta Cedergren and David Sankoff. Their probability model has added greatly to the theoretical coherence of this representation and opened up new prospects for quantitative analysis which should have profound effects on linguistic theory.

Chapter 4 owes a great deal to the insights of Harris Savin, whose contributions to the analysis of *any* are the basis of section 6 of that chapter, which is greatly revised from the original analysis in CRR 3288.

During the initial stages of the preparation of this book, I benefited from a fellowship from the Guggenheim Foundation, and I would like to acknowledge their assistance with thanks. In the final past year, I have acted as Research Professor with the Center for Urban Ethnography at the University of Pennsylvania. The support of the Center has made it possible to complete this book. I am particularly indebted to Erving Goffman, whose initial impetus and strong encouragement is responsible for its existence.

Language in the Inner City

Part I

THE STRUCTURE
OF THE
BLACK ENGLISH
VERNACULAR

1 Some Sources of Reading Problems for Speakers of the Black English Vernacular

IN the past ten years, a number of linguists have turned to the study of the nonstandard English spoken by black people in the inner city: the black English vernacular (BEV). From this study, linguists have learned a great deal about the nature of language, and chapters 2-4 of this volume document the impact of this data on linguistic theory. But it remains to be seen how much society can profit from what linguists have learned. These studies were made possible by public and private agencies that hoped linguistic knowledge would help solve the enormous educational problems of the inner city. In the first year that we began the exploration of the BE vernacular in south-central Harlem, we presented the analysis in this chapter to the National Council of Teachers of English.[1] It is addressed squarely to the most critical problem: in what way can an understanding of structural differences between BEV and the standard language help teachers of reading?

It seems natural to look at any educational problem in terms of the particular type of ignorance which is to be overcome. In this chapter, we will be concerned with two opposing and complementary types:

> Ignorance of standard English rules on the part of speakers of nonstandard English
> Ignorance of nonstandard English rules on the part of teachers and text writers

1. Reprinted by permission from A. Frazier (ed.), *New Directions in Elementary English* (Champaign, Ill., National Council of Teachers of English, 1967), pp. 140-67. The material has been slightly revised.

In other words, the fundamental situation that we face is one of reciprocal ignorance, where teacher and student are ignorant of each other's system, and therefore of the rules needed to translate from one system to another.

The consequences of this situation may be outlined in the following way. When the teacher attempts to overcome the first kind of ignorance by precept and example in the classroom, she discovers that the student shows a strong and inexplicable resistance to learning the few simple rules that he needs to know. He is told over and over again, from the early grades to the twelfth, that -ed is required for the past participle ending, but he continues to write:

> I have live here twelve years.

and he continues to mix up past and present tense forms in his reading. In our series of interviews with Harlem youngsters from 10 to 16 years old, we asked them to correct to classroom English such sentences as the following:

> He pick me.
> He don't know nobody.
> He never play no more, man.
> The man from U.N.C.L.E. hate the guys from Thrush.

Words such as *man* and *guys* are frequently corrected, and *ain't* receives a certain amount of attention. But the double negative is seldom noticed, and the absence of the grammatical signals -s and -ed is rarely detected by children in the fifth, sixth, or seventh grades. It seems reasonable to ask what connection there is between this lack of attention to English inflections and the fact that most of them have difficulty in reading sentences at the second grade level.

There are many reasons for the persistence of ignorance. Here I will be concerned with the role played by the second type: the fact that the child's teacher has no systematic knowledge of the nonstandard forms which oppose and contradict standard English. Some teachers are reluctant to believe that there are systematic principles in nonstandard English which differ from those of standard English. They look upon every deviation from schoolroom English as inherently evil, and they attribute these mistakes to laziness, sloppiness, or the child's natural disposition to be wrong. For these teachers, there is no substantial difference in the teaching of reading and the teaching of geography. The child is simply ignorant of geography;

he does not have a well-formed system of nonstandard geography to be analyzed and corrected. From this point of view, teaching English is a question of imposing rules upon chaotic and shapeless speech, filling a vacuum by supplying rules where no rules existed before.

Other teachers are sincerely interested in understanding the language of the children, but their knowledge is fragmentary and ineffective. They feel that the great difficulties in teaching black and Puerto Rican children to read are due in part to the systematic contradictions between the rules of language used by the child and the rules used by the teacher. The contribution which I hope to make here is to supply a systematic basis for the study of the nonstandard English of black and Puerto Rican children, and some factual information, so that educators and text writers can design their teaching efforts with these other systems in mind.

Priority of Problems

Within the school curriculum, there seems to be an order of priority of educational problems that we face in large urban centers. Many skills have to be acquired before we can say that a person has learned standard English. The following list is a scale of priority that I would suggest as helpful in concentrating our attention on the most important problems:

a. Ability to understand spoken English (of the teacher).
b. Ability to read and comprehend.
c. Ability to communicate (to the teacher) in spoken English.
d. Ability to communicate in writing.
e. Ability to write in standard English grammar.
f. Ability to spell correctly.
g. Ability to use standard English grammar in speaking.
h. Ability to speak with a prestige pattern of pronunciation (and avoid stigmatized forms).

I would revise this list if it appeared that the teacher could literally not understand the speech or writing of the child; weaknesses in *c* or *d* could conceivably interfere with the solution to *b*. But considering all possibilities, this list would be my best estimate, as a relative outsider to the field of elementary education; it is of course subject to correction by educators.

In dealing with children from English-speaking homes, we usually assume *a*. In the extreme cases where the child cannot understand the literal meaning of the teacher, we have to revise our approach to teach this ability first. For the most part, however, we take the first academic task of the child to be *b*, developing the ability to read and comprehend. Certainly reading is first and most urgent in terms of its effect on the rest of learning, and it is most seriously compromised in the schools of the ghetto areas in large northern cities. The problem of reading is so striking today that it offers a serious intellectual challenge as well as a pressing social problem. One must understand why so many children are not learning to read or give up any claim to understand the educational process as a whole.

Structural vs. Functional Conflicts

We have dealt so far with a series of abilities. Obviously the desire to learn is in some way prior to the act of learning. Our research for the Office of Education was concerned with two aspects of the problem:

1. Structural conflicts of standard and nonstandard English: interference with learning ability stemming from a mismatch of linguistic structures.
2. Functional conflicts of standard and nonstandard English: interference with the desire to learn standard English stemming from a mismatch in the functions which standard and nonstandard English perform in a given culture.

In this chapter and the three following, we will be concerned only with the first type of conflict; the second will be the focus of the rest of this volume.

We should also consider whose speech, and whose learning problems, must be analyzed. Here again there is an order of priority, based on the numbers of people involved, the extent of neglect, and the degree of structural differences involved. In these terms, the educational problems of the black children in large cities must be considered most pressing; secondly, those of Puerto Rican and Mexican children from Spanish-speaking homes; and third, the problems of white youth from Appalachian backgrounds and other underprivileged areas.

Is there a black speech pattern? This question has provoked a great deal of discussion in the last few years, much more than it deserves. At many meetings on educational problems of ghetto areas, time which could have been spent in constructive discussion has been devoted to arguing the question as to whether a black dialect exists. The debates have not been conducted with any large body of factual information in view, but rather in terms of what the speakers wish to be so, or what they fear might follow in the political arena.

For those who have not participated in such debates, it may be difficult to imagine how great are the pressures against the recognition, description, or even mention of black speech patterns. For various reasons, many teachers, principals, and civil rights leaders wish to deny that the existence of patterns of black speech is a linguistic and social reality in the United States today. The most careful statement of the situation as it actually exists might read as follows: Many features of pronunciation, grammar, and lexicon are closely associated with black speakers—so closely as to identify the great majority of black people in the northern cities by their speech alone.

The match between this speech pattern and membership in the black ethnic group is of course far from complete. Many black speakers have none—or almost none—of these features. Many northern whites, living in close proximity to blacks, have these features in their own speech. But this overlap does not prevent the features from being identified with black speech by most listeners: we are dealing with a stereotype which provides correct identification in the great majority of cases and that therefore has a firm base in social reality.[2] Such stereotypes are the social basis of language perception; this is merely one of many cases where listeners generalize from the variable data to categorical perception in absolute terms. It may be socially useful to correct these stereotypes in a certain number of individual cases, so that people learn to limit their generalizations to the precise degree that their experience warrants, but the overall tendency is based upon very regular principles of human behavior, and people will continue to identify as black speech the pattern which they hear from the great majority of the black people that they meet.

In the South, the overlap is much greater. There is good reason

<hr>

2. For empirical research on such subjective reactions to speech, see CRR 3288:4.6, and Shuy, Baratz, and Wolfram 1969.

to think that most features of the black speech pattern have their origin in dialects spoken by both blacks and whites in some parts of the South. Almost every feature of BEV can be found among some white speakers in the South.[3] But many such forms are more frequent among black speakers: for example, it seems most likely that the small incidence of the deletion of *is* among whites is the result of black influence on white speech. Beyond this, there are many structural aspects and marginal phenomena of BEV which point to a strong Creole influence or origin, or at least indicate that in the past this vernacular was more different from other dialects than it is today (Stewart 1968, 1970). Given that some process of alignment or de-Creolization has occurred, the immediate historical background of BEV is that it was formed as a southern regional pattern and became aligned with the grammar and phonology of other southern dialects before it emerged as the uniform pattern we find in northern cities. The black speech pattern that we are dealing with in northern cities is therefore a regional speech pattern. We might stop speaking of black speech and begin using the term "southern regional speech" if that would make the political and social situation more manageable. But if we do so, we must not deceive ourselves and come to believe that this is an accurate description of the current situation. The following points cannot be overlooked in any such discussion:

1. For most northern whites, the only familiar example of southern speech is that of the black people they hear, and these southern features function as markers of black ethnic membership, not southern origin.

2. Many characteristic features of southern speech have been generalized along strictly ethnic lines in northern cities. For example, the absence of a distinction between /i/ and /e/ before nasals (*pin* equal to *pen*) has become a marker of the black group in New York City, so that most young black children of northern and southern background alike show this feature while no white children are affected.

3. In this merger of northern and southern patterns in the northern black communities, a great many southern features are being elimi-

---

3. There have been a number of reports on southern speech that show whites using invariant *be* and deleting *is*. James Sledd (pers. comm.) has observed one white southerner who always dropped *is* after *This*. James K. Bachman has shown that white school children in Alexandria, Va., delete *is* as well as blacks but much less often.

nated. Thus in New York and other northern cities, we find that young black people do not distinguish *four* and *for, which* and *witch;* while monophthongization of *high* and *wide* is common, the extreme fronting of the initial vowel to the position of *cat,* or near it, is less and less frequent; the back upglide of *ball* and *hawk,* so characteristic of many southern areas, is rarely heard; grammatical features such as the perfective auxiliary *done* in *he done told me,* or the double modal of *might could,* are becoming less common. As a result, a speaker fresh from the south is plainly marked in the northern black communities, and his speech is ridiculed. Black speech is thus not to be identified with southern regional speech.

4. The white southern speech which is heard in many northern cities—Chicago, Detroit, Cleveland—is the southern mountain pattern of Appalachia, and this pattern does not have many of the phonological and grammatical features of black speech.

5. Many of the individual features of black speech can be found in northern white speech, as we will see, and even more so in the speech of educated white Southerners. But the frequency of these features, such as consonant cluster simplification, and their distribution in relation to grammatical boundaries, is radically different in black speech, and we are forced in many cases to infer the existence of different underlying grammatical forms and rules.

6. There are some features of BEV which are indeed unique to this dialect and which seem to reflect an organization of the tense and aspect system different from other dialects. Whereas the habitual invariant *be* in *He always be doing that* is found among some white speakers, it is much rarer to find recognition and understanding of *been* in *I been know your name,* meaning 'I have known for a long time and still do.'

We can sum up this discussion of the southern regional pattern by saying that we are witnessing the transformation of a regional speech pattern with possible Creole origins into a class and ethnic pattern in the northern cities. This is not a new phenomenon; it has occurred many times in the history of English. According to H. Kökeritz (1953) and H. C. Wyld (1936), such a process was taking place in Shakespeare's London, where regional dialects from the east and southeast opposed more conservative dialects within the city as middle-class and lower-class speech against aristocratic speech. We see the same process operating today in the suburbs of New York City; where the Connecticut and New Jersey patterns meet the New

York City pattern, the New York City pattern becomes associated with lower socioeconomic groups.[4]

The existence of a black speech pattern must not be confused of course with the myth of a biologically, racially, exclusively black speech. The idea that dialect differences are due to some form of laziness or carelessness must be rejected with equal firmness. Anyone who continues to endorse such myths can be refuted easily by such subjective reaction tests as the Family Background test which we used in our research in Harlem (CRR 3288, Vol. 2:266). Sizable extracts from the speech of 14 individuals are played in sequence for listeners who are asked to identify the family backgrounds of each. So far, we find no one who can even come close to a correct identification of black and white speakers. This result does not contradict the statement that there exists a socially based black speech pattern: it supports everything that I have said above on this point. The voices heard on the test are the exceptional cases: blacks raised without any black friends in solidly white areas; whites raised in areas dominated by black cultural values; white Southerners in Gullah-speaking territory; blacks from small northern communities untouched by recent migrations; college-educated blacks who reject the northern ghetto and the South alike. The speech of these individuals does not identify them as black or white because they do not use the speech patterns which are characteristically black or white for northern listeners. The identifications made by these listeners, often in violation of actual ethnic membership categories, show that they respond to black speech patterns as a social reality.

Relevant Patterns of Black Speech

One approach to the study of nonstandard black speech is to attempt a complete description of this form of language without direct reference to standard English (SE). This approach can be quite revealing and can save us from many pitfalls in the easy identifica-

---

4. Such a phenomenon can be observed in suburban Bergen County, along the boundary of the New York City dialect area. In Closter, N.J., for example, the socioeconomic differentiation of speakers by r-pronunciation seems to be much more extreme than in the city itself: middle-class children may pronounce final and preconsonantal /r/ consistently, while working-class children will be completely r-less, and this difference is maintained over a wide range of stylistic contexts.

tion of forms that are only apparently similar. But as an overall plan, it is not realistic. We are far from achieving a complete description of standard English, to begin with; the differences between BEV and other dialects are slight compared to their similarities; and finally, some of these differences are far more relevant to reading problems than others. Let us therefore consider some of the most relevant patterns of black speech from the point of view of reading problems.

Some black-white differences are plainly marked and easy for any observer to note. In the following examples, the black forms are patterns which frequently occur in our recordings of individual and group sessions with boys from 10 to 17 years old—ranging from careful speech in face-to-face interaction with adults to the most excited and spontaneous activity within the primary (closed network) group:

Black	*White*
It don't all be her fault.	It isn't always her fault.
Hit him upside the head.	Hit him in the head.
The rock say 'Shhh!'	The rock went 'Shhh!'
I'm a shoot you.	I'm g'na shoot you.
I wanna be a police.	I wanna be a policeman.
Ah 'on' know. [a o no]	I d'know. [aᴵdnoᵁ]

Now consider the following examples, in which black-white differences are less plainly marked and very difficult for most people to hear:

Black	*White*
He [pæsɨm] yesterday.	He [pæsdɨm] yesterday.
Give him [ðeᵀ] book.	Give him [ðɛ⊥] book.
This [jɔːɣ] place?	This [jɔːᵊ]place?
[ðæs] Nick boy.	[ðæᵗs] Nick's boy.
He say, [kæːᵉl] is.	He says, [kærəl] is.
My name is [bu].	My name is [buʔ].

This second series represents a set of slight phonetic differences, sometimes prominent, but more often unnoticed by the casual listener. These differences are much more significant than the first set in terms of learning and reading standard English. In truth, the differences are so significant that they will be the focus of attention in the balance of this paper. The slight phonetic signals observed here indicate systematic differences that may lead to reading problems and problems of being understood.

Corresponding to the phonetic transcriptions on the left, we can and do infer such grammatical constructions and lexical forms as:

> He pass him yesterday.
> Give him they book.
> This you-all place?
> That's Nick boy.
> He say, Ca'ol is.
> My name is Boo.

Each of these sentences is representative of a large class of phonological and grammatical differences which oppose BEV to SE. The most important are those in which large-scale phonological differences coincide with important grammatical differences. The result of this coincidence is the existence of a large number of homonyms in the speech of black children which are different from the set of homonyms in the speech system used by the teacher. If the teacher knows about this different set of homonyms, no serious problems in the teaching of reading need occur; but if the teacher does not know, there are bound to be difficulties.

The simplest way to organize this information seems to be under the headings of the important rules of the sound system which are affected. By using lists of homonyms as examples, it will be possible to avoid a great deal of phonetic notation and to stay with the essential linguistic facts. In many cases, the actual phonetic form is irrelevant: it is the presence or absence of a distinction which is relevant. Thus, for example, it makes no difference whether a child says [pɪn] or [pɪ³n] or [peː³n] or [pɛn] for the word *pen;* what counts is whether or not this word is distinct from *pin.* The linguistic fact of interest is the existence of contrast, not the particular phonetic forms that are heard from one moment to another. A child might seem to distinguish [pɪn] and [pɛn] in northern style in one pair of sentences, but if the basic phonemic contrast is not present, the same child might reverse the forms in the next sentence, and say [pɪn] for *ink pen* and [pɛn] for *safety pin.* A linguistic orientation will not supply teachers with a battery of phonetic symbols, but rather encourage them to observe what words can or cannot be distinguished by the children they are teaching.

Some Phonological Variables and
Their Grammatical Consequences

1. r-lessness

There are three major dialect areas in the eastern United States where the r of spelling is not pronounced as a consonant before other consonants or at the ends of words: eastern New England, New York City, and the South (Upper and Lower). Thus speakers from Boston, New York, Richmond, Charleston, or Atlanta will show only a lengthened vowel in *car, guard*, or *for*, and usually an obscure centering glide [ə] in place of r in *fear, feared, care, cared, moor, moored, bore*, or *bored*. This is what we mean by r-less pronunciation. Most of these areas have been strongly influenced in recent years by the r-pronouncing pattern which is predominant in broadcasting, so that educated speakers, especially young people, will show a mixed pattern in their careful speech.[5] When the original r-less pattern is preserved, we can obtain such homonyms as the following:[6]

guard	= god	par	= pa
nor	= gnaw	fort	= fought
sore	= saw	court	= caught

and we find that *yeah* can rhyme with *fair*, *idea* with *fear*.

Black speakers show an even higher degree of r-lessness than New Yorkers or Bostonians. The r of spelling becomes a glide or disappears before vowels as well as before consonants or pauses. Thus in the speech of most white New Yorkers, r is pronounced when a

---

5. In New York City, the correlation of (r) and stylistic context follows a very regular pattern (*Social Stratification, Sociolinguistic Patterns*). Black speakers are especially sensitive to the prestige status of /r/. The systematic shift indicates the importance of controlling the stylistic factor, as well as socioeconomic factors, in gathering data on speech patterns.

6. In many cases, pairs such as *guard-god, nor-gnaw* are differentiated by vowel quality. For most black speakers in northern cities, they are identical. Pairs such as *sore-saw* or *court-caught*, which oppose M.E. closed o before r to long open o, are differentiated more often by vowel quality, especially among older people. In any case, the lists of homonyms given here and elsewhere are given as examples of possible homonyms illustrative of large classes of words that are frequently identical.

It should be noted that words with mid-central vowels before r do not follow the r-less patterns discussed here; r appears much more frequently in such words as *work, shirt, bird*, even when it is not used after other vowels.

vowel follows in *four o'clock*; even though the r is found at the end
of a word, if the next word begins with a vowel, it is pronounced
as a consonantal [r]. For most black speakers, r is still not pronounced
in this position and so is never heard at the end of the word *four*.
The white speaker is helped in his reading or spelling by the existence of the alternation: [fɔːfiːt, fɔrəklak], but the black speaker has
no such clue to the underlying (spelling) form of the word *four*.
Furthermore, the same black speaker may not pronounce intervocalic r in the middle of a word, as indicated in the dialect spelling
inte'ested, Ca'ol. He has no clue, in his own speech, to the correct spelling form of such words, and may have another set of possible homonyms besides those listed above:

> Carol   = Cal
> Paris   = pass
> terrace = test

Another aspect of the r-less pattern is the deletion of postconso-
nantal /r/ before back rounded vowels. Thus /r/ is deleted particularly in *throw, through, threw, throat*, and occasionally after other
initial consonants. The result of this pattern is not so much homonymy with other words as the difficulty in reading words or looking
them up in the dictionary. In some areas (e.g., Philadelphia) there
is an additional tendency to affricate *tr-* so that it merges with /tʃ/,
giving as possible homonyms

> trial   = child
> trolley = Charlie
> true   = chew

2. l-lessness

The consonant *l* is a liquid very similar to *r* in its phonetic nature.
The chief difference is that with *l* the center of the tongue is up,
and the sides are down, while with *r* the sides are up but the center
does not touch the roof of the mouth. The pattern of *l*-dropping is
very similar to that of *r*, except that it has never affected entire
dialect areas in the same sweeping style. When *l* disappears, it is
often replaced by a back unrounded glide, sometimes symbolized
[ɣ], instead of the center glide that replaces *r*; in many cases, *l*
disappears entirely, especially after the back rounded vowels. The
loss of *l* is much more marked among the black speakers we have

interviewed than among whites in northern cities, and they therefore
have much greater tendencies towards such homonyms as:

toll	= toe	all	= awe
help	= hep	Saul	= saw
tool	= too	fault	= fought

3. Simplification of Consonant Clusters

One of the most complex variables appearing in black speech is
the general tendency towards the simplification of consonant clusters
at the ends of words. A great many clusters are involved, primarily
those which end in /t/ or /d/, /s/ or /z/.[7] We are actually dealing
with two distinct tendencies: (1) a general tendency to reduce clusters
of consonants at the ends of words to single consonants, and (2) a
more general process of reducing the amount of information provided after stressed vowels, so that individual final consonants are
affected as well. The first process is the most regular and requires
the most intensive study in order to understand the conditioning
factors involved.

The chief /t,d/ clusters that are affected are (roughly in order of
frequency)/-st, -ft, -nt, -nd, -ld, -zd, -md/. Here they are given in
phonemic notation; in conventional spelling we have words such as
*past, passed, lift, laughed, bent, bend, fined, hold, poled, old, called,
raised, aimed.* In all these cases, if the cluster is simplified, it is the
last element that is dropped. Thus we have homonyms such as:

past	= pass	mend	= men
rift	= riff	wind	= wine
meant	= men	hold	= hole

If we combine the effect of *-ld* simplification, loss of *-l*, and monophthongization of /ay/ and /aw/, we obtain

  [šiwa: ɤ]   She wow! = She wild!

and this equivalence has in fact been found in our data. It is important to bear in mind that the combined effect of several rules will

---

7. When the /t/ or /d/ represents a grammatical inflection, these consonants are
usually automatic alternants of the same abstract form *-ed*. Phonetic rules delete the
vowel (except after stems ending in /t/ or /d/), and we then have /t/ following
voiceless consonants such as /p, s, š, k/ and /d/ in all other cases. In the same way
/s/ and /z/ are coupled as voiceless and voiced alternants of the same *-s* inflection.
But in clusters that are a part of the root, we do not have such automatic alternation.

add to the total number of homonyms, and even more, to the unexpected character of the final result:

  told = told = toe

In addition, there are two clusters ending in other consonants
which are frequently reduced: -sp and -sk in wasp, ask, desk, etc.
Together with -st, these clusters lose the final stop much more often
than any of the others given above, so that they can actually be dealt
with as part of a separate rule (CRR 3288:3.2). Simplification is
obligatory for black speakers when a final -s is added, so that the
plurals of wasp, test, desk never show the clusters -sps, -sts, -sks.
The major forms that are heard are wasses, tesses, desses [wɑsɪz,
tɛsɪz, dɛsɪz] or was', des', tes' with occasional [wɑspɪz, wɑpsɪz]. The
effect of these processes can give such homonyms as

  best = Bess
  guest = guess
  asks = ask   = ass

More importantly, the simplification of -sp, -st, -sk clusters may be
so strong that children do not have the same underlying forms as
SE standard forms of these words (see below).

The first impression that we draw from casual listening is that
black speakers show much more consonant cluster simplification
than white speakers. But this conclusion is far from obvious when
we examine the data carefully. Table 1.1 shows the total simplifica-

TABLE 1.1.
OVERALL SIMPLIFICATION OF /t,d/ CONSONANT
CLUSTERS FOR TWO NEW YORKERS

Consonant cluster	BF (black)		AO (white)	
	Number simplified	Total clusters	Number simplified	Total clusters
/-st/	29	37	18	23
/-ft/	7	9	0	2
/-nt/	8	16	14	29
/-nd/	8	14	8	14
/-ld/	8	15	2	4
/-zd/	5	8	3	4
/-md/	2	3	0	1
other	4	4	1	4
Total	71	106	46	81

tion of consonant clusters for two speakers: BF is a black working-class man, 45 years old, raised in New York City; AO is a white working-class man, of Austrian-German background, 56 years old, also raised in New York City but with little contact with blacks.

The overall percentage of simplification for BF is 67 percent, not very much more than for AO, 57 percent. Furthermore, the individual clusters show remarkably similar patterns; for the larger cells, the percentages are almost identical. It is true that the social distribution of this feature is wider for blacks than for whites, but the sharpest differences are not in this particular phonetic process. As we shall see below, it is the nature of the grammatical conditioning that restricts the deletion of the final consonant.

The other set of clusters which seem to be simplified are those ending in /-s/ or /-z/, words like *axe* /æks/, *six* /siks/, *box* /baks/, *parts* /parts/, *aims* /eymz/, *rolls* /rowlz/, *leads* /liydz/, *besides* /bisaydz/, *John's* /džanz/, *that's* /ðæts/, *it's* /its/, *its* /its/. The situation here is more complex than with the /t,d/ clusters, since in some cases the first element of the cluster is lost, and in other cases the second element.[8] Furthermore, the comparison of the same two speakers BF and AO shows a radical difference (see Table 1.2).

TABLE 1.2.
OVERALL SIMPLIFICATION OF /s,z/ CONSONANT
CLUSTERS FOR TWO NEW YORKERS

BF (black)			AO (white)		
1st Cons. dropped	*2nd Cons. dropped*	*Total clusters*	*1st Cons. dropped*	*2nd Cons. dropped*	*Total clusters*
31	18	98	6	4	69

This overall view of the situation is only a preliminary to a much more detailed study, but it does serve to show that the "simplification" of the /s,z/ clusters is much more characteristic of black speakers than of white speakers. The comparison of these two

8. The loss of the first element—that is, assimilation to the following /s/—is most common in forms where the /s/ represents the verb *is* or the pronoun *us* as in *it's*, *what's*, *that's* and *let's*. In none of these cases is there a problem of homonymy, even in the case of *let's* where there is no likelihood of confusion with *less*. This type of simplification will therefore not be considered in any further detail. It should be noted that "simplification" in regard to the loss of final /s/ is merely a device for presenting the data: we will be forced to conclude that the /s/ is not there to begin with in many cases.

speakers is typical of the several hundred black and white subjects that we studied.

In one sense, there are a great many homonyms produced by this form of consonant cluster simplification, as we shall see when we consider grammatical consequences. But many of these can also be considered to be grammatical differences rather than changes in the shapes of words. The /t,d/ simplification gives us a great many irreducible homonyms, where a child has no clue to the standard spelling differences from his own speech pattern. Though this is less common in the case of /s,z/ clusters, we can have such extreme mergers as

$$
\begin{array}{ll}
\text{six} = \text{sick} & \text{Max} = \text{Mack} \\
\text{box} = \text{bock} & \text{mix} = \text{Mick}
\end{array}
$$

as possible homonyms in the speech of some black children.

4. Weakening of Final Consonants

It was noted above that the simplification of final consonant clusters was part of a more general tendency to produce less information after stressed vowels, so that final consonants, unstressed final vowels, and weak syllables show fewer distinctions and more reduced phonetic forms than initial consonants and stressed vowels. This is a perfectly natural process in terms of the amount of information required for effective communication, since the number of possible words which must be distinguished declines sharply after we select the first consonant and vowel. German and Russian, for example, do not distinguish voiced and voiceless consonants at the ends of words. However, when this tendency is carried to extremes (and a nonstandard dialect differs radically from the standard language in this respect), it may produce serious problems in learning to read and spell.

This weakening of final consonants is by no means as regular as the other phonological variables described above. Some individuals appear to have generalized the process to the point where most of their syllables are of the CV type, and those we have interviewed in this category seem to have the most serious reading problems of all. In general, final /t/ and /d/ are the most affected by the process. Final /d/ may be devoiced to a [t]-like form, or disappear entirely. Final /t/ is often realized as glottal stop, as in many English dialects, but more often disappears entirely. Less often, final /g/ and /k/

follow the same route as /d/ and /t/: /g/ is devoiced or disappears, and /k/ is replaced by glottal stop or disappears. Final /m/ and /n/ usually remain in the form of various degrees of nasalization of the preceding vowel. Rarely, sibilants /s/ and /z/ are weakened after vowels to the point where no consonant is heard at all. As a result of these processes, one may have such homonyms as:

Boot = Boo[9]	seat = seed = see	
road = row	poor = poke = pope[10]	
feed = feet	bit = bid = big	

It is evident that the loss of final /l/ and /r/, discussed above, is another aspect of this general weakening of final consonants, though of a much more regular nature than the cases considered in this section.

5. Other Phonological Variables

In addition to the types of homonymy singled out in the preceding discussion, there are a great many others which may be mentioned. They are of less importance for reading problems in general, since they have little impact upon inflectional rules, but they do affect the shapes of words in the speech of black children. There is no distinction between /i/ and /e/ before nasals in the great majority of cases. In the parallel case before /r/, and sometimes /l/, we frequently find no distinction between the vowels /ih/ and /eh/. The corresponding pair of back vowels before /r/ are seldom distinguished: that is, /uh/ and /oh/ fall together. The diphthongs /ay/ and /aw/ are often monophthongized, so that they are not distinguished from /ah/. The diphthong /oy/ is often a monophthong, especially before /l/, and cannot be distinguished from /ɔh/.

Among other consonant variables, we find the final fricative /θ/ is frequently merged with /f/, and similarly final /ð/ and /v/. Less frequently, /θ/ and /ð/ become /f/ and /v/ in intervocalic position.

9. This homonym was troublesome to us for some time. One member of the Thunderbirds is known as "Boo." We did not notice the occasional glottal stop which ended this word as a functional unit for some time; eventually we began to suspect that the underlying form was "Boot." This was finally confirmed when he appeared in sneakers labeled BOOT.

10. The word *poor* is frequently pronounced with a mid-vowel [po] even by those who do not have a complete merger of such pairs as *sure-shore, moor-more*. One of our Gullah-influenced South Carolina informants on Saint Helena Island is named Samuel Pope or Polk, but we cannot determine which from his pronunciation.

Initial consonant clusters which involve /r/ show considerable variation: /str/ is often heard as /skr/; /šr/ as [sw, sr, sɸ]. In a more complex series of shifts, /r/ is frequently lost as the final element of an initial cluster.

As a result of these various phonological processes, we find that the following series of homonyms are characteristic of the speech of many black children:

pin	= pen	beer	= bear	poor	= pour
tin	= ten	cheer	= chair	sure	= shore
since	= cents	steer	= stair	moor	= more
		peel	= pail		

find	= found	= fond	boil = ball
time		= Tom	oil = all
	pound	= pond	

Ruth	= roof	stream	= scream
death	= deaf	strap	= scrap

Changes in the Shapes of Words

The series of potential homonyms given in the preceding sections indicate that black children may have difficulty in recognizing many words in their standard spellings. They may look up words under the wrong spellings in dictionaries and be unable to distinguish words which are plainly different for the teacher. If the teacher is aware of these sources of confusion, she may be able to anticipate a great many of the children's difficulties. But if neither the teacher nor the children is aware of the great differences in their sets of homonyms, it is obvious that confusion will occur in every reading assignment.

However, the existence of homonyms on the level of a phonetic output does not prove that the speakers have the same sets of mergers on the more abstract level which corresponds to the spelling system. For instance, many New Yorkers merge *sore* and *saw* in casual speech, but in reading style, they have no difficulty in pronouncing the /r/ where it belongs. Since the /r/ in *sore* reappears before a following vowel, it is evident that an abstract //r// occurs in their abstract understanding of the word.[11] Thus the standard spelling

11. The // // notation encloses morphophonemic forms—that is, forms of words which are the most abstract representation underlying the variants that occur in particular environments as determined by some regular process. English spelling is,

system finds support in the learned patterns of careful speech and in the alternations which exist within any given style of speech.

The phonetic processes discussed above are often considered to be "low-level" rules—that is, they do not affect the underlying or abstract representations of words. One piece of evidence for this view is that the deletable final /r, l, s, z, t, d/ tend to be retained when a vowel follows at the beginning of the next word. This effect of a following vowel would seem to be a phonetic factor, restricting the operation of a phonetic rule; in any case, it is plain that the final consonant must "be there" in some abstract sense, if it appears in this prevocalic position. If this were not the case, we would find a variety of odd final consonants appearing, with no fixed relation to the standard form.[12]

For all of the major variables that we have considered, there is a definite and pronounced effect of a following vowel in realizing the standard form. Fig. 1.1 shows the effect of a following vowel on final /-st/ in the speech of four black and three white subjects. In every case, we find that the percentage of simplification of the cluster falls when a vowel follows.

The same argument, however, can be used to argue that the black speakers have underlying forms considerably different from those

---

on the whole, morphophonemic rather than phonemic: the stem *academ-*, for example, is spelled the same way even though it is pronounced very differently in *academy*, *academic*, *academe*, and *academician*.

(The situation in regard to r is not quite this regular in white working-class speech. "Intrusive r" does appear at the end of *saw* in *I saw a parade*, and consonantal [r] is sometimes not pronounced in *sore arm*. But the general pattern indicated above prevails and provides enough support for the spelling forms.)

12. This is precisely what does happen when final consonants are lost in words that have no spelling forms, no correlates in careful speech, and no regular morphophonemic alternation. Terms used in preadolescent culture will occur with a profusion of such variants (which may be continued in the adolescent years). For example, in Chicago the term for the base used in team versions of Hide-and-Seek is the *goose*. This is derived from the more general term gu:l with loss of final /l/—a dialect form of *goal*. (For example, the alternation *Gould* and *Gold* in proper names.) A similar phenomenon occurs in New York City, where the same item is known as the *dent*— related to older *den*. It is worth noting that both of these cases are characteristic of language change among the black speakers we are discussing, and illustrate the unchecked consequences of the homonymy we are considering. A more extreme case may be cited: in one group of black teenage boys, the position known elsewhere as *War Lord* (the member who arranges the details for gang fights) has shifted to a term with the underlying form //war dorf//, or possibly //waldorf// or //wardof//.

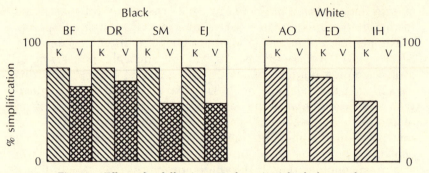

Fig. 1.1. Effect of a following vowel on /-st/ final clusters for
four black and three white speakers.

of white speakers. The white speakers showed almost as much
overall simplification of the clusters before a following consonant,
but none at all before a following vowel: in other words, their
abstract forms were effectively equivalent to the spelling forms. The
black speakers showed only a limited reduction in the degree of
simplification when a vowel followed.

We can explore this situation more carefully when we consider
grammatical conditioning. But we can point to one situation which
suggests the existence of nonstandard underlying forms. In the most
casual and spontaneous speech of the young black people whose
language we have been examining, the plural //-s// inflection is
seldom deleted. It follows the same phonetic rules as in standard
English: (1) after sibilants /s, z, š, ž/, the regular plural is [əz]; (2)
after other voiceless consonants, [s]; and (3) elsewhere, [z]. The
regular form of the plural after a word like *test, desk,* is [s], as in
[desks]. If the rules were so ordered that we began with the abstract
form //desk//, added the //-s//, and then deleted the /k/ in the
consonant cluster simplification process, we would find the final
phonetic form [dɛs:]. We do in fact sometimes find this form, in a
context which implies the plural. But more often, we find [dɛsəz,
gosəz, tosəz] as the plurals of *desk, ghost,* and *toast.*

A form such as [dɛsəz] is consistent with an order of the rules
which begins with //des//, or reduces //desk// immediately to
/des/. Then the plural //-s// is added, and the phonetic rules give
us [dɛsəz]. It should be emphasized that those speakers who use this
form do so consistently, frequently, and in the most careful speech;
it is not a slip of the tongue. On the contrary, clusters such as *-sps,*

-sts, -sks are almost impossible for many black children to articulate. Even with direct modeling, they find it extremely difficult to repeat the standard forms of *wasps, lists,* or *desks* (CRR 3288:3.9). It is quite common for children to produce under pressure such forms as [lɪstsəsəsəs], a recursive process, as a result of their efforts to produce the *-sts* cluster.

Forms such as singular [dɛs], plural [dɛsəz] give no support for an underlying spelling form *desk.* It is true that they are not inconsistent with a spelling *desk,* for an automatic rule simplifies *-sks* in 100 percent of the cases, changing *-sk + s* to *-s + s.* But there is no way for the black child to differentiate *mess, messes* from *des', desses,* on the basis of his own native speech forms. Therefore he can only memorize from school lessons which words have final consonants after *-s.* In the case of verbs such as *test,* and their derived nouns, there is no problem, for the form *testing* normally preserves the final *-t;* but most words in this class have no derived forms or inflectional forms in which a vowel follows the stem. When the next word begins with a vowel, the effect is often not strong enough to bring out the underlying final consonant in the speech of adults, and the listener does not hear the full form as regularly as he does in *testing.* There are, of course, dialects which resolve this problem in other ways by changing the rules for epenthetic vowels, yielding *deskes, testes* and *waspes,* but this is more characteristic of white Appalachian speech than southern black speech.

Grammatical Correlates of the Phonological Variables

As we examine the various final consonants affected by the phonological processes, we find that these are the same consonants which represent the principal English inflections. The shifts in the sound system therefore often coincide with grammatical differences between nonstandard and standard English, and it is difficult at first to decide whether we are dealing with a grammatical or a phonological rule. In any case, we can add a great number of homonyms to the lists given above when we consider the consequences of deleting final /r/, /l/, /s/, /z/, /t/, and /d/.

1. The Possessive

In many cases, the absence of the possessive //-s// can be interpreted as a reduction of consonant clusters, although this is not the most likely interpretation. The //-s// is absent just as frequently after vowels as after consonants for many speakers. Nevertheless, we can say that the overall simplification pattern is favored by the absence of the //-s// inflection. In the case of //-r//, we find more direct phonological influence: two possessive pronouns which end in /r/ have become identical to the personal pronoun: [ðeɪ] book, not [ðɛːə] book. In rapid speech, one cannot distinguish *you* from *your* from *you-all*. This seems to be a shift in grammatical forms, but the relation to the phonological variables is plain when we consider that *my, his, her,* and *our* remain as possessive pronouns. Speakers of the BE vernacular do not say *I book, she book* or *we book,* though there are reports of such forms from young children, especially where there has been heavy West Indian influence or other Creole influence. *He book* is not as uncommon among young children, though again it seems to be concentrated heavily in certain areas. This form is subject to the same phonological processes as those noted for *you book* and *they book,* though the phonetic motivation is much weaker than with *their* and *your.* The phonetic basis for *they book* is strengthened somewhat by the observation that some white southern dialects use *they* for dummy *there* in *They's a difference* (BEV uses *it* for this item and does not therefore find internal support for phonetic processes at this point).

It is obvious that there are two possible routes by which *they book* and *you book* could be derived. There are (1) the phonetic processes noted above, and (2) the process of de-Creolization in which the forms which wound up most different from other English dialects are stigmatized first and dropped. Both would have to come into play in de-Creolizing as BEV is becoming aligned more closely with other dialects, since the perception of the similarity of *they book* and *their book* is equivalent to the assumption that the phonetic rules of r-vocalization and deletion of postvocalic glides are operating.

2. The Future

The loss of final /l/ has a serious effect on the realization of future forms:

you'll = you	he'll = he
they'll = they	she'll = she

In many cases, therefore, the colloquial future is identical with the colloquial present. The form *will* is used in its full form quite often compared to other dialects, e.g., *I will be there,* without the necessary emphatic or formal connotation which this full form often has elsewhere. Various forms derived from *going to* are quite frequent:

gonna, gon', 'on', gwin, and with *I, I'm'na* and *I'ma* [amənə, amə].
(CRR 3288:3.5.2). The grammatical category of the future is therefore
quite secure.[13] In fact, black children appear to have much more
difficulty in reading contracted forms like *I'll* than the full form *I
will;* text writers who are trying to achieve an informal style are now
shifting to such contracted forms, but for black children they would
do better to avoid them.

3. The Copula

The verb forms of *be* are frequently not realized in sentences such
as *you tired* or *he in the way.* If we examine the paradigm, we find
that it is seriously affected by phonological processes:

I'm	$\neq$ I	we're	= we
you're	$\simeq$ you	you're	$\simeq$ you
he's	? he	they're	= they

The loss of final /z/ after vowels is not so frequent as to explain
the frequency of the absence of *-s* in *he's,* and it is reasonable to
conclude that grammatical rules have been generalized throughout
the paradigm—still not affecting *I'm* in the same way as the others,
as we would expect, since phonological rules are not operating to
reduce /m/. (See Chapter 3 for a detailed discussion of the copula.)

4. The Past

Again, there is no doubt that phonological processes are active
in reducing the frequency of occurrence of the /t,d/ inflection.

pass	= past = passed	pick	= picked
miss	= mist = missed	loan	= loaned
fine	= find = fined	raise	= raised

At the same time, there is no question about the existence of a past
tense category. The irregular past tense forms, which are very frequent in ordinary conversation, are plainly marked as past no matter
what final simplification takes place.

I told him [atoɪm]   He kept mine [hikɛpmaɪn]

13. Joan Fickett has recently suggested that *I'ma* has a different meaning from *I'm
gonna,* signifying immediate future as against more remote. This seems plausible at
first sight, since *I'ma* is often used in this way. But it seems to be the natural con-
comitant of greater condensation, and we can find such counterexamples as the
observation of the lion to the monkey in Saladin's version of Signifying Monkey "Now
Mr. Monkey, now I see/ you the one tha's been talkin' shit about me./ If I was you,
Mr. Monkey, I'd mend my ways/ 'cause *I'ma* kill you black ass one of these days."
(CRR 3288:4.2.2).

The problem which confronts us concerns the form of the regular suffix //-ed//. Is there such an abstract form in the structure of the vernacular English spoken by black children? The answer will make a considerable difference both to teaching strategy and our understanding of the reading problems which children face. To approach this problem, we have used a variety of methods which it may be helpful to examine in detail.

The Problem of the -ed Suffix

The first approach to this problem is through a study of the quantitative distribution of the forms as spoken by black and white subjects in a variety of stylistic contexts. We contrast the simplification of consonant clusters in two situations: where the /t/ or /d/ represents a part of the root form itself (KD_{MM}) and where the /t/ or /d/ represents the grammatical suffix of the past tense (KD_P). Fig. 1.2 shows the results for the speakers BF and AO who were first considered in Tables 1.1 and 1.2.

The black speaker BF shows almost the same degree of consonant cluster simplification when the /t,d/ represents a past tense as when it is a part of the original root. On the other hand, the white speaker AO simplifies very few past tense clusters. We can interpret these results in two ways: (a) BF has a generalized simplification rule without grammatical conditioning, while AO's simplification rule is strongly restricted by grammatical boundaries, or (b) BF's underlying grammar is different. If we were to rewrite his grammar to show -ed morphemes only where phonetic forms actually appear, his

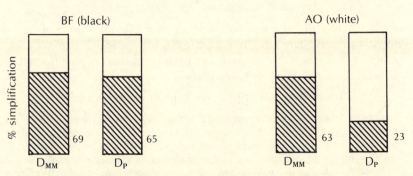

Fig. 1.2. Effect of grammatical status on /t,d/ of final clusters for one black and one white speaker.

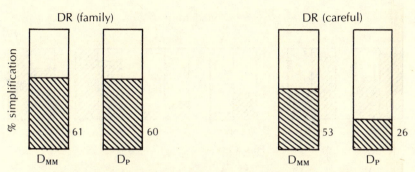

Fig. 1.3. Effect of stylistic level and grammatical status on /t,d/ of final clusters for one black speaker. KD_{MM}: /t,d/ final in monomorphemic (root) clusters. KD_P: /t,d/ final as past tense *-ed* morpheme.

consonant cluster rule would look much the same as AO's. Without attempting to decide this issue now, let us examine a black speaker in several styles, and see if the *-ed* is affected by the shift.

Fig. 1.3 shows the percent of /t,d/ clusters simplified by DR, a black woman raised in North Carolina. On the left, we see the simplification of both KD_{MM} and KD_P in intimate family style, discussing a recent trip to North Carolina with a close relative. The pattern is similar to that of BF, with no differentiation of KD_{MM} and KD_P. But on the right we find a sharp differentiation of the two kinds of clusters: this is the careful style used by DR in a face-to-face interview with a white stranger. Fig. 1.3 shows us that the grammatical constraint which DR uses in careful speech is quite similar to the pattern used by the white speaker AO.

Stylistic context is obviously important in obtaining good information on the underlying grammatical system of black speakers. We may therefore profit from considering data where this factor is controlled. Fig. 1.4 shows the overall consonant cluster simplification patterns for two groups of black adolescent boys: the Thunderbirds, 10 to 12 years old, and the Cobras, 14 to 16. These are two peer groups which form closed networks. Most of the boys are poor readers, and they represent the groups which respond least to middle-class educational norms. In the interviews which provided these data, the groups were recorded in circumstances where they used the most excited and spontaneous speech, interacting with each other, in the group sessions described in the Introduction (p. XIX). Each boy

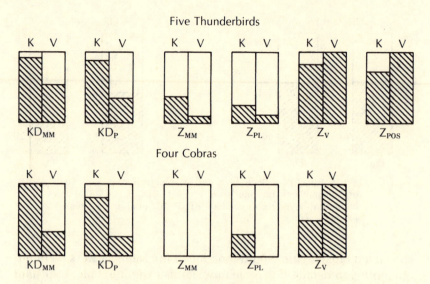

KD_MM: /t,d/ final in monomorphemic (root) clusters

KD_P: /t,d/ final as past tense -ed morpheme

Z_MM: /s,z/ final in monomorphemic (root) clusters

Z_PL: /s,z/ final as plural morpheme

Z_V: /s,z/ final as 3rd person singular marker

Z_POS: /s,z/ final as possessive morpheme

Fig. 1.4. Simplification of /t,d/ and /s,z/ final clusters for two groups of black adolescent boys from south-central Harlem.

was recorded on a separate track, from a microphone placed only a few inches away from his mouth. (Recordings made with a single group microphone are of little value for this type of group interaction since only a small part of the data is recovered.)

The Thunderbirds show a very high percentage of simplification of clusters before consonants: 61 out of 63 for nongrammatical clusters and 21 out of 23 for grammatical clusters. But before following vowels, only 7 out of 14 nongrammatical clusters were simplified, and even fewer—3 out of 13—for grammatical clusters.

We can conclude from these figures that there is a solid basis for the recognition of an -ed suffix: grammatical status does make a difference when the unfavorable phonological environment is set aside. Secondly, we can see that there is a good basis for approximating the lexical forms of standard English: 50 percent of the root clusters conformed to the standard forms in a favorable environment. From another point of view, however, one might say that in half the cases, the boys gave no evidence that they would recognize such spellings as *test* or *hand* as corresponding to their [tɛs] and [hæn].

The Cobras, some four years older, are very similar in their /t,d/ pattern. The phonological conditioning has become even more regular—that is, the effect of the following vowel is more extreme. All of the root clusters are simplified before consonants, but only a small percentage before vowels. The effect of grammatical status is no stronger, however. We may conclude that the process of growing up has brought better knowledge of the underlying lexical forms of standard English, but the status of the *-ed* morpheme is still about the same.

Perception Testing

A second approach to the problem of the *-ed* suffix is through perception testing. It is possible that the speakers are not able to hear the difference between [pɪk] and [pɪkt], [mɛs] and [mɛst]. If the phonological reduction rule was regular enough, this might be the case. We explore this possibility by a perception test of the following form. The subject listens to a series of three words: [mɛs, mɛst, mɛs], and is asked to say which one is different. The test is repeated six times, with various random combinations of the two possibilities. Then a second series is given with /-st/ before a vowel: [mɛsʌp, mɛstʌp, mɛsʌp], etc. A person who can hear the distinctions will give a correct response in six out of six, or five out of six trials.

The Thunderbirds had no difficulty with the perception test. Three of the boys had perfect scores, and only one showed definite confusion—in fact, the one boy who came closest to standard English norms on the other tests described below. It is true that many black youngsters have great difficulty in perceiving phonemic contrasts which are not made in their own dialect; but in this particular case, perception of the /-t∼-st/ distinction has less relevance to the grammatical status of *-ed* than any of the other means of investigation.

Classroom Correction Tests

A third means of approaching the grammatical status of *-ed* is through the classroom correction tests mentioned earlier (CRR 3288:4.4). The subjects are asked to change certain sentences to correct schoolroom English, starting with easy examples like *I met three mens*. Several sentences are relevant to the *-ed* problem:

> He pick me.
> I've pass my test.
> Last week I kick Donald in the mouth, so the teacher throwed me out the class.

As a whole, results on the classroom correction tests show that the Thunderbirds and the Cobras have little ability to detect the absence of *-ed* as a grammatical element to be corrected. They focus upon *ain't*, or *man* in *He never play no more, man*, but not upon the *-ed*. Among the Thunderbirds, only one of the five boys had this ability to supply *-ed*, and the Cobras showed no greater perception of the status of this element.

The -ed Reading Test

The most effective way of determining the grammatical significance of *-ed* for the groups we have been working with is through a series of sentences in the reading texts used in our interviews. The relevant sentences are as follows:

a. Last month I read five books.
b. Tom read all the time.
c. Now I read and write better than Alfred does.
d. When I passed by, I read the posters.
e. When I liked a story, I read every word.
f. I looked for trouble when I read the news.

These sentences depend upon the unique homograph *read* to indicate whether the reader is interpreting the *-ed* suffix as a past tense signal. The first three sentences show whether the reader can use the time indicators *last month, now*, and the absence of *-s* to distinguish correctly between [ri:d] and [rɛd]. In sentences *d, e*, and *f* the reader first encounters the *-ed* suffix, which he may or may not pronounce. If he interprets this visual signal as a sign of the past tense, he will pronounce *read* as [rɛd]; if not, he is apt to say [ri:d]. The distance between the *-ed* suffix and the word *read* is kept as short as possible in sentence *d*, so that here at least there is no problem of understanding *-ed* and then forgetting it.

The overall results of this test show that *-ed* is interpreted correctly less than half the time by the Thunderbirds—less often than the *-ed* suffix is pronounced. The Cobras show no material improvement in this respect. For each group, only one boy was able to approximate the standard English performance in this test.

Figure 1.5 shows the correlation of reading skill and success in interpreting past tense signals for 46 BEV speakers. The solid upper line shows success in transferring adverbial past meanings to the correct pronunciation of *read* in sentences like *a, b, c.* There is obviously a high degree of success and an upward movement with a rise in reading test scores. The dotted lower line shows success in transferring *-ed* to the pronunciation of *read* in sentences *d, e, f.* There is no greater than chance score and no upward movement with reading test scores. (Labov 1971c, CRR 3288:3.2).

We can conclude that the original inferences drawn from Fig. 1.4, based on linguistic performance in spontaneous speech, are sup-

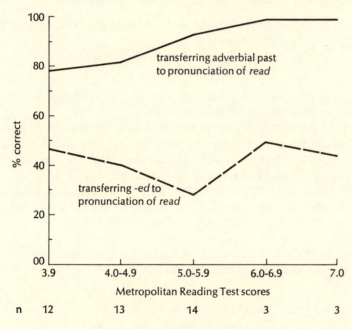

Note: upper line: % correct for sentences 1, 2, and 8;

Fig. 1.5. Correlation between Metropolitan Reading Test scores and reading of the -ed suffix for 46 BEV speakers. Reprinted from *Basic Studies on Reading*, eds. H. Levin and J. Williams, by permission of Basic Books, Inc.

ported by various other approaches to the *-ed* problem. The degree
of uncertainty registered in the KD_P column for consonant clusters,
even before vowels, indicates that the *-ed* cannot function as an
effective marker of the past tense for many children. Though the
Cobras are four years older than the Thunderbirds, they show little
change in their use of *-ed*. It is also true that some children—a
minority in this case—can recognize *-ed* as a past tense marker, and
use it effectively in reading, even though they usually do not pronounce it.

Grammatical Status of the //-s// Suffixes

The same quantitative method which was effective in interpreting
the status of *-ed* can be used to analyze the various *-s* suffixes used
by black children. Fig. 1.4 provides information on consonant cluster
simplification as it affects four different categories of *-s*:[14]

Z_{MM} monomorphemic *-s* in root clusters: *axe, box*
Z_{PL} the plural *-s*
Z_V the 3rd person singular marker of the verb
Z_{POS} the possessive *-'s*

For each category, we can compare the extent of simplification
before consonants and before vowels.

In the case of root clusters, the Thunderbirds show only a moderate tendency to drop the final element before consonants, and a very
small tendency before vowels. In other words, the standard forms
are intact. For the Cobras, this *-s* is always present.

The plural is rarely lost and shows the usual effect of the following
vowel. We can conclude that the plural inflection is the same for
the Thunderbirds, the Cobras, and standard English.

In the case of the 3rd person singular marker and the possessive,
an extraordinary reversal is found. For the Thunderbirds, the situation can be summarized as follows:

Z_V	_K	_V
simplified	17	12
not simplified	4	0

---

14. Two other types of //-s// can be isolated: the adverbial /s/ of *besides, sometimes,* etc., and the various contracted forms mentioned above: *that's, it's* and *let's.*
The first is not frequent enough to provide good data for the small groups discussed
here, and the second type shows a loss of the first element of the cluster with no
grammatical effect.

Not only is the extent of simplification higher in Z_V than for Z_{PL}, but the direction of influence of a following vowel is reversed. No clusters at all appeared in the most favorable environment for the phonological rule. We can infer that this is no longer effectively described as consonant cluster simplification, but rather as a grammatical fact. The 3rd person singular marker //-s// does not exist in the particular grammar being used here. The same argument holds for the possessive //-s// marker, though as noted above, we cannot extend this argument to infer a loss of the possessive in general.

A striking fact about this situation is that the older group has gained in several respects as far as approximation to standard English forms is concerned, but their development has not affected the grammatical status of the 3rd person singular marker.

Consequences for the Teaching of Reading

Let us consider the problem of teaching a youngster to read who has the general phonological and grammatical characteristics just described. The most immediate way of analyzing his difficulties is through the interpretation of his oral reading. As we have seen, there are many phonological rules which affect his pronunciation, but not necessarily his understanding of the grammatical signals or his grasp of the underlying lexical forms. The two questions are distinct: the relations between grammar and pronunciation are complex and require careful interpretation.

If a student is given a certain sentence to read, say *He passed by both of them,* he may say [hi pæs baɪ bof ə dɛm]. The teacher may wish to correct his bad reading, perhaps by saying, "No, it isn't [hi pæs baɪ bof ə dɛm], it's [hi pæst baɪ boθ əv ðɛm]." One difficulty is that these two utterances may sound the same to many children—both the reader and those listening—and they may be utterly confused by the correction. Others may be able to hear the difference, but have no idea of the significance of the extra [t] and the interdental forms of *th-*. The most embarrassing fact is that the boy who first read the sentence may have performed his reading task correctly and understood the *-ed* suffix just as it was intended. In that case, the teacher's correction is completely beside the point.

We have two distinct cases to consider. In one case, the deviation in reading may be only a difference in pronunciation on the part of a child who has a different set of homonyms from the teacher. Here, correction might be quite unnecessary. In the second case, we may be dealing with a boy who has no concept of -ed as a past tense marker, who considers the -ed a meaningless set of silent letters. Obviously the correct teaching strategy would involve distinguishing these two cases and treating them quite differently.

How such a strategy might be put into practice is a problem that educators may be able to solve by using information provided by linguists. But there does emerge from our work two principles that have been neglected in previous approaches to the teaching of reading:

1. Teachers of reading should distinguish each deviation from standard English in oral reading as either a mistake in reading or a difference in pronunciation.

2. Teachers in the early grades should be ready to accept the existence of a different set of homonyms in the speech of black children, at least in their speech production. Such acceptance may preserve the children's confidence in the phonic code and therefore facilitate their learning to read. There are in addition some basic strategies which teachers can follow which are indicated here in our work.

In the early stages of teaching reading and spelling, it may be necessary to spend much more time on the grammatical function of certain inflections, which may have no function in the dialect of some of the children. In the same way, it may be necessary to treat the final elements of certain clusters with the special attention given to silent letters such as b in lamb.

3. A certain amount of attention given to perception training in the first few years of school may be extremely helpful in teaching children to hear and make standard English distinctions. But perception training need not be complete in order to teach children to read. On the contrary, most of the differences between standard and nonstandard English described here can be taken as differences in the sets of homonyms which must be accepted in reading patterns. On the face of it, there is no reason why a person cannot learn to read standard English texts quite well in a nonstandard pronunciation. Eventually, the school may wish to teach the child an alternative system of pronunciation. But the key to the situation in the early grades is for the teacher to know the system of homonyms of nonstandard English, and to know the grammatical differences that separate her own speech from that of the child. The teacher must be prepared to accept the system of homonyms for the moment, if

this will advance the basic process of learning to read, but not the grammatical differences. Thus the task of teaching the child to read -ed is clearly that of getting him to recognize the graphic symbols as a marker of the past tense, quite distinct from the task of getting him to say [pæst] for *passed*.

If the teacher has no understanding of the child's grammar and set of homonyms, she may be arguing with him at cross purposes. Over and over again, the teacher may insist that *cold* and *coal* are different, without realizing that the child perceives this as only a difference in meaning, not in sound. She will not be able to understand why he makes so many odd mistakes in reading, and he will experience only a vague confusion, somehow connected with the ends of words. Eventually, he may stop trying to analyze the shapes of letters that follow the vowel and guess wildly at each word after he deciphers the first few letters. Or he may lose confidence in the alphabetic principle as a whole and try to recognize each word as a whole. This loss of confidence seems to occur frequently in the third and fourth grades, and it is characteristic of many children who are effectively nonreaders.

The sources of reading problems discussed in this chapter are only a few of the causes of poor reading in the ghetto schools. We do not believe that these structural differences are major causes of the problem; on the contrary, the major conclusion of our research is that reading failure is primarily the result of political and cultural conflict within the classroom. Chapters 5 and 6 document the immediate situation and later chapters will give us deeper insight into the cultural differences involved. But the structural differences cited here are quite specific and easily isolated. If they are not recognized, they can become the symbolic issues around which other conflicts arise. The information provided in this chapter may then have immediate application in the program of improving the teaching of reading to children in inner city schools.

2 | Is the Black English Vernacular A Separate System?

EVERY step that we take in approaching the black English vernacular will be influenced by our fundamental attitude to the question: how different is BEV from other dialects of English? There is a great deal of evidence to indicate that BEV is more different from most other English dialects than they are from each other, including the standard English of the classroom. If we do not accept the fact that BEV has distinct rules of its own, we find that the speech of black children is a mass of errors and this has indeed been the tradition of early education research in this area (Loban 1966). In our early study of the Lower East Side of New York City, it quickly became apparent that black speakers had many more "nonstandard" forms than any other group by a factor of ten or more. It is confusing and uneconomical to approach these forms in terms of their deviation from other standards.

In the last chapter, we showed that BEV had a distinctly different organization of the English sound system from the white NYC vernacular though we did not go into the rules that produced this result. In this chapter we will examine briefly the nature of some of these rules and see what relation they have to comparable rules in other dialects in contact with BEV. Is BEV a separate language, so that standard English has to be taught to black children as a different system with the same techniques that are used to teach French and Spanish? Or is the BEV system basically a variant of other English systems, that can easily be placed in relation to it? Black children in the school system use language that is quite variable, showing some features of BEV and some features of SE. Is this a mixture of two different systems, or is it one of the intermediate stages in a single system that embraces both BEV and SE?

36

The question of one unit vs. two is fundamental to linguistic operations. In basic linguistic courses, most of the initial exercises concern the decision as to whether two sounds are members of a single phoneme or represent two different phonemes: whether the difference between these two sounds can be used to distinguish two different meanings. Is [ɨ] in *chicken* [cɨkn] really the "same" as [ɪ] in *chick* [čɪk]? The classic question of "one phoneme or two" concerns a higher level question: since an affricate like [č] in *chicken* can also be represented phonetically as [tʃ], can it be shown on the phoneme level as a sequence of two phonemes, /t/ and /ʃ/ equal to the sequence in *night shirt* [naɪtʃɚt]? In studying the structure of words, the basic operation is again one of cutting: can *slurp,* for example, be cut into two parts, *sl-* and *urp,* each with its own meaning?

The question of one system vs. two has not been given the same attention, although the term *system* bulks very large in linguistic thinking. An important paper of Fries and Pike (1949) on "Co-existent systems . . ." raised the question as to whether certain sounds borrowed from Spanish into an American Indian language could be set aside as part of a separate but "co-existent" system. In general, linguists have not developed criteria for answering this question, which now becomes crucially important for a proper view of the place of the black English vernacular in the American speech community.

To say that BEV is a system completely different from other English systems is of course absurd. The great majority of the rules of BEV are the same as the rules of other English dialects. But within that overall similarity, there may be subsets of rules which are not easily integrated into other English grammars, and some of these subsets may be located at strategic points, close to the grammatical core. The linguistic motto that language is a system where everything hangs together (*tout se tient*) has been shown to be a gross overstatement by many studies, most importantly by Gumperz in Kupwar (1971). Gumperz showed that in this multilingual community some components of co-existent languages had become identical, while other components had become even more differentiated. So too, the vocabulary, phrase structure, and most transformations of BEV might be identical with neighboring dialects, and yet the grammatical subsystem of tense and aspect be completely different. Instead of trying to focus on the system as a whole, I will examine here particular rules of BEV which are different from the white New York City vernacular (WNS) and from standard English (SE). We will look for (1) systematic relations between the BEV rules and others and (2) systematic relations between different BEV rules. To the extent that BEV is a separate subsystem, we should see internal cohesion of BEV rules. Homans' image of a system in equilibrium applies here (1955): if we sit on a mattress, the spring underneath us does not go down as far as it would if we sat on any given spring alone, since its connections with other springs prevent it from moving as far from its position of rest. Similarly, there may be rules in BEV which cannot be easily moved or altered individually. Their systematic connections with other rules may hold them in place, so that several rules must shift together. We can speak then of a degree of systematicity in BEV, meaning systematic interrelations of BEV rules, rather than the larger and emptier question as to whether BEV is a different "system" as a whole.

If we consider that a language is a set of rules for transforming meaning into sound patterns (or graphic forms) then of course it becomes important to decide if BEV is operating on the same set of meanings as other dialects. Our chief concern will be with the central grammatical systems: the tense and aspect system, negation, quantifiers, and the transformations that operate on these units. Since there is no agreement on the semantics of English tense and aspect in general, it is unlikely that linguists will suddenly agree on the semantics of the BEV system, whether or not they are native speakers of the dialect. There will be points of divergence between BEV and other dialects in this area, and we will consider them in the final section of this chapter. But first we will approach the issues by looking at the formal units that are actually found in BEV, observing how they behave, inferring what underlying forms exist, and then seeing what rules govern their appearance and disappearance in a variable rule. The present chapter must be considered a trial balance in the direction of a final accounting of the systematic relations of BEV and other dialects.

Before we consider the variables of BEV which affect the central grammatical system, it will be instructive to look at one which is essentially a part of the sound pattern and not so centrally located. The vocalization of (r) in BEV has been discussed in chapter 1, and its intersection with grammatical elements indicated. Frequent deletion of *are* and the use of *they book* and *you book* are related to the basically r-less character of the dialect, though as we pointed out before, the reinterpretation of these forms as being related to r-vocalization may be quite recent.

Table 2.1 shows the social and stylistic stratification of three subvariables in the r-complex. The first—(r)—is the general vocalization of final and preconsonantal /r/ in car, card, bear, beard. The second and third cases concern intervocalic /r/. The (r# #V) variable concerns word-final /r/ when the next word begins with a vowel, as in four o'clock. The third—(VrV)—is the vocalization of /r/ between two vowels within a word (when the first vowel is stressed), as in Carol, Paris, borrow. Each of these variables is shown in several different styles: A is the style closest to the vernacular of everyday life, recorded in group sessions with youth and extracted from casual speech in individual interviews with adults. Style B is the main bulk of an interview, relatively careful conversation. C is reading style, and D the reading of isolated word lists.

The values for four black peer groups are given at the top of Table 2.1, then five subclasses of 28 adult speakers drawn from our sample of 100 adults in south-central Harlem; and finally the control group

TABLE 2.1.
SOCIAL AND STYLISTIC STRATIFICATION OF
AVERAGE (R) INDICES FOR BEV AND WNS GROUPS

Group	(VrV) Style			(r# #V) Style		(r) Style			
	A	B	D	A	B	A	B	C	D
Thunderbirds (5/8)*	98%	98%	100%	15%	04%	01%	00%	10%	23%
Aces (4)		100	100		06	00	00	03	26
Cobras (5/9)	97	93	100	00	04	00	02	13	24
Jets (12/13)	100	96	80	11	02	00	00	19	07
Adults									
Middle class (10/14)	100	95	100	52	77	10	25		67
Working class									
—upper									
Northern (4)		89	100	21	40	00	08		61
Southern (7)		78	100	23	40	09	11		34
—lower									
Northern (5)	79	80	100	22	06	01	05		44
Southern (8)		79	100	37	12	(08)	09		37
Inwood (6)	⊲100	100	100	95	80	00	00	00	13

*Numbers in parentheses represent numbers of subjects in Style B or Style A/Style B

of white adolescents from the Inwood section of upper Manhattan.

The values of the variable given here are percentages of consonantal (r-1) of the total occurrences of /r/ in each environment. As we look down the first column, style A for (r), it is obvious that all of these groups are basically r-less. Only a few of the adult groups show any significant amount of consonantal (r-1) here.[1] The middle-class groups show (r)-10, and a comparable figure appears for the southern working-class groups.[2] But in more formal styles, we observe that all groups move regularly upward in a uniform pattern. This is what we have come to expect in many studies of (r) in New York City (see *Social Stratification* and *Sociolinguistic Patterns*). The upward movement is relatively slow for all but the middle-class adults, who follow a pattern typical of white middle-class speakers in other studies. In style B, careful speech, this group is the only one to show a clear increase. All groups show higher values for (r) in more formal styles, especially in reading isolated words. The white working-class Inwood group does not differ sharply from the blacks and uses less (r-1) in style D. As we have seen before, (r) is an even more important stylistic marker for blacks than for whites in New York City.

However, we can see a sharp difference between white and black in the second subvariable, (r##V). The Inwood group shows very little vocalization of word-final /r/ when the next word begins with a vowel, but for all of the black groups the vocalization rule operates here at least 50 percent of the time. This variable does not respond to stylistic shifting for any black groups except the middle and upper working-class adults.

Finally, under (VrV), we see that the white group never vocalizes intervocalic /r/ but that all black groups do so occasionally in connected speech. There are thus sharp qualitative differences between blacks and whites. The black speakers are quite similar and are opposed in their pattern to the white speakers, who agree generally in their behavior with the much larger number of whites sampled in the Lower East Side study (*Social Stratification*). In the

1. The notation (r-1), (r-0) etc. indicates specific values of the variable. (r-1) is used for any type of consonantal constriction and (r-0) for the absence of such constriction.

2. This reflects the existence of two separate prestige norms in the South: for one, (r-1) is a prestige feature, and for the other, it is a lower-class vernacular feature. The working-class adults raised in the North are r-less in the vernacular as we would expect.

larger pattern, there are no significant differences between peer-group members and adults—even the adults who match the white pattern for (r). The case of (r # #V) is particularly significant because as we pointed out in chapter 1, this is the feature which makes it difficult for black children to be sure of the underlying forms of many words. If *four* is vocalized [fɔ:] in *four days*, but [fɔr] in *four o'clock*, there can be no question that the underlying form in the speaker's dictionary will be /for/, and he will be able to draw on this knowledge in reading and writing. But if *four* is normally [fɔ:] or [fo] in all environments, then the speaker must draw on a small number of cases to establish the existence of the variable class of words ending in /r/. There is in fact a good deal of hypercorrection as people make wrong guesses about which is which, but on the whole the identity of the classes remains intact. Otherwise we would not see the clear pattern of Table 2.1.

How does this situation affect our view of the relations of BEV and WNS? To answer this we have to see what are the underlying rules which generate the pattern of Table 2.1. To begin with, we note that all speakers are participating in the same sociolinguistic pattern of (r). The intricate regularities of this table reflect the kind of class and stylistic stratification we have observed for many other stable variables—the initial consonant of *thing* and *three*, or of *this* and *that;* the form of unstressed (ing); and so on (*Sociolinguistic Patterns*). Certain general principles emerge from all of these patterns:

1. The variable differentiates speakers at different age and class levels at each stylistic context.

2. All adult speakers use the variable in the same way: at each stylistic level, they shift the same direction.

3. The stylistic shift of the middle-class speakers is more extreme than that of working-class speakers.

When we pass beyond (r), we find the community differentiated. For whites, (VrV) is not a variable, and whites and blacks operate at very different levels for (r # #V). We can construct a matrix that shows the relatively higher position of blacks in the scale of r-lessness: Table 2.1′ shows how often r-vocalization applies to the vernaculars of various speakers.

The natural tendency of linguists trained in the traditional categorical view is to explain the variation in the use of /r/ as the product of "dialect mixture": the intersection of two consistent systems. Relations of more or less cannot be shown within this view:

TABLE 2.1.'
APPLICATION OF *R*-VOCALIZATION RULE
TO FOUR VERNACULARS

Vernacular	(VrV)	(r##V)	(r)
BEV	low	high	obligatory
BE middle class	low	moderate	high
WNS	no	low	obligatory
White middle class	no	low	moderate

we must then describe these original dialects by saying that the rule never applies, always applies, or is in free variation. Thus we would have to rewrite Table 2.1′ to look like Table 2.1″.

This table differentiates the three dialects, though it corresponds to the facts of Table 2.1 only in a very rough way. But it does not show at all how style shifting can operate or how one moves from one of these "pure dialects" to an intermediate form. The relations of more or less that we find in Table 2.1 are actually a part of the structure which we can capture if we write variable rules. The formal interpretation of these rules will be presented in the next chapter. Here we will simply note that angled brackets around the element to the right of the arrow indicate a variable rule, and angled brackets around an element in the environment after the slash indicate variable constraints which favor the rule. An asterisk indicates that when that feature is present in the environment, the rule always applies.

The WNS vernacular rule for the vocalization of /r/ which brings together all three subvariables would then be written informally as

1 $$r \rightarrow \langle \vartheta \rangle / \underline{\qquad} \begin{Bmatrix} (\#\#)^* \langle \sim V \rangle \\ \#\# \end{Bmatrix}$$

TABLE 2.1.″
APPLICATION OF *r*-VOCALIZATION RULE
ACCORDING TO THE CATEGORICAL RULE

Dialect	/VrV/	/r##V/	/r/
Dialect 1 (BEV)	no	optional	obligatory
Dialect 2 (WNS)	no	no	obligatory
Dialect 3 (SE)	no	no	no

This rule states that /r/ is always vocalized in preconsonantal and final position. In the remaining case, when the next word begins with a vowel, the rule can apply variably. The level of the rule at that point will be set by the level of the input probability p_o (see next chapter).

The rule for BEV is remarkably similar. We can achieve the changes indicated in Table 2.1′ by simply writing

$$2 \qquad r \rightarrow \langle \partial \rangle / \underline{} \begin{Bmatrix} (\#\#)^* \langle \sim V \rangle \\ \langle \#\# \rangle \end{Bmatrix}$$

Here the word-boundary symbol $\#\#$ is placed in angled brackets, indicating that it is a variable constraint which favors the rule but need not be present. If it is not present, and a vowel follows the /r/ directly, the rule can still apply but at a level to be registered with a low p_o. To move from this form of either vernacular rule to the more formal styles in which some (r-1) is used for (r), we need only remove the semicategorical symbol * and write (for BEV):

$$2' \qquad r \rightarrow \langle \partial \rangle / \underline{} \begin{Bmatrix} (\#\#) \langle \sim V \rangle \\ \langle \#\# \rangle \end{Bmatrix}$$

The two variable constraints are now ordered by their vertical position: this tells us that the rule will apply most often in final and preconsonantal position, next before $\#\#V$ and least often when it is directly before V. The WNS rule is adjusted in the same way.

To register the style shifting of (r), we make p_o a function of contextual style and age. The use of the asterisk notation in 1 and 2 could be dispensed with if we set up the probabilities for the variable constraints in 2′ to approach 1 as closely as we like. But for the purposes of the semiquantitative version given here, the asterisk notation captures an important difference in the expectation of the listener: with an asterisk constraint, the rule applies so often that its absence is marked and is socially significant.

These qualitative differences in the use of (r) can therefore be easily accounted for by a simple adjustment in the rules. This is the type of formal operation which would justify the claim that BEV and WNS can be fitted into a single system, along with SE and other dialects. Substantively, the close relation of rules 1 and 2 suggests that speakers of WNS would be able to extrapolate from their own rules to see how BEV might operate and so understand the possibility of saying *Ca'ol* for *Carol*, even when *Carol* and *Cal* merge.

Let us now turn from this relatively simple case to the simplification of consonant clusters, especially those ending in *-t,d* which were the main focus of the last chapter. We have seen that there are four distinct major environments which are regularly differentiated:

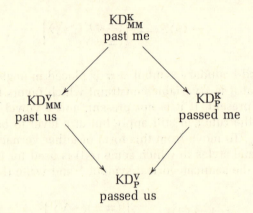

For all speakers, the rule applies most often for monomorphemic forms before a consonant and least often for past tense forms before a vowel. For all speakers, the rule applies more often before a consonant than before a vowel and more often with monomorphemic forms than for *-ed* clusters.

How, then, are the speakers differentiated? In all these respects, BEV speakers and WNS speakers are the same. Table 2.2 shows the use of deletion of final *-t,d* for a number of groups in two contextual styles A and B. This table shows that the following rule governs all speakers:

3 $$t,d \rightarrow \langle \emptyset \rangle / C \langle \emptyset \rangle \underline{\qquad} \# \# \langle \sim V \rangle$$

Rule 3 states that *t* or *d* is variably deleted after another consonant at the end of a word, more often if it is not followed by a vowel, and more often if there is no (past tense) boundary between it and the preceding word.

Though the general rule 3 applies to BEV, WNS, and many other dialects, we can differentiate BEV from WNS by observing the

TABLE 2.2.
SOCIAL AND STYLISTIC STRATIFICATION OF t,d DELETION

Group	Style A KD_{MM} __K	__V	KD_P __K	__V	Style B KD_{MM} __K	__V	KD_P __K	__V
T-Birds (5/8)	97%	36%	91%	23%	91%	59%	74%	24%
Aces (4)					98	64	85	43
Cobras (5/9)	98	45	100	12	97	76	73	15
Jets (14/13)	98	82	60	05	90	49	44	09
Oscar Br. (6/6)	97	54	85	31	97	69	49	17
Inwood (3/8)	67	09	14	04	68	26	30	03
Adults								
Middle cl. (14)	79	32	30	00	60	28	19	04
Working cl.								
U/No. (4)	90	56	84	25	90	40	19	09
U/So. (7)	93	21	41	18	89	40	47	32
L/No. (5)	87	45	49	16	61	35	33	05
L/So. (8)	98	46	61	35	93	70	72	32

relative weights of the two variable constraints shown here. In Table 2.2 we can see that the two mixed cases KD_{MM}^V and KD_P^K reveal these relative weights quite clearly. In style A, all the BEV groups except the Jets show a greater effect of the phonological constraint, and several of the adult groups show the two constraints about equal. In style B, every group shifts in the direction of a heavier weight for the grammatical constraint. If we plot the two mixed cases in the two-dimensional diagram of Fig. 2.1, we see that the BEV groups are well differentiated from adult speakers and from the white groups. Here each of the individual group members is shown separately: their clustering shows how compelling the pattern is. Most of the younger BEV speakers—the T-Birds, the Cobras and the Aces, are located in the upper right. The Jets and the adults are located more in the center, and in the lower left we have plotted a number of other dialects, southern and northern, American and British. It is evident that all of the speakers of the English language treat the -t,d deletion rule in the same way, giving more recognition to the grammatical clusters in more formal styles and always preserving enough -ed clusters to demonstrate their knowledge of the language.

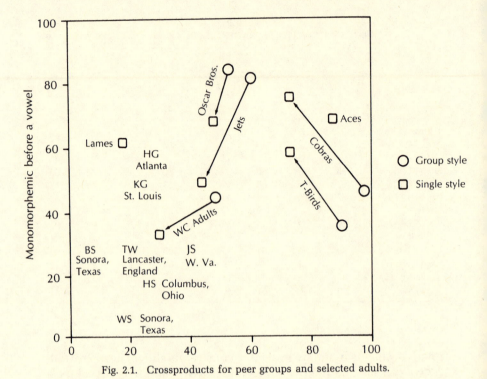

Fig. 2.1. Crossproducts for peer groups and selected adults.

We can register the differentiation of these groups by weighting the variables:

3a   BEV $t,d \rightarrow \langle \emptyset \rangle / C \ ^{\beta}\langle \emptyset \rangle \underline{\quad\quad} \# \# \ ^{\alpha}\langle \sim V \rangle$

3b   WNS $t,d \rightarrow \langle \emptyset \rangle / C \ ^{\alpha}\langle \emptyset \rangle \underline{\quad\quad} \# \# \ ^{\beta}\langle \sim V \rangle$

These rules presuppose that the -ed suffix is inserted as the representation of the past tense by a regular rule of grammar long before the t,d deletion rule begins to operate. This rule would have the general form:

4                          $PAST \rightarrow was/ \underline{\quad\quad} \begin{Bmatrix} NP \\ Prog \end{Bmatrix}$

                               $\rightarrow -ed/ \underline{\quad\quad} [+REG]$

Residual PAST symbols would then be interpreted by dictionary entries for the irregular verbs such as *kept* or *told*. At this point we can see evidence of systematicity in the BEV rule system in the interaction between the past tense, the present tense marker, and the historical present.

In most dialects, the historical present is used quite freely to convey the sense of more vivid narrative, to retell dreams, plots, tell jokes, etc. In BEV, the historical present is used much less than in other dialects. For many of the groups and speakers we have worked with, it is not used at all. A few forms like *come* and *say* can give the impression of the use of the historical present, but that is only because the same form serves for both past and present. And it is also because much -ed is deleted by rule 3. But if we look at the common irregular verbs like *lost, kept, told, did,* we find that they appear in their past forms. To explain this, we can consider the following paradigm:

	Present		Past	
WNS	he kicks	he tells	he kicked	he told
BEV	he kick	he tell	he kick	he told

In WNS and other white dialects, the present is usually clearly differentiated from the past by the third singular -s, irregular past forms, and the -ed suffix. The latter is only occasionally dropped. If the speaker switches to historical present, his switch is immediately signalled by the absence of -ed or ablaut and the presence of -s. But in BEV, there is no -s in the present as we have seen. The -ed in the past can be dropped as often as 90 percent of the time. A switch to the historical present would then be very poorly marked and would not be clearly differentiated from the older, West Indian type of system that uses an invariant form for past and present alike.[3]

It is possible that the preference of BEV for the past in narrative is the result of an historical stage when it was moving away from the unmarked forms. But in any case, the historical present is more limited in BEV today, and one can see that if it were to be used, in the majority of cases it would be invisible and inaudible for all regular verbs. It is therefore not too much to argue that the abstention from the historical present by BEV speakers is connected with the

3. In the West Indian Creole system, the present can be marked optionally by the auxiliary *does.*

absence of third singular -s and the high rate of application of -t,d deletion in past tense morphemes.

The general problem which we face in relating BEV to other dialects is how to evaluate differences in the overt expression of grammatical categories. Are the observed differences in surface structure indications of even greater differences in the deep structure, or merely the result of low-level realization rules, lexical inputs, phonological and late transformational rules? Our own investigations have regularly pointed to the latter alternative. We have frequently encountered cases where sentences differ strikingly from standard English in their surface structure, yet in the final analysis appear to be the result of minor modifications of conditions upon transformational rules or late stylistic options. The case of -ed is one of the simplest and clearest examples of how a superficial difference is created by low-level phonological rules. Only those who are most remote from the speakers and the speech of BEV would claim that the -ed suffix is not present in the grammar (Loflin 1967a). The briefest attention to tape recorded conversations will show the phonological conditioning registered in rule 3. But just as phonological rules can be conditioned by grammatical facts, so these rules can have grammatical consequences, as our discussion of the historical present indicates.

We can now approach the problem of the copula in BEV. One of the most well-known characteristics of this dialect of English is the absence of the copula in the present before predicate nouns and adjectives, locatives and comitative phrases, and the parallel absence of the forms of *to be* in the auxiliary *be . . . ing*:

> He a friend.
> He tired.
> He over there.
> He with us.
> He working with us.

This pattern is paralleled and reinforced by the frequent absence of *is* and *are* in questions: *Why he here? He with you?*

Some linguists would like to produce such sentences by phrase structure rules in which no copula or auxiliary *is/are* appears (Stewart 1966). The arguments for and against the presence of these elements in the underlying phrase structure might be tabulated as follows:

For	*Against*
+1. *ain't* appears in the negative: *He ain't there.*	−1. *ain't* is merely a negative carrier, not a copula.
+2. *was* appears in the past: *He was here.*	−2. *was* is merely a past tense marker, not a copula.
+3. *'m* remains in the 1st person: *I'm here.*	−3. *I'm* is an allomorph of *I*, found in equative sentences.
+4. *'s* appears in *that's, it's, what's* [dæs, ɪs, wʌs]	−4. These are single morphemes.
+5. *be* appears after modals, and in infinitival complements	−5. *be* represents the distinct verb found in *He be good,* as opposed to *He good.*
+6. *is* and *are* appear in tags, *He ain't here, is he?*	−6. automatic *is*-support parallel to automatic *do*-support.
+7. *is* and *are* are never deleted when they appear clause-finally in the surface structure, where standard English does not permit contractions: *There he is, That's what you are, I'm smarter than he is.*	−7. same as 6.

The problem of the copula is the subject of chapter 3, where arguments 1–7 will be presented in greater detail. To most linguists, the case presented here would prove to their satisfaction that the copula is present, and they would reject the arguments against the copula as relatively flimsy and miscellaneous. However, these arguments cannot be discounted, as many of them can be shown to have weight for some speakers of BEV or in other Creoles which are not unrelated. The fact that these negative arguments *can* be put forward suggests that BEV may indeed be showing a Creole ancestry and may have passed through a period when the copula was inserted by a late rule optionally instead of being inserted by an early rule automatically and deleted by a late phonological process.[4]

4. In this discussion I am much indebted to W. Stewart whose vigorous arguments for a Creole background of BEV have illuminated my own thinking on the topic for the past several years.

Argument −1 against the copula runs into difficulties when we
consider that *ain't* alternates with zero forms just like *is* and *are*.
He ain't here ∼ *he not here* is parallel to *He is here* ∼ *he here*. If
we call *ain't* a simple alternant of *not*, we then have to explain why
it occurs only where the tense marker is present, but not without
it, as in *I told you not to do that* but not **I told you to ain't do that*.
Argument −2 runs into the same problem, since *was* is confined to
situations where the tense marker is present. Nevertheless, both −1
and −2 can be maintained if we are willing to call *ain't* and *was*
tense-restricted alternants of NEG and PAST.

Argument −3 finds considerable support in the fact that young
black children frequently find it difficult to segment *I'm* into *I am*.
Stewart's observations were confirmed by Jane Torrey's work in
Harlem. When she challenged five- and six-year-olds with the statement "You're not Robert!" the answer was very often *Yes I'm am*
or *Yes I'm is* as well as *Yes I am*. In one series of tests she obtained
the following results: of 10 black children in the second grade tested,
3 replied *I'm is*, 4 *I'm am*, 1 *I is*, and only 2 *I am*. Four white children
of the same age all said "I am". This response indicates that the form
I'm is not easily segmented, but serves as an allomorph of *I* in
equative sentences for these young children. Nevertheless, the fact
that they produce some form of *to be* in elliptical forms shows that
they recognize the presence of the copula in grammar but have not
mastered the particular forms of *I am*. Secondly, it is not accidental
that *'m* is the only one of the present tense forms of *be* which is
consistently present (well over 95 percent, see chapter 3). There is
no phonological process in BEV which deletes final nasal -m.

Argument −4 is tenable, especially in the light of the fact that
other Creoles, like Hawaiian Creole, also show *tha's* even though
the copula does not have as secure a place as in the grammar: it
is most likely inserted optionally without phonological conditioning
(Day to appear). Three arguments, −5, −6, and −7, have no such
empirical support, but they are not impossible analyses. We conclude
that no abstract analysis in the style of traditional grammar can prove
conclusively that the BEV grammar has the same basic copula and
be mechanism as WNS or SE. Many Creoles which do not have a
single *be* copula have incorporated bits and pieces of the English
copula in fixed forms like *tha's*. To demonstrate the position of the
copula in BEV we must go beyond such abstract arguments and
examine the actual use of the forms in conversation. There we find

a series of alternations that are conditioned by grammatical and, most importantly, phonological factors. The absence of hyper-correction and the existence of phonological conditioning provide the basic evidence for locating the copula in the BEV grammar. In chapter 3 we will show that the copula deletion rule is tightly bound in with a series of other phonological rules. Though BEV may have passed through a stage when forms of *be* were inserted individually and variably, as implied by arguments −1 through −7, it is now aligned so closely with other English dialects that the basic phrase structure and transformations that insert *be* are the same, and the differences are located in the phonological component.

We cannot escape the fact, however, that BEV contains elements in its copula system which are missing from other dialects. The invariant *be* in *He be always fooling around* generally indicates "habitual" behavior: durative or iterative depending on the nature of the action. We will differentiate this invariant *be* as be_2 and use be_1 to refer to the ordinary finite *be* which alternates with *am, is, are,* etc.

5   So you know it all don't be on her; it be half on me and
        half on her.—*Lettie, 12, Chicago*

This be_2 is always [bi:] and does not alternate with the irregular forms as be_1 does. It requires *do*-support as shown in 5. It is not obligatory in any context and can alternate with zero forms or finite forms of be_1:

6   She be standin' with her hand in her pocket, and her
        friend is standin' there, and a man is messin' with her
        friend, . . .—*15, Oscar Brothers, #584*
        If you be beatin' him and he down and he say, "Man, I
        quit," and you get up and walk away, he'll hitcha.—*15,
        Oscar Brothers, #584*

The meaning of be_2 and its uses are discussed in CRR 3288:3.4.1 and in many other articles (Stewart 1966; Fasold 1969). We are here concerned with how the presence of be_2 makes the copula system of BEV a different system from other dialects. Be_2 provides no strong argument for a Creole origin: the closest analogy is with the Anglo-Irish *be*, stemming from the Celtic "consuetudinal" or habitual copula. Nevertheless, it plays an important role in BEV grammar and shows no sign of weakening or disappearing among younger speakers.

The habitual be_2 illustrates again a certain systematicity in BEV rules. We find that it occurs two to five times more often in environments where other dialects have *are* than in *is* environments.

percentage *be* in environment of

	is	*are*
Thunderbirds	07	37
Cobras	15	32
Jets	06	29
Oscar Brothers[5]	00	16

There may be good semantic reasons for this. We may speak of habitual actions by plural subjects more often than singular ones.[6] But we cannot ignore the fact that *are* is deleted about twice as often as *is*. Thus a comparable table of deletion in *is* and *are* shows the parallel:

percentage deletion of

	is	*are*
Thunderbirds	43	85
Cobras	50	74
Jets	42	80
Oscar Brothers	48	89

Here we again observe a subtle systematicity in relations of BEV rules. The deletion of *are* has reached such a high point that it is effectively zeroed out for many speakers. The morpheme be_2 cannot be affected by the phonological processes that attack *are*, so that be_2 naturally falls into the hole left by *are*. To put it more simply, it is easier to put something in where something is not than where something is.

5. The lower figures for be_2 among the Oscar Brothers are typical of the changes observed in BE among older speakers. Overtly marked morphemes like *be* or *done* appear less often among adult speakers than among adolescents, and the Oscar Brothers, 18 and 19 years old, are emerging into adult status.

6. The obvious solution is to test *you* (sg) against *you* (pl) for frequency of be_2, but this has not yet been done.

The use of be_2 is quite irregular from one individual to another: it is a form that is heavily favored by certain speakers and not by others. Yet it is clearly a part of the competence of all BEV speakers, and as far as we can tell, the whole range of black English speakers naturally understand and evaluate be_2 even if they do not use it. We might raise the question as to whether this be_2 can appear in the grammars of other speakers of English as a potential element that could be understood and evaluated even if not used. That is, does BEV require a separate grammar if only to provide for the presence of be_2, or is there a place in general English grammar to show that be_2 is the equivalent of some other element in other dialects?

We are currently conducting research into the possibility and limits of a "pan-dialectal grammar" in the sense advanced by C.-J. Bailey (1972) but answers on be_2 are not yet clear. Whether or not speakers of other dialects are capable of understanding be_2 and locating an equivalent in their grammar remains to be seen. But there is another element of the BEV tense and aspect system which is plainly and simply outside of the competence and understanding of other dialects: the remote perfect *been*.

The position of the present perfect *have* in BEV is skewed by phonological processes and hypercorrection; but in some environments it is quite regular, especially with the negative (CRR 3288:3.4.10). The past perfect with *had* is very common and gives support to *have* in general: but we also have *done* as a perfect marker (carrying "intensive" meaning as well—see CRR 3288:3.5.7). This *done* is a feature of other southern dialects, but appears to be receding in the BEV of northern cities; it is used much less frequently than be_2, for example. A third form *been* appears quite often in contexts that makes it seem as if *have* might have been deleted: *He been gone*. But it also appears in contexts where *have* could not be underlying and the verb could not be a past participle: *I been know your name, I been own one of those*. This form is not common in New York City, though it is recognized and understood there, but it is very common in other areas, e.g., Philadelphia.[7] *Been* in these contexts means 'have for a long time' and implies 'and do so now'. It may be glossed as a 'remote present perfect' since it combines the

7. I am especially indebted to John and Angela Rickford who have called my attention to the common use of *been* in Philadelphia and explained its current meaning with ample evidence from their participant-observation in West Philadelphia.

functions of *used to* and *have . . . ed.* Its relevance to the present
is very strong and this leads to considerable misunderstanding; it
is normally not understood at all by speakers of other dialects. A
psychologist once introduced me to a six-year-old member of his
reading program in West Philadelphia; the boy Samuel who said
hello to me and then turned to the psychologist Paul (I was recording the conversation):

8   Samuel (to Paul):   I been know your name.
         Paul: What?
         Samuel: I *been* know your name.
         Paul: You better know my name?
         Samuel: I *been* know your name.

Samuel meant 'I have known your name for some time and know
it now' was not conveyed by Samuel to Paul. We have pursued this
use of *been* into our studies of pan-dialectal grammars, where we
ask among other questions the following:

a. Someone asked, *Is she married?* and someone answered, *She* <u>been</u>
    married. Do you get the idea that she is married now?
            Yes ____
            No ____
b. A teacher said, *Do you know your number facts?* and a boy
    answered, *I* <u>been</u> *know them.* Do you get the idea that
            he's all ready to take the test ____
            he has to brush up on this stuff ____
c. So what do you think *been* means in *I* <u>been</u> *know them?*
    used to know   ____
    know right now   ____
    knew but can't quite remember ____
    have known for a long time   ____

So far, we find that only those who were raised in the black community or have had some contact with blacks get such questions consistently right. To speakers of other dialects, the unqualified *been*
married implied that 'she is not now married'—that the condition
is terminated. But in BEV it definitely indicates that she is still
married, just as *I been know your name* means that 'I still know
it.' The correct answers as black speakers generally give them are
a: yes; b: he's all ready; c: have known for a long time. In our first
study of 23 subjects, none of the white subjects gave such answers
to similar questions. In a second study of 24 subjects in Kansas, 3

white subjects answered the three questions above correctly: one was raised in Georgia and Florida, the other two said they had learned about *been* from blacks. In a third series of 51 subjects, 9 of 12 blacks gave the answers listed above; 3 were different only on the first question. Of the 39 white subjects, 7 gave the above answers; 5 said they had learned about *been* from blacks, one was a resident for a year and half in the South, and one was an apparent exception.

We conclude that this remote present perfect *been* is not recognized, evaluated, or understood by speakers of other dialects. It will not appear in other grammars, even the widest kind of pan-dialectal grammar, but it is a specific grammatical category of BEV. There are therefore at least two elements of BEV deep structure which are not present in other dialects,—*been* and be$_2$—and there may very well be others which have not yet been reliably identified and demonstrated.

The case of *done* raises an interesting problem parallel to a whole range of phenomena in BEV which I have called elsewhere "tense transfer" (CRR 3288:3.5.5). At first glance these are unconnected disturbances in the grammar or hypercorrections which seem to show irregular patterns in BEV quite different from other dialects. But they turn out to be extensions of the general process represented by *done*.

Done normally occurs before the verb in the same position as the auxiliary *have* and can usually be seen as an equivalent of *have*:

9   I done told you on that.—*13, Jets*
10   But you done tol' em, you don't realize, you d— you have
               told 'em that.—*39, New York City*

It is frequently reinforced with *already*, emphasizing its perfective meaning:

11   She done already cut it up.—*13, Chicago*

It might therefore seem possible to write in a general grammar of English the form *done* as an alternant of *have*, restricted to southern dialects and BEV. In this sense, *done* would have no importance in establishing BEV as a separate system. However, we find that *done* has also an 'intensive' meaning which is not equivalent at all to *have* in other dialects:

12   After you knock the guy down, he done got the works,
               you know he gon' try to sneak you.—*13, Jets*

13   I forgot my hat! I done forgot my hat! I done forgot it!—*an
            elderly black man in a restaurant in Ohio*

Furthermore, we find that the formal properties of *done* are not
equivalent to *have:*

14   'Cause I'll be done put—stuck so many holes in him he'll
            wish he wouldna *said* it.—*17, Cobras*
15   I done about forgot mosta those things.—*46, North
            Carolina*

Done has for all intents and purposes become an adverb, functioning
sometimes like *already* or *really*, and lost its status as a verb. The
same thing has happened to southern *like to* meaning 'almost' but
also with intensive significance:

16   My father liketo kill me.—*15, Oscar Brothers*
17   I was liketo have got shot.—*29, South Carolina*

It is possible that *liketo* is derived from *liked to*, with a past tense
form *-ed*, but it is a fixed form and *-ed* was long since neutralized
and zeroed out for phonological reasons. The same thing has happened in many dialects to *supposed to* and *used to*.

18   'Cause I was supposed to had had it done long time
            ago.—*17, Oscar Brothers*

Supposed to (normally pronounced [posta]) requires *do*-support as
supposed to don't or *don't supposed to:*

19   . . . when he don't supposed to hit me with it.—*9, T-Birds*
20   Indians don't supposed to have those on.—*9, T-Birds*

We observe the same pattern with *useta* which usually does not carry
the tense marker:

21   He useta was workin'.—*10, T-Birds*
22   She useta hadda pick at me.—*35, South Carolina*
23   My mother useta wanted me to be a doctor.—*29, Alabama*

A similar pattern can be observed with *happened to* [hæpənə]:

24   He happened to made the club up.—*16, Cobras*
25   I just happened to wen' over there.—*16, Cobras*

The adverb *better* shows the same loss of auxiliary verbal status and no longer carries the tense marker. This pattern is common to many nonstandard dialects:

26   She better had been fair with me.—*16, Jets*
27   He better hadda moved out.—*16, Jets*

The speaker assigns the tense marker to the next element in the verb phrase. In 26 *have* takes the past tense marker, but in 27 *hadda* is treated as an adverb, and the tense is shifted to the first clearly recognizable verb, *move*, which becomes *moved*.

We find *do*-support supplied for many elements in BEV which do not require *do*-support in other dialects.

28   You must didn't read it too good!—*ca., 50, New York City*
29   . . . to don't throw bottles and rocks.—*11, New York City*

Furthermore, we find finite forms of various verbs appearing in places where other dialects would find them very odd indeed, so that they look like gross mistakes in English syntax:

30   We *did* went to school.—*15, Cobras*

All of these patterns can be clarified if we examine an important aspect of southern syntax, the double modals, and see what extensions occur in BEV. The double modals are well known features of southern grammar, though they have never been studied in the detail that they deserve. At first glance, they seem to defy the canonical rule of English phrase structure, that one modal cannot follow another and would thus require some serious revisions in the most fundamental rules of the auxiliary.

31   If you can find that cancelled check, I may can go out there and get it.—*Florida*

Might would, might could, may can, useta could are used in various combinations by white speakers throughout the South. Rebecca Moreton of Jackson, Mississippi, reports to us from her own experience that *may can* and *may could* are acceptable colloquial style; that *might* is coupled with *could (have), can, would (have),* and *ought to;* that *must(a), ought(a),* and *supposed(a)* can precede *could;* and *useta* can precede *could* or *would.* Any of these are negativized by adding *'nt* to the second modal. But *must don't* and *might don't* are marked for her as characteristic of black speakers only.

Note that the first forms of the double modals are those which have "zero" tense markers in other dialects. *Can* and *could* differentiate past from present (not in BEV or in New York City) and have a -*d* ending, but they function only as a second member. *May* and *might* are both nonpast, but formally none of these first members of "double modals" have any mark that could be identified with a tense signal.

If this analysis is correct, question forms would have to be

32   He might could do that → Could he might do that?

But no clear evidence on yes-no questions or tag forms have been obtained. Intuitions of southern speakers are very weak on this point and we have no evidence from speech.

In BEV, we find many examples of the double modal pattern:

33   I might can't get no more fines, neither.—*12, New York City*

This can be translated into northern SE by substituting the nonfinite *be able to* for the finite forms, just as in 31. But there are many forms that cannot be treated this way.

34   In deep water, I might can get hurt.—*14, New York City*
35   Even in the streets, people useta would ask us to sing.—*37, South Carolina*

Here *might can* seems to equal 'might' and *useta would* equals either 'useta' or 'would', and these seem to be pleonastic forms. We also get extensions of the various patterns of other southern dialects, as in the future:

36   Can you get your civil rights without getting your head busted? You might will in the long run.—*29, Alabama*

We also get *must* used as the first form of a double modal:

37   Well, you must can't fuck good, then.—*26, N.J.*

Now we also find that the pattern is extended by supplying *do* + NEG after a modal instead of *can* + NEG as in 37. This appeared already after *must* in 28. We also find:

38   If they gon' walk around the street with holes in they pants, they must don't have too much in they wardrobe, right?—*17, Oscar Brothers*

39   She still might don't even like the thing.—*39, New York City*

40   You might could go to the church and pray a little, but you—that still might don't help you.—*13, Jets*

Here it has become clear that *might* and *must* are functioning formally as adverbs, without a tense marker. This is not surprising in the light of the fact that they have no formal mark, do not participate in flip-flops in questions in colloquial English, do not contract, or show the other properties of the first member of the auxiliary which contains a tense marker. We do not get the same kind of loss of auxiliary status with *will, have, do,* or *can,* which are identified by the yes-no transformation and (in the case of *will* and *have*) can be contracted (see chapter 3 for the identification of tense marker by the contraction rule).[8] Our conclusion is that all of these phenomena can be seen as examples of a single on-going process: the loss of tense marker in the underlying grammar for items that do not have an overt phonological mark.

done	better
liketo	may
hafta	might
useta	must
supposta	

These items would then appear in the dictionary as adverbs. No change in the grammar is actually required, since we now find that they behave like other adverbs: *probably, maybe, always.* The rules for adverb placement are different in southern syntax and BEV, and they have not yet been worked out, but it is plain that the various rules of yes-no question, tag formation, contraction, which affect the first members of auxiliaries containing the tense marker will not affect these elements. Since they generally precede that first element, the tense marker and *do* support will be supplied after them.

We conclude that no systematic change in the grammar of BEV is required by "double modals," and in other southern dialects we may also be able to account for them by changing the status of the first element to an adverb.

8. There is some evidence for a lack of clarity in the identification of *can* as carrying the tense marker from the hypercorrection of third singular *-s* as in *He can goes out.* But there are so many other odd placements of *-s* that we cannot take this as a specific response to *can* (see CRR 3288:3.3.5).

Turning now to a more complex aspect of BEV syntax, we can consider negative inversion:

41   Ain't nothin' happenin' 'n' shit.—*Jets, 16*
42   Ain't nobody gon' let you walk all around town to find somebody to whup them.—*Jets, 15*
43   Ain't no white cop gonna put his hands on me.—*Jets, 16*
44   Ain't nobody in my family Negro.—*12, T-Birds*

These forms differ strikingly from standard English in that the inverted order associated with questions is here used in a declarative statement, equivalent to WNS, *Nothin' ain' happenin' 'n' shit*. It is possible to analyse 40–43 as derived from a deletion of dummy *it*:

41'   It ain't nothin' happenin' 'n' shit.

equivalent to WNS *There isn't nothin' happenin'*. But this analysis breaks down for other examples where along with the tense marker and negative we have a modal or *do* being inverted:

45   Don't nobody break up a fight.—*12, Chicago*
46   Doesn't nobody really know that it's a God, you know.—*16, Jets*
47   Can't nobody tag you then.—*12, Chicago*

Such modal inversion is common in other southern dialects. The relation between BEV and these other dialects is approximately the same as for double modals: BEV extends the normal southern forms several steps further. Beginning with the inversion of modals as in 47, we add the movement of a simple tense marker with *do*-support and the forms of *be* with the negative in 41–44. There is no difficulty in integrating all of these processes into a single grammar of English, since we already have the basic mechanism for inversion in standard forms. In Standard Literary English (SLE) it is possible to bring negative adverbs to the front of a sentence, at the same time reversing the position of tense marker and subject. We observe this in our interviews with middle-class speakers of black English:

48   Not until he came into the United States did they decide to get married . . .—*31, Bronx*
49   The Negro doesn't know about the Negro, and neither does the white know about the Negro.—*26, Ohio*

The closest SLE analogy to forms 41–44 is 41″

41″   Nor is anything happening.

which is a bit stiff but still a part of the machinery of English. The extension of the process we see here is limited largely to cases with subject indeterminates, as it is clearly related to negative concord (see chapter 4). We can then differentiate BEV from SLE by saying that negative inversion freely applies when the speaker has an indeterminate *any* quantifier, and instead of moving negative adverbs to the front, he can move the first member of the auxiliary along with the negative participle. The full description of the rule systems involved has not yet been worked out (see CRR 3288:3.6.5), but it is clear that there is no major obstacle towards integrating the BEV rules with those of other dialects. From the study of these various cases, we can come to the following conclusions:

1. BEV is a distinct system from other dialects in several important grammatical categories of the tense and aspect system.
2. BEV extends many of the rules of other dialects by including new environments and raising output probabilities in older environments. No new transformations are required to account for the special forms of BEV involving negation, quantifiers, modals, and other functional elements of the grammatical mechanism.
3. BEV shows its systematic character in a set of interrelations between rules of types 1 and 2 such that they operate jointly to preserve the major grammatical and semantic functions of language.

Given the properties of the BEV system, let us now consider what happens when direct contact is made between it and other grammars. In the course of our studies in south-central Harlem, we discovered that repetition tests with adolescent boys could yield a great deal of information, showing what happened when speakers of BEV tried to absorb and repeat back SE forms, and when WNS speakers tried to absorb and repeat BEV forms. The full report on these "Memory Tests" is given in CRR 3288:3.9; further studies of this sort have since been carried out by Baratz (1969) and Garvey and McFarlane (1968).

The memory tests were given to several groups of BEV speakers that we had known for some time. A complicated betting system insured that everyone was trying as hard as possible, and subjects (who were tested individually) returned to the group with a report on how many nickels they had won. In all of these tests, we find

a remarkable transformation occurring when BEV speakers are faced
with SE sentences containing embedded yes-no questions.

> *Test pattern:* I asked Alvin if he could go.
>
> *Boot:* I as' Alvin could he—could he go.
>
> *Test pattern:* I asked Alvin whether he knows how to
> play basketball.
>
> *Boot:* (*1st*): I asked Alvin—I asked Alvin—I can't—I didn't
> quite hear you.
>
> (*2nd*): I asked Alvin did he know how to play
> basketball.
>
> (*3rd*): I asked Alvin whether—did he know how to
> play basketball.

About half of the Thunderbirds produce responses like Boot's. Even
if the standard sentence is said very slowly and repeated many times,
the BEV form is repeated back with very different word order and
grammatical machinery. This has no relation to general memory or
ability to repeat: many longer sentences are repeated back rapidly
and accurately if they do not contradict BEV rules.

This behavior leads us to a more far-reaching conclusion about
the linguistic structure available to our subjects. We can ask what
linguistic competence is required to explain the rapid repetition:

> A: I asked Alvin if he knows how to play basketball.
>
> B: → I aks Alvin do he know how to play basketball.

In the most obvious view, we can observe that the subject failed
to perform the task required. But we cannot overlook the fact that
B is the correct equivalent of A; it has the same meaning and is
produced by the nonstandard rule which is the nearest equivalent
to the standard rule. In the standard form, the order of the yes-no
question is re-reversed when it is embedded with the complementizer *if* it means 'whether or not'.

> A1: I asked Alvin-#-Q-he knows how to play basket-
> ball #
>
> A2: I asked Alvin-#-Q-does he know how to play bas-
> ketball #
>
> A3: I asked Alvin if he knows how to play basketball.

In the nonstandard form, the order of the yes-no question is preserved when it is embedded without a complementizer.

> B1: I aks Alvin-#-Q-he knows how to play basketball #
> B2: I aks Alvin-#-Q-do he know how to play basket-
> ball #
> B3: I aks Alvin do he know how to play basketball.

Thus the original Q of the deep structure is represented in the standard sentence as *if,* and in the nonstandard sentence as reversal of auxiliary and subject-noun phrase. The nonstandard rules differ from the standard only in the absence of the *if*-complementizer placement A3.

Since the listener does perform the translation, it is clear that he does understand the standard sentence. He then rapidly produces the correct nonstandard equivalent B3. Understanding here must mean perception, analysis, and storage of the sentence in some relatively abstract form. If the nonstandard were converted to standard, it would mean the *addition* of the *if*-complementizer rule. Since standard is converted to nonstandard, we can only infer that the perceived sentence is decoded at least to the depth of A2-B2 from the point of view of production, but at least to A1-B1 from the point of view of perception and understanding.

From these considerations, it is clear that the listener is perfectly competent in (at least this) aspect of the standard grammar. The overall linguistic structure which describes his competence is rather complex:

$$
\begin{array}{ll}
\textit{Perception} & \textit{Production} \\
\rightarrow A3 \rightarrow A2 \rightarrow A1 \Big\} & \\
\rightarrow B3 \rightarrow B2 \rightarrow B1 \Big\} & B1 \rightarrow B2 \rightarrow B3 \rightarrow
\end{array}
$$

This asymmetrical situation is apparently well-formed in the sense that the listener-speaker will use this set of rules persistently and reliably as indicated in the test situation, and we can infer that his behavior in school is not very different as he decodes the teacher's speech production or printed texts in reading.

This view of the relations of BEV and SE in the competence of black speakers shows that they do indeed form a single system. Some SE forms may be outside of the competence of BEV speakers—*whether* seems to be one of these in the examples given above. But it cannot be said that the SE rules for yes-no questions lie outside of the BEV system. Though we have indicated above the ways in which BEV shows internal cohesion, it is best seen as a distinct subsystem within the larger grammar of English. Certain parts of the tense and aspect system are clearly separate subsystems in the sense that they are not shared or recognized by other dialects, and we can isolate other such limited areas. But the gears and axles of English grammatical machinery are available to speakers of all dialects, whether or not they use all of them in everyday speech. In the next two chapters, we will explore in detail the ways in which BEV utilizes this machinery in its own productive system and write detailed rules which show the specific relations between this grammar and other dialects.

3 | Contraction, Deletion, and Inherent Variability of the English Copula

THE study of the black English vernacular (BEV) provides a strategic research site for the analysis of English structure in general.[1] BEV differs from standard English (SE) in many subtle and unexpected ways. In this chapter we will examine one of the most intricate and challenging problems: the appearance and disappearance of the copula in the vernacular. As in any study of variability, our basic problem is to locate the source of that variation: what is varying? At what level of the grammar does the copula appear first and what controls its disappearance? Does this variation have any relation to processes in other dialects of English?

It is important to note here that we are dealing with the synchronic description of the structure of BEV as it is spoken today in the black population centers of the United States.[2] The origins of BEV, its earlier history, and its relation to the Creole continuum are matters of great interest, and some of the findings of this chapter are relevant to them. I will indicate at various points where the data touches on the Creole hypothesis (Stewart 1968, 1970; Dillard 1971) and develop further the observations made in the last chapter. Recent studies of the Creole continuum in Guyana (Bickerton 1971) and Hawaii (Day

---

1. This chapter first appeared in *Language* 45: no. 4 (Dec. 1969) and is reprinted here by permission of the Linguistic Society of America. The present version includes a number of modifications of the formal interpretation of variable rules and additions to the corroborating data from other studies.

2. As noted in the introduction, our own studies include exploratory interviews in most of the major cities of the United States. The geographical origin of the adult speakers quoted gives further indication of the generality of BEV grammar. The detailed investigation of Detroit by Wolfram (1969) and others will be cited below to further illustrate the stability and generality of our findings and the uniformity of BEV grammar.

1972) illuminate the situation we are describing, both in their similarities and their differences. We must recognize that youth growing up in the inner cities today is not in contact with that Creole continuum. Their language, like any other, is the product of an historical development which can be traced only through the most probable interpretation of a limited body of residual data. But the black English vernacular which they hear, learn, and produce today is available for precise description through an unlimited body of data drawn from everyday conversation. That vernacular is the topic of this chapter.

The main body of data for this study of variation is obtained from our long-term participant-observation of black peer groups in south-central Harlem. We will refer to peer-group members, lames, adults of various class backgrounds, and white control groups. The methods for recording in group sessions and individual interviews are discussed in the introduction and in greater detail in CRR 3288:2.1. The validity of what is said here about BEV depends upon the fact that our methods did indeed capture the basic vernacular and solve the Observer's Paradox (*Sociolinguistic Patterns*, chapter 8). The effects of the recording situation are of course never absent, but they can be overridden by more powerful social controls exerted by peer-group members in excited and rapid interaction. Quotations from the group sessions in the introduction will give some orientation on this point, but more complete familiarity with the style of peer-group interaction can be obtained from chapters 8 and 9.

In attacking these questions, we will introduce a series of BEV rules in the context of some general rules of English phonology; some of these have not been analyzed before. The articulation of the BEV rules with higher-level rules of English will give added support to proposals that have been put forward in generative phonology. The analysis will be carried out within a generative framework, moving from syntactic arguments to phonological ones. At some points, intuitions on standard English will be called on. This "SE" is first the colloquial style of the author and his co-investigators, but no great reliance is placed on intuitions unchecked by observation. Since this analysis was originally presented (at the Linguistic Society of America in 1967) I have gathered additional data from interviews and observations of speakers in many areas, white and black, as well as from my own speech.

In this chapter and the next I have tried to put forward a model of linguistic analysis which combines evidence from the observation of speech, experimentation, and formal elicitation. (*Sociolinguistic Patterns*, chapter 8). Central to this analysis is the quantitative study of variation, which will occupy the major part of our attention. In this chapter, the formal statement of *variable rules* will be developed in detail. A revised version of the mathematical interpretation of variable rules will be presented, following the suggestions of Cedergren and Sankoff (1972).

1. The Status of the Copula in BEV

In this section, the techniques of standard generative grammar will be used to examine the position of the copula and auxiliary *be* in BEV.[3] It is well known that BEV frequently shows the absence of *be* in a variety of syntactic environments such as those in 1–12.

—NP

    1 She the first one started us off.—*35, S.C., 729*[4]

    2 Means he a faggot or sump'm like that.—*18, Oscar Bros., 570*

—PA

    3 He fast in everything he do.—*16, Jets, 560*

    4 I know, but he wild, though.—*13, T-Birds, 451*

—Loc

    5 You out the game.—*10, N.Y.C., 362*

    6 We on tape.—*16, Chicago, 471*

—Neg

    7 But everybody not black.—*15, Jets, 524*

    8 They not caught.—*11, T-Birds, 429*

3. The awkward disjunction "copula and auxiliary *be*" is necessary here since the *be* of the progressive and future is usually not considered the same grammatical form as the copula before noun phrases and predicates. At various points in the discussion, *copula* is used as a shorter way to refer to both where no ambiguity is likely. As the discussion progresses, it will be obvious that the issue is not an important one for the rules we are investigating, since it is the finite forms of *be* which are involved in the phonological component of the grammar. The distinction between copula and auxiliary will however reappear in terms of the influence of the following grammatical environment on the variable rules which contract and delete these forms.

4. The three items following each quotation identify the speaker: his age; his peer-group membership in New York City, or other geographical background (area raised in the years 4–13); and tape number on which the quotation can be heard. These tapes are available for further research, investigation, and comparison to all those interested in the study of language in its social context.

___Ving

    9 He just feel like he gettin' cripple up from arthritis.—*48, N.C., 232*

    10 Boot always comin' over my house to eat, to ax for food.—*10, T-Birds, 451*

___gon

    11 He gon' try to get up.—*12, T-Birds, 451*

    12 'Cause we, we gon' sneak under the turnstile.—*13, Cobras, 488*

These examples of missing *be* have led several observers to conclude that there is no present copula or auxiliary *be* (see Stewart 1966). This would seem to be a reasonable inference in view of the fact that a great many languages show no present copula—e.g. Hungarian or Hebrew. The French Creole of the Caribbean (Solomon 1966) shows the same pattern (13–14), and so does the English Creole of Trinidad (15–16).

13	mwē ā čwizin.	15	I in the kitchen.
14	mwē esit.	16	I here.

The English Creole of Jamaica (Bailey 1966) shows no copula in some of the environments of 1–12, as for example before predicate adjectives:

17	*im sik bad* 'She is very sick.'
18	*di tiicha gud* 'The teacher is good.'

Furthermore, the sentences used generally by children 18 to 24 months old show no copula (Bloom 1970), and there seems to be little basis for constructing one in the underlying phrase structure:

19	That a lamb.	23	Man in blocks.
20	That a bear book.	24	Tiny balls in there.
21	It a my book.	25	Mommy busy.
22	Kathy in there.		

The suggestion that BEV has no copula or auxiliary *be* is therefore plausible in that this is a very common pattern, particularly in languages which may have had considerable contact with and influence on BEV; in this analysis, BEV would differ from SE in a high-level rule of the grammar.

The question raised here is not the same as the question as to whether the copula appears in the phrase structure of SE or BEV. There are many ways to introduce the copula into the early rules of English grammar; it is not at all necessary that this be done by a phrase structure rule. The rule given by Chomsky (1965:107) shows a copula in the phrase structure:

$$26 \qquad VP \rightarrow \left\{ \begin{array}{l} \text{Copula} + \text{Predicate} \\ V \left\{ \begin{array}{l} \text{(NP)} \quad \text{(PP)} \quad \text{(PP)} \quad \text{(Manner)} \\ S' \\ \text{Predicate} \end{array} \right. \end{array} \right\}$$

However, Bach's suggestion (1967) that the copula should be introduced by an early transformation such as 27 whenever it is followed by a bare predicate appears quite reasonable, since it is obviously predictable in this environment:

$$27 \qquad \begin{array}{llll} T^{ob} \text{ cop: } X - \text{Aux} - \text{Pred} - Y \\ \quad\quad\quad\quad 1 \quad\quad 2 \quad\quad 3 \quad\quad 4 \rightarrow 1 \quad 2 + be \quad 3 \quad 4 \end{array}$$

Another possible approach is that of Rosenbaum 1968; here the auxiliary *be* is introduced by a segmentalization transformation from features of the following element, and the copula could plainly be handled by the same device:

$$28 \qquad \begin{array}{lll} X - [+\text{prog}]_{VB} - Y \\ 1 \quad\quad\quad 2 \quad\quad\quad 3 \rightarrow 1 \quad \begin{bmatrix} +\text{prog} \\ +\text{COP} \end{bmatrix} + 2 \quad 3 \end{array}$$

Whichever method we select for treating the copula, the issue is whether BEV has such high-level rules as 26, 27, or 28, or whether BEV differs from SE in not having such a rule. The evidence of the following section supports the former alternative.

2. Environments in Which Forms of be *Regularly Appear in BEV*

Despite the fact that the copula and auxiliary *be* frequently do not appear in BEV in the variety of environments shown in 1–12, there is a wide variety of other environments in which these forms regularly do appear. The following examples are typical of a large number produced by our grammatical searching of many interviews and group sessions. For most of these environments, the forms of *be* appear in the overwhelming majority of cases, and contrary examples are extremely rare: in effect, the appearance of *be* obeys a categorical rule.

The first examples concern forms of *be* other than *is* and *are;* these forms are rarely deleted. In the past, *was* appears regularly:

29   I was small; I was sump'm about one years o' baby.--*12, Aces, 464*

30   She was likin' me . . . she was likin' George too.—*18, Oscar Bros., 556*

It can be contended that this is a simple past tense marker, having no connection with SE *be.* Similarly, one might argue that the *ain't* which regularly appears is merely a negative marker:

31   It ain't no cat can't get in no coop.—*15, Cobras, 490*

32   My sons, they ain't but so big.—*26, N.Y.C., 840*

However, a simple negative *not* frequently appears as in 7–8, evidently the representative of the negative without the copula. If *ain't* does not represent *is* plus *not,* then we must conclude that there are two negative markers in free variation or search for some possible semantic difference between *They not black* and *They ain't black.*

In the first person, the form *I'm* is regularly found:

33   I'm tired, Jeannette.—*48, N.C., 232*

34   I'm not no strong drinker.—*15, N.Y.C., YH44*

This form occurs with overwhelming frequency, despite the fact that it is possible to find rare instances of plain *I, I is,* or even *I'm is.* If the task of writing a grammar for a nonstandard speech community is that of finding the regular linguistic patterns, we must conclude that the form *I'm,* which occurs in well over 99 percent of the cases, represents the pattern here.[5]

5. In the last chapter (page 50) we cited evidence which supports Stewart's objection to this argument. While it is true that *I'm* is the overwhelmingly predominant form in natural conversation (960 out of 1000 cases), young black children have difficulty in segmenting *I'm* into *I + am.* In natural conversation, we recorded only three cases of *I'm is* among older children, but this was a common response among six-year-olds along with *I'm am* when the investigator said "You're not David!" (and he was). One eight-year-old insisted that the written form AM contained the letter S, not M because she was convinced that the copula was spelled I-S. White children of the same age do not seem to share this difficulty in reconstructing the full form of *am.* The data shows of course that young children are fully aware of the copula in their system but have not yet absorbed all of the context-restrictions. See Torrey 1972 for evidence that young children use more full forms of *is* than older children. The difficulty with *I'm* is one of the pieces of evidence that points to a possible Creole origin of present day BEV, or at least to a period when BEV was more different from SE than it is today.

The cases of *i's*, *tha's*, and *wha's* provide other examples in which the copula is frequently represented:

35   I's a real light yellow color.—*15, Cobras, 490*
36   Tha's my daily routine: women.—*14, Cobras, 497*
37   Wha's a virgin?—*12, Jets, 637*

While we occasionally do get plain *it*, as in *It always somebody tougher than you are*, these forms [ɪs], [ðæs], and [wʌs] are again found in the great majority of cases and assume considerable significance for the final statement of the rule which operates in 1–12.

We also find the form *be* without exception wherever the SE copula would follow a modal or appear in the infinitive form:

38   You got to be good, Rednall!—*15, Jets, 524*
39   His wife is suppos' a be gettin' money for this child.—*48, N.C., 232*

It would seem obvious that the declarative form *You good, Rednall!* corresponds to the modal form (38). There is no way to convert *You good* into **You got to good* without realizing the underlying *be*. The same situation prevails with imperatives:

40   Be cool, brothers!—*15, Jets, 524*
41   Don't be messin' with my old lady!—*16, Jets, 560*

We now consider environments in which the forms *is* and *are*, which do not appear in 1–12, do appear regularly in BEV. Under emphasis, we find:

42   Allah *is* God.—*16, Cobras, 648*
43   He *is* a expert.—*12, T-Birds, 396*

The finite forms of *be* also appear in yes-no questions, e.g.:

44   Is he dead? is he dead?—Count the bullet holes in his motherfucking head.—*16, Jets, 560*
45   Are you down?—*13, Jets, 497*
46   Are you gon' give us some pussy?—*13, Jets, 632*

We also obtain yes-no questions without *is* and *are*; the problem of the question transformation and the base forms of questions must be considered elsewhere. But in the large number of cases where *is* and *are* do appear in questions, we must relate them to underlying declarative sentences with copula *be*. The examples chosen here are deliberately selected to show that these are vernacular forms: to explain these examples as "dialect mixture" or as importations from standard English would be an extremely unlikely hypothesis.

In the case of tag questions, the finite forms of *be* are required; e.g.:

47   Is that a shock? or is it not?—*13, Cobras, 493*

Again we find that *is* occurs in the most excited and spontaneous interaction in group sessions.

The most interesting examples, from the syntactic point of view, are those in which we find *is* and *are* in clause-final position, as the result of several transformational processes. In elliptical responses:

48   (You ain't the best sounder, Eddie!) I ain't! He is!—*12, Cobras, 489*

After ellipsis in comparative constructions:

49   He is better than the girls is, now.—*35, S.C., 729*
50   It always somebody tougher than you are.—*25, Fla., 825*

In embedded questions, after WH-attraction:

51   That's what he is: a brother.—*14, Cobras, 492*
52   I don't care what you are.—*16, Jets, 580*
53   Do you see where that person is?—*15, N.Y.C., YH35*

In all of these frequent forms, we find the finite forms *is* and *are* without exception.

It is possible, with sufficient ingenuity, to provide an explanation for each of the cases in this section, and to claim that there is no connection between these forms and the sentences of 1–12 (see page 49 of chapter 2). Some of these arguments are ad hoc and unconvincing, such as the claim that the infinitive *to be* is really the habitual *be*$_2$ of BEV and not the copula. Others are defensible and plausible alternative explanations of the data, such as the claim that *I'm* is a single morpheme for younger speakers. However, it will be obvious to all familiar with the logic of transformational grammar that the evidence given here points to the existence of an underlying copula and auxiliary *be* which is deleted in the specific environments of 1–12. The question then remains, by what kind of rule are these finite forms of *be* deleted? Is it a transformational rule which deletes the copula, or a separate set of rules which delete *is* and *are*? Or is it a phonological rule which operates at a lower level in the grammar? We will now proceed to specify the nature of this deletion rule more precisely.

3. The General Nature of the Deletion Rule and Its Relation to Contraction

First, we can observe a number of signs of phonological influence upon the deletion rule. *Is* and *are* are deleted, but *'m* is not: there are phonological processes which operate upon final [z] and [r] in BEV, but not upon final [m]. *Ain't* and *be* are phonologically distinct from *is* and *are* in that they contain tense vowels which are not reduced to shwa or contracted. *Was* and *were* begin with a consonant which is not generally deleted. The forms *i's* [ɪs], *tha's* [ðæs], and *wha's* [wʌs] are plainly the result of some low-level process of assimilation, which transforms them in such a way that they are protected from the deletion rule. It follows that the deletion rule is ordered after the processes which change *it is* to *i's* [ɪs].

But the most important suggestion which proceeds from the examples of section 2 is the relation between contraction and deletion. We find that the following general principle holds without exception: wherever SE can contract, BEV can delete *is* and *are,* and vice versa; wherever SE cannot contract, BEV cannot delete *is* and *are,* and vice versa. This intimate relationship between contraction and deletion will be illustrated by the examples below.

3.1. *The rule for contraction of the English auxiliary.* To the best of my knowledge, the rules for SE contraction have never been explored in print in any detail. It is therefore necessary to look into the conditions under which contraction can occur and to specify the form of the contraction rule in order to understand its relation to deletion and the form and position of the deletion rule itself.

Just as SE cannot contract in final position, so BEV cannot delete. These examples illustrate the parallel:

	SE	BEV
54	* He's as nice as he says he's.	* He's as nice as he says he.
55	* How beautiful you're!	* How beautiful you!
56	Are you going? * I'm.	Are you going? * I.
57	* Here I'm.	* Here I.

The patterns shown by the data are so absolute that I feel justified in placing asterisks in the BEV column to indicate that the form is impossible, even without asking for intuitive judgments of native speakers. From these examples, it would appear that the rule is simply that contraction is impossible in final position. But 58–61 show that there is more to the matter than this:

	SE	BEV
58	* Who's it?	* Who it?
59	Who's IT?	Who IT?
60	* What's it?	* What it?
61	What's it for?	What it for? Wha's it for?

We cannot say 58 with dummy *it*, although we can say 59 with lexical *IT* ('the person who is IT in a game'). We cannot say 60, with dummy *it*, but we can say 61, when stressed *for* follows. It would seem then that a stressed syllable must follow the *is* or *are* if it is to be contracted or deleted. Still, 62–64 show that the situation is more complex:

	SE	BEV
62	* He's now.	* He now.
63	* He's unfortunately.	* He unfortunately.
64	He's unfortunately here.	He unfortunately here.

In both 62 and 63, there are stressed forms following the copula, yet we cannot delete or contract. In 64, after the addition of *here*, we can contract and delete. It is evident at this point that the grammatical relations between *is* and *are* and the following elements are important to the rule. Such grammatical relations figure in the stress assignment rules provided by Chomsky and Halle 1968, and these allow us to state the initial conditions which govern contraction. The Chomsky-Halle rules are used here with only one modification: the weak word rule.[6] The following set of three rules operate to provide these conditions:

6. Chomsky and Halle do not discuss *be* or the copula in detail; but *The Sound Pattern of English* (p. 22, fn. 11), makes it clear that primary stress will not be assigned to auxiliaries or the copula by the main stress rule as has been done here. On p. 240, they apply this rule only before brackets labeled with the major categories N, A, V, S, or P, but not *Aux*. The # boundary is automatically inserted at the beginning and end of every string dominated by a major category (p. 366): thus we have surface structures such as $[_s\#[_{NP}\#[_N\#John\#]_N\#]_{NP}[_{VP}\#$ is $[_A\#crazy\#]_A\#]_{VP}\#]$s. The auxiliary or copula is thus not a "phonological word" in the sense introduced by Chomsky and Halle and does not receive main stress and the vowel of *is* is automatically reduced unless contrastive stress intervenes. After the ellipsis transformation

65        $\begin{bmatrix} \text{1stress} \\ \text{V} \end{bmatrix} \rightarrow [\text{1stress}]/\overset{1}{\text{V}} \cdots \underline{\hphantom{xxx}} \cdots]_\alpha$

                                                              Nuclear stress rule

66        $\begin{bmatrix} +\text{W} \\ \text{3stress} \\ \text{V} \end{bmatrix} \rightarrow [-\text{stress}]$ Weak word rule

67        $\begin{bmatrix} -\text{stress} \\ -\text{tense} \\ \text{V} \end{bmatrix} \rightarrow \text{ə}$ Vowel reduction

---

which removes *crazy*, we would presumably have a surface structure $[_S \# [_{NP} \# [_N \#$ *John* $\#]_N \#]_{NP} [_{VP} \#$ *is* $\#]_{VP} \#]_S$; the main stress rule, which assigns primary stress to *crazy* without ellipsis, assigns primary stress to *is* in these elliptical forms. This treatment would provide a simpler mechanism than the weak word rule and allow us to do away with the special feature [+W] and so predict the behavior of *is* and *was* from the general stress rules. This would mean that the main stress rule should apply to verb phrases as well as verbs, for the nuclear stress rule will only apply to items which have already received primary stress. Without ellipsis, *is* will never receive stress and will automatically be reduced and be subject to contraction: no further consideration of the transformational cycle is required.

There is good evidence that auxiliaries do receive primary stress by the main stress rule and are reduced by the transformational cycle. The application of the Chomsky-Halle stress rules sketched above will yield the wrong result when there are several auxiliaries in an elliptical sentence: *He may have;* *He may have been.* Contraction would then apply to first elements containing the tense marker, yielding *He's been;* *He'll have been.* But this contraction and these stress patterns are as impossible as any we have yet encountered. The actual result is a primary stress on the first auxiliary and an even series of secondary or tertiary stresses on the others: *He may have been;* *He will have; He has been.* We cannot explain the even noncontrastive stress which appears in the second and third members of the series unless we assume that stress has been applied by the main stress rule and reduced only one step by a single application of the transformational cycle. The fact that nuclear stress falls on the first element can be provided for by extending the compound rule to include auxiliaries as well as nouns and verbs: [*may have been*] $_{AUX}$ is thus a compound like [*hot dogs*]$_N$ or [*comparison shop*]$_V$.

Finally, it should be pointed out that the category of "weak words" and the feature [+W] are independently motivated by the rules for tensing of short *a* in many dialects of English. Paul Cohen (1970) has shown that this feature allows us to account for the oppositions *an* ∼ *Ann, have* ∼ *halve, can* (Aux) ∼ *can* (verb, noun), *as* ∼ *razz,* by the use of the single feature [+W], where other alternatives are much more complex.

The nuclear stress rule (cf. Chomsky and Halle 1968:17–18, rules 9–10) is a cyclical rule which reassigns primary stress to the last lexical item within each phrase marker, by convention reducing the stress assignment of all other items by one unit. The subscript alpha here stands for any label except *N*, *A*, or *V*. The phrase marker boundaries are then erased, and the rule applies to the next larger phrase. The weak word rule operates so that words which can occur with shwa as their only vowel are reduced to [−stress] from [3stress], whereas other syllables will be reduced to [−stress] only from [4stress] or [5stress], and weaker. The vowel reduction rule (67) is the last rule in the Chomsky-Halle series. Contraction then follows: it is the removal of a shwa which occurs initially in a word before a lone consonant. The operation of these rules is illustrated in the examples of Fig. 3.1. In *Tom is wild*, the nuclear stress rule operates twice, reducing *is* to [3stress]; then the weak word rule makes this [−stress], vowel reduction and contraction apply, yielding *Tom's wild*. In the elliptical form *Tom is*, there is only one cycle with full stress on *is* (or if emphatic stress is placed on *Tom*, with [2stress] on *is*). No contraction is possible. In *Tom is wild at night*, there are again two cycles, and the rules yield *Tom's wild at night*. But after ellipsis of *wild*, as in *Bill is wild during the day, and Tom is at night*, the copula *is* is not in construction with *at night*, and there is only one cycle for the nuclear stress rule.[7]

3.2. *The problem of* what I mean. The general principle underlying the discussion so far is that the possibility of contraction in SE is

---

7. In a recent study of auxiliary reduction in English, Zwicky (1970) argues that stress considerations are not sufficient to predict the contractability of *is*. His critical cases involve the application of *Glide Deletion* (which operates only on unstressed elements) but not contraction. The examples cited are *Tweedledum has gobbled more oysters than Tweedledee (h)as* and *Gerda has been to North Dakota as often as Trudi (h)as*. Zwicky states that "in my speech the vowel of *has* in these examples is reducible, so that *has* may appear as [əz] but not as [z]" but adds that "there are speakers of English who disagree with me on this point." This situation has since been used as the basis of an argument for derivational constraints (Lakoff 1970). It seems unwise to base an important theoretical claim on such subjective and disputed data, especially when we note that both involve the application of contrastive stress to the item immediately preceding *has*. If contrastive stress operates in the same fashion as normal stress assignment, it regularly reduces the stress of other elements in the phrase, which may be responsible for the marginal behavior of the auxiliary here. I do not believe that the same claim would be made for *I told him about the difficulty that George has* which does not show contrastive stress.

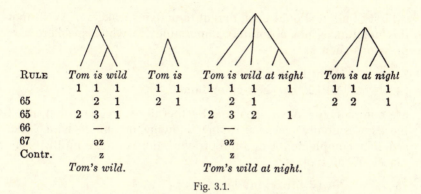

RULE	Tom is wild			Tom is		Tom is wild at night				Tom is at night		
	1	1	1	1	1	1	1	1	1	1	1	1
65		2	1	2	1		2	1			2	2	1
65	2	3	1			2	3	2	1				
66		—			—								
67		əz			əz								
Contr.		z			z								
	Tom's wild.			*Tom's wild at night.*									

Fig. 3.1.

in a one-to-one correlation with the possibility of deletion in BEV. However, the following quotation seems to be a blunt contradiction of the principle:

68   What I mean by bein' destroyed, they was brought up into they rightful nature.—*29, N.J., 737*

This is a case of clause-final *is*, produced by WH-attraction, and the rules of stress assignment and vowel reduction presented above will not allow this to be contracted:

69   * What I mean by being destroyed's, they was brought up into they rightful nature.

There is nothing in the development so far to indicate that this principle can be variable. The contraction rule is dependent on the categorical stress assignment and reduction rules, and if contraction does not occur, we have argued, deletion cannot occur.

    Example 68 is not a rare phenomenon in BEV; we have many other examples.

70   All I knowed, that I was in the hospital.—*13, T-Birds, 458*
71   All I could do, as' him what he's tryin' to do.—*16, N.Y.C., YH33*
72   But next thing I knew, he was on the ground.—*16, Jets, 560*

Careful examination of these examples shows that the deletion of *is* is not the product of the deletion rule, but a very different process. The evidence for this depends upon several empirical and theoretical points.

First of all, it should be apparent to native speakers of WNS that this deletion is not absolutely impossible for white speakers. Expressions such as

73   What I mean, he's crazy.
74   All I know, he's going home.

are common for WNS speakers. Furthermore, we note that all of these cases involve verbs of *saying, knowing, meaning*—which take sentence complements, and the pro-verb *do*. We have no BEV sentences of the type

75   *All I broke, my leg.

and WNS does not find this acceptable either. It is possible that *All I broke* sentences go back to underlying structures with *is* as the main verb. There are also many related foregroundings such as *The only thing is, I broke my leg*, which also allow, *The only thing, I broke my leg*. Where *is* can thus be deleted, *was* can be too, as in 70, which indicates that we are not dealing with a phonological process.

The fact that white speakers can delete this *is*, but no other *is* in sentences of the type 29–53, makes us suspect that we are dealing with a different mechanism than the deletion rule itself. We are of course concerned with the surface structure, rather than the deep structure, since the former determines the application of the stress rules; but the deep structure will ultimately determine the operation of the critical transformations involved. One approach is to trace sentences of the type 73 to the intermediate structure of Fig. 3.2, after WH-attraction has applied.

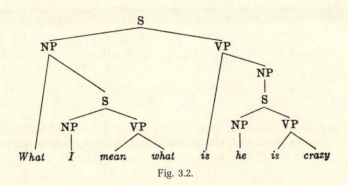

Fig. 3.2.

The WH-attachment that is shown here in the subject would be the same WH which produces exclamations (*What an idea it is!*), free relatives (*This is what I mean*), or, when relative clauses are appended, sentences such as 73 or *What I broke was my leg*. After the object *what* of the relative clause is removed and the *that* complementizer is placed before the complement sentence, we have the constituent structure

76   [What [I mean]$_S$]$_{NP}$ [is [that he is crazy]$_S$]$_{VP}$

where the main verb of the sentence is *is*, appearing before a sentence. According to the analysis that we have given so far, this particular *is*, in construction with a following sentence, should be contractable, just like other copulas before sentence complements:

77   My home's where I want it.

Yet most people do not easily accept

78   * What I mean's he's crazy.

A cleft sentence like 79 can be contracted to 80, but not to 81—

79   What he is is smart.
80   What he is's smart.
81   * What he's is smart.

—even though 81 seems much easier to say than 80 from the phonetic point of view. All of these considerations make us suspect that Fig. 3.2 is not the correct analysis of the sentence structure. There is an alternative analysis of 73, as in Fig. 3.3.

Here the main verb is *mean*, and the *is* is the verb of the relative clause. The rule which deletes *is* is then the same rule which operates to reduce *the book that is yellow with age* to *the book yellow with age*: it is a transformation needed for all dialects of English, applying much earlier and quite independent of the phonological processes discussed above. If this is indeed the structure of 73, we can understand why both white and black speakers can delete the *is*, although it cannot be contracted. The same reasoning applies to 79–80. If the first *is* is the main verb of the sentence, it no longer stands in construction with its object *what*, which has been moved to the front by WH-attraction and therefore has the same status as sentences of the type *That's what he is.*

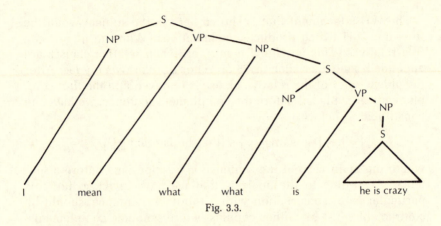

Fig. 3.3.

3.3. The form of the contraction rule, therefore, will show that it represents the removal of an initial shwa before a lone consonant as in *am, is, are; have, has,* and *had* will be included after a general rule removes the initial *h; will* is included, apparently in the form of a lexical alternant without the initial *w,* since there is now no general rule to delete this consonant. But unstressed *as* cannot be contracted, even though it has the requisite phonological form [əz]. We know this because voicing assimilation, which occurs automatically after contraction, does not apply to *as* in *like as not* or *hot as can be:* no matter how ephemeral the shwa seems to be, we do not say [laɪksnɑt] or [hɑtskənbi]. Nor are *his, him,* or *her* contracted, although the rule which removes the initial *h* applies to them as well as to *has, had, have.*

It appears from these examples that contractability may be a lexical property of these verbs or auxiliaries: some variation may be noted in the verb *have,* which is contracted in British English (as in *They'd a great deal of money*), but not in American English. Despite this idiosyncrasy of *have,* there is a general feature of the context that determines contractability and shows why *as, him, his, her* do not contract while both auxiliaries and copula generally do. Contraction requires the presence of the type or tense marker. The critical case is found in *They may have.* This can be written as *They may've,* but the apostrophe only indicates the deletion of the *h-.* Contraction has not applied, as we can tell from the fact that *They may've* does not rhyme with *knave.* When contraction does operate to remove the shwa, we obtain a single syllable: *They've* does rhyme with *knave*. Thus contraction occurs only when the tense or type marker is incorporated in the verb or auxiliary, and the form of the contraction rule has this general shape.[8]

82 $$\mathfrak{e} \rightarrow (\emptyset)/ \cdots \# \# \begin{bmatrix} - \\ +T \end{bmatrix} C_0^1 \# \# \cdots$$

The dots imply that there are further constraints upon contraction which will be discussed below. We have developed the contraction rule as far as we can within the framework of categorical, invariant rules. There are deeper problems and important constraints upon contraction which can only be handled with an enlarged concept of "rule of grammar."

3.4. *Relations of order between contraction and deletion.* One such further problem concerns the relations between the contraction rule, as sketched above, and the deletion rule of BEV. There are four possible relations of order between contraction and deletion:

Case 1	*Case 2*	*Case 3*	*Case 4*
1. C	1. D	$1. \begin{Bmatrix} C \\ D \end{Bmatrix}$	1. C(D)
2. D	2. C		
$\mathfrak{e}z \rightarrow z/\cdots$	$\mathfrak{e}z \rightarrow \emptyset/\cdots$	$\mathfrak{e}z \rightarrow \begin{Bmatrix} z \\ \emptyset \end{Bmatrix}/\cdots$	$\mathfrak{e}z \rightarrow z \rightarrow \emptyset/\cdots$
$z \rightarrow \emptyset/\cdots$	$\mathfrak{e}z \rightarrow z/\cdots$		

Case 1 is that contraction occurs first, deletion second. Case 2 is the reverse: deletion first optionally, contraction second. It is apparent from the forms suggested that no particular relation between the two rules is implied by Case 2; for many reasons, this order will appear the least likely. Case 3 shows deletion and contraction as simultaneous alternates of the same rule, with only one set of environmental constraints. Case 4 has deletion as an extension of contraction—contraction gone wild, as it were—again with only one set of envi-

---

8. Although the tense marker must be present for contraction to take place in most English dialects, there are dialects where this constraint is not present. In dialects of northeastern New England (Maine), the lower south (Atlanta), northern England (Leeds) and others, it is normal to contract *as* and *to*, *the* and *a*. When the vowel of *to* is deleted, consonant cluster simplification may follow which removes this formative entirely, as in *I used' go* [aɪjusgoʊ]. The remaining consonant of *the* is often converted to a glottal stop (or zero), yielding *get out' way* [gɛtæo?wei], and of course when *a* is contracted nothing at all remains. This extension of the contraction rule thus leads to striking differences in surface structure which may be mistaken at first glance for differences in syntactic rules.

ronmental conditions. Our task is now to discriminate among these four possibilities of order, and to specify in detail the form of the deletion rule.

4. *Inherent Variability of Deletion*

So far, I have presented forms 1–12 of section 1 as if this were the pattern of BEV. This is the pattern which is most frequently noticed, for it is marked by its deviation from SE. However, deletion of the copula is an inherent variable for all of the BEV speakers whom we have studied. We will now explore the internal structure of this variable characteristic in order to solve the problems of ordering raised in the preceding section.

The study of variation is necessarily quantitative, and quantitative analysis necessarily involves counting. At first glance, counting would seem to be a simple operation, but even the simplest type of counting raises a number of subtle and difficult problems. The final decision as to what to count is actually the solution to the problem in hand; this decision is approached only through a long series of exploratory maneuvers.

First, one must identify the total population of utterances in which the feature varies. There are always some parallel cases where the variable feature is not variable at all—as, for example, the environments of 48–53, where we find that *is* is never deleted. If all the environments of 29–53 were included in a quantitative study of the variable deletion rule, the frequency of application of the rule would appear much lower than it actually is; a number of important constraints on variability would be obscured, since they would appear to apply to only a small portion of the cases; and the important distinctions between variable and categorical behavior would be lost.

Second, one must decide on the number of variants which can be reliably identified and set aside those environments in which the distinctions are neutralized for phonetic reasons. In the case of *is*, we decided to isolate full, contracted, and deleted forms, but not to attempt to distinguish the degree of stress or reduction of the vowel in the full form. Furthermore, sentences such as *Boot is seventeen* must be set aside, since the contracted form cannot be distinguished from the deleted form in [butsɛvntin] or [but·sɛvntin].

Third, one must identify all the subcategories which would reasonably be relevant in determining the frequency with which the rule in question applies. In this case, there are many grammatical and phonological characteristics of the preceding and following element which determine the frequency of contraction and deletion of *is:* few of these can be predicted from any current theory or knowledge about contraction. Such subcategories emerge from the ongoing analysis as a result of various suspicions, inspections, and analogies. There is of course no simple procedure for the isolation of the relevant subcategories: the end result is a set of regular constraints which operate upon every group and almost every individual. When the three operations outlined above are carried out with accuracy and linguistic insight, the regularities are so evident that statistical analysis is superfluous.

In this section we will focus upon the quantitative analysis of the forms of *is* in the environments of 1-12. Among all BEV speakers in our sample (or in our exploratory work in Washington, Philadelphia, Cleveland, Detroit, Chicago, and Los Angeles), there are none at any age level, in the most excited and spontaneous interaction, who always (or never) delete *is* in these environments. Full, contracted, and deleted forms are all characteristic of BEV. The contracted but undeleted form is least typical of BEV and most characteristic of WNS and SE. On the analogy of the SE and WNS feeling that contracted forms are "natural" and that full forms are "careful," one might be tempted to argue that the full forms are importations from SE in "careful" style. However, as we move from single, face-to-face interviews to spontaneous group sessions, we find that the percentage of full forms generally increases. The feature which is correlated with style shift from single to group sessions is the ratio of deleted to originally contracted forms—that is, $D/D + C$. In other words, BEV speakers do not necessarily contract more in excited interaction, but they delete more of the forms which have been contracted. These stylistic shifts are minor effects among the preadolescent and adolescent peer groups and only begin to assume importance with older adolescents and adults.[9]

---

9. Although BEV has a relatively constant set of grammatical and phonological rules throughout the age range of the Thunderbirds, Cobras, and Jets, a number of subtle changes in the structures of the rules take place in the shift from preadolescence to adolescence—principally a gain in the knowledge of the underlying forms of certain words and a cleaning up of certain phonological rules; as we will see below, some of the basic phonological constraints upon the rules do not appear in the youngest speakers. In late adolescence, there are other changes which reflect an enlargement of stylistic range and a growing knowledge of the norms of social evaluation of speech in the community.

TABLE 3.1
PERCENTAGES OF FORMS OF *IS* WITH PRONOUN SUBJECT vs. OTHER NOUN-PHRASE SUBJECT

	T-Birds		Cobras		Jets		Oscar Bros.		Adults		Inwood	
	NP	pro	NP	pro	NP	pro	NP	pro	NP	pro	NP	pro
Single style												
Full	63	05	56	04	67	00	85	25	75	04	26	00
Contracted	25	44	26	29	15	39	11	60	17	80	74	100
Deleted	12	51	18	67	18	61	04	15	08	16		
Total	100	100	100	100	100	100	100	100	100	100	100	100
N:												
Forms	124	212	35	106	145	189	45	47	187	118	54	61
Subjs.	13		9		15		3		17		8	
Group style												
Full	44	07	45	00	54	00	51	04	61	01	41	01
Contracted	15	33	19	23	19	42	23	33	26	72	59	99
Deleted	42	60	36	77	27	58	26	64	14	27		
Total*	101	100	100	100	100	100	100	101	101	100	100	100
N:												
Forms	53	43	85	30	113	75	73	80	170	112	110	81
Subjs.	5		9		11		4		15		7	

*Totals are occasionally more than 100 percent because of rounding.

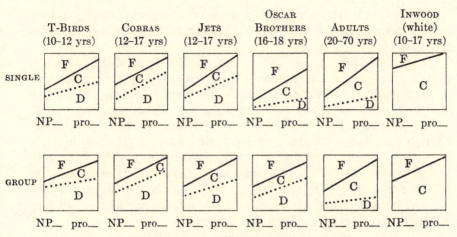

Fig. 3.4. Percentages of full, contracted, and deleted forms of *is* with pronoun subject vs. other noun-phrase subject for six groups in single and group (casual) style.

The single most important constraint on deletion in BEV, and upon contraction in SE and BEV, is one which we did not expect:[10] whether or not the subject is a pronoun or some other noun phrase. Table 3.1 and Fig. 3.4 show the percentages of full forms (F), contracted forms (C), and deleted forms (D) for six groups that have been studied closely: the preadolescent Thunderbirds, the adolescent Cobras, Jets, and (somewhat older) Oscar Brothers; a sample of one quarter of the working-class adults in the Cobra and Jet areas from the larger random sample of 100 adults; and the combined records of two white working-class groups, preadolescent and adolescent, from the Inwood neighborhood of upper Manhattan.

On the left of each square in Fig. 3.4 is the percentage of full, contracted, and deleted forms after noun phrases; on the right, after pronouns. In every case, the percentages of deleted and contracted forms are greater when a pronoun precedes. The upper line of squares shows the pattern for single interviews; the bottom, for group

10. We originally began to investigate the effect of a pronoun subject because Brown and Bellugi's study showed that the copula appeared more often after pronouns than after noun phrases, apparently as a fixed form similar to *I'm* noted above. We were surprised to find a powerful effect in the opposite direction in mature speakers.

interaction.[11] Though there is a general increase in the ratio of deletion to contraction, the basic pattern is the same in both styles, for all groups.

In these diagrams, deletion is shown as occurring after contraction (Case 1 of section 3.4); that is, the total percentage of contracted forms includes those forms which were afterwards deleted. The pattern for contraction shown here is similar for the BEV groups and for the Inwood WNS groups, who do not delete. Contraction and deletion thus respond to the same syntactic constraint. The fact that this pattern repeats regularly in six different groups, in each style, indicates how pervasive and regular such variable constraints are. We are not dealing here with effects which are so erratic or marginal that statistical tests are required to determine whether or not they might have been produced by chance.

The relationship between contraction and deletion can be explored more deeply by considering the effect of the following grammatical category. Again, we find that both rules respond to the same set of syntactic constraints. Table 3.2 and Fig. 3.5 show this pattern for the

11. In the case of the adults, the lower diagram shows "casual speech" as isolated in the single interviews. The criteria for determining the shift to casual style are contrastive changes in "channel cues"—pitch, volume, tempo, and rate of breathing (which includes laughter). For black speakers, increases in pitch range are taken as the primary criteria, being relatively much more important than with white speakers.

TABLE 3.2
PERCENTAGES OF FORMS OF IS, ACCORDING TO GRAMMATICAL
CATEGORY OF COMPLEMENT FOR TWO GROUPS IN ALL BEV STYLES

	__NP	__PA	__Loc	__V + ing	__gon
Thunderbirds (13 subjs.)					
Full	40	25	30	04	00
Contracted	37	27	34	30	12
Deleted	23	48	36	66	88
Total	100	100	100	100	100
No. of forms	210	67	50	46	40
Jets (29 subjs.)					
Full	37	34	21	07	03
Contracted	31	30	27	19	03
Deleted	32	36	52	74	93
Total	100	100	100	100	99
No. of forms	373	209	70	91	58

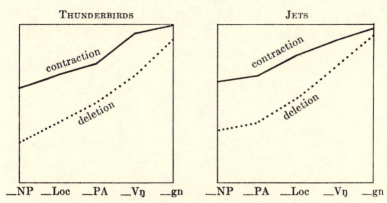

Fig. 3.5. Percentages of full, contracted, and deleted forms of *is* according to grammatical category of complement.

Thunderbirds and the Jets, for single and group styles combined. The relationships as shown here are essentially the same for the other groups.[12] The least deletion and contraction take place before a following noun phrase; more occur before predicate adjectives and locatives; both rules apply with even greater frequency before a following verb with the progressive *-ing* and with the highest frequency before the future form *gon'* or *gonna*. Here contraction is again shown as taking place on the full population of full forms, but the population upon which the deletion rule operates is limited to the pool of forms already contracted.

Figure 3.6 shows the consequences of treating contraction and deletion as independent processes. Here the percentage of contraction for the Jets is shown in terms of the actual numbers of contracted forms recorded: the result is a minor tendency which responds in just the opposite way to syntactic constraints. Furthermore, there is no connection at all between contraction in BEV and contraction

12. In the quantitative studies shown here, the amount of data presented varies. In these initial variables, the patterns for six different groups in two styles are shown, so that the full regularity of the variable relations may appear. In later variables, only limited portions of the available data are presented; and when certain cross-correlations are necessary, some of the categories shown here as separate are combined. Not all of the speakers in most groups have been studied completely, and there are more data available which have not yet been transcribed, so it is possible that some of these data may later lead to changes at points of our analysis; but in almost every case the regular relations are so apparent that if only half or quarter of the data presented here is taken, the relationships remain constant.

JETS

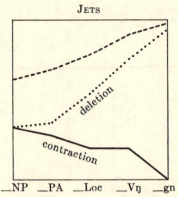

_NP _PA _Loc _Vŋ _gn

Fig. 3.6. Independence of contraction and deletion.

in WNS: Fig. 3.7 shows the contraction pattern of the Inwood groups, quite similar to the "cumulative" contraction pattern of Fig. 3.5 (indicated on Fig. 3.6 with a dotted line). If we should insist on regarding contraction and deletion as completely unrelated, we would then find that the syntactic constraints which operate upon them have very different effects and that contraction for BEV has nothing to do with contraction for WNS. This is a very implausible result, and we can proceed upon the assumption that the cumulative diagram of Fig. 3.5 represents the actual situation.

Given these quantitative relations, we can now return to the problem of the particular form of ordering which holds between the contraction and deletion rules. The four cases of possible ordering

INWOOD

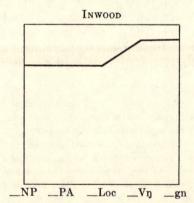

_NP   _PA   _Loc   _Vŋ   _gn

Fig. 3.7. Contraction for the Inwood groups.

presented above can now be simplified. Case 2, with deletion first and contraction second, would not fit any of the quantitative results shown above, for there is no reason for the contraction of some undeleted [əz] to be dependent upon the deletion of some other [əz]: that is, it would be quite unreasonable to insist that contraction operates upon a pool of already deleted forms. The other three cases can be represented by the abstract quantitative models of Figs. 3.8a–c.

The application of the variable contraction and deletion rules is logically governed by two factors. First is an input variable which sets the overall frequency with which the rule is selected. Second, there are variable constraints which differentiate the frequencies with which the rule applies according to the syntactic and phonological features of the environment.[13] Figures 3.8a–c represent various combinations of these two factors. For Case 3, with contrac-

13. And third, of course, there are sociolinguistic factors such as age, sex, ethnic group, social class, and contextual style; but we will not be considering these here. Our focus is upon the relatively constant grammars of black adolescent boys, 10–17 years old, who are integral members of the peer groups in which the vernacular culture is maintained.

If these rules are compared to algebraic expressions, we can consider that in a linear expression $y = ax + b$, the selection of the constant b represents the variable input and the factor a the slope which relates the dependent variable y to some other variable x. Here, however, we will not have a continuous function y, but a specific series of environmental constraints which give us a characteristic profile for the application of the rule to any given individual, group, or speech community. It is an extraordinary result that these profiles are essentially the same for all the peer groups studied—that is, the rule is a part of a single grammar which we can construct for this speech community.

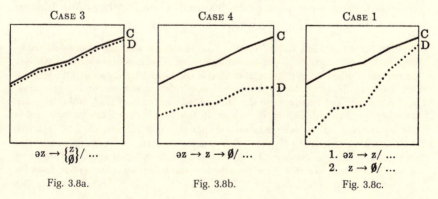

CASE 3

əz → $\begin{Bmatrix} z \\ \emptyset \end{Bmatrix}$ / ...

Fig. 3.8a.

CASE 4

əz → z → ∅/ ...

Fig. 3.8b.

CASE 1

1. əz → z/ ...
2. z → ∅/ ...

Fig. 3.8c.

tion and deletion as alternative right-hand members of a single rule, the rule is selected only once, and there is therefore only one variable input and one set of variable constraints. The spectrum of frequencies with which the contraction and deletion rules apply should therefore be the same, as shown in Fig. 3.8a. If, on the other hand, deletion is thought of as an extension of contraction (Case 4), we might have two selections and two variable inputs, but only one set of variable constraints. Deletion would then be a fixed percentage of contraction in all environments—say 50 percent, as suggested by Fig. 3.8b. The third possibility is that we have two selections (with variable inputs), and two sets of variable constraints. This is equivalent to Case 1, with the rule for contraction applying first, and the rule for deletion applying second. Here the quantitative pattern would be that of Fig. 3.8c, where the variable constraints apply twice. This pattern shows more extreme or exaggerated constraints upon deletion than upon contraction; it is in fact the actual pattern which appears in the empirical data of Fig. 3.5 for both the Thunderbirds and Jets and one which is repeated for the other peer groups as well.[14] We can conclude from this quantitative evidence that contraction and deletion are separate though similar rules which apply in the order stated.

The grammatical status of adjacent elements are only two of the many constraints upon the contraction and deletion rules; we have not yet considered here the effects of the phonological environments. However, before proceeding further it will be necessary to investigate the relative independence of the preceding and following environments. It is possible that one is conditioned by the other: that the effect of a following noun phrase, for example, might be entirely different when a pronoun precedes than when another noun phrase

14. In Fig. 3.9, the Jets differ from the T-birds and the Cobras in the relationship between the following noun phrase and following adjectives and locatives, when a noun phrase precedes; but this relationship is the same after a pronoun. In general, we find that the differentiation between following noun phrases, on the one hand, and adjectives and locatives, on the other, is not as constant from group to group as other features, although in a given group this profile does allow us to examine the specific relations between deletion and contraction. In all cases, the $D/C + D$ line follows the pattern of the $C + D/F + C + D$ line: instead of remaining constant as in Case 4, it rises, as one would expect in Case 1. In the final version of the rules given in section 7, we will leave the effect of the following noun phrase open for further analysis.

precedes. Or going even further, one of these effects could be nothing but the result of unequal distribution of forms in the other environment: e.g., a following verb phrase might favor contraction and deletion simply because pronouns occur more frequently before predicates with *Verb + ing* than they do before predicates with *NP*.

Figure 3.9 resolves this question by displaying the two variable conditions independently. On the left, 3.9a–c show the effect of the following grammatical category for all sentences with subject noun phrase; on the right, 3.9d–f show the data for sentences with subject pronouns. Because the total number of forms is considerably reduced for each group (even when single and group styles are combined), the following predicate adjectives and locatives are given together. Some of the cells are still too small to be reliable, as the table for N at the bottom shows: for the T-Birds, for example, there are only six cases of a following verb after a noun-phrase subject, and only eight cases of following *gon'* or *gonna,* which may be responsible for the irregularity of the pattern at this point.

Fig. 3.9 demonstrates that neither of the environmental constraints, preceding or following, is dependent upon the other. There is some degree of irregularity in the patterns with preceding noun phrase: for the Jets, for example, we see that the order of effects of following locatives and predicate adjectives vs. following noun phrases is reversed in Fig. 3.9c. We do not know as yet whether this reversal is constant or reproducible; the data presented here do not exhaust all the material which is available for the Jets and Cobras, and further analysis will answer such questions.

Fig. 3.9 shows a remarkable regularity across the three groups, especially in the case of a preceding pronoun. The effect of a preceding pronoun upon contraction is almost categorical for all three groups—that is, the contraction rule goes almost to completion; but the deletion rule operates variably and regularly across a wide range of frequencies.

Most importantly, all six sections of Fig. 3.9 conform to the model of Fig. 3.8c—showing that contraction and deletion are governed by similar constraints. Contraction and deletion follow the same pattern even when there is a reordering in the constraints, as in the *NP ~ PA-Loc* situation for the Jets in 3.9c. With this parallelism, we observe that contraction and deletion have distinct variable inputs and distinct variable constraints which reapply to deletion after they have applied to contraction. Case 1, in which a contraction rule is

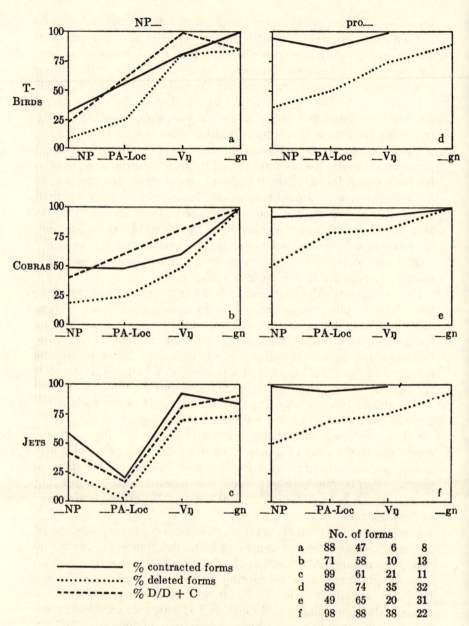

Fig. 3.9. Percentages of full, contracted, and deleted forms of *is*
according to preceeding and following environments.

followed by a deletion rule, receives ample confirmation: for each group, deletion diverges from contraction on the left and converges on the right. If one assumes that the deletion rule operates upon the pool of already contracted forms, then the frequency of deletion $D/D + C$ (indicated by a line of dashes in Figs. 3.9a–c) should regularly rise from left to right, as it does (see Table 3.4). In Figs. 3.9d–f, contraction is virtually independent of the following environment—only traces of variability before noun phrases and predicate adjectives remain. This may be considered the normal result of a variable constraint moving to a higher level and producing the semicategorical pattern shown here.

5. The Formal Expression of Variable Rules

The goal of our analysis is to incorporate such variable rules as contraction and deletion into the main body of generative rules needed for a full description of BEV or SE. By absorbing the data of section 4 on systematic variation into the rules, we will be able to resolve questions of ordering and rule form which would otherwise remain undecidable. Furthermore, it will be possible to enlarge our current notion of the "linguistic competence" of a native speaker. To achieve this goal, it is necessary to write single rules for contraction and deletion incorporating the relationships found in Figs. 3.4–3.9: certain innovations in formal notation will be required which will reflect this enlargement of the concept "rule of grammar." We will develop the argument both with abstract schemata and with the example of the contraction rule. The formal interpretation of variable rules given here incorporates modifications of Cedergren and Sankoff (1972) based upon a probability model which solves a number of mathematical problems in the original version and develops the quantitative treatment to a higher level of accountability.

Linguistic rules are currently conceived in generative grammar as having the general form

83          $X \rightarrow Y/A\_B$
          Contraction: $\vartheta \rightarrow \emptyset/ \#\# [\_, +T] C_0^1 \#\#$

where X is always rewritten as Y in the stated environment but is never rewritten as Y otherwise. This is a *categorical* instruction—the only type of rule which is permitted in any of the traditional approaches to formal grammar. When one is faced with the fact of variation—that the rule does *not* always apply, then it is possible to say that the rule itself is optional—that it may or may not be applied at the discretion of the speaker. We can represent such optionality by writing parentheses around the right-hand member of the rule:

84          $X \rightarrow (Y)/A\_\_B$
            Contraction: $\partial \rightarrow (\emptyset)/ \#\# [\_\_, +T] \, C_1^0 \#\#$

However, if we interpret this notation as meaning no more than the conventional label "optional," it will hardly allow the facts of systematic variation presented above to be accommodated in the grammar of BEV. The label "optional" is no more useful in this respect than the label "free variation." It is true that we would come closer to the actual situation in BEV by writing optional contraction and deletion rules rather than obligatory ones. But in so doing, we would be portraying BEV as nothing more than a mixture of random possibilities—a notion quite consistent with the usual concept of "dialect mixture." It is not the object of sociolinguistic analysis to reduce the precision of linguistic rules or to add to the vagueness with which linguistic structure is perceived. If the data of the preceding sections are to be utilized in formal rules, it must be shown that the study of variation adds to our knowledge of linguistic structure and simplifies the situation rather than reducing the precision of the rules by uncontrolled and unaccountable notations.

The variable rules to be presented here are intended to achieve a higher level of accountability than unconstrained free variation will allow. They depend upon a more general *principle of accountability* which we require in the analysis of linguistic behavior: *that any variable form (a member of a set of alternative ways of "saying the same thing") should be reported with the proportion of cases in which the form did occur in the relevant environment, compared to the total number of cases in which it might have occurred.* Unless this principle is followed, it is possible to prove any theoretical preconception by citing isolated instances of what individuals have been heard saying. Speech is perceived categorically, and linguists who are searching for an invariant, homogeneous dialect will perceive even more categorically than most. The problem is most severe in the study of nonstandard dialects. Unwanted variants will first be set aside as examples of "dialect mixture" and only the forms most different from the standard will be reported. Gradually even the linguist perceives only the marked or exceptional form, when in fact these forms may occur with vanishingly small frequency. The principle of accountability is motivated by a conviction that the aim of linguistic analysis is to describe the regular patterns of the speech community, rather than the idiosyncrasies of any given individual.[15]

The first step in the formal recognition of the principle of accountability is to associate with each variable rule a specific quantity φ which denotes the probability of the rule applying. This probability predicts the ratio of cases or frequency with which the rule actually does apply to the total population of utterances in which the rule would apply in the specified environment if it were a categorical rule of the type 83. It is not the output frequency which is a part of the rule, but rather this probability φ which as we will see is a function of several linguistic and sociolinguistic factors.[16] The probability φ thus ranges between 0 and 1; for categorical rules, such as 83, $\varphi = 1$. A variable rule is then an optional rule viewed in this perspective; it will be symbolized in formal notation by the use of angled brackets around the output to the right of the arrow, indicating that considerations of more "$\rangle$" and less "$\langle$" are linguistically significant.

84' $X \rightarrow \langle Y \rangle / A\_\_B$
           Contraction: $\vartheta \rightarrow \langle \emptyset \rangle / \# \# [\_\_, + T] \, C_1^0 \, \# \#$

5.1. *Input probability.* Although a great many rules do apply categorically, without exception, there are cases in which some

15. It is true that a variable rule cannot be checked by any one instance, and therefore it would seem to have deprived us of that principle of accountability which is the mainstay of generative grammar. The disproof of a variable rule requires the analysis of utterances, for each of a small group of speakers. Fortunately, the regularity of linguistic behavior is so great that these groups can be quite small. The patterns shown here emerge reliably in sets of utterances as small as five or ten; and since they hold for almost every speaker, a group of five speakers is more than sufficient.

16. This is the basic change in formulation of variable rules introduced by Cedergren and Sankoff. In the earlier version, (Labov 1969), φ stood for the output frequency of the rules, and had to be interpreted as a mean value from several samples or a general tendency to approach an unspecified limit. Formally, φ was specific to any given sample. When φ is properly seen as the *probability* of the rule applying, it is now evident that φ is a stable and abstract property of a rule characteristic of the language of the speech community. For a discussion of the status of φ in "competence" and the knowledge of variable rules possessed by native speakers, see below.

factor interferes with or impedes the full application of the rule so that it is not categorical. It is thus convenient to show φ as

85 $$\varphi = 1 - k_0$$

where k_0 is the limiting factor which constrains the application of the rule. With categorical rules of the type 83, it follows that there is no variable input, and $k_0 = 0$; that is, there is no impediment to the operation of the rule. If $k_0 = 1$, then of course the rule does not apply at all.

The limiting factor is itself determined by a series of factors of the general form $(1 - x)$. These are the factors which favor the rule, ranging between 0 and 1.

86 $$k_0 = (1 - x)(1 - y)(1 - z) \cdots$$

This product model of Cedergren and Sankoff has the important property that the constraints on k_0 are independent of each other.[17] If in a given case the factor x is absent or equal to 0, then it will have no effect upon k_0 or upon the probability φ of the rule. Only if a factor $x = 1$ will it interfere with the effect of the other factors since in that case it will zero out k_0 altogether, and the rule will apply categorically.

The first of these probability factors which favors the rule is the *input probability* p_0. In the absence of all other constraints, $k_0 = 1 - p_0$, and p_0 will have the same properties as φ cited above. If $p_0 = 0$, the rule will not apply at all; if $p_0 = 1$, the rule applies categorically. For a variable rule, $0 < p_0 < 1$. This value must vary if the rule is involved in the process of linguistic change: it will thus be a function of the age of the speaker or group whose language is governed by the rule. The variable input is also governed by such sociolinguistic factors as contextual style, socioeconomic class, sex, and ethnic group. In this chapter, we will not consider formally the development of the function p_0 since our main focus is on the relatively uniform vernacular of male black members of the street culture in the inner cities. But enough data on the other groups will

17. The assumption of independence is of course only an hypothesis and is subject to empirical verification (see below). But a defect of the original additive model was that values were not independent (as one variable constraint grows larger in an additive model, others must necessarily diminish if the fixed sum is 1). This could only be adjusted to the facts of independent constraints by ad hoc conditions for interpreting values of φ greater than 1.

be given to show the influence of sociolinguistic factors, and in chapter 6 it will appear that p_o for the contraction rule is relatively unaffected by group membership or distance from the BEV culture, while p_o for the deletion rule is directly correlated with this distance. Some semiquantitative functions for p_o involving style, class, and linguistic security are given in *Sociolinguistic Patterns,* chapter 8.

5.2. *Variable constraints.* The data of section 4 showed that variation in contraction and deletion is governed by a set of constraints such as the effect of a preceding pronoun or a following verb. These variable constraints are features of the environment which are indicated in a variable rule by angled brackets:

87
$$X \rightarrow \langle Y \rangle \, / \, \left\langle \begin{array}{c} \text{fea}_i \\ \vdots \end{array} \right\rangle \left\langle \begin{array}{c} \overline{\text{fea}_j} \\ \vdots \end{array} \right\rangle \left\langle \begin{array}{c} \text{fea}_k \\ \vdots \\ \text{fea}_n \end{array} \right\rangle$$

Features which must be present in the environment if the rule is to apply (minimal features) will be indicated as usual by square brackets. Thus we may indicate that contraction is favored by a following verb and a preceding pronoun by

88
$$\vartheta \rightarrow \langle \emptyset \rangle / \langle +\text{Pro} \rangle \, \# \# \left[\frac{}{+T} \right] C_0^1 \, \# \# \, \langle +\text{Vb} \rangle$$

In this form, the rule 88 states that contraction is the variable deletion of a schwa. There are minimal features of the environment if the rule is to apply: we see that the schwa must be preceded by a word boundary, incorporate the tense marker, and be followed by no more than one consonant and a word boundary. There are also variable constraints: we see that the rule is favored if the preceding word is a pronoun or the following word is a verb.

In general, if we indicate the contribution to the probability of the rule applying from any given variable constraint $\langle \text{fea}_i \rangle$ as v_i, then

89
$$k_o = (1 - p_o)(1 - v_i)(1 - v_j) \cdots (1 - v_n)$$

and φ is then determined by

90
$$\varphi = 1 - (1 - p_o)(1 - v_i)(1 - v_j) \cdots (1 - v_n)$$

and in the case of 88,

91
$$\varphi = 1 - (1 - p_o)(1 - v(+\text{Pro}\underline{\ \ }))(1 - v(\underline{\ \ }+\text{Vb}))$$

5.3. *The invariance condition.* In many variable rules, we find that there is a feature of the environment which favors the rule so strongly that whenever it is present the rule applies in every case, or in almost every case. This is an important aspect of linguistic change; rules typically go to completion in the most favored environments first, while they are still variable in other environments. In the stable situation of the contraction rule, we find that *I'm* is for all practical purposes invariant in BEV; for most speakers, contraction applies 98 to 99 percent of the time in the relevant environment marked in rule 88. When v_i approaches 1 so closely, the effect is to make *I am here* an unexpected or exceptional form. The same may be said for the retention of the *-t* in *just now* (see chapter 2) and many other examples of semicategorical rule environments. In some cases, we are dealing with truly categorical behavior. In BEV, the cluster in *wasps, tests, desks* is always simplified, and most speakers cannot prevent the application of the deletion rule even when their full attention is turned to the effort (chapter 1).

Our general notation for variable rules will not incorporate probabilities directly, but indicate only relations of more or less. But the categorical or semicategorical effect of a given environment is a qualitative difference, since it neutralizes the effects of other variable constraints. When $v_i = 1$ or approaches very close to 1, we will designate feature$_i$ with an asterisk.

$$92 \qquad X \rightarrow \langle Y \rangle / \left\langle \begin{matrix} \text{fea}_i \\ \vdots \end{matrix} \right\rangle \left\langle \overline{\phantom{\text{fea}_m}} \atop \text{fea}_m \atop \vdots \right\rangle \begin{matrix} {}^*\langle \text{fea}_k \rangle \\ \left\langle \text{fea}_m \atop \vdots \right\rangle \end{matrix}$$

Whenever a given $v_i = 1$, the occurrence in the environment of fea$_i$ has the effect of zeroing out k_0, and so the probability of the entire rule is 1. In the case of contraction, we can indicate for many speakers that the rule always applies if the following consonant is a nasal.

$$93 \qquad \text{ə} \rightarrow \langle \emptyset \rangle / \langle +\text{Pro} \rangle \,\#\# \left[\frac{}{+T} \right] \,{}^*_{\langle +\text{nas} \rangle} \, \overset{C_0^1}{} \,\#\# \langle +\text{Vb} \rangle$$

Whenever the sign, of the invariant feature is + or the notation indicates presence rather than absence of a feature, we can abbreviate 93 to

$$93' \qquad \text{ə} \rightarrow \langle \emptyset \rangle / \langle +\text{Pro} \rangle \,\#\# \left[\frac{}{+T} \right] \,\overset{C_0^1}{\langle {}^*\text{nas} \rangle} \,\#\# \langle +\text{Vb} \rangle$$

If the value of the fea$_i$ which triggers invariant application of the rule is negative, we can follow a similar convention of writing $\langle * - \text{fea}_i \rangle$. The interpretation of the * notation will be the same: if fea$_i$ is present when the rule reads $\langle * \text{fea}_i \rangle$ or it is absent when the rule reads $\langle * - \text{fea}_i \rangle$, the value of the variable constraint will be 1 and the rule will always apply. The probability of application of 93 is then

94 $\quad \varphi = 1 - (1 - p_o)(1 - v(\text{Pro}\underline{\quad}))(1 - v(\underline{\quad}\text{nas}))$
$$(1 - v(\underline{\quad}\text{Fut}))(1 - v(\underline{\quad}\text{Vb}))$$

where $v(\underline{\quad}\text{nas}) = 1$. Given sentences of the type *I am your brother, I am Killer-Diller, I am gonna go*, the third factor will be $1 - 1 = 0$ and the rule will always apply. If however we have sentences of the type *He is here, She is my sister*, $v(\underline{\quad}\text{nas}) = 0$ and this factor will have no effect upon the probability of the rule.

5.4. *Ordering of variable constraints.* The development of the variable rule notation in 87 and 92 must be seen as independent of the quantitative interpretation in terms of probability functions in 90 and 94. The variable rules present certain relations which are seen as linguistically significant: that the rule applies more often in one environment than another, that it applies categorically in a given environment. These variable constraints are normally binding on all members of the community, and their effect is so strong that it appears regularly with very small numbers of cases. But the relative strengths or influence of these constraints may also be linguistically significant, though not necessarily the same for all members. We saw in the last chapter that a crucial difference between BEV speakers and others was the relative ordering of the phonological and grammatical constraint on -t,d deletion. But as a rule the ordering of variable constraints within a segment is more regular than ordering across segments. Thus in the centralization of (ay) and (aw) on Martha's Vineyard (Sociolinguistic Patterns, chapter 1) the basic mechanism of change was a reordering of variable constraints in the following segment. The intermediate stages of the change showed as usual a wide range of ordered variable constraints, involving most of the features of the consonant system; in the final stages, the effect of a following ⟨+tense⟩ feature became dominant, could finally be written as ⟨*tense⟩, and produced the same kind of categorical rule that we observe in Canada or Virginia: centralization before tense consonants, uncentralized forms elsewhere.

In this notation, ordering within a segment will be indicated by vertical position. Invariance conditions designated by * will of course be listed first. Ordering across segments can be indicated by the use of Greek letters to the upper left of the left-hand angled bracket. Thus we can indicate that the effect of a preceding pronoun on contraction is greater than the effect of a following verb.

95          $\mathrm{\vartheta} \rightarrow \langle\emptyset\rangle/^{\alpha}\langle+\mathrm{Pro}\rangle \,\#\# \begin{bmatrix} \\ \hline +\mathrm{T} \end{bmatrix} \begin{smallmatrix} \mathrm{C}^1_0 \\ \langle^*\mathrm{nas}\rangle \end{smallmatrix} {}^{\beta}\langle+\mathrm{Vb}\rangle$

The Greek letters can indicate + or − as in the usual paired convention for indicating "same feature" in generative phonology. Since they will only be used to discriminate ordering here, rather than indicate equal status, there will never be more than one α or one β and so we will not risk confusing the two notations if we abbreviate 95 as

95′ $\mathrm{\vartheta} \rightarrow \langle\emptyset\rangle/\langle\alpha\mathrm{Pro}\rangle \,\#\# \begin{bmatrix} \\ \hline +\mathrm{T} \end{bmatrix} \begin{smallmatrix} \mathrm{C}^1_0 \\ \langle^*\mathrm{nas}\rangle \end{smallmatrix} \langle\beta\mathrm{Vb}\rangle$

As we have seen above, the direction of the variable constraints is constant for all groups, but the ordering of these constraints does show some variation from group to group, even within BEV. A following adjective generally favors contraction and deletion more than a following noun phrase, but there are exceptions in some environments for some groups. The phonological constraint of a following consonant is a marginal or inconsequential effect for younger groups, but gradually assumes more importance with age, as does the grammatical constant for -t,d deletion considered in the last chapter.

An important aspect of the present notational convention is that it is not necessary to indicate such ordering across segments.[18] It is thus possible to write rules for the entire speech community which show the direction of the variable constraints without entering into the reorderings that mark specific dialects. The general rule for -t,d

18. I am indebted to Bruce Fraser for this simplifying suggestion, which makes it possible to describe variable constraints without reference to specific ordering across segments. If we want to abstain from ordering within segments, we can use braces within the angled brackets, as in the rules for r-vocalization in the last chapter. We may also want to use a linear formulation, where three ordered variable constraints may be written $\langle\mathrm{fea}_i\rangle\mathrm{fea}_j\rangle\mathrm{fea}_k\rangle$ and three unordered constraints as $\langle\mathrm{fea}_i, \mathrm{fea}_j, \mathrm{fea}_k\rangle$.

deletion given in the last chapter (page 44) thus describes the language used by all members of the English speech community. Particular dialects can be indicated by the Greek letter convention when necessary. We can thus use more or less delicacy in our exploration of constraints on free variation. Normally, we will be most interested in the ordering of variable constraints when we are studying change. Change in the order of variable constraints represents a basic mechanism of linguistic development for the individual as well as for the community. But this chapter is confined to the major relations of order within a relatively uniform grammar. For this purpose, one more variable constraint upon contraction and deletion must be presented: the effect of a preceding vowel as against a preceding consonant.

6. The Effect of a Preceding Vowel

There are a number of phonological constraints upon the operation of contraction and deletion, but the most important, from the standpoint of magnitude and linguistic significance, is whether or not the preceding element ends with a consonant or a vowel. Most subject pronouns end with stressed vowels,[19] but other noun phrases can be subclassified in many ways according to their final segments. The most useful subcategories of the environments for the contraction and deletion of *is* are as follows:

a. — S__ After noun phrases ending in sibilants.
b. — K^0__ After noun phrases ending in nonsibilant voiceless consonants.
c. — K^v__ After noun phrases ending in nonsibilant voiced consonants.
d. — V__ After noun phrases ending in vowels.[20]

It is no accident that the first three of these categories are the same

19. *That, what, it, lot,* and *one* are the chief exceptions; but the first three obey special rules discussed below to yield *i's, tha's,* and *wha's. One* and its derivatives are the only pronouns which would allow us to examine the deletion rule left in this class. Impersonal *one* does not occur in colloquial speech, and the other forms are not common enough to yield reliable data at this time.

20. The "vowels" we are speaking of here are vowels in the underlying representation. At a lower level of phonetic output, they are usually represented as ending in glides or semivowels.

as those used to describe forms of the English {Z} morpheme.[21] But whereas the usual rules can treat categories *c* and *d* as one (the "elsewhere" or "other voiced segment" category), the distinction between *c* and *d* will be critical in the analysis of contraction and deletion.

Table 3.3 shows the percentages of full, contracted, and deleted forms for all six groups studied in section 4 according to the phonetic form of the preceding element. Examining the percentages of full forms, we can immediately state the following:

(1) In all cases, there are fewest full forms after pronouns; contraction is, therefore, almost categorical after pronouns, as observed in section 4.

(2) In all cases, there are fewer full forms after noun phrases ending in vowels than after those ending in consonants, but more than after pronouns. In other words, the fact that pronouns end in vowels accounts for some, but by no means all, of their effects upon contraction.

(3) In all cases but one,[22] there is a small but distinct tendency for more full forms to occur after voiceless consonants than after voiced.

(4) There are almost no contracted forms after sibilants, although, contrary to the usual concept, a few can definitely be observed. But quite a few forms of *is* have apparently undergone both contraction and deletion after sibilants. If we assume that forms such as *The fish is* . . . will follow the same rules as the rest of the other BEV sentences, then it appears that deletion is practically categorical after sibilants.

Table 3.4 reanalyses these data in terms of the operation of the contraction and deletion rules. Since noun phrases are relatively sparse as compared to subject pronouns, the numbers for all of these subcategories are not large enough for us to study the operation of

21. The set of rules developed below shows that, after contraction of *is*, the resulting [z] behaves very much like the plural {Z} in BEV and the 3rd person singular, possessive, and adverbial {Z} of SE. An epenthesis rule will apply across inflectional boundaries and across the word boundary which separates the contracted [z] from the preceding material. Although it is possible to show the various inflectional morphemes with underlying forms of /əz/ or /əs/, the parallels shown in section 7 make the /z/ presentation more reasonable and economical.

22. This exception, the Cobras, is based upon a relatively small number of cases, and it is possible that further data will alter the picture; in any case, voicing is not a major effect.

TABLE 3.3
PERCENTAGES OF FULL, CONTRACTED, AND DELETED FORMS
ACCORDING TO PHONETIC FORMS OF PRECEDING ELEMENT
FOR SINGLE AND GROUP STYLES COMBINED

Group	$-K^o\_$	$-K^v\_$	$-S\_$	$-V\_$	pro__
Thunderbirds					
Full	83	70	62	43	05
Contracted	05	28	00	30	42
Deleted	12	02	38	27	53
Total	100	100	100	100	100
N:	24	92	21	79	255
Cobras					
Full	54	58	67	10	03
Contracted	08	09	06	53	28
Deleted	38	33	27	37	69
Total	100	100	100	100	100
N:	13	33	18	32	136
Jets					
Full	89	58	80	42	00
Contracted	00	14	00	45	39
Deleted	11	28	20	13	61
Total	100	100	100	100	100
N:	28	65	29	69	269
Oscar Brothers					
Full	93	71	68	40	04
Contracted	00	21	12	40	54
Deleted	07	08	20	20	42
Total	100	100	100	100	100
N:	15	14	41	37	95
Working-class Adults					
Full	75	69	88	45	39
Contracted	08	21	03	45	47
Deleted	16	10	09	10	14
Total	99	100	100	100	100
N:	48	100	75	83	200
Inwood groups					
Full	42	30	97	13	00
Contracted	58	70	03	87	100
Deleted	00	00	00	00	00
Total	100	100	100	100	100
N:	12	46	34	65	61

TABLE 3.4
FREQUENCY OF OPERATION OF DELETION AND CONTRACTION
RULES WITH PRECEDING CONSONANT OR VOWEL FOR SIX BEV
GROUPS IN SINGLE AND GROUP STYLES COMBINED

Group	f_C $\dfrac{C + D}{F + D + C}$	N	f_D $\dfrac{D}{C + D}$	N
Thunderbirds				
−K__	.28	116	.16	32
−V__	.57	79	.47	45
pro__	.95	255	.56	241
Cobras				
−K__	.41	46	.80	20
−V__	.90	32	.41	29
pro__	.97	136	.71	132
Jets				
−K−	.32	93	.70	30
−V−	.58	69	.22	40
pro−	1.00	269	.61	269
Oscar Brothers				
−K__	.17	29	(.40)	5
−V__	.59	37	.33	22
pro__	.96	95	.44	91
Working-class adults				
−K__	.30	148	.38	59
−V__	.55	83	.18	46
pro__	.61	200	.77	99
Inwood groups				
−K__	.67	58	.00	39
−V__	.87	65	.00	60
pro__	.99	142	.00	141

deletion within them. Table 3.4 therefore combines $-K^o\_\_$ and $-K^v\_\_$ into a single category $-K\_\_$. The contraction rule is seen as having operated upon full forms to produce the contracted and deleted forms, with deletion then operating upon the resulting pool of contracted forms. These tables now show the frequency with which the contraction and deletion rules operate, which we will designate f_C and f_D, indicating the particular frequency for a given sample f as opposed to the general probability of the rule applying in all samples, φ.

$$96 \qquad f_C = \frac{C + D}{F + C + D} \qquad f_D = \frac{D}{C + D}$$

For the Cobras, Jets, Oscar Brothers and adults, it appears that a preceding vowel favors contraction, while exactly the opposite situation prevails with deletion: the rule applies more frequently when a consonant precedes. Fig. 3.10 shows the striking character of this reversal, which runs counter to the parallelism of contraction and deletion that has prevailed up to this point. The Inwood groups show no deletion, but we observe that contraction is also favored by a preceding vowel in their case. Only the youngest group, the Thunderbirds, does not show this effect: for them, a preceding vowel favors both contraction and deletion.[23]

23. As noted at several points in the discussion, this absence of phonological conditioning of the younger group is characteristic of the general tendency for rules to develop more phonological conditioning with age.

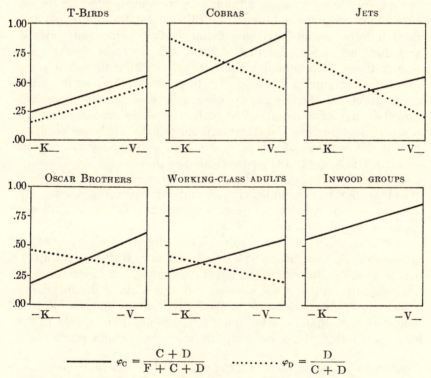

Fig. 3.10. Effect of a preceeding consonant or vowel upon operation of the contraction and deletion rules for six groups, single and group styles combined.

The prevailing pattern can be elucidated by these examples:

97
$$\frac{\text{Joe}}{\text{CV}} \frac{\text{is}}{\text{VC}} \frac{\text{here}}{\text{CVC}} \xrightarrow{\text{C}} \frac{\text{Joe's}}{\text{CVC}} \frac{\text{here}}{\text{CVC}} \xrightarrow{\text{D}} \frac{\text{Joe}}{\text{CV}} \frac{\text{here}}{\text{CVC}}$$

98
$$\frac{\text{Stan}}{\text{CVC}} \frac{\text{is}}{\text{VC}} \frac{\text{here}}{\text{CVC}} \xrightarrow{\text{C}} \frac{\text{Stan's}}{\text{CVCC}} \frac{\text{here}}{\text{CVC}} \xrightarrow{\text{D}} \frac{\text{Stan}}{\text{CVC}} \frac{\text{here}}{\text{CVC}}$$

In the case of a subject noun ending in a vowel, we see that contraction acts to reduce a CVVC sequence to CVC. (It is true that the first vowel may be diphthongized so that a glide interposes between the two vowels in the actual phonetic output, but this is not always the case in BEV.) On the other hand, when contraction operates upon a subject noun ending in a consonant, the result is a consonant cluster. There are a number of rules operating throughout BEV which reduce consonant clusters, although there is no single rule for all cases. In general, it can be said that BEV, like standard English and most Indo-European languages, disfavors final consonant clusters, and there are many examples of historical processes operating to reduce them. This tendency runs strongly in BEV, though it is by no means extreme in this respect.[24] In any case, the way in which contraction and deletion are opposed with respect to the preceding vowel clearly demonstrates that both contraction and deletion are phonological processes; furthermore our original analysis that deletion is the removal of a lone consonant produced by contraction receives strong confirmation from the data presented here. We have thus arrived at the point farthest removed from the original suggestion that BEV has no underlying *be* and corresponding *is;* even the suggestion that it is the morpheme *is* which is deleted would not account for the data provided here.

It is also apparent from Table 3.4 that the effect of a preceding pronoun upon contraction and deletion is in part dependent upon, but in part distinct from, the effect of a preceding vowel. Almost all pronouns end in tense vowels, and it is plain that contraction is heavily favored when the subject is a pronoun. But the effect is much stronger than for other noun phrases ending in vowels. In the case of deletion, it can be seen that the rule operates much more

24. There are individual speakers of BEV who extend the usual rules of consonant cluster simplification to extremes and also carry further the weak tendency to delete final single consonants, thus arriving at a high proportion of CV syllables.

often when a pronoun precedes than when another noun phrase ending in a vowel precedes. Therefore the effect of a preceding pronoun will be one of the variable constraints upon deletion, though not necessarily the primary one.

To this point, we cannot be sure that the effect of a preceding vowel or consonant is not the product of some odd distribution of noun phrases before various complement categories, since the data of Tables 3.3 and 3.4 treat all such categories alike. As we have seen in Table 3.2, a following verb strongly favors both contraction and deletion, and it is possible that the noun phrases which precede verbs are different from those which precede predicates. Table 3.5 shows the percentages of contraction and deletion, on the same basis as Table 3.4, but with the proportions for four following grammatical categories shown separately. Since the numbers necessarily become quite small, the figures for the four adolescent BEV groups are grouped together: the T-Birds, the Cobras, the Jets, and the Oscar Brothers. The result shows that the opposing effect of a preceding vowel and consonant holds for all syntactic environments, except in the case of a following future in *gonna*, where both contraction and deletion are close to categorical, and the numbers are very small.[25] In the other cases, we again observe that the effect of a

25. The position of *gonna* is not quite as regular as that of the other constraints; in some cases, it seems as if it is a categorical feature, yet in others we find it behaving as a variable increment to __Vb. The reason seems to be that *gonna* can be interpreted as a quasimodal, comparable to *wanna* and *hafta*. This is one of the many processes of lexicalization referred to below, which intercept phonological processes and reinterpret their results.

TABLE 3.5.
FREQUENCY OF OPERATION OF DELETION AND CONTRACTION RULES ACCORDING TO PRECEDING AND FOLLOWING ENVIRONMENTS FOR FOUR ADOLESCENT BEV GROUPS, IN GROUP STYLE ONLY.

	___NP				___PA-LOC				___Vb				___gon			
	f_c	N	f_D	N	f_c	N	f_D	N	f_c	N	f_D	N	f_c	N	f_D	N
—K__	.37		.62		.25		.50		.65		1.00		.89		.87	
		35		13		32		8		14		9		9		8
—V__	.80		.29		.70		.37		.86		.33		1.00		1.00	
		64		51		23		16		14		12		6		6
pro__	.94		.40		.98		.56		.97		.79		1.00		.96	
		32		30		65		64		32		33		23		23

preceding pronoun is semicategorical for contraction and that deletion is much stronger with a preceding pronoun than with a noun
ending in a vowel. Table 3.5 thus provides us with additional confirmation of our analysis of the relations between contraction and
deletion.

As one illustration of the power of the probability model to predict
the output of variable rules, Cedergren and Sankoff examined the
twelve cells of Table 3.5 which show the output of the contraction
rule. Utilizing the statistical method of maximum likelihood through
a program developed by Sankoff, they estimated the values for the
input probability and the seven parameters which generate this table.
The following probabilities were derived:

$$p_o = 0.25 \qquad\qquad v(\underline{\quad}Vb) = 0.49$$

$$v(Pro\underline{\quad}) = 0.95 \qquad\qquad v(\underline{\quad}gon) = 0.89$$

$$v(V\underline{\quad}) = 0.65 \qquad\qquad v(\underline{\quad}PA, Loc) = 0$$

$$v(K\underline{\quad}) = 0 \qquad\qquad v(\underline{\quad}NP) = 0.16$$

Sankoff's method requires that one of the values for each segment
be .00, so altogether six values are needed to predict the twelve cells
of Table 3.5. Table 3.6 shows that the model is quite successful in
predicting this data. Column 1 is the number of instances, Column
2 the number of contracted (and deleted) cases which show the
contraction rule in operation; and Column 3 is the number predicted.
The prediction is made by inserting the parameters given above into
the general formula 90 to derive the probability φ of the rule applying
in any one instance, and multiplying by Column 1. Cedergren and

TABLE 3.6.
PREDICTION OF CONTRACTION IN TABLE 3.5 BY
CEDERGREN AND SANKOFF MODEL

	Succeeding environments											
	__NP			__PA-Loc			__Vb			__gonna		
Preceding	1	2	3	1	2	3	1	2	3	1	2	3
environment	N	found	pred.	N	found	pred.	N	found	pred.	N	found	pred.
K__	35	22	21.9	32	24	24	14	5	5.3	9	1	0.8
V__	64	13	14	23	7	6	14	2	1.9	6	0	0.2
Pro__	32	2	1	65	1	2.3	32	1	0.6	23	0	0.1

Sankoff have also predicted the deletion values of Table 3.5 and applied this procedure to a number of other variable rules, including the pharyngealization of Panamanian Spanish (R) and the deletion of *que* in Montreal French. All of their initial trials have confirmed to a large extent the hypothesis that the variable constraints are independent. In Table 3.6 the confirmation is striking; in other cases there is some evidence of lack of independence which requires further investigation.

In the particular data taken by Cedergren and Sankoff, the weighting of the following noun phrase over the following adjective is the exceptional rather than the general case. Furthermore, they have taken as their variable constraints the surface syntactic forms rather than the underlying features such as [+ Vb] which are present in several environments (i.e., *gonna* and *Verb*). With these limitations, the fact remains that their quantitative model is an extraordinary step forward in establishing the empirical foundations of linguistic theory. The importance of their work goes considerably beyond variable rules.

The basic activity of the linguist consists of noting particular cases, writing the general rules that govern these cases, and then assembling these general rules into rule schemata. Chomsky and Halle (1968) emphasize that the selection of the proper abbreviatory conventions—braces, brackets, subscripts, and the methods of unfolding these schema—give us our clearest view of linguistic structure. The language-learning facility of the native speaker is said to be just that ability to assemble data into rules and combine rules into rule schema (1968: 331). Yet the test of the proper conventions involves some internal evaluation measure that has not yet been worked out to anyone's satisfaction, and it is still possible for someone to assert that *simplicity* has never yet proved anything.[26] Many linguists feel that we have not given empirical justification for our engagement in this activity: the assembling of subrules into larger rules, extracting as much redundancy as possible at the cost of considerable cost in intelligibility. (e.g., see the Main Stress Rule of Chomsky and Halle 1968: 240).

---

26. In G. Lakoff's introduction to *Linguistics and Natural Logic* (1970) he notes (footnote 2) that the only explicit application of an internal evaluation measure in syntax is Chomsky's analysis of the auxiliary in *Aspects* (1965) and in the light of Ross's refutation of this, argues that "there is not the slightest reason to believe that evaluation measures play any role in the theory of grammar at all, much less in the innate biological mechanisms of the child.

Given the importance of the issues, the weight of Cedergren-and Sankoff's demonstration should be evident. If the variable rule for contraction which underlies Table 3.6 were to be dismantled into its individual components such as the specific subrule 95'

$$95' \qquad \mathrm{\partial} \rightarrow \langle \emptyset \rangle / \begin{bmatrix} +\mathrm{Pro} \\ +\mathrm{V} \end{bmatrix} \# \# \begin{bmatrix} \underline{\quad} \\ +\mathrm{T} \end{bmatrix} \begin{matrix} \mathrm{C}^1 \\ [-\mathrm{nas}] \end{matrix} \# \# \begin{bmatrix} +\mathrm{Vb} \\ -\mathrm{Fut} \\ -\mathrm{NP} \end{bmatrix}$$

there would be no room for variable constraints, but rather a table of individual output frequencies (or probabilities) for each case. These might be arranged in some kind of implicational scale, so they would not be without structure. But the six probabilities derived by Cedergren and Sankoff would not exist; instead we would have twelve empirically derived values for φ. This step would be necessary despite the loss in economy if the hypothesis of the independence of the variable constraints was not empirically justified by the ability of the Cedergren-Sankoff model to predict Table 3.6. In other words, the hypothesis of the independence of variable constraints is equivalent to the hypothesis that assembling rules into rule schema is a legitimate linguistic activity: that this activity reflects the nature of linguistic structure rather than the tastes of the linguist. The theoretical organization of the rule schema in section 5 thus matches the empirical demonstration of independence in section 4 and goes considerably beyond.

It seems to me that this is a remarkable example of the power of quantitative analysis to resolve critical problems in linguistic theory.

7. The Rules for Contraction and Deletion

We can now incorporate the quantitative data of sections 4 and 6 into the logical development of ordered rules for contraction and deletion of sections 1–3, using the formal apparatus of section 5. The outline which follows shows a series of 17 phonological rules of BEV in which the contraction rule (10) and the deletion rule for *is* (13) are included. The contraction and deletion rules are given in full; other rules are shown in enough detail to illustrate their general character and their relation to 9 and 13 (these are discussed in detail in CRR 3288: Vol. 1).

Only a few of these rules are peculiar to BEV. Half of them are part of the basic machinery of SE and operate in exactly the same fashion in BEV; they are marked with double asterisks. The nuclear

Seventeen Phonological Rules of BEV

** 1. Nuclear stress rule

$$\begin{bmatrix} 1\text{stress} \\ V \end{bmatrix} \rightarrow 1\text{stress}/V \cdots \underline{\quad} \cdots]_\alpha$$

** 2. Weak word rule

$$\begin{bmatrix} +W \\ 3\text{stress} \\ V \end{bmatrix} \rightarrow [-\text{stress}]$$

** 3. Syllabification of r

$$V \rightarrow \langle \emptyset \rangle / \begin{bmatrix} -\text{low} \\ -\text{tens} \end{bmatrix} \begin{bmatrix} +\text{cen} \\ +\text{cons} \end{bmatrix} \langle +\text{cons} \rangle$$

** 4. Vowel reduction

$$\begin{bmatrix} -\text{stress} \\ -\text{tense} \\ V \end{bmatrix} \rightarrow [+\text{cen}]$$

5. Vocalization of r

$$[+\text{cen}] \rightarrow [-\text{cons}]/[-\text{cons}] \underline{\quad} \begin{matrix} (\#\#) \\ \langle \#\# \rangle \end{matrix} \langle^* -\text{syl} \rangle$$

6. Loss of postvocalic shwa

$$[+\text{cen}] \rightarrow \langle \emptyset \rangle / \begin{matrix} \begin{bmatrix} +\text{voc} \\ -\text{cons} \end{bmatrix} \\ \langle +\text{high} \rangle \end{matrix} \underline{\quad} \#\# \cdots$$

** 7. Loss of initial glide

$$h \rightarrow \langle \emptyset \rangle / \underline{\quad} \partial \, C_0^1 \#\#$$

8. -t,d deletion

$$[-\text{cont}] \rightarrow \langle \emptyset \rangle / \langle +\text{cons} \rangle \langle \emptyset \rangle \underline{\quad} \#\# \langle -\text{syl} \rangle$$

9. Vocalization of l

$$l \rightarrow \langle \tfrac{1}{2} \rangle / [-\text{cons}] \underline{\quad} (\#\#) \langle -\text{syl} \rangle \cdots$$

** 10. Auxiliary contraction

$$\begin{bmatrix} +\text{voc} \\ -\text{str} \\ +\text{cen} \end{bmatrix} \rightarrow \langle\emptyset\rangle / \left\langle \begin{matrix} +\text{Pro} \\ -\text{cons} \end{matrix} \right\rangle \#\# \left[\overline{+\text{T}} \right] \underset{\langle *\text{nas}\rangle}{C_0^1} \#\# \left\langle \begin{matrix} +\text{Vb} \\ +\text{Fut} \\ -\text{NP} \end{matrix} \right\rangle$$

11. Loss of postvocalic ł

$$\underset{\sim}{\text{ł}} \rightarrow \langle\emptyset\rangle / \left\langle \begin{matrix} [+\text{voc}] \\ +\text{round} \\ : \end{matrix} \right\rangle \underline{} \#\# \cdots$$

12. Assibilation of t

$$[-\text{cont}] \rightarrow \begin{bmatrix} +\text{cont} \\ +\text{strid} \end{bmatrix} / \left[\overline{+\text{Pro}} \right] \#(\#) \, [+\text{strid}] \quad \#\#$$

13. Auxiliary deletion

$$[+\text{cons}] \rightarrow \langle\emptyset\rangle / \left\langle \begin{matrix} *\text{strid} \\ +\text{cons} \\ +\text{Pro} \end{matrix} \right\rangle \#\# \begin{bmatrix} -\text{nas} \\ +\text{cont} \end{bmatrix} \#\# \left\langle \begin{matrix} +\text{Vb} \\ +\text{Fut} \\ -\text{NP} \end{matrix} \right\rangle$$

14. Simplification of $-\text{sK}$ clusters

$$[-\text{cont}] \rightarrow \langle\emptyset\rangle / [+\text{strid}] \underline{} \#(\#) \left\langle \begin{matrix} *\,\text{strid} \\ -\text{syl} \end{matrix} \right\rangle$$

** 15. Epenthesis

$$\emptyset \rightarrow \begin{bmatrix} +\text{cen} \\ -\text{cons} \end{bmatrix} / [+\text{strid}] \, \#(\#) \underline{} [+\text{cont}] \, \#\#$$

** 16. Voicing assimilation

$$[-\text{voc}] \rightarrow [\alpha\text{voice}] / [\alpha\text{voice}] \, \#(\#) \underline{} \#\#$$

** 17. Geminate simplification

$$X_1 \rightarrow \emptyset / X_1 \, \#(\#) \underline{}$$

** = rules common to other English dialects

stress rule 1 operates well before any of the others to provide conditions for vowel reduction, as discussed above; the weak word rule 2 and vowel reduction 4 provide the [ə] upon which rule 10 operates. Rules 3, 5, 6, 7, 9, and 11 are relevant to other contractable items such as *have, has, will,* and *are,* and will be considered briefly below.

Rule 8 is concerned with the simplification of -t/d clusters which intersect with the grammatical category of the past tense (discussed in some detail in CRR 3288:3.2.) Rule 14 is the special case of -sp, -st, -sk clusters (for the justification for writing a separate rule, see the same reference.) Once we establish the basic conditions for contraction by rules 1, 2, 4, the behavior of *is* is governed by the five rules 10, 12, 13, 15 and 16, which we examine below.

7.1 Form of the contraction and deletion rules. Rule 10 appears as the removal of a shwa which stands before (no more than) a single consonant in a word which incorporates the tense marker.[27] The preceding environment shows two variable constraints: the rule is favored if the subject is a pronoun, and if it ends in a nonconsonantal segment—vowel or glide. The residual case is the least favored: a noun phrase which ends in a consonant. The following environment shows three variable constraints. Most important is whether or not the following element is a verb. Here we find restored in part the distinction between the copula and the *be* of the progressive, and it seems likely that the deletion of that *be* (in its finite forms) is connected with its redundant relation to the following -*ing* form. Instead of showing *gonna* as the most favored form, we abstract its [+Future] feature, the increment which makes it most favored among verbal forms, and show that feature as the second variable constraint. The third is the most problematical: ⟨−NP⟩, which registers the fact that if the following element is not a noun phrase—i.e., an adjective, locative, etc.—the rule will be favored more than if it is a noun phrase. There are some cases where this constraint is reversed, but they are in the minority, and we tentatively add this constraint subject to further investigation.

The deletion rule 13 appears as the removal of a lone oral continuant between word boundaries. It might well include the deletion of the /d/ from *would* and *had*, but we have not investigated the relatively small number of cases in which this stop disappears. The nasal /m/ of *I'm* is definitely excluded. In addition to the [z] from *is*, the rule also deletes the [v] from *have*, though it is not clear to

---

27. For details on contraction of other auxiliaries, see Zwicky 1970. As Zwicky points out, *is* and *has* are the only auxiliaries which contract with preceding elements of all phonetic shapes; *would, had, will, have* and *are* are much more restricted. But as we have seen, Zwicky overstates the case when he writes "The reduction of *is* and *has* takes place regardless of the nature of the preceding word." (1970:331).

what extent this deletion obeys the constraints determined for *is*. Turning to the preceding environment, we note that the rule operates categorically when a strident is present. We did not block contraction from operating when the subject ended in a sibilant or strident; but the data shows that if a cluster of two sibilants is formed, the second one is categorically deleted. We also note that the ⟨+Pro⟩ constraint is present, as in rule 10. But the consonantal constraint is reversed: whereas contraction is favored by a preceding vowel or glide, deletion is favored by a preceding obstruent or liquid. The configuration of the following environment is the same as for the contraction rule.

Thus the contraction and deletion rules are parallel but distinct rules of the phonological component. They are alike in four variable constraints—all representing the influence of the grammatical environment. They are dissimilar and even opposed in their effect upon the phonetic structure of the phrase, and we find accordingly that the variable phonetic constraints are diametrically opposed. Both the similarities and the differences of the contraction and deletion rule confirm the view that absence of *is* in BEV is due to the deletion of the lone segment [z] remaining after contraction.

The quantitative data presented in this chapter are sufficient to establish the major variable constraints upon these rules—constraints which are independent of each other and which recur regularly in almost all styles and peer groups. It will no doubt be possible to modify this presentation in the future, as more data are accumulated; there are many interesting questions to be investigated concerning the role of various predicate types. But the purpose of this type of analysis is not to explore every conceivable constraint upon a variable rule to the limits of reproducibility, but rather to apply the logic of these converging (and diverging) patterns to establishing the place, form, and order of the deletion and contraction rules of BEV.

One of the first and most obvious arguments for order springs from the predominance of *i's, tha's,* and *wha's* [ɪs, ðæs, wʌs] as the BEV phonetic output of underlying *it is, that is,* and *what is*. At first glance it seems that the assimilation of the /z/ to the preceding voiceless stop has produced an [s] which is not subject to the deletion rule, and therefore deletion does not apply.[28] In the light of this evidence,

28. The literary convention of writing *i's* with the apostrophe before the *s* indicates that the unreflecting approach to this form does see this *s* as the descendant of an original *is*. As we will see below, this is true only in the sense that the *s* reflects the presence of the copula, but in a nonlinear fashion.

one might order the voicing assimilation rule before the deletion rule, with derivations such as the following:

99   ɪt##ɪz
     ɪt##əz vowel reduction
     ɪt## z contraction
     ɪt## s voicing assimilation
         (deletion—does not apply to [s])
     ɪs## s assibilation
     ɪ ## s reduction of geminates

After a sibilant, one could obtain either *The fish is dead* or *The fish dead* depending on whether or not contraction applies:

	A	B	
100	fɪš##ɪz	fɪš##ɪz	
	fɪš##əz	fɪš##əz	vowel reduction
		fɪš## z	contraction
		fɪš## s	voicing assimilation
		fɪš##	deletion

One's first tendency is to deny that contraction can take place after sibilants, but a few contracted forms are heard. Further, the existence of a sizeable number of zero forms makes it seem clear that route B is in fact followed. Deletion of /s/ after a sibilant must therefore be semicategorical, as indicated in rule 13 by ⟨*strid⟩ __.

However, the case of the plural *fishes* would then pose a difficult problem:

101   fɪš#z
     fɪš#s voicing assimilation (deletion does not apply
         across inflectional boundary)
   *fɪš#əs epenthesis

This result is plainly wrong, and we are forced to conclude that voicing assimilation is ordered after epenthesis, so that it will not assimilate /z/ to a preceding voiceless sibilant. But epenthesis must come *after* deletion, since the entire force of the evidence in sections 4 and 6 indicates that deletion is the removal of a lone consonant; we do not find any remnants of an epenthetic vowel in expressions

such as *That des' [e] mine or *One fish [e] on my line.[29] And assibilation must precede deletion if forms such as i's are to survive as
regularly as they do. Therefore the correct order must be

> contraction
> assibilation
> deletion
> epenthesis
> voicing assimilation.

It is an attractive notion to place the rule of voicing assimilation
last, since this is actually a very general constraint upon the form
of final clusters which contain morpheme boundaries. But this order
is contrary to the notion expressed above, that in i's /z/ is assimilated
to [s] before deletion. The contradiction lies in the assumption that
the [s] of [ɪs] is derived from is, as indicated by the practice of writing
i's in dialect literature. It now seems clear that this [s] is the assibi-
lated [t] of it: the verb is has entirely disappeared, leaving behind
its footprint on the preceding pronoun, in the following fashion:[30]

102   ɪt # #ɪz
           ɪt # #əz   vowel reduction (4)
           ɪt # # z   contraction (10)
           ɪs # # z   assibilation (12)

We have already seen that deletion must be categorical after sibilants, so it follows that the last step is necessarily

           ɪs # #   deletion (13).

The order 10–12–13–15–16, as shown in the rules, therefore gives the
correct results. Rule 12 shows that assibilation is restricted to words
with [+Pro]; there are four such pronouns ending in -t: it, that, what,
and lot. This is a rule which applies with a somewhat lower φ for
other (WNS) dialects of English. Neither BEV nor WNS uses
[pæsgʊd] for Pat's good; this does not seem to rhyme with [ðæsgʊd]
That's good. But it is possible that the restriction of the assibilation
rule to pronouns and one /z/ is too sharp: the rule may apply to

29. One might think that such schwas would be indistinguishable from reduced
forms of are; but in BEV person-number disagreement of is and are is very rare, and
there is practically no vestige of are occurring in singular contexts.

30. I am indebted to Joshua Waletzky for this solution to the problem posed
by i's.

other frequent forms ending in -t, such as *outside*. We do not have enough evidence at present to judge whether the rule operates regularly in cases such as these, and intuitions are quite unreliable in these areas of morphological condensation.

Given the rule order shown above, we have the derivations

103   A   B   C
             fish is   *fish is*   *fish (pl.)*
             fıš##ız   fıš##ız   fıš#z
             fıš##əz   fıš##əz   vowel reduction (4)
             fıš## z   contraction (10)
             fıš##   deletion (13)
                                            fıš#əz   epenthesis (15)

The form *fish is* can follow route A or B, depending on whether contraction applies, yielding *The fish good today* or *The fish is good today*. The plural *fishes* appears only as [fıš#əz], since deletion does not apply across an inflectional boundary.

One prominent characteristic of BEV morphology is that final clusters in -*sts*, -*sps*, and -*sks* are necessarily simplified, so that an underlying form //test// (which shows up in the verb form *testing*) cannot have a plural [tɛsts].[31] The phonetic form which does appear is chiefly [tɛsəz]. This form is derived by the following sequence:

104   tɛst#z
             tɛs #z   simplification of -sK clusters (14)
             tɛs #əz   epenthesis (15)

It should be noted that many BEV speakers do say [tɛs] for this plural, which can only indicate a different ordering of the epenthesis rule. If 15 comes *before* 14, we then get [tɛs#z] without epenthesis; voicing assimilation (16) then applies, and geminate simplification (17), yielding [tɛs]. This seems to be a genuine case of alternation through rule reordering, rather than a choice of different options. In either case, [tɛsts] is impossible, for the simplification of -sK clusters is categorical when a sibilant follows, as indicated in 14. If the sibilant

31. In the following discussion we will take the cases where the general -*t/d* deletion rule 9 has not applied and where the latter -*sK* rule deletes the final consonant. The -*sKs* clusters are categorically simplified: they pose particular difficulties for BEV speakers who find it difficult to articulate them even in the most careful speech. Extreme effort produces such recursive forms as (tɛstsəsəsəs). (See chapter 1 and CRR 3288: sections 3.2.4, 3.9.5.)

is derived from a separate word, as in *The test is . . .* , no reordering is required to obtain [tɛs] as the output, for after contraction the deletion rule (13) applies:

105		
	tɛst # #ɪz	
	tɛst # #əz	vowel reduction (4)
	tɛst # # z	contraction (10)
	tɛst # #	deletion (13)
	tɛs # #	simplification (14)

But the contraction rule is not categorical here; when it does not apply, the simplification of -sK clusters now takes place before a following vowel, and it is possible to get either A or B:

	A	B	
106	tɛst # #ɪz	tɛst # #ɪz	
	tɛst # #əz	tɛst # #əz	vowel reduction (4)
	tɛs # #əz		simplification (14)

Thus there is a high degree of ordering in the rules discussed so far. Stress assignment (1) is followed by the weak word rule (2) which removes stress. Vowel reduction (4) is dependent on 1 and 2, since only unstressed vowels are reduced. Contraction (10) in turn depends upon reduction, since it removes the shwas so provided. Assibilation (12) occurs only after contraction and necessarily precedes deletion (13) if it is to leave any trace at all. The simplification of -sK clusters (14) must follow the optional deletion rule (13), for otherwise we would obtain [-sts] clusters in *The test's O.K.* when 13 does not apply. Epenthesis (15) must of course follow the -sK rule (14) to insert the shwa in [tɛsəz]. Finally, voicing assimilation (16) must follow epenthesis (15) if we are not to derive [tɛsəs].

7.2. *Other contractable verbs.* Rules 3, 5, 6, 9, and 11 operate upon liquids /r/ and /l/ as general phonological rules of BEV and affect other verb forms that are later contracted and deleted—chiefly *are* and *will.* The vocalization of these consonants is a process which occurs in somewhat different form in many other English dialects, but the loss of the resulting vocalic glide by rules 6 and 9 is quite characteristic of BEV.

As we have seen in chapter 2, the general rule for the vocalization of r in New York City and other r-less areas is weaker than the BEV rule. It is missing the second variable constraint in 5 which states that BEV favors the environment __ # #V over __V, but does not exclude __V. In contrast, the WNS rule must begin by excluding __V with the minimal feature [−syl] directly after the r: that is, a vowel cannot follow immediately without a word boundary intervening.

107         $r \rightarrow \langle \partial \rangle / [-\text{cons}]$ _____ $\genfrac{}{}{0pt}{}{[-\text{syl}]}{(\#\#)\langle \begin{Bmatrix} C \\ \emptyset \end{Bmatrix} \rangle}$

Below this minimal feature appears the variable constraint which says that the rule is favored if consonant or pause follows, whether or not a word boundary intervenes. This then favors the cases of __##C, __##, and __C over __##V, which is the residual case, __V already being excluded. The BEV version in rule 5 has as its first variable constraint the same configuration symbolizing "final and preconsonantal" but with the * notation indicating that it is categorical. The second constraint ⟨##⟩ then favors __##V over __V, which is not excluded.

In studying these vocalization processes, it becomes evident that they represent the sudden or gradual loss of a single feature; [+consonantal] gives way to [−consonantal]. It is therefore essential that weakly constricted [r] and [ə] should differ only in that one feature. These two segments might be shown here as sharing the feature [+central], which differentiates [r] and [ə] from [l] and the back lateral glide [ɫ]. This feature organization is indicated in rules 5 and 6 as well as rule 10.

The lateral *l* on rules 9 may also be shown as [−cen, +voc, +cons] and the glide in rule 11 as [−cen, −voc, −cons], but these rules are only lightly sketched in for our discussion of contraction + deletion of the copula.

The glides are removed by variable rules 6 and 11 when they follow vowels, producing the well-known lower prestige southern forms *po'* [po] and *do'* [do] for [poə] and [doə]. Rule 6 also affects the glide of *there, their,* and *your,* a process which has led to phonetic forms homonymous with *they* and *you.* Here we are concerned with the effect of 5 and 6 upon *are:*

108   ##ăr##   weak word rule (2)
          ##ər##   vowel reduction (4)
          ##əə##   vocalization of r (5)
          ##ə ##   loss of postvocalic ə (6)
          ##   ##   contraction (9)

Contraction of *are* is therefore equivalent to deletion; there is nothing left for Rule 13 to apply to. If contraction does not apply to some forms, the deletion process is very likely to eliminate them. In any case, the net result is that far fewer *are* forms survive in BEV than *is* forms: for many speakers, deletion of *are* is (semi)categorical. This might be indicated by placing an asterisk next to the zero subscript of C_0^1 (for quantitative comparisons of the contraction and deletion of *is* and *are*, see chapter 2).[32]

Rules 9 and 11 operate upon the noncentral liquid *l* in a parallel fashion, so that when the auxiliary in *I will be here* is contracted, it is to all intents and purposes eliminated. The vocalization of *l* is a later and less regular process than the vocalization of *r*: otherwise we would have vocalic *l* after consonantal *r* in *Charles*, i.e. * [čarl̩]— whereas we actually have the reverse [čaːl̩z] or [čaːlz]. (The symbol [ɫ] stands for a back, unrounded, possibly lateral, glide.) The vocalization of *l* must also follow the general *-t,d* simplification rule, for *d* behaves like a consonant cluster in *old* and *told*, rather than like a glide and lone consonant as in *card* and *cared*. Thus we have:

109	## wĭl ##	weak word rule (2)
	## wəl ##	vowel reduction (4)
	## əl ##	$w \to \emptyset$ (7?)
	## əl̩ ##	vocalization of *l̩* (9)
	## l̩ ##	contraction (10)
	## ##	loss of final *l̩* (11)

Rule 11 follows contraction, for we rarely obtain simple [ə] for the future (except in the condensation of *I am going to* → *I'ma*) (see CRR 3288:3.5). There is probably no general process which removes

---

32. One indication that this analysis of *are*-contraction is correct is the fact that working-class white Southerners do omit *are* in such expressions as *You gettin' the salad?* and *Cucumbers? We out of them* (from my own observations in Georgia and North Carolina). On the other hand, there is no evidence of white Southerners deleting *is*, and the intuitive response of a number of southern linguists and laymen is that this is not possible for a white speaker. This is not an arbitrary selection of *are* rather than *is*, but rather a reflection of the fact that white Southerners do occasionally use Rule 6 to yield *po'* (seemingly in the same stylistic contexts as the absence of *are*), but have no deletion rule for *is*. Another indication is in the results of Wolfram's Detroit study (1969): the frequencies of zero forms for *are* are considerably lower in Detroit than in New York City (though still higher than for *is*), clearly reflecting the less categorical vocalization of *r* in this *r*-pronouncing area.

Note that if neither rules 5 or 6 apply to *are*, the resulting geminate [əə] automatically is simplified to [ə] by the regular rule 17.

the *w* in BEV or SE: a special lexical alternation for *will* may be required to produce the equivalent of 7. This rule removes *h* whenever it occurs before a shwa and one or no consonant; thus the *h* in *his, her, him* is deleted, as well as in *have, has,* and *had.* The form *has* is not characteristic of BEV; although there is person-number agreement in the forms of *be,* we find that the forms *do, have,* and *was* predominate in all persons over *does, has,* and *were.*

Contraction does not of course operate upon the pronouns *his, her,* and *him,* since they do not contain the tense marker. The apostrophe used in literary conventions indicates merely the deletion of the *h.* Contraction does operate upon *have* when it contains the tense marker; in the rule given here, only the undifferentiated C_0^1 is shown for the consonant remaining. A fuller form would specify variability before oral consonants. The resultant $\#\#v\#\#$ will be deleted by Rule 13:

110      $\#\#hæv\#\#$

           $\#\#h\breve{æ}v\#\#$ weak word rule (4)

           $\#\#\ \ \ əv\#\#$ vowel reduction (5)

           $\#\#\ \ \ \ \ v\#\#$ contraction (9)

           $\#\#\ \ \ \ \ \ \ \#\#$ deletion (13)

The deletion rule 13 now shows that a lone oral continuant is removed: that is, [v] and [z], but not [d] or [m], although Fasold has pointed out that [d] may be deleted in expressions such as *He be mad right then* and elsewhere. We do not have complete data on any of the other verb forms as yet, but there seems to be little question but that the grave member [v] favors deletion more than [z]. This is particularly true, of course, before labial consonants, so that *I've been* would be among the rarest of BEV forms.

A word of caution is in order before accepting all of these rules as productive processes in the BEV grammars of any given speech community. For many speakers, the *have* before *been* may no longer exist as a synchronic fact. In general, phonological processes are reversible: if an auxiliary disappears through the vocalization of /r/, it can reappear if that phonological rule no longer operates or is reversed. But it appears that irreversible change can take place when phonological change identifies one lexical item with another so that the underlying forms alter. This may indeed be the case with *they book* or even with the zero form of *We crazy,* for some speakers. In the first case, we find that rules 5 and 6 operate upon the underlying possessive as follows:

111   ðe + r
           ðe + ə   vocalization of r (5)
           ðe +   loss of postvocalic ə (6)

The last item falls together with [ðeᵛ¹], the phonetic output of the pronoun *they*; and even when Rule 5 is strongly restricted by the influence of a surrounding r-pronouncing community, the form [ðeᵛ ¹] may still be used in attributive position. In effect, speakers may have reanalysed the phonetic form as equivalent to that which appears in subject position as *they*; the absence of a possessive /z/ suffix may reinforce this analysis. Yet it is clear that we are dealing with what was, originally at least, a phonological process: in southern white dialects which use dummy *there* in *There's a difference*, the form /ðer/ undergoes the same process to produce a phonetic form equivalent to *they*, without any involvement of the possessive category. The extent to which such lexicalization has taken place is a topic for empirical study through the techniques of accountable, quantitative investigation outlined above.

These brief notes on verb forms other than *is* are not intended to give a definitive account of their treatment in BEV; that is not possible without the same type of quantitative data which we have supplied for *is*. This broader view of the operation of the system allows us to show how the rules for contraction and deletion of *is* are embedded in a more general set of processes which govern the phonetic form of the BEV verbal system. The construction of such broader rules raises questions which can be resolved by more detailed investigations of variable rules. For example, closer study of the relation of *v*-deletion to *z*-deletion will allow us to determine whether the comparative infrequency of the *have* perfect in BEV (as compared to the relatively common *had* pluperfect) is due to phonological processes or to less frequent use of the grammatical category itself (see chapter 2 on the status of *have*). The 17 rules presented here have been discussed only insofar as they relate to contraction and deletion. The constraints upon ordering for the entire set of auxiliaries are almost as tight as those discussed above in relation to *is*. Table 3.7 gives an overall view of some of the derivations given above for the first 15 rules and the order inherent in them.[33]

33. For speakers who habitually say [tɛs] for *tests*, the order of rules 14 and 15 is reversed; thus the *t* may be deleted without epenthesis, and the geminate simplification rule (17) gives the results [tɛs].

TABLE 3.7.
EXAMPLES OF PHONOLOGICAL DEVIATIONS OF SELECTED LEXICAL ITEMS.

1. Nuclear stress rule	wórker	wil^3	ar^3	ar^3	.hǽv^3	fíš##iz^3	ft##íz^3	tést###iz^3	tést###iz^3	tést#z	tést#z
2. Weak word rule	wɜker	wĭl^3	ăr^3	ăr^3	hǽv^3	fíš##íz^3	ft##íz^3	tést###iz^3	tést###iz^3	tést#z	tést#z
3. Syllabification of r	wɜker										
4. Vowel reduction	wɜkər	wəl	ər	ər	həv	fíš##əez	ft##æz	tɜst###əez	tɜst##əez		
5. Vocalization of r	wɜkəe		ee	ee							
6. Loss of postvocalic ə	wɜkə	e									
7. Loss of initial glide		el			ʌe						
8. -t/d deletion		əĭ								ze#sɜ	tes#z
9. Vocalization of l		ɬ̃/			v	fíš##z	ít##z	tést###z	tes##z	tes#z	ze#sɜ
10. Contraction		∅				fíš##z	ít##z	tést###z	tes##z	tes#z	ze##sɜ
11. Loss of postvocalic ɬ		∅									
12. Assibilation of -t							ís##z				
13. Auxiliary deletion					∅	fíš#	ís	tɜs			
14. Simplification of -sK clusters								tɜs##z	tɜs##z	tes#z	ze#sɜ
15. Epenthesis										tɜs#z	ze##sɜ
16. Voicing assimilation			ə								
17. Geminate simplification											
Phonetic output	[wɜkə]	∅	[ə]	∅	[fíš]	[ís]	[tɛsiz]	[tɛs]	[tɛsiz]		

123

8. The General Implications of the Study of Variable Rules

This chapter has presented a systematic exploration of a particular problem in the grammar of BEV, using controlled data from the speech community in a formal rule system adequate for the purpose. More generally, the chapter is directed at the methodological problem which seems to me of overriding importance in linguistics at the moment: to connect theoretical questions with a large body of intersubjective evidence which can provide decisive answers to those questions. In the first statements of generative grammar, it was proposed that theories could rest upon a great number of clear cases where intuitive judgments on well-formedness were uniform throughout the community—and that the theory would then decide the marginal cases. But the number of papers based upon idiosyncratic and uncertain judgments has multiplied rapidly as the questions become sharper and the analysis more detailed.[34] No matter what help the theorist's intuitions may give him in formulating his hypotheses, it is clear that his own intuitions are the only kinds of data which are *not* allowable as evidence, for no one can estimate the degree to which such judgments are influenced by the universal and understandable desire to prove oneself right. In any case, the construction of complete grammars for "idiolects," even one's own, is a fruitless and unrewarding task; we now know enough about language in its social context to realize that the grammar of the speech community is more regular and systematic than the behavior of any one individual. Unless the individual speech pattern is studied within the overall system of the community, it will appear as a mosaic of unaccountable and sporadic variation.

The data that we need cannot be collected from the closet or from

34. Among Chomsky's first published statements on this point (1955:14), we read: "In many intermediate cases we shall be prepared to let the grammar itself decide, when the grammar is set up in the simplest way so that it includes the clear sentences and excludes the clear nonsentences." It should then be possible to avoid presenting intermediate cases as evidence. However, a great many recent arguments in syntax have hinged upon sentence types which are evidently intermediate in grammaticality, in the sense that there is widespread disagreement or "variation" in judgments on grammaticality. The techniques employed here to deal with inherent variation may prove applicable to these cases of marginal grammaticality, where speakers' judgments vary according to some unknown constraint. See chapter 8 of *Sociolinguistic Patterns* for more data on these problems, and Carden 1972 for a suggestion on applying variable rules to the continuum of NEG-Q and NEG-V judgments.

any library, public or private; fortunately for us, there is no shortage of native speakers of most languages, if we care to listen to them speak. Without such empirical data, we are now in the process of producing a great many well-formed theories with nothing to stand on: beautiful constructions with ugly feet. The test of simplicity—some internal evaluation measure which is in the continuous process of revision—has not satisfied many linguists to date. It is reasonable to ask that alternative analyses of the data on hand prove their value by pointing to further data which can conclusively resolve the alternatives proposed.

It seems necessary at this point to refer to the distinction between competence and performance, primarily because it is so widely discussed. I am not sure whether this is a useful distinction in the long run. There seem to be some limitations of speakers which have to do with memory span, or difficulties in articulation, which are outside the linguistic system proper. Surely no one would want to use the notion of performance as a wastebasket category, in which all inconvenient data on variation and change can be deposited; we have any number of labels such as "free variation" or "dialect mixture" which are readily available for this purpose. Are the variable constraints discussed in this chapter limitations on performance rather than competence? For some types of consonant cluster simplification, we might be tempted to answer yes. But the variable rules themselves require at so many points the recognition of grammatical categories, of distinctions between grammatical boundaries, and are so closely interwoven with basic categorical rules, that it is hard to see what would be gained by extracting a grain of performance from this complex system. It is evident that rules 1–17 of section 7 are a part of the speaker's knowledge of the language, and if some of these rules are cast in a different form than traditional categorical rules, then we must clearly revise our notions of what it means to "know" a language.

It should be equally clear that we are in no way dealing with statistical statements or approximations to some ideal or true grammar. We are dealing with a set of quantitative *relations* which are the form of the grammar itself. A grammar in which all of the variable rules of 1–17 suddenly became categorical would have no direct relation to the language we have described; a number of reorganizations and striking changes in the system would be certain to take place. (*Sociolinguistic Patterns,* chapter 8).

The study of variable rules will enable us to make progress in five general areas of linguistic theory which arise in the study of any language or speech community:

1. What is the most general form of linguistic rule? That is, what notations, conventions, schemata, and interpretations allow us to account for the productive and regular patterns of linguistic behavior?

2. What relations hold between rules in a system? What principles of ordering, combination, and parallelism prevail in systems such as rules 1–17?

3. How are systems of rules related? What is the range of possible differences between mutually intelligible dialects? How do languages, originally diverse, combine within a bilingual speech community?

4. How do systems of rules change and evolve? This historical question is of course closely related to the last point:

5. How are rule systems acquired? How does the individual's system of rules change and develop as he acquires the norms of the speech community?[35]

This chapter has been concerned with specific questions within the first and second areas, but further extensions into the third and

35. The theoretical problems outlined here are not at all irrelevant to some immediate problems of applied linguistics, in teaching the reading and writing of SE to speakers of BEV. Although the primary obstacles in the schools are social and cultural factors, there are some linguistic differences which have profound effects—not because BEV is so different from SE, but because it is so similar (see chapter 1). The conclusion reached in this chapter should make it immediately evident that the task is not so much to inhibit deletion as to teach contraction to BEV speakers—not the abstract contraction rule, but rather the control of contraction without immediately ensuing deletion. There is no English program currently in use which focuses on this critical point, since it would never occur to an SE or WNS speaker that contraction needs to be taught. When the BEV speaker says *He wild,* the teacher would normally correct with *He is wild,* thinking that this is the equivalent translation. But as we have seen, the BEV speaker would have said *He is wild* if that is what he meant. What he intended to say is equivalent to SE *He's wild,* and that equivalence must be explicitly taught. When it comes to reading, speakers have a great deal of trouble with printed contractions. In the commendable desire to make primers less formal, some authors have begun to insert contractions *I'll, we're,* without realizing what difficulties they are creating for BEV readers, for whom full forms *I will* and *we are* are perfectly natural—much more so than for WNS readers. Thus, in more than one way, a knowledge of the abstract rule system of BEV is essential for the right approach to educational problems.

fourth areas of investigation have been indicated at many points. The particular problem investigated here has been to determine the form and order of the rules which control the appearance of the copula and auxiliary *is* in BEV. We began with a wide range of possible solutions: total absence of the copula; deletion of abstract *be;* deletion of the formative *is;* alternative contraction and deletion of *is;* or contraction, then deletion of a single consonant. The evidence clearly shows that the last alternative is the correct one. We combined the techniques of generative grammar with quantitative analysis of systematic variation in BEV to arrive at this result, and in so doing necessarily enlarged the concept of "rule of grammar." This enlargement and our methods of analysis may seem novel or even challenging to those who are convinced that linguistic theory has little to learn from the study of linguistic behavior. But I do not regard these methods or this formal treatment as radical revisions of generative grammar and phonology. On the contrary, I believe that our findings give independent confirmation of the value of generative techniques in several ways. First, I do not know of any other approach which would allow us to work out this complex series of ordered rules, in which both grammatical and phonological constraints appear. Secondly, the stress assignment rules of Chomsky and Halle seem to yield precisely the right conditions for vowel reduction and the contraction rule. Since the contraction rule has never been presented before in detail, we must consider this independent confirmation on the basis of discrete data, clearer evidence than we can obtain from the continuous dimensions of stress or vowel reduction. We also find independent confirmation of the position and role of the tense marker, even where it takes a zero form. Third, we find abundant confirmation of Chomsky's general position that dialects of English are likely to differ from each other far more in their surface representation than in their underlying structures. This concept of ordered rules is particularly well designed to discover and display such complex sets of relations in a relatively simple way.

Even more encouraging than this theoretical fit is the fact that these quantitative relations, once discovered, reappear in other accountable studies of BEV. Table 3.8 shows some comparable data from Wolfram's study of 48 black subjects in Detroit (1969). Wolfram's careful analysis proceeded within a different formal framework than the one presented here, but provided full confirmation of each of

TABLE 3.8.
EFFECT OF GRAMMATICAL ENVIRONMENT ON DELETION OF
THE COPULA FOR BLACK SPEAKERS IN DETROIT

		Preceding environment			
Middle class	N__	Pro__			
Upper	1.8	6.2			
Lower	6.3	13.8			
Lower class					
Upper	18.9	40.7			
Lower	30.1	63.1			

	Following environment				
	__N	__PA	__Loc	__Ving	__gn
Middle class	1.6	4.2	13.3	11.3	33.3
Lower class	36.5	47.3	44.4	50.0	78.9

This table is adapted from Wolfram 1969:209, 211.

the basic qualitative and quantitative relations presented in this paper, including even fluctuations in the ordering of __ PA and __ Loc as following grammatical environments.[36] Wolfram's work confirms the environments in which the copula can be deleted; the relation between SE contraction and BEV deletion; the inherent variability of deletion; the stylistic shift and the effect of a preceding pronoun; the effect of the following grammatical environments; the quantitative relations of the contraction and deletion process; and the relations of am, is, and are. Further reflections of the same variable constraints can be seen in Mitchell-Kernan's close analysis of two adults from the San Francisco black community; in Henrie's work with young black children in the same area (1969); in the work of Legum and his associates at SWRL with young black children in Los Angeles (Legum et al. 1971); and in Jane Torrey's work in Harlem with younger children (1972). The convergence of such intricate quantitative findings on this abstract level is a compelling demonstration of the force of sociolinguistic method and theory.

Cumulative and convergent results of this nature confirm my belief that intersubjective knowledge about abstract linguistic structures

36. Wolfram was aware of the findings presented here, as they appeared in CRR 3288, and deliberately chose to examine some of the same variables.

is within the grasp of linguistic theory. In addition to solving this particular problem or enlarging a particular theoretical framework to deal with variation, the work described in this chapter aims to provide a model for linguistic research which will arrive at decisive solutions to theoretical questions through the use of data from the speech community, and I believe that this mode of work can provide the stability and sound empirical base which is a matter of some urgency in linguistics today.

4 | Negative Attraction and Negative Concord

1. A Semantic Contradiction

THE following sentence poses a difficult problem for linguistic analysis, since it has two directly opposite meanings, depending on who hears it.[1]

1   It ain't no cat can't get in no coop.

This is a sentence of the black English vernacular spoken by Speedy, the 15-year-old leader of the Cobras, recorded in a discussion of pigeon flying during a group session in the course of our studies in south-central Harlem. For speakers of other dialects, 1 has the meaning of standard English

2   There isn't any cat that can not get into any (pigeon) coop.

But the meaning intended by Speedy will be clear if we place 1 in a larger context:

3   CR: Do cats . . . ever get in your cage?
           Speedy: They never got in one of mine.
           Junior: No; they scree—unless they got th—one of them
                    jive coops! (general laughter)
           Speedy: (chuckle) It ain't no cat can't get in no coop.

1. This chapter is scheduled to appear in *Language* in a forthcoming issue. The analysis reflects original contributions by Paul Cohen and discussions with Edward Klima, Charles Fillmore, Bruce Fraser, C.-J. Bailey, and Harris Savin, whose assistance is gratefully acknowledged. The analysis of the semantic features of *any* in section 6 is particularly indebted to recent work of Harris Savin whose views provide the point of departure for the logical characterization of the quantifiers given there.

Speedy's meaning is plainly 4, the direct opposite of 2.

4   There isn't any cat that can get into any (pigeon) coop.

Whatever the historical origins of BEV may be, it is now a dialect of English. In case after case, we find that striking differences from other dialects may be traced to minimal adjustments in English phonological and grammatical rules. There are differences in the selection of redundant elements, different choice of dummy elements, and extensions of old rules to new areas. But on the face of it, 1 poses a much more dramatic difference which seems to be quite apart from aspect, emphasis, or style. For one surface structure we have two contradictory interpretations which must correspond to the deep structure difference.

This is not an isolated case. As we will see (section 4) it is one of a half-a-dozen examples where the BEV rules of negative concord produce forms that are interpreted with exactly the opposite meaning by white listeners. The immediate problem for the linguist—or for speakers of other dialects who would like to understand BEV—is to discover the nature of the rule which produces such an effect. What are the conditions under which BEV speakers can duplicate a negative in a following clause without changing the meaning of the sentence? What process of change could have produced a sentence which means X in dialect A and not-X in dialect B? And how do speakers of A and B come to understand each other if this is the case? The problem has even greater interest for our understanding of linguistic evolution, since we do not yet understand the ways in which dialects in close contact diverge to the point of unintelligibility and become distinct languages (Labov 1971a).[2]

It appears that the problem of dialect differences in negative concord has not been properly appraised. The naive view is that the nonstandard dialects simply have too many negatives. Historically-minded linguists and dialectologists point out that multiple negation is the traditional pattern and that our standard form is a rule imposed on English by grammarians in the 18th century. More recently,

2. In some ways, BEV is converging with other dialects of English and reflects a Creole origin with structures more different from English than we now observe. But in the rules of negative concord and negative attraction, we are looking at the further development of traditional, well-established English rules with no reflection in Creole structures. We are therefore examining a divergence of dialect rules responsible for such a phenomenon as 1.

students of syntax have pointed out that standard *any* in *He doesn't know anything* already reflects the presence of a negative (or other affective element) commanding it, so that *He doesn't know nothing* simply does with the second *no* what SE does with *any*. These dialect differences are summarized by Stockwell, Schachter, and Partee:

> The question of grammaticality for double negation is complicated by the existence of a substandard dialect which, like Chaucerian English, converts all *some*'s directly into *no*'s in negative sentences, rather than leaving all but one of them as *any*'s. (1968 Vol. 1:272)

As we will see, there are many dialects of English which convert some *any*'s into *no*'s, differing from the standard in a variety of ways, but there is no dialect which converts all *any*'s in negative sentences into *no*'s. In other words, dialect differences cannot be encapsulated by a *some-no* suppletion rule opposed to a *some-any* rule. In the course of our analysis of negative transfer rules, we will encounter other evidence that dialect differences in the handling of negation are more extensive than these authors suggest.

The problems posed by real language phenomena can best be handled with a three-pronged attack. In this chapter, I will combine the abstract analysis of intuitive data with naturalistic observation of language in use and supplement these with experimental tests of well-defined variables. This chapter will attempt to solve the semantic and grammatical problems posed by sentence 1, using several kinds of data to converge upon a single solution. Sections 2, 3 and 4 will present the basic linguistic and dialectal data on three kinds of negative transfer: negative attraction to subject *any*, negative postposing to indeterminates, and negative concord. In section 5 we will consider the possibility of combining these three rules into a single transformation. From a purely formal point of view this is not impossible. But when deeper questions are asked about what these transformations accomplish for speakers of the language, it appears that we are dealing with two radically different kinds of grammatical operations. The strongly obligatory character of negative attraction provides a puzzle in itself, and in section 6 we will be forced to undertake an analysis of the semantics of *some, any, each,* and *all* to understand this categorical rule. This chapter therefore stands as complementary to the last. In chapter 3 our main concentration was on the variability of the copula, while here our main concern will be to explain the strongly obligatory character of negative attraction. When the analysis of section 6 is completed we will engage the variable nature of negative concord, and it will appear that the contrast between categorical and variable rules lies at the heart of the problem first posed. Section 8 integrates these findings into an overall view of negative transfer rules, and from this overall pattern, the answer to the problem raised by sentence 1 will be found.

2. Negative Attraction

We must begin with the analysis of the *no* in *it ain't no cat*, since this contains the semantic features which govern the transformational rules operating in 1. It is generally agreed that the *no* in *no cat* represents an underlying indefinite *any* combined with a negative which has been attracted to it from elsewhere in the sentence. To understand the movement of negatives in sentences such as 1, we must deal with the whole range of rules which govern negative attraction in English. These include the obligatory attraction of the negative to subject indefinites, as in

5   * Anybody doesn't go → Nobody goes

the optional postposing of the negative to object indefinites

6   He doesn't like anything ∽ He likes nothing

nonstandard negative concord

7   He doesn't like anything ∽ He don't like nothing

and various forms of negative inversion

8   He didn't ever go ∽ Never did he go

9   Nobody saw it ∽ Didn't nobody see it

These rules all involve the attraction of NEGATIVE to the "indeterminates" *any, ever,* and *either.* This chapter is concerned principally with these elements, without taking up the problems associated with adverbs, prepositions, and conjunctions that contain the negative feature.[3] The label *indeterminate* was first applied by Klima (1964)

---

3. There are also other indefinites and quantifiers involved in these rules; we will necessarily be involved with *some,* and touch briefly on *much* and *many* which lie on the periphery of the rules being studied.

to distinguish *any, ever,* and *either* from other indefinites like *some,* primarily on the basis of their co-occurrence with negative and question features.

The analysis of the quantifier *no* in *no cat* into NEG + *any* is a fundamental given for our investigation. Klima (1964) assembles a great deal of evidence on this point, which can hardly be questioned if one gives any weight to relatedness between sentences. Typical is the alternation between active and passive forms of sentences that contain two indeterminates and one negative.

10a   No cook spoiled any broth.
10b   * Any broth was spoiled by no cook.
10c   No broth was spoiled by any cook.

There is no reason to think that most speakers would be aware of the underlying *any* in *no,* but there is evidence from linguistic pathology that a deep-seated knowledge of this fact may be present in native speakers. There is a particular schizophrenic verbal pattern of reversing positive and negatives in a consistent and predictable way. A patient described by Laffal (1965) was exceptionally gifted in the use of this rule.

11   *Doctor:* Can you tell me now who invented the airplane?
            Patient: I do know.
            Doctor: You do know.
            Patient: Yes, I know . . .
            Doctor What you mean to say is that you don't know.
            Patient: I do know. If I don't know, I, I, I, I wouldn't be
                able to tell you.
            Doctor: You're not able to tell me, though, are you?
            Patient: Yes I am, for I do know.

The patient could of course reverse meaning simply by adding a negative to every sentence. But he operated instead at a more abstract level, reversing the negative modality of each underlying sentence by an alpha rule:

12          $[\alpha \text{NEG}] \rightarrow [-\alpha \text{NEG}]$[4]

The effect is to remove any realization of an underlying negative.

4. This is one of the phenomena which justify the use of the feature notation [+NEG], implying the existence of a [−NEG]. This person's behavior could not easily be formalized without the use of [−NEG].

When the same patient was performing a word association test, he responded:

13   Home . . . there's any place like.

demonstrating an unconscious knowledge of the *NEG + any* analysis of *no* through the production of this totally ungrammatical sentence.

The negative is then normally attracted to the indeterminates *any* and *ever*, realized as *no* and *never*. This attraction is obligatory for subject indeterminates, but optional with others, so that we have the alternation:

14a   He didn't know anything about anybody.
14b   He   knew nothing about anybody.

But no indeterminate can be skipped:

15a   * He   knew anything about nobody.
15b   * He ever knew nothing about anybody.

The English NEGATTRAC rule can be summed up informally by saying that in standard English the negative is attracted to the first indeterminate, obligatorily if it is a subject. The simplest form of transformation that will accomplish this, following Fillmore (1967), operates upon the negative in its sentence initial position as modality or type marker.[5] Our first approximation to this transformation would then be 16. (The category *Indet* stands for a set of features to be developed in section 6; the symbol "[" stands for "contains" and "∼[" for "does not contain").

16   NEGATTRAC I
            W − [+NEG] − X − Indet
            1   2   3   4 → 1   3   2 + 4
            Conditions: a. Obligatory if 3 = ∅
                        b. 3 ∼[Indet

5. Negative attraction and concord are shown in 16 as a rightward movement from a leftmost abstract constituent, but this view will not survive in the present analysis. These transformations will eventually be seen as leftward and rightward movements following negative placement in the unmarked preverbal position. The ultimate location of constituents such as NEG or Q in the underlying structure is of course currently in dispute. Recent views of NEG and Q as predicates of higher level sentences, reflected in Carden (1970) are consistent with the analysis here, although it is neutral on this issue as it does not rely upon the formal presence of higher level S, NP, and VP nodes which require an operation of quantifier or NEG lowering.

Condition *b* insures that 4 is the first indeterminate, and condition *a* is merely a first approximation to the statement of when NEG-ATTRAC is obligatory. If 16 does not apply, then the negative will be transferred to preverbal position by the usual rule. Even when 3 is null and we are dealing with a subject indeterminate, there are still many conditions under which NEGATTRAC is not obligatory. We will want to examine these marginal cases in order to come to grips with the central phenomenon of the categorical nature of negative attraction. For when NEGATTRAC is obligatory, it is one of the most mysteriously compelling obligations of all. On the face of it, there seems to be no reason why anybody cannot say

17   * Anybody doesn't sit there any more.

But we can't say it, we don't say it, we won't say it; we reject it without hesitation or reservation. For most listeners, 17 has a curiously ill-formed, fascinatingly perverse character.

We get used to some ungrammatical sentences, and as we repeat them, we can almost see how we might have said them ourselves. We can certainly imagine someone saying

18   * This bed was eaten potato chips in.[6]

If 18 is not already acceptable in some dialect, we would enjoy meeting the man who had the imagination to say it. But we cannot imagine why anyone would say 17, which becomes worse as we repeat it. We cannot even imagine why we cannot imagine it; and if someone were to say it, we would not be at all anxious to meet him.[7]

2.1 Conditions Suspending the Obligatory Character of NEGATTRAC

Let us then consider some conditions where NEGATTRAC to subject indeterminates is not obligatory with the hope that the

---

6. This sentence cannot be reduced to the proper analysis for the passive transformation, $N_1 - AUX - Vb - NP_2$. There is considerable latitude in the analysis of various verb plus particle, verb plus preposition combinations as *Vb*; thus we have *this bed was slept in, this wall was stood beside*. But the only *Vb + N + Prep* combinations which can fit into this analysis are idioms which have been lexicalized, like *make fun of, take umbrage at*. The acceptance of 18 involves accepting for the moment that *eat potato chips in* is such a *Vb*.

7. For empirical evidence on the compelling nature of negative attraction and hearers' inability to comprehend violations, see section 6 below.

exceptions will help us to understand the rule. First we should note that a negative in the previous sentence has the effect of making NEGATTRAC optional. Thus we can say without hesitation

19   I don't say that anyone didn't go.

In place of the explicit negative of *don't*, we are also entitled to use the implicit negatives in *deny* or *doubt* or the presupposed negatives in *regret, am sorry,* or *apologize* with the same effect on the rule. As we might suspect, there is a wide range of acceptability of the incomplete or implicit negatives in suspending negative attraction. A feature of AFFECT combined with the negative seems to have greater effect. In a series of test questions submitted to 52 student subjects,[8] we observed the following pattern of judgments:

20	Gramma- tical	Question- able	Ungram- matical
a. I hated for anyone not to eat in my mother's restaurant.	56%	33%	11%
b. I expected anyone not to eat in my mother's restaurant.	4	8	88

It is of course essential that the preceding negative be in the correct structural position to influence the NEGATTRAC rule; a preceding negative in a coordinated clause has no such effect.

21   *I didn't go and predicted anyone else wouldn't either.

The necessary condition is that the [+NEG] in W of 16 must command the indeterminate in Langacker's sense—that is, must be a member of an S which dominates the indeterminate and is not dominated by the indeterminate.[9] We can then amend condition *a* of 16 to read as follows:

8. The tests were carried out at Columbia University by a group of students, who submitted them to a range of nonlinguistic subjects. They are therefore cited as relevant evidence but by no means conclusive, as the subject population was not chosen systematically or the tests administered in a uniform manner. Research cited in section 6 below on variation in grammaticality judgments has provided additional evidence to confirm and develop these findings.

9. The conditions for removing the obligatory character of negative attraction are quite similar to those which govern the replacement of *some* by *any* cited in Stockwell et al. 1968:262ff.

a   Obligatory if $3 = \emptyset$,

$$1 \sim [\,[+\text{NEG}] \text{ commanding } 4$$

In addition to this condition, there are three other sets of environments in which a subject indeterminate does not necessarily attract the negative. These are quite different on the surface, but on deeper analysis they can be seen as governed by a single feature that may be added to condition a. Starting from the ungrammatical *Anyone can't go we have

22   HYPOTHETICALS
            a. If anyone can't go . . .
            b. When anyone can't go . . .
            c. Should anyone not be able to go . . .
23   RESTRICTED INDEFINITES
            a. Anyone can't go who drinks.
            b. Anyone who drinks can't go.
            c. Anyone can't go unless he swears off drinking.
            d. Anyone who is anyone won't go.
24   EMBEDDINGS
            a. For anyone not go was a shame.
            b. It's a shame for anyone not to go.
            c. (?) Anyone's not going was a shame.

The hypotheticals of 22 are all easily and clearly acceptable. They involve the presence of a common feature which we may indicate provisionally as [+HYP]. In 23, the subject indeterminate is limited by a restricted relative clause. Traditionally, relative clauses on any have also been understood as reduced hypotheticals (Karttunen 1971):

23a'   If there's anyone who drinks, he can't go.

If we follow this derivation, both 22 and 23 can be accounted for by adding to condition a of 16 the requirement that the type marker must not contain [+HYP] if the rule is to be obligatory.

The nominalizations of 24 pose some difficult questions of syntactic and semantic analysis. First we may note that 24a and b are much more acceptable than 24c, which is marginal. These reactions are supported in our set of test questions.

25	Gramma- tical	Question- able	Ungram- matical
a. Anyone doesn't eat in my mother's restaurant.	0%	4%	96%
b. Anybody's not eating in my mother's restaurant is a shame.	31	55	14
c. For anybody not to eat in my mother's restaurant is a shame.	73	27	0

This is merely one of many findings which show that the POS-ING and FOR-TO nominalizers are not equivalents but differ in subtle and pervasive semantic effects. One explanation for the effect of FOR-TO in eliminating the obligatory character of NEGATTRAC is suggested by Klima (pers. comm.): that such embedded sentences are almost always subjects of negative or negative-affective predicates. Since it has already been demonstrated that this category plays an important role in the syntax of indefinites (Klima 1964), the possibility should be considered. However, the test results show surprisingly little difference between the positive "O.K." and the negative-affective "shame."

26	Gramma- tical	Question- able	Ungram- matical
For anybody not to eat in my mother's restaurant is a shame.	73%	27%	0%
For anybody . . . is O.K.	65	35	0

Whatever the affective character of *shame* may contribute here, it is obviously a smaller effect than that of embedding with the FOR-TO complementizer. For example, if the predicate *O.K.* is used with a *that* complementizer (*It's O.K. that anyone*), the corresponding percentages are 42, 56, 2. Or as we see above in 25, switching to a POS-ING complementizer produces changes of comparable magnitude in judgments of grammaticality. The overall pattern of the various constraints inhibiting the obligatory force of negative attraction can be seen in Table 4.1, which lists sentence types in order of increasing acceptability.

TABLE 4.1.
GRAMMATICALITY JUDGMENTS OF 52 SUBJECTS ON
CONDITIONS FOR OBLIGATORY NEGATIVE ATTRACTION

	Grammatical	Questionable	Ungrammatical
1. Anyone doesn't eat in my mother's restaurant.	0%	4%	96%
2. I expected anybody not to eat in my mother's restaurant.	4	8	88
3. It's not true that anybody doesn't eat in my mother's restaurant.	35	29	36
4. Anybody's not eating in my mother's restaurant is a shame.	31	55	14
5. I hated anybody's not eating in my mother's restaurant.	56	33	11
6. It's O.K. that anybody doesn't eat in my mother's restaurant.	56	42	2
7. For anybody not to eat in my mother's restaurant is O.K.	65	35	0
8. For anybody not to eat in my mother's restaurant is a shame.	73	27	0
9. It's O.K. for anybody not to eat in my mother's restaurant.	79	17	4
10. It's a shame for anybody not to eat in my mother's restaurant.	85	15	0

The factors which favor the suspension of NEGATTRAC are combined in sentence 10 of Table 4.1: an affective implicit negative commands the indeterminate,[10] and it is embedded in a subject with the FOR-TO complementizer. Clearly the most heavily weighted condition is the use of the FOR-TO complementizer in sentences 7–10, as opposed to the POS-ING or THAT complementizers in sentences 3–6. How is this differentiation of FOR-TO and POS-ING to be understood? Our intuitive response would be that the FOR-TO embedding suspends most completely any actual predication, has the least "predicating" effect of the three complementizers, and is therefore closest to the IF clause, while THAT with its finite tense marker is the furthest in the other direction. This general impression fits in with the efforts of the Kiparskys (1970) to correlate the com-

10. Extraposition plays a clear but minor role in promoting the acceptability of these sentences. Sentence 10 may be compared with sentence 8 in this respect, and sentence 9 with 7. The gain in acceptability is approximately the same: a shift of 10 to 15 percent out of the "questionable" column into the "grammatical" column.

plementizers with factive and nonfactive predicators. While the data here are variable and at times contradictory, there are enough clear cases to lend weight to the argument.

We find that nonfactive predicators like *want, prefer, believe,* tend to take the FOR-TO complementizer while POS-ING regularly goes with such factives as *regret, approve, dislike.* There are some verbs which take either complementizer, and the difference in assertiveness becomes obvious:

27a   I liked Albert to scratch his back.
27b   I liked Albert's scratching his back.

The second appears to make it much clearer that Albert *did* scratch his back. In general, we can say that whenever there is an option, the POS-ING complementizer implies that the event took place while FOR-TO makes no such claim.

There is a grammatical feature that sentences 24a, b, and c share with 22 and 23 which is weaker and more general than [HYPO-THETICAL]: it is a superordinate of [+HYP] which we will designate [±FACT]. The feature [+FACT] is to be found in predicates containing preterits, progressives, and perfects in the indicative, but sentences with subjunctive or optatives, conditionals or hypotheticals will show [−FACT]. A sentence embedded with a FOR-TO complementizer, without a tense marker, is clearly nonfactive and is to be assigned [−FACT]. Thus we can say that negative attraction is not obligatory in 22, 23, or 24 since the W of 16 contains [−FACT] commanding the negative and the indeterminate.

It is not necessary for [−FACT] to appear in the same clause as the negative and indeterminate but only that it appear in a clause dominating them. The obligatory character of NEGATTRAC is effectively cancelled in 22d:

22d   If John says that anyone shouldn't go, he's exceeding his
          authority.
22e   *Anyone shouldn't go.

since the [+HYPOTHETICAL] *if,* implying the presence of [−FACT] in the higher clause, commands the negative and indeterminate.

The situation is not so clear with POS-ING complementizers. The "questionable" reactions to sentences 4 and 5 in Table 4.1 match my own question mark in 24c. We are simply not sure if POS-ING is [−FACT] or not. It is clear that POS-ING is more assertive than

FOR-TO, as in 27a and b. But on the other hand 27b asserts that Albert did scratch his back much less clearly than 27c.

27b   I liked Albert's scratching his back.
27c   I liked it that Albert scratched his back.

Rather than invent a new feature for POS-ING, it is best to say that in so far as POS-ING is perceived as containing [−FACT], it suspends the obligatory character of NEGATTRAC. That is, we have a match between two variable elements—the factual character of POS-ING and its effect on NEGATTRAC.[11]

Finally, we must not fail to include one condition that can suspend the obligatory character of NEGATTRAC: the presence of stress on *any*. The violations of NEGATTRAC cited, as in 17, become more acceptable when we use stressed *ány* and perfectly grammatical if *ány* is preceded by *just*.

17′a   * Anybody can't eat there.
17′b   ?Ánybody can't eat there.
17′c   Just ánybody can't eat there.

We will refer to both the *b* and *c* possibilities as the presence of [+STRESS], which relieves the strongly obligatory character of NEGATTRAC. Many linguists would prefer to consider this stressed *ány* as a different item altogether (Lakoff 1969: fn 1). But such a strategy is appropriate only when we have no explanation as to how stress added to *any* produces this effect. In section 6 such an explanation will be submitted, and we will accordingly proceed as if we were dealing with a single *any*. Condition *a* of 16 must therefore indicate that *any* is unstressed if NEGATTRAC is to be obligatory.

We will thus rewrite condition *a* as follows:

16′   Condition a: Obligatory if 3 = Ø,
                          4 is [−STRESS], and
                          1 ∼[[+NEG] or [−FACT]
                          commanding 2 and 4.

---

11. There are several examples in this discussion of features which are perceived to a degree in specific lexical items, with uniformly vague reactions for many speakers. These phenomena are more challenging to our system of discrete distinctive features than arguments for n-ary as against binary features. Negative or nonfactive features seem to be perceived as present to a certain degree in some words or constructions.

This condition defines the profoundly ungrammatical core of NEGATTRAC violations as exemplified by sentences 1 and 2 of Table 4.1. There is a penumbra of questionable sentences which surround this core, as in sentences 22-27 where NEGATTRAC is less strongly obligatory. We have analyzed this variable character as depending upon our variable perception of a discrete feature, [−FACT]. Though more might be said about this variable area, it is sufficient here to note the minimal conditions under which the categorical nature of NEGATTRAC is suspended, which we have done in 16′. We can paraphrase this condition in a general statement that also includes condition *b:*

28   Whenever an unstressed indeterminate *any,* without a negative feature of its own, is not commanded by a negative or nonfactive feature, it may not be followed by a negative.

3. Negative Postposing

Let us now consider in greater detail the optional displacement of the negative to an indeterminate when X in rule 16 is not zero— that is, to the first object indeterminate after the verb. We will refer to this operation as *negative postposing.* No special conditions need be stated as long as negative and indeterminate are within the same clause.

29a   I didn't find a proof of the theorem in any of these texts.
29b   I   found a proof of the theorem in none of these texts.

In most cases, the operation of negative postposing produces a marked form. Both 14a and 29a seem to be neutral conversational forms, while 14b and 29b are emphatic, perhaps formal or literary. There are some postposed expressions which seem quite straightforward, even unmarked:

30a   That isn't anything new.
30b   That's nothing new.

But these seem confined to the simplest and most common expressions involving the contraction of the copula and other auxiliaries. Thus *There's nothin' to it, He's nowhere at all, You're nobody to talk* all show the same unmarked character as 30b. It is possible that these do not represent negative postposing at all but rather a different option at the level of contraction rules, yielding 's no- in place of isn't any. In any case, the vast majority of productive forms follow the pattern of 29a and b, with negative postposing as the marked form.

When the indeterminate is contained in a following clause, the situation becomes more complex. In some cases, the postposed negative allows both interpretations—that the negative originated in the earlier or the later clause. This is the case with 31, where b is ambiguous in this respect.

31a   I didn't tell John to paint any of these.
31b   I told John to paint none of these.

As long as we are dealing with infinitival complements of the verb, it seems that such negative postposing can reach, with some strain on the imagination, many clauses down from the original verb.

32a   He didn't order George to tell Arthur to ask Sam to do
           anything like this.
32b   He ordered George to tell Arthur to ask Sam to do nothing
           like this.

When the next clause is finite, negative postposing seems far more difficult. It takes considerable imagination to give 33b the same reading as 33a.

33a   I didn't say that John painted any of these.
33b   I said that John painted none of these.

When the indeterminate is in a relative clause, the situation becomes impossible for negative postposing.

34a   I'm not going to sign a petition that any half-baked Stalin-
           ist wrote.
34b   I'm going to sign a petition that no half-baked Stalinist
           wrote.

There seems to be no way that 34b could be derived from 34a; it is not clear if 34b means anything at all. We are dealing here with the inverse of Ross's Complex NP Constraint (1967), since we are prevented from moving a negative into a sentence dominated by a lexical head noun.

We thus have at least two additional constraints on X in 16 beyond the fact that it cannot contain an indefinite: the "Inverse Complex NP Constraint" and the "Finite Complement Constraint." Both are difficult to state formally and both show exceptions and ragged edges. This is to be expected, because negative postposing is an odd, irascible, cranky kind of transformation that has very shallow roots in speaker intuitions.[12] To cover these two conditions, we can add to 16 the following approximations to a formal statement:

Condition c. Inverse Complex NP Constraint: 4 cannot be dominated by an S dominated by a lexical NP which does not dominate 2.

Condition d. Finite Complement Constraint: 4 cannot be dominated by an S adjoined to THAT and commanded by 2.

Both of these constraints could be examined in greater detail, but it should be obvious that the conditions which control NEGATTRAC when X is not zero are very different from those which operate when X is zero as discussed in section 2. Conditions b, c, and d which control negative postposing share no features in common with condition a which governs negative attraction to subject indeterminates.

4. Negative Concord

In various nonstandard dialects of English, our formulation of negative attraction must be extended to account for *negative concord*. Instead of saying that the negative is attracted to the first indeterminate, we might say for these dialects that the negative is attracted to indeterminates generally. Thus the nonstandard equivalents of 29–34 are

29'   I didn't find a proof of the theorem in none of these texts.
30'   That ain't nothin' new.
31'   I didn't tell John to paint none of these.
32'   He didn't order George to tell Arthur to ask Sam to do nothing like this.

---

12. We would expect negative postposing to have a weak intuitive base because it is so much a part of the literary pattern learned as a superposed variety. This in turn reflects its origin in the normative patterns imposed upon standard English grammar.

33'   I didn't say that John painted none of these.
34'   I'm not going to sign a petition that no half-baked Stalinist
           wrote.

Teachers and other opponents of nonstandard dialects may argue
that these sentences reverse the meaning of 29–34. But this is mere
rhetoric; for any speaker of English, no matter how refined, is familiar with the existence of negative concord and realizes that 29'–34'
intend the same meaning as 29–34. When an underlying double
negative is intended, speakers of nonstandard dialects use the same
device as speakers of standard English: heavy stress on both negatives.

31''   I *didn't* tell John to paint *none* of these; I wanted to get
           some of them painted at least.

(See 145 in section 8 for an example of this type of double negation
in BEV.)

The ordinary meaning of 29'–34' is therefore recognized by
speakers of all dialects, and these sentences do not produce the
reversal of expected meaning that we observed in section 1. The
general nonstandard rule which operates here can be written as a
simple pleonastic transformation, copying instead of chopping the
negative:

35   NEG CONCORD I
           W – [+NEG] – X – Indet
           1   2   3   4 → 1   2   3   2 + 4
           Conditions: a. Obligatory if 3 = $\emptyset$,
                                      4 is [–STRESS], and
                                      1 ~[[+NEG] or [–FACT]
                                         commanding 2 and 4

Here we must repeat the same condition *a* that was worked out for
rule 16, since it applies to nonstandard dialects as well as SE. Condition *b* on 16, which governs negative postposing, is missing. So too
is the finite complement constraint *d*, as indicated by sentence 33'.
None of the difficulty or strain in negative postposing to remote
infinite complements that we felt in 32 or 33 appears here—as indicated in 32' and 33'. Even the inverse complex NP constraint *c* does
not apply, as 34' shows.

It would be going too far to say that there are no constraints on negative concord. We find that we cannot transfer a negative to an indeterminate in a relative clause if the indeterminate is a direct object and not a subject. 34 and 34' show negative concord to a subject indeterminate in a relative clause, possible for nonstandard negative concord but impossible for standard negative postposing. With object indeterminates in relative clauses any negative transfer is prohibited:

36a They wouldn't fire a man who could fix anything in a
    Ford.
36b They would fire a man who could fix nothing in a Ford.
36c They wouldn't fire a man who could fix nothing in a Ford.

All three of these sentences have different meanings. We therefore have to state a condition c on negative concord as:

> Condition c. 4 cannot be directly dominated by a VP dominated
>   by an S dominated by a lexical NP which does not
>   dominate 2.

Except for this one condition, we can say that negative concord applies much more regularly than negative postposing and without the finite complement constraint and the whole series of marginal judgments involved in it. We can easily construct such extreme examples as 37, with eleven pleonastic negatives in the surface structure all dependent upon a single negative in the deep structure:

37   I ain't (1) gonna sit here in no (2) chair and let no (3) crazy
    lawyer never (4) tell me no (5) lies about no (6) law that
    no (7) judge told no (8) smart-ass clerk to look up in
    no (9) book that no (10) smart politician wrote or
    nothin' (11) like that nohow (12).

Here we see that the negative can be reduplicated in coordinate structures (3), in subject indeterminates in relatives (7) and (10), and also in oblique object indeterminates in relative clauses (9). But copying onto a direct object indeterminate in a relative clause seems to lie just outside the operation of this rule.

Is there an equivalent of condition b for NEGCONCORD? That is, can we state that X cannot contain an indeterminate? If we can establish enough parallels in the conditions on 16 and 35, then it might seem practical to combine both into a single transformation showing the overall system of English negative transfer. If 35 applies to its own output, successively transferring the negative rightward, then we could write such a condition *b*. But that would require that no indeterminate be skipped in the regular application of the rule. At this point, intuitions cannot be relied upon, and we have to examine what speakers of nonstandard dialects actually say. From the Outer Banks of North Carolina, we have:

38   We don't ever see none of them guys.—*Monnie O., 35, Wanchese*

And from a railroad foreman in East Atlanta:

39   From then on, I didn't have any trouble at school, no more.—*Henry G., 60*

And from a black speaker raised in the lower South:

40   Ain't nobody ever thought about pickin' up nothin'.—*William T., 25, Florida*

Since it is possible to skip an indeterminate, then 35 can apply to any indeterminate anywhere in the sentence, and there can be no constraint parallel to condition *b* of 16.

4.1 Negative Concord to Preverbal Position

In addition to the transfer of negatives to indeterminates, we also have the possibility of negatives appearing in the usual preverbal slot as well. There are many nonstandard dialects which do not allow this and reject such sentences as *Nobody don't know*.[13] But this is a regular construction in many nonstandard dialects throughout the United States. It is used in the white southern dialect of the speaker quoted in 39.

41   Nobody don't like a boss hardly.—*Henry G., 60, E. Atlanta*

We have not yet mapped all the dialects which permit transfer to the preverbal position as against those which do not. Northern New Jersey seems to permit this, while the white New York City vernacu-

---

13. In Bellugi's "The Acquisition of Negation" we note that the children acquired a "thick layer" of negation in the later stages of their development (1967:143). In his fourth year, Adam began to use negative concord from subject indefinites to preverbal position, as for example, *No one can't even find me; But nobody wasn't gonna know it*. Bellugi argues that this is an internal generalization, since it is not found in any adult dialect. But as shown here, adult models are available for this pattern.

lar definitely does not. We will use the cover terms WNS_1 and WNS_2 to refer to the groups of dialects which respectively prohibit and permit negative transfer to preverbal position.

Since white New Yorkers are members of the WNS_1 group, they contrast sharply on this point with black speakers in the same city. Negative transfer to preverbal position is quite common in black English vernacular.[14]

42   Down here nobody don't know about no club.—*William T., 25, Florida*

43   None of our friends don't fight 'im.—*Larry H., 15, Jets*
44   Nobody don't know where it's at—*Douglas S., 17, Cobras*
45   None of 'em can't fight.—*Ray L., 14, Jets*

We can adjust our rule systems in one of two ways to account for this extension. In 35 we can show *Vb* as well as *Indet* as the locus of transfer.

35′

$$W - [+NEG] - X - \begin{Bmatrix} \text{Indet} \\ \text{Vb} \end{Bmatrix}$$

$$1 \qquad 2 \qquad 3 \qquad 4 \rightarrow 1 \quad 2 \quad 3 \quad 2+4$$

The other possibility for dealing with preverbal negatives is to let the usual rule of negative placement put the negative before the verb in *Nobody don't know*. Since that is a simple categorical rule, it will always apply. But then we will have to change the NEGATTRAC rule 16 to make it a chopping rule for most dialects and a copying rule for WNS_2 and BEV. Furthermore, the copying will have to be optional, for negative concord to preverbal position is variable in all dialects. To insert this kind of variability into the NEGATTRAC rule is contrary to its uniform, nonaffective character. It is far more plausible to make this preverbal option a feature of the negative concord rule, since it shares the variable and affective character of that rule.

We have no choice in the matter when we observe that there also exists a dialect which transfers the negative to preverbal position in a *following* clause.

14. In the citations given, speakers are identified by their age and the area where they were raised from 4 to 13 years, except for members of the peer groups in south-central Harlem. These (all New Yorkers) are identified with the names of the peer groups: Jets, Cobras, Thunderbirds, Aces, and Oscar Brothers.

For almost all speakers of English, this is an impossibility. If a negative appears with a verb in a following clause, it is inevitably interpreted as referring to a second deep structure negative.

46   None that I had, I never had any that I couldn't break yet.—*Mike G., 15, Sonora, Texas*

This sentence is rightly interpreted to mean that there is no horse that Mike could *not* break. The fact that negatives in following clauses are necessarily understood as independent is registered in our rule system by adding to 35′ the condition that 2 and 4 must be clause mates—that is, there is no S which dominates 2 which does not dominate 4 and vice versa.

But this constraint does not hold for black English vernacular. We can see that 1 is an example which violates it: the negative in *can't* is copied from the first clause and has no independent meaning of its own.

1   It ain't no cat can't get in no coop.

This is not an isolated instance. We have collected a number of parallel examples in our work with BEV. A sales clerk in Harlem remarked one day:

47   When it rained, nobody don't know it didn't.

That is, nobody knew that it rained when it *did*, not when it didn't. A 29-year-old man raised in the Bronx said:

48   Back in them times, there ain't no kid around that ain't— wasn't even thinkin' about smokin' no reefers.

That is, there wasn't any kid who *was* even thinking about smoking reefers. And in one of the long epic poems of black folklore, "The Fall," we have the following description of the central character:[15]

49   Like a sex machine, she stood between
            Raindrops, snow and hail,
            She stood on hot bricks to lure her tricks
            Come cyclone, blizzard or gale.

---

15. The version of "The Fall" given here is that of Saladin, as recorded by John Lewis. Saladin is the most skilled and knowledgeable of all masters of the oral literature that we have met.

> She tricked with the Frenchmen, torpedo men 'n' hench-
> men,
> To her they were all the same,
> She tricked with the Greeks, Arabs and freaks,
> And breeds I cannot name.
> She tricked with the Jews, Apaches and Sioux,
> She even tricked in the house of God,
> For there wasn't a son of a gun who this whore couldn't
> shun,
> That claimed to play a rod.

The meaning of the next to last line is plainly that 'there wasn't a son of a gun who *could* shun this whore', and we have the same reversal of the expected meaning as in 1, 47 and 48. We also recorded the following interchange between John Lewis and Derek, one of the verbal leaders of the Cobras:

50   *JL:* What about the subway strike?
            Derek: Well, wasn't much I couldn't do.

Here Derek plainly meant that there wasn't much that he *could* do. No indeterminates are involved here; this is a case where the negative concord rule must transfer the negative to the next clause (possibly governed by the quantifier *much*—see section 7.3 below) and again there is no way that the regular rule of negative placement could account for it.

It should be emphasized that such extrapositions of the negative to following verb phrases are relatively rare. The normal construction in black English vernacular is not to apply the negative concord rule in this environment.

51a   It wouldn't of been nothing I could do.—*Larry H., 15, Jets*
51b   Ain't nothin' you can do for 'em.—*Roy M., 56, South Carolina*

Furthermore, speakers of black English vernacular have no difficulty in using the negative position in a following clause for an underlying negative with independent meaning.

52   I was writin' for fun 'cause I ain't do it till nothin' was
            happenin'.—*Florence, 13, West Philadelphia*

Here Florence is explaining that she didn't write with a red grease

pencil on a car until there was nothing happening in the neighborhood.

Nevertheless, the possibility of using negative concord with a
following verb phrase is open to all speakers of BEV, who interpret
1 and 47–50 correctly and automatically.

There is no way to account for this possibility if we transfer the
negative to preverbal position by the usual cyclical rule of negative
placement, since that rule could not possibly transfer a negative to
a following clause. We therefore conclude that 35′ is the correct
expansion of negative concord, and we must limit the condition that
2 and 4 are clause mates to WNS_2 and not to BEV.

We can sum up this view of the distribution of negative concord
by an expanded version of rule 35, following the same order of
conditions that we used with negative attraction and negative postposing.

53   NEG CONCORD II

$$W - [+NEG] - X - \begin{Bmatrix} \text{Indet} \\ \text{Vb} \end{Bmatrix}$$

1   2   3   4 → 1   2   3   2 + 4

Conditions: a. Obligatory if 3 = ∅

                                    4 = Indet, [−STRESS]

                                    1 ∼[[+NEG] or [−FACT]

                                       commanding 2 and 4

        b. —

        c. 4 cannot be directly dominated by a VP
           in an S dominated directly by an NP
           which does not command 2

        d. —

        e. 4 = Vb in WNS_2 and BEV only; in WNS_2,
           2 and 4 must then be clause mates

5. One Negative Transfer Rule?

At this point we may feel compelled by principles of economy
or a belief in one overall system of English grammar to write a single
rule for negative attraction, negative postposing, and negative concord, combining 16 and 53. We can do this by making the pleonastic
element variable:

54   NEGTRANSFER

$$W - [+NEG] - X - \begin{Bmatrix} \text{Indet} \\ (Vb)_1 \end{Bmatrix}$$

1   2   3   4   →   1 $(2)_1$ 3 $2+4$

Conditions: a. Obligatory if $3 = \emptyset$

$4 = \text{Indet}, [-\text{STRESS}]$

$1 \sim [\,[+\text{NEG}]$ or $[-\text{FACT}]$

commanding 2 and 4

b. $X \sim [$ Indet if $(\ )_1$ is not realized

c. 4 cannot be (directly dominated by a VP)$_1$ in an S dominated directly by an NP which does not command 2

d. 4 cannot be dominated by an S adjoined to THAT and commanded by 2 if $(\ )_1$ is not realized

e. $(\ )_1$ not in SE

$4 = \text{Vb}$ in WNS$_2$ and BEV only, in WNS$_2$ only if 2 and 4 are clause mates

This combined rule effects some economies, although certain conditions are awkward to write. The pleonastic operation of concord is represented by an option in parentheses, with a subscripted cross-reference to the preverbal possibility. This has an additional set of parentheses, indicating that it is optional even if the subscripted option 1 is taken.

Conditions *b* and *d* are cumbersome to state because they are constraints only on the standard rules, and we have to mark them formally as operating only if option 1 is not taken.[16] On the other hand, the subscripted insert on condition *c* condenses the conditions for standard and nonstandard rules with considerable economy.

Condition *e* uses ad hoc dialect labels. We could resolve these into a set of features, beginning with $[\pm\text{STD}]$ and $[\pm\text{BEV}]$. We would then have to add a feature $[\pm\text{NS}]$ to differentiate WNS$_1$ and WNS$_2$,

---

16. The subscripted parentheses indicate optional elements that co-occur. But the finite complement constraint is also a variable constraint; to state it more precisely we would use subscripted angled brackets to indicate that the rule operates more often with nonfinite complements, but is not confined entirely to them.

although there is no match with "northern states" versus "southern states" in this distribution.[17] We would then have:

54'   NEGTRANSFER

$$S - [+NEG] - X - \begin{Bmatrix} \text{Indet} \\ (Vb)_{-NS} \end{Bmatrix}$$

1   2   3   4 $\rightarrow$ 1 $(2)_{-STD}$ 3   2 + 4

Conditions: a. Same as (54)
b. $X \sim [\ \text{Indet}/[+STD]$
c. 4 cannot be (directly dominated by a $VP)_{-STD}$ in an S dominated directly by an NP which does not command 2
d. 4 cannot be dominated by an S adjoined to THAT and commanded by 2/[+STD]
e. If 4 = Vb, 2 and 4 clause mates/[−NS, −BEV]

This set of features gives us a more economical and less awkward representation than 54. It is possible that such a limited set of features will be satisfactory, but it is more likely that as our knowledge of negative concord grows, the number of subclassifications will increase rapidly. Rather than a set of conditions, we will want to set up matrices of the kind to be developed in section 8.

One difficulty with 54' is that the registration of dialect options makes it awkward to show variable constraints on the rule, and we will eventually want to do this. A deeper understanding of negative concord must include the fact that in some environments, the rule applies more often than in others—as for example, more often when 4 = Indet than when 4 = Vb.

The effort to produce a single rule schema can be rewarding in that it forces us to define the precise nature of the differences between dialects. If it also showed us interactions between conditions, it might actually explain why the rule develops as it does. Those who believe in internal evaluation measures would also believe that this condensation effort will help us select the correct form of the grammar and even give us such explanations. (see fn 26, chapter 3). But without a direct demonstration of such a claim, we must admit

17. We would eventually want to replace the arbitrary designation WNS_2 with a series of dialects located in space or time, filling out the paradigm suggested in Bailey 1971.

that 54' explains very little. In fact, it obscures. A fundamental objection to 54' is that it combines two opposing grammatical processes: negative attraction on the one hand and negative postposing and concord on the other. Negative attraction is an obligatory process governed by abstract, conceptual constraints. Negative postposing and concord are optional, emphatic transformations. Since the argument in this chapter will be seen to revolve about the difference between these two types of rules, the major point would be lost in such a global formulation.

In the next two sections we will examine the distinct semantic character of these distinct types of grammatical rules. Section 6 will explore the logical basis for negative attraction, which will allow us to unify and simplify the conditions which govern the obligatory application of this rule. Section 7 will then examine the affective character of negative concord, and place this rule within a larger context of devices for reinforcing negation.

6. The Nature of Negative Attraction

At the end of section 2 we arrived at a general principle 28, which summarized the conditions under which negative attraction is obligatory:

28   Whenever an unstressed indeterminate *any*, without a negative feature of its own, is not commanded by a negative or hypothetical feature, it may not be followed by a negative.

While this output condition will produce the correct results, it is both miscellaneous and unmotivated. It is not clear why stress, hypotheticals, and negatives should appear together as a list of exceptions to the obligatory character of negative attraction; and there is nothing here which helps us to understand why violations of the obligatory core of the rule are uninterpretable or why they produce an incurable confusion in listeners of every age and background.

The generality and force of negative attraction to subject indefinites cannot be overstated. It is equally strong in all of the English dialects we have studied. So far we have considered data from the abstract analysis of our own intuitions and from the observation of natural speech. We can also bring to bear the results of experiments with repetition tests which reveal the uniform character of the negative attraction rule. These tests were carried out with groups of adolescent speakers of black English vernacular, who showed that deep-seated rules of the vernacular influenced perception and production more than had been realized (see CRR 3288:3.9). For a central core of vernacular speakers, BEV forms were repeated back verbatim and certain SE forms were immediately translated into the corresponding BEV forms. However, sentences which violated negative attraction produced a different response: profound confusion. Here is the record of three subjects' attempts to repeat a sentence that violated the output constraint 28.

55   *Anybody doesn't sit there anymore, do they?*
            Boot (1st trial): Anybody—Hey, you goin' too fas'!
                (2nd trial): Any—I can't say it; I owe you a nickel.
            David (1st trial): Hunh?
                (2nd trial): That don't sound right!
            Money (1st trial): Anybody—eh—what is that?
                (2nd trial): Anybody ever sits there d—any more,
                    do they?
                (3rd trial): Anybody nev—ever sits there—

Boot and David respond with total confusion. Money tries to solve the problem by removing the negative element; a fourth member of the group followed the same pattern, producing *Anybody ever sits there anymore, do they?*

Recent work with a wide range of English dialects shows that this confused response is not limited to BEV speakers: violations of NEGATTRAC are hard to focus on and impossible to interpret. Though subjects know what referential meaning would be intended, they cannot understand why anything would be said in that way. Here are some responses to violations of negative attraction which were presented to middle-class white subjects in Philadelphia in a series to be rated for grammaticality.[18]

            Anybody doesn't like him.
            Ralph: That's confusing. At least, it is for me. If someone
                said that to me, you know, in some context, I'd probably
                have to repeat it, or explain it in some other way.

18. I am indebted here to Mark Baltin, who did the interviewing in these explorations of intuitive judgments and provided many insights into the theoretical issues involved.

Anybody didn't leave.

Karen: That doesn't make any sense. You can say, "Nobody left," but "Anybody didn't leave. . ."?

Anybody didn't arrive.

Mel: That's just awkward. It doesn't make sense. It doesn't sound natural.

Laurie: I don't know what that means.

Wendy: It doesn't make a lot of sense. I suppose I could get a meaning from that, but I'm not sure what.

Ginny: That doesn't make any sense. Who's *anybody?* Joe Anybody didn't arrive!!

Perhaps the most vivid view of someone struggling to understand violations of negative attraction can be gotten from this exchange with Tom.

Interviewer: Anybody didn't arrive.

Tom: Anybody didn't arrive?

Interviewer: Yeah.

Tom: Anybody didn't arrive.

Interviewer: Yeah.

Tom: I don't understand it actually. Anybody didn't arrive? I just don't understand it. I would say, "Nobody arrived", but it seems to me that the person is sort of beating around the bush, saying, "Anybody didn't receive an invitation."

6.1. The Semantic Features of any in Positive Sentences

Responses to violations of negative attraction suggest the presence of deep-seated logical incoherence which is not easily resolved by listeners trying to interpret such sentences. It will therefore be necessary to consider the general semantic features of *any*, first of all in positive sentences. This is an extraordinarily complex area with a long history of resistance to analysis, and only some of the problems will be considered here. The discussion will be directed at uncovering just those central features of the quantifiers which are responsible for the phenomena we have outlined above.

Our current approach to the study of language in context is based on the strategy of a regular interplay between observations of natural behavior, the exploration of intuitions, and experimental testing (*Sociolinguistic Patterns*, chapter 8; Labov 1972c). The analysis in this section departs from the empirical findings of the use of negative attraction and negative concord in various dialects and adds to it data from my own intuitions and those of other linguists, along with the evidence and arguments of scholars and philosophers. Some of the intuitive data will rest on a firm foundation of general agreement, using only well-known examples. But other sentence types may touch on unexpected areas of variability in judgment and may contain uncorrected biases produced by the theoretical notions themselves. Recognizing the possibility of such a bias, we present this analysis with the hope that it will illuminate the earlier studies and lay the foundation for further empirical investigation.

Klima (1964) originally assigned the label *Indeterminate* to the class of *any* and *ever* on the basis of the formal properties we have noted in section 2. His analysis of the behavior of *any* had semantic implications, since he noted its co-occurrence with *WH-* and verbs such as *wonder* which he marked with the general semantic feature [+AFFECT]. Nevertheless, Klima saw *any* in negative sentences as a formal suppletive alternant of *some*, usually obligatory but occasionally optional with unanalyzed semantic consequences. Fillmore (1967) distinguished two senses of *some* as [±SPECIFIC]; he argued that it is the [−SPECIFIC] which alternates regularly with *any*. In this view, *any* remains an automatic suppletive alternant in negative sentences which does not convey information of its own. Stockwell, Partee, and Schachter (1968) review these various possibilities and point out difficulties with the [±SPECIFIC] hypothesis, but conclude that this is the most plausible account we can now give of the matter. Accordingly, the *some-any* suppletion transformation is represented there with a structural analysis

$$56 \qquad X - [+\text{AFFECT}] - X - \begin{bmatrix} -\text{SPEC} \\ -\text{INDET} \end{bmatrix} - X$$

and instructions to change [−INDET] to [+INDET]. This formal analysis of *any* is missing the substantive semantic elements which would account for a large body of linguistic facts, including the obligatory character of negative attraction. The feature [−INDET] is simply a label; if "indeterminate" had any significance at all, [−INDET] would be oddly redundant. In a paper on "Some reasons why there can't be any *some-any* rule," R. Lakoff (1969) demonstrated the existence of meaningful alternation between *some* and *any*. Typical are the oppositions:

57a	Who wants some beans?
57b	Who wants any beans?
58a	Do you think those men want to do some work?
58b	Do you think those men want to do any work?

Lakoff argues that *some* has a positive presupposition, *any* a negative one and that this must be entered into the formal description by some mechanism not yet elaborated.[19]

These are some of the many considerations which would lead us to believe that *any* embodies a set of semantic features distinct from *some* in questions and negatives as well as in positive declarative sentences. As a quantifier, *some* is a limiter and designator of the extent of reference of the nominal being modified.[20] *Some* is an indefinite quantifier as opposed to definite quantifiers such as *three* and partitive as opposed to *all* and *every* which are nonpartitive. We can sum up these characteristics in feature notation by saying that *some* is [+QUANTIFIER, −DEFINITE, +PARTITIVE] or refer to it in logical terms as the existential quantifier which binds variables in propositions $(\exists x)(Fx)$.

Any is also [+QUANTIFIER, −DEFINITE], but it differs from *some* in at least three other semantic features; [+DISTRIBUTIVE], [−PARTITIVE], and [−FACT]. We will consider these three features in positive contexts before going on to examine their interaction with the negative.

a. [+DISTRIBUTIVE]. *Any* is [+DISTRIBUTIVE] in that it considers items one at a time. *Any* shares this property with *each*, as against *some* which is [−DISTRIBUTIVE]. When only one person can do a given activity, the difference comes out strongly. If you have three bridge players you can turn to a crowd at the other end of the room and ask

59   Can any of you make a fourth at bridge?

But you cannot ask

60   *Can some of you make a fourth at bridge?

---

19. She notes that there appear to be some "purely syntactic constraints" on the positive use of *any* as in *Anyone left*. The analysis given below shows this constraint as a regular product of the semantic features of *any* and the preterit.

20. In a recent discussion of logical properties of quantifiers, Keenan (1971) proposes three characteristic properties: binding, relative scope, and predication; all of the items discussed here satisfy these requirements.

By the operation of the same semantic feature, you would be inviting trouble if you asked

61   Can some of you play bridge?

b. [−PARTITIVE]. *Any* is generally equivalent to *every, each,* and *all* in its universal [−PARTITIVE] feature as opposed to the existential [+PARTITIVE] character of *some, a,* and other quantifiers. In terms of truth values, *any* and *every* are equivalent in

62a   Any boy can run a mile.
62b   Every boy can run a mile.

These statements apply both to the class of all boys and to each and every boy; for one to be true, the other must be true. There are also ambiguous occurrences of *any* which make it seem that there is a [+PARTITIVE] *any* in hypothetical sentences. The following pair cited by Fillmore (pers. comm.) illustrates such ambiguity.

63a   If John can do it, anyone can do it. [−PARTITIVE]
63b   If anyone can do it [±PARTITIVE], John can do it.

In 63a, the conclusion is that "everyone" can do it, and it is plainly a derogatory one. In 63b, there are two readings. The [+PARTITIVE] one is complimentary to John: 'If there exists any one person who can do it, that person is John.'[21] The [−PARTITIVE] meaning has the same derogatory interpretation as in 63a: 'If everyone can do it, John can do it.' The ambiguity is then quite discrete, since the one meaning of *any* is a knock and the other is a boost.

This ambiguity of *any* is present in any hypothetical clause but can be seen most readily when we construct different consequences to the same antecedent.

64a   If John can sleep with any of these girls, then at least he'll
             have a roof over his head. [+PARTITIVE]
64b   If John can sleep with any of these girls, then he'll have
             a decision problem. [−PARTITIVE]

One way to display the specific difference between these two uses

21. There is a further ambiguity in the [+PARTITIVE] reading of 63b: 'If any one person can do it, then John can do it (also)' vs. 'If any one person can do it, then John is that one person'. The logical representations of these are quite different: $(\forall x)$ $(x$ can do it $\supset$ John can do it) vs. $(\forall x)$ $(x$ can do it $\supset$ John is $x)$. Both of these are examples of the extended [+PARTITIVE] use of *any*, and both will be analyzed as the result of the extended rather than limited scope of *any*.

of *any* is to consider what we would have to do to test the validity
of 64a and 64b. In 64a the consequence must be tested each time
that a girl says yes and the antecedent holds; if each girl who says
yes has an apartment, then 64a is true. But for 64b, no test of the
consequence is relevant or necessary until the condition is seen to
hold for each and every individual: after all the girls say yes, we
could then test 64b by seeing if John indeed had trouble deciding
what to do.

This view of the matter is consistent with the analysis of the
ambiguity of *any* proposed by Harris Savin in which 64a and 64b
differ in the relative scope of the quantifier. Thus we can represent
64a in the logical configuration of 65:

65         $(\forall x)$ (John can sleep with $x \supset$ John will have a roof over
           his head).

where the scope of the universal quantifier extends over both the
antecedent and the consequent. This is the characteristic property
assigned to *any* by Reichenbach: "its scope is always the whole
formula" (1947:106).[22] But 64b shows a different scope for *any*—in
this case the more limited scope which Reichenbach restricts to
every,

66         $((\forall x)$ (John can sleep with $x)) \supset$ (John will have a decision
           problem).

In this analysis, *any* is always a universal quantifier, or [−PARTI-
TIVE] in our feature notation, and the ambiguity is a structural rather
than a substantive one. The ambiguity of 63b would then be represented as

63b′ $((\forall x)$ $(x$ can do it$)) \supset$ (John can do it)
63b″ $(\forall x)$ $(x$ can do it $\supset$ John can do it)

But the fact that we can differentiate the two *any*'s by scope is not
decisive. For 64a and 65 are of the general form $(\forall x)$ $(Fx \supset \alpha)$ where
α is a constant, and this is equivalent to the formula with an existential quantifier with limited scope, $(\exists x)$ $(Fx) \supset \alpha$, so that we can rewrite 65 as

22. Although Reichenbach identified the extended scope of *any* as opposed to the
limited scope of *every*, he does not refer to that use of *any* which has the same limited
scope as *every* and is therefore responsible for the ambiguities noted here. He argues
(1947:106ff.) for an invariant interpretation of *any* with a categorical rule of maximally
extended scope.

65' $(\exists x)$ (John can sleep with x) $\supset$ (John will have a roof over
             his head)

which we can paraphrase as 'If there is any girl that John can sleep
with, then he'll have a roof over his head.' We can therefore express
the ambiguity of *any* as an operator with limited scope which is
either a universal [−PARTITIVE] quantifier equivalent to *every* or
an existential [+PARTITIVE] quantifier and so maintain the
[±PARTITIVE] analysis. Simplicity considerations alone do not
easily resolve the situation in favor of a conjunctive definition with
variable scope or a disjunctive definition with constant scope. But
the variable scope proposed by Savin also explains certain peculiari-
ties in the restrictions on *any* with preterits and progressives to be
examined below and will also allow us to simplify greatly the statement of obligatory negative attraction.

   c. [−FACT]. *Any* cannot be used in positive sentences with progressives and preterits, but it can be used with modals, the general
present, the future, and any tense which does not assert that an event
actually occurred.

67a   * Anyone is going to his party.
67b   * Anyone went to his party.
67c   Anyone can go to his party.
67d   Anyone goes to his party.
67e   Anyone will go to his party.
67f   Anyone might have gone to his party.

This set of properties can be summarized by saying that *any* is
incompatible with predicates which make particular existential
statements asserting that a given factual state of affairs is the case.
It is compatible with any lesser or more general degree of assertion.
We identified this feature as [−FACT] in section 2 and will continue
to use this notation. In one sense, *Anyone can go* can be considered
a statement of fact, since it can be factually disproved by finding
someone who cannot go. But it is neutral in regard to whether anyone
in fact did go.[23]

   In section 2, it appeared that the obligatory character of negative
attraction to *any* was relieved by complementizers such as FOR-TO
which are strongly selected in turn by the [−FACT] predicates

---

23. The lawful generalizations expressed by *any* may be considered facts of a kind,
though not statements about a particular state of affairs. To make this point clear,
Savin uses the feature [−MEREFACT].

(Kiparsky and Kiparsky 1970; Karttunen 1971). The mechanism of this connection remains to be elucidated, but if we are dealing with the same semantic feature, then *any* should be incompatible with [+FACT] predicates in general. The most obvious cases are

68a   * Anything is forgotten.
68b   * Anything is finished.
68c   Anything is possible.
68d   Anything is available.

where predicate adjectives containing perfective features, necessarily [+FACT], are incompatible with *any*, but those containing the semantic features of modality or modal suffixes are. Adjectives neutral in regard to [±FACT] do not conflict with *any*.

68e   Anything is interesting.

The obverse of the [−FACT] feature is that *any* is used to make lawful statements about general conditions. Savin has pointed out that *any* makes predictions about counterfactual conditions which *every* does not make.

69a   John spoke to everyone who came.
69b   John spoke to anyone who came.

Here 69a is a factual assertion from which nothing else follows. But it follows from 69b that if one more person had come, John would have spoken to him. There is therefore a strong interaction between the quantifier and the predicate, in that *any* is incompatible with a [+FACT] predicate and also imposes a sense of lawful generalization upon it.[24] The feature [−FACT] is therefore not a property of *any* but rather something required in the environment of *any*; that

---

24. Reichenbach argues that *any* statements like *anything goes* are best shown without the universal quantifier as free variables, of the form Fx and that this gives the support of natural language to operations with such formulas by logicians. It would follow that *any* is thus opposed to *every* and *all* as the absence of a quantifier, rather than as an indefinite quantifier. But Reichenbach also states that Fx "means the same" as $(\forall x)Fx$ and this is a necessary intermediate for his interpretation of *any* sentences with extended scope. Furthermore, the distributive property of *any* is best shown logically as the ordering of quantifiers: $(\forall x)(\exists y)Fxy$ instead of $(\exists y)(\forall x)Fxy$. However, Reichenbach's argument for free variables may be relevant to the ultimate analysis of our problem, since the negation of Fx is not interpreted $\sim(\forall x)Fx$ but rather $(\forall x) \sim Fx$. This implies the possibility of a further logical motivation for the constraint on *All the boys didn't leave* or *Any boys didn't leave,* though the connection between the logical facts and the surface constraint is certainly not clear.

is, a transfer feature (Weinreich 1966). Transfer features can be seen operating in temporal adverbs like *ago* which transfer a temporal feature to the noun phrase with which they are in construction: symbolically [+TEMP → ⟨NP⟩]. The metaphor *a grief ago* does not yield a reinterpretation of *ago* but rather imposes a temporal feature on *grief*. The transfer feature of *any* can thus be formalized provisionally as [−FACT → ⟨PRED⟩], leaving open for the moment how we identify the particular predicate phrase to be affected.

We noted in 21-24 four sets of conditions which removed the obligatory character of negative attraction: a preceding negative, preceding hypothetical, following relative clause, or embedding with nonfinite predicates. All of these also operate to remove the constraint that *any* cannot be used with preterits and progressives. The case of the negative we will consider in the following section. In the positive cases we see that *any* in such environments is compatible with preterit and progressive verbs.

22′   HYPOTHETICALS
        a. If anyone went to his party, they had a good time.
        b. When anyone went to his party, they had a good time.
        c. Should anyone be going to his party, they will have
           a good time.

23′   RESTRICTED INDEFINITES
        a. Anyone who was anybody went to his party.
        b. Anyone who is anybody is going to his party.

24′   EMBEDDINGS
        c. For anyone to have gone to his party was amazing.
        d. For anyone to be going to his party is astonishing.

In all of these examples, the [−FACT → ⟨PRED⟩] feature of *any* is transferred to some other predicate higher than *went* or *is going*. They all have the general form $(\forall x)(Fx \supset Gx)$. The logical representation of both 22′a and 22′b would be

70          $(\forall x)$ (x went to his party $\supset$ x had a good time).

There is no difficulty in reducing 23′ to the same form, since as noted above it is generally agreed that this must be interpreted logically as equivalent to 'If there was anyone who was anybody, he went to John's party', giving us

71          $(\forall x)$ (x was important $\supset$ x went to John's party).

Here the scope of the universal quantifier is the entire sentence. Since both antecedent and consequent are [+FACT] predicates, we must conclude that it is not necessary for *any* to be compatible with either. The transfer feature must therefore apply to the *if-then* element of the sentence, which would then be interpreted as the highest predicate if our [−FACT → ⟨PRED⟩] notation is to be maintained. We would then have to establish the formal convention that the [−FACT] feature is to be transferred to successively higher predicates (perhaps in the course of the cycle) until it agrees with one.

72   I said that if John knew [−FACT] that Harry invited anyone to the party, he told me a lie.

The scope of *any* here extends up to the conditional clause.

72'   I said that (∀x) (John knew that Harry invited x ⊃ John told me a lie).

But if there is no predicate which will accept the [−FACT] transfer feature, then the use of *any* will be ungrammatical.

73   * I said that John knew that Harry invited anyone to the party when he told me a lie about it.

If the Savin analysis of the ambiguity of *any* is correct, we should be able to find only one meaning in 22'–24'. A limited scope for *any*, confined to the antecedent, would be impossible because of the incompatibility of *any* with preterits and progressives. This seems to be the case; we cannot maintain the 'every' meaning of 64a if we change the antecedent to a preterit or progressive. Thus 64b' has lost entirely the meaning that John had slept with all of the girls:

64b'   If John slept with any of these girls, then he had a decision problem.

This finding shows that the [±PARTITIVE] theory is inadequate to account for the ambiguity of *any* in 63b and 64. If the scope of *any* was limited to the antecedent in both 64a and 64b, there would be no way to explain that only one of these meanings—the [+PARTITIVE] one—was compatible with a preterit or progressive verb, as in 64b, and is the only meaning which emerges when we change the antecedent of 63b to a preterit:

74   If anyone did it, John can do it.

Since *any* is incompatible with *did* in 63b', its scope must necessarily extend beyond the antecedent, and no ambiguity is possible. The scope explanation proposed by Savin is the only one consistent with these facts.

The embedded sentences of 24' show an extended scope for *any*. It is possible to interpret the sentences of 24' as *if-then* conditions, and it seems more likely that it is necessary for *any* to be compatible with the main predicate, as in the case of *amazing* or *unlikely*. These involve negative presuppositions: that *someone did not believe that anyone would go*. The problem of apparently neutral predicates like *O.K. with me*, raised in connection with negative attraction in 26, seems to involve a more indirect type of presupposition: *for someone it is not O.K. for anyone to go*, but for me it is. An exact formulation of the conditions which permit *any* in these and parallel constructions is beyond the scope of this analysis, though presumably not beyond the scope of any analysis. They seem to involve all of the semantic features we have identified in *any* and perhaps more.

We can sum up our characterization of *any* in positive sentences by paraphrasing *any* X as a prediction of the form:

75   If [−FACT] you select [+QUANTIFIER], one at a time
          [+DISTRIBUTIVE], all [−PARTITIVE] of the items
          designated X, no matter which [−SPECIFIC] or how
          many [−DEFINITE], you will find that . . .

The combination of [+DISTRIBUTIVE, −PARTITIVE] is usually realized as *each*, so that we can reduce this to 'If you select each of the items designated X, no matter which . . .' *Any* is thus opposed to *each* in its indefinite feature and to *all* by its distributive and indefinite features; since *every* is [±DISTRIBUTIVE], its relation to *any* may be the same as *all* or as *each*. The transfer feature [−FACT] is not needed to distinguish these quantifiers minimally.

76   Universal [−PARTITIVE] Quantifiers

	[+DEFINITE]		[−DEFINITE]
[+DISTRIBUTIVE]	each	every$_1$	any
[−DISTRIBUTIVE]	all	every$_2$	

In section 2, we observed that stress on *any*, with or without an attributive *just*, diminished the obligatory force of NEGATTRAC.

It is therefore surprising to find that stress or *just any* has no such effect in eliminating the restriction against using *any* with preterits and progressives.

77a   *Anyone* is going to his party.
77b   *Just *anyone* went to his party.[25]

6.2. Any With Negatives

We now turn to the way in which *any* behaves in negative sentences and reconsider the obligatory rule of negative attraction in an effort to understand its strongly obligatory character in terms of the semantic features we have isolated. There is a general output constraint (28) which gives us a rather heterogeneous list of conditions under which negative attraction is optional. Otherwise, we find that (1) negative attraction is uniform in all dialects of English, (2) violations do not occur in natural speech, (3) violations constructed by the linguist are not interpretable and do not become more acceptable on repetition. It is not our purpose to explain here the existence of the rule in English: it is the end result of the interaction between the properties of the negative and *any* as they have developed over the course of time. But in properties 1–3, NEGATTRAC contrasts sharply with negative postposing and negative concord. Our main focus is on the contrast between categorical (strongly obligatory) and variable rules, and our analysis is designed to illuminate properties 2 and 3.

We have noted above that the first generative formulations considered *any* a mere formal, suppletive variant of *some* in negative sentences. Klima's analysis (1964) implies the following series:

78a   I want some.
78b   I don't want any.
78c   *I want any.
78d   *I don't want some.

A careful reading of Klima's original discussion shows that he did not explicitly mark sentences of the type 78d as ungrammatical, and many writers have since pointed out that they are quite acceptable

---

25. Although *Just anyone went* is not acceptable in isolation, it seems more natural as the amplification of a negative response to *Did Jackie go to his party? No, just ányone went.* Here the mechanism seems to involve the overt denial of the [—SPECIFIC] feature of *any*, that it is not the case that it does *not* matter which of the members of the class are selected.

in a wide range of contexts. As noted above, R. Lakoff 1969 has shown many meaningful alternations of *some* and *any* in questions.

There is no shortage of empirical evidence to show that 78d is grammatical. Among our BEV speakers we find many examples of *some* in negative sentences:

79   I don't want some more.—*Keith W., 9, Thunderbirds.*
80   I don't give my friends some.—*David H., 13, Thunderbirds*
81   We don't sometime use that.—*Kenneth S., 12, New York City.*

What then is the basis of the feeling behind Klima's formulation which marks *I don't want some* as at least awkward or unlikely in unmarked contexts and *I don't want any* as much more natural? It seems to me that those who declare 78d ungrammatical are unconsciously treating it as the contradiction of 78a, and the full contradiction of an indefinite existential statement is a universal negative.

Consider someone looking out of a window who suddenly says

82   There are some rabbits in that field.

If a friend comes to the window, he cannot deny the statement as quickly as it was made. Since the location of the rabbits is indefinite, he must now scan the entire field before he observes

83   There aren't any rabbits in that field.

If he takes a quick look at one corner of the field and hastily observes

84   I don't see some rabbits in the field

he has made a true observation, but he has not contradicted 82. It is necessary to search the entire field and obtain class closure to contradict an indefinite statement,[26] shown diagrammatically in Fig. 4.1.

The correspondence of *some* ↔ NEG + *any* is thus a product of discourse considerations, rather than an automatic suppletive fact. We are dealing with a discourse strategy which established the sequence of 78a and b, rather than an obligatory rule of grammar. If the *any* in 78b were simply a formal alternant of *some*, we would

26. The strong denial with [−PARTITIVE] *any* is opposed to the weak denial with [+PARTITIVE] *some* in the same way that a strong denial with the present perfect can be opposed to a weak denial with the preterit. *You never ate asparagus!* can be denied weakly *Yes, I did*, meaning 'at least once', but denied strongly as *Yes I have* meaning 'indefinitely many times'.

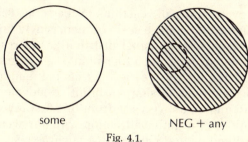

some   NEG + any

Fig. 4.1.

expect to find the semantic features of *some*, such as [+PARTITIVE]. But by the argument advanced above, *any* is selected just *because* it contrasts with *some* in being [−PARTITIVE]. We have every reason to believe that *any* in negative sentences is the same universal quantifier that we have just examined in positive sentences.

It is now generally understood that the negation of sentences with quantifiers can take several forms and that some surface structures with quantifiers and negatives are ambiguous in this respect. Carden 1970 explains the two interpretations of *All the boys didn't leave* by readings of the deep structure with either the quantifier as the highest predicate (NEG-V) or the negative as the highest (NEG-Q). Logically, these two interpretations would be opposed as

85a   NEG-V $(\forall x)(\sim Fx)$
85b   NEG-Q $(\sim\forall x)Fx.$

Carden finds that some subjects find both readings, some only one, but for everyone NEG-V is rendered more naturally by *None of the boys left*. There seems to be general agreement on the following series for $(\forall x) \sim Fx$ readings:

86a   All the boys didn't leave.
86b   Every boy didn't leave.
86c   ?Each boy didn't leave.
86d   *Any boy didn't leave.

While 86a and 86b are awkward but grammatical for most speakers, 86c is questionable or more than questionable and as we have seen, 86d is impossible for everyone. If the [+DISTRIBUTIVE] feature of *each* is responsible for 86c being worse than 86a, then 86b should be intermediate; some subjects should react to the [+DIS-TRIBUTIVE] alternant of *every*.

Empirical investigation of reactions to the series 86a–86d shows
that they do indeed lie along a scale of increasingly ungrammatical
status. Table 4.2 shows the actual distributions of responses of 19
subjects to these four types on a four-point scale of grammaticality.
This is Phase I, the first of a series of tests that employed a range
of contextual conditions to sharpen intuitive judgments.[27] The responses to *any* quoted above were from this first investigation. On
all tests, violations of negative attraction with *any* were at the most
ungrammatical end of the scale. As we might expect, *every* shows
the most variation, since its position intermediate between *all* and
each depends upon its ambiguity as [±DISTRIBUTIVE]. Table 4.3
shows similar results in Phase V of this series, this time on a seven-
point scale of "native" status. These results confirm the view that
there is a stable series of subjective responses to the quantifier series

TABLE 4.2.
NEGATIVE ATTRACTION TO
FOUR QUANTIFIERS (PHASE I)

Quantifier	Grammaticality			
	1	2	3	4
All	8	10	1	0
Every	4	6	7	2
Each	2	2	6	9
Any	1	1	5	12

Quantifier sentences:
All the men didn't come.
Every man didn't arrive.
Each of the men didn't leave.
Anybody didn't arrive.

Scale of grammaticality:
1. I would say it without qualms
2. Awkward, but can conceive of saying it
3. Other native speakers might conceivably say it
4. No native speaker would say it

27. The investigation of *any-each-every-all* was only one of the issues studied in
this series of investigations, carried out by Mark Baltin. Subjects were drawn from
middle-class and working-class Philadelphians, with more emphasis on the former,
at shopping malls, the airport, and college lounges. Phase V drew subjects from the
Baldwin School and from shoppers at the Cedarbrook Mall.

in ($\forall$x) $\sim$ Fx constructions and gives support to the feature analysis proposed.

All four quantifiers are replaced by *None of the boys left* to allow the NEG-V reading. The restriction on ($\forall$x) $\sim$ Fx is directed entirely against that reading; the alternation with NEG-Q is confined entirely to the [−DISTRIBUTIVE] quantifiers *all* and *every*. Perhaps the explanation for the greater acceptability of 86a and 86b is that there are these alternate readings available and so the surface forms are heard.

We occasionally do get reactions to *all* and *every* in these constructions which resemble the violently confused reactions to *any* quoted above, from the Phase I series.

> *All of the boys didn't leave.*
> *Marsha:* Doesn't sound like correct grammar, but I'm not exactly sure why. It just sounded funny . . . wait a minute. *It sounds like nothing.*
>
> *Every man didn't arrive.*
> *Marsha:* That sounds like the "All of the boys didn't leave" one. I can't put my finger on what it is.

TABLE 4.3.
NEGATIVE ATTRACTION TO FOUR QUANTIFIERS (PHASE V)

Quantifier	Grammaticality							Total	Mean
	1	2	3	4	5	6	7		
All	1	5	2	3	2	1		14	3.2
Every		2	3	5	2	2		14	3.9
Each		2	3	4	1	1	3	14	4.5
Any				2	2	3	7	14	6.1

Quantifier Sentences:
All the guys didn't leave.
Everybody didn't do the dishes.
Each of the guys didn't wear a red shirt; some of them wore a brown one.
Anybody doesn't like him.

Scale of grammaticality:
1. Any native speaker would say it.
4. Some native speakers might say it.
7. No native speaker would say it.

From our analysis of the feature system of these quantifiers in 76 it would seem that it is the interaction or cumulative effect of the nonpartitive, indefinite, and distributive character of *any* which is responsible for the force of negative attraction here. That is, [−PARTITIVE] + NEG is awkward (*all, every*); [−PARTITIVE, +DISTRIBUTIVE] + NEG is objectionable (*every, each*); and [−PARTITIVE, +DISTRIBUTIVE, −FACT → ⟨PRED⟩] + NEG is impossible. The total effect of *Any boys didn't leave* is that of going up an indefinite number of garden paths, one after the other, and knowing all the time that there is nothing at the end of any of them. It should be borne in mind that a logical equivalent of the universal negation 85a is the existential negation

87              $(\sim\exists x)Fx$

which is parallel to the equivalent surface structures

88a   None of the boys left.
88b   No one of the boys left.
88c   Not one of the boys left.
88d   There was not one of the boys that left.
88e   There wasn't any boy that left.

In all of these versions of 87, the negative precedes the indefinite and therefore satisfies the constraint 28. It is not likely that there is a one-to-one correspondence between logical representations 85 and 87, and surface structures 86 and 88. Nevertheless, the parallel is so striking that we might rewrite 28 as

28′   If a linguistic structure is interpreted as a positive universal quantifier applied to a simplex negative predicate, then the negative precedes or is incorporated with the quantifier in the surface structure, more often when the quantifier contains a distributive feature, and always when it is hypothetical.

This new constraint is broader than 28 since it includes all the quantifiers in 86. But it seems to be lacking the list of exceptions to the categorical operation of negative attraction on *any*—that NEGATTRAC may not apply when the quantifier is commanded by another negative, commanded by a hypothetical, or stressed. We can now use our analysis of *any* in positive sentences to show that these specifications are not needed in the new version 28′.

Commanded by another negative. When a second negative commands the indefinite quantifier, as in our example

19   I don't say that anyone didn't go

the logical structure is not that of 28' but rather

89          $\sim((\forall x) \sim Fx)$

that is, 'I say that it is not the case that anyone didn't go'. In 19, negative raising is added to 89; the effect of a preceding negative without negative raising is seen in 3 of Table 4.1 (p. 140). Such explicit negatives as *it is false* do relieve the categorical nature of negative attraction, but as noted in section 2 are not as effective as the implicit negatives in *regret, apologize, am sorry, hate.* It is not clear why these indirect negatives have a stronger effect.

Commanded by a hypothetical. These are the cases listed under 22 and 23 and analyzed in section 6.1 in their positive counterparts. From this discussion it is clear that the logical structure of *If anyone can't go* . . . and 23 *Anyone can't go who drinks* are not of the form $(\forall x) \sim Fx$ but rather of the forms

90a $(\forall x)(\sim Fx \supset Gx)$
90b $(\forall x)(\sim Fx \supset \alpha)$

and neither of these are specified in 28'. In the case of the embedded sentences of 24 *For anyone not to go* . . . the structure is either 89 or 90b, and it is difficult to decide which. That is, 24b *It's a shame for anyone not to go* may be read as

91          $(\forall x)(\exists y)(\sim(x \text{ go}) \supset \text{shame } y)$

or we can refer to the presupposition of 24b: *someone doesn't want anyone not to go.*

92          $(\forall x)(\exists y)(\sim(y \text{ like} \sim (x \text{ go}))$

Stress. In all the previous cases cited, the scope of *any* naturally expands to cover the entire proposition. We observe that in

17'   Just *anybody* can't eat there

the stress protects against the force of negative attraction. But it is also clear that the meaning is quite different from *Nobody can eat there*. The logical representation would be equivalent to the NEG-Q reading of 85b:

93          $(\sim \forall x)(x \text{ can eat there})$

where the negative has a larger scope than the quantifier. This is not the normal scope for *any*; the limited scope shown here is more characteristic of *all* and *every*, as in *Not every boy can eat there*. But the stress on *any* has the effect of limiting its scope, so that the negation applies directly to the quantifier.[28] There is no need for any special representation of the effect of stress on *any*; contrastive stress normally focuses the semantic force of negation on the stressed particle so that the negative commands it. In

94   The *E-string* didn't break

we assert that it was *not* the E-string but some other string which broke. And in 17′ we assert that it is not *any* body who can sit there but only members of some other, less inclusive set.

The mechanism of contrastive stress involved here does not operate without a negative feature. It is therefore understandable that the parallels between the constraints on *any* in positive and negative sentences comes to an end here, and that stress on *any* does not make it compatible with preterits and progressive verbs.

6.3. Limits of the Logical Representations

Though we should not attempt to make any direct connection between the logical representations and the relatively superficial rule of negative attraction, it is evident that this transformation is governed both by logical configurations and abstract conceptual features of the sentence. These considerations are quite distinct from the emphatic, affective, and socially marked features of negative postposing and negative concord, and fully justify our treating NEGATTRAC as a separate transformation.

Although the informal logical representations given above are quite revealing, it is clear that they are not sufficient to show the

28. In the representations used by Carden 1970, this difference would be shown as a deep structure with the quantifier as the predicate of the highest level sentence vs. a structure with the NEG as the predicate commanding the quantifier.

meaning of *any*. *Any* is more than a universal quantifier; we would have to enlarge our representation of *any one can go* to read.[29]

95          $(\forall x)$ (x can go)
            $[-\text{FACT}] \rightarrow$ $\langle \text{PRED} \rangle]$
            $[+\text{DISTR}]$

If we were to incorporate these features into a transformation, we might be able to capture the generalization expressed in 28′ and simplify the statement of obligatory conditions. Since 28′ plainly contains a variable rule, we would have to utilize the notation developed in chapter 3 reflecting the findings of Tables 4.2 and 4.3.

95′   NEGATTRAC II

$$\begin{bmatrix} +\text{QUANT} \\ -\text{PART} \\ \left\langle \begin{matrix} +\text{DISTR} \\ {}^*-\text{FACT} \end{matrix} \right\rangle \end{bmatrix} - \text{Nom} - [+\text{NEG}] - \text{VP}$$

           1   2   3   4 $\rightarrow$ 3 + 1   2   4

We would not need any further conditions on when the transformation is obligatory if we could formalize the notion of a "simplex negative predicate" presented in the preceding pages. In the final version of the transformations involving negative attraction and negative concord we will return to the more conventional notation involving only the indeterminates. But the generalization expressed in 95′ might well form the basis of future investigations.

Whatever formalism we use, negative attraction will be clearly differentiated from other rules by the reactions of native speakers to violations. Given the rules of English, we expect that an un-

---

29. That is, features such as [+DISTRIBUTIVE], [−DEFINITE], [−FACT →
⟨PRED⟩] are not normally shown in a logical representation. As noted above, [+DIS-
TRIBUTIVE] can be shown logically as the difference between $(\forall x)(\exists y)Fxy$ and
$(\exists y)(\forall x)Fxy$, but not for one-place predicates such as *Anyone can go*. The [−DEFI-
NITE] feature may be shown by the absence of a quantifier, as indicated in footnote
24. The nonfactual transfer feature might ultimately be reduced to a consequence of
this free variable formula. Whether or not all the semantic features of the quantifiers
can be reduced to a logical representation is still an open question; an answer will
of course require a proof of such suggestions with an explicit connection between
logical formulas and the grammatical end result.

stressed, unmodified, subject indefinite introduces a positive sentence. Violations of negative attraction, *Anyone can't go, therefore begin with what should be a positive sentence and then confront the hearer with a negative. Without the presence of a hypothetical feature, or a modifying clause which may be interpreted as a hypothetical feature,[30] or stress to limit the scope of *any*, the sentence remains an uninterpretable reversal of our expected pattern. It is possible that all universal and compelling prohibitions of this type involve abstract conceptual features with unexpected reversals of meaning. In any case, we have no choice but to regard NEGATTRAC as an entirely different rule from the rightward movements of the negative particle. To clarify further the distinction between obligatory and variable rules, we will now consider the way in which negative postposing and negative concord operate, and see what semantic or discourse functions can be assigned to these transformations.

7. The Nature of Negative Concord

The semantics of negative concord are a much simpler study than those of negative attraction. To begin with, we note that negative concord is an optional rule for almost all dialects of English. In this respect, it resembles negative postposing of the standard language.

---

30. The property of *any* which allows the interpretation of modifiers as hypotheticals is of considerable interest and may be of value for the exploration of the semantic value of various nominalizing processes of sentence reduction. We can construct a series of sentences with decreasing acceptability:

> Any boy who received an invitation went to his party.
> ?Any boy receiving an invitation went to his party.
> ?Any boy with an invitation went to his party.
> ?Any boy invited went to his party.
> ?Any boy on his block went to his party.
> ?Any boy here went to his party.
> *Any boy went to his party.

A purely logical representation will show the last item as a general hypothetical as readily as the first: $(\forall x)$ (x is a boy $\supset$ x went to his party). But the grammar seems to reject this interpretation, just as it would reject the interpretation of *Anyone went* as $(\forall x)$ (x is [+HUMAN] $\supset$ x went). If we accept this extremely analytical approach, we must conclude that any indefinite expression which contains a semantic feature in addition to the quantifier is to be interpreted as a hypothetical, and logical interpretation would be at the mercy of the number of distinctions made in the pronoun paradigm.

Both represent rightward movements of the negative beyond the verb and they seem to share a strongly emphatic character:

96a   I owe you nothing!
96b   I don't owe you nothin'!

Jespersen points out (1924:331) that the system of 96b is the normal one for most languages, that negation is typically cumulative, not multiplicative. It is the cumulative character of negative concord, along with the postposing, which seems to put strong emphasis on the negation itself. It is not necessary to base such observations on intuitive speculation. When the pattern typical of careful speech gives way to the vernacular, negative concord is used by speakers to make their strongest points stronger. The use of negative concord can be illustrated by an interview with a 60-year-old woman from a working-class family in East Atlanta, Georgia. Mrs. Gratton had only a grade school education, but she was self-educated to the point of controlling most SE features when she wanted to. In the entire face-to-face interview she used the standard rules for negatives with indeterminates 32 times (including three examples of negative postposing); she used negative concord only 12 times. For the first 20 minutes, Mrs. Gratton regularly used such standard forms as the following:[31]

> TL: How do you keep it [the skillet] from getting rusty?
> Mrs. G.: Well—uh—I haven't ever thought anything about it. I jus' wash it an' put it back [laugh], an' clean it and that's all.
> TL: Do you keep it on top of the stove?
> Mrs. G.: No—I usually put it up. Now you see, I haven' put up anything.

But a little later, the conversation touched on a theme that produced a sudden switch to negative concord:

> TL: Do you make 'em (biscuits) from scratch?
> Mrs. G.: Make 'em from scratch (chuckle).
> ⎰TL: Wow! Do you measure the things when you put—
> ⎱Mrs. G: *I don't measure nothin'!*
> ⎰TL: Never, even when you first . . . ?
> ⎱Mrs. G: *I never have measure' nothin'.*
>   *I have never measured—*

---

31. I am indebted to Teresa Labov, who was the interviewer here, for initiating this exchange.

The emphatic character of Mrs. Gratton's response shows up in the repeated, strident overlap of speakers as well as her repetitions on the same theme. When this theme—cooking without measuring—comes up later in the interview, it is again given emphatic treatment. (Note that the cultural feature [−book learning] coincides with the use of nonstandard grammar at this point and reinforces the use of negative concord.) As the discussion continues, Mrs. Gratton switches back to standard forms:

> TL: How'd you learn how to make biscuits?
> Mrs. G.: Well . . .
> TL: Do you remember?
> Mrs. G.: No I didn'. I didn' know how to do anything when I cooked. But—I could make 'im corn bread. That's about th'easies' thing anybody can do, can make corn bread; i's nothin' to that.

Negative concord in other white dialects typically has this emphatic character.

97   We wouldn't never have took it!—*Marie C., 39, Hackney, London*

98   You don't have to know too much of nothing.—*Monnie O., 34, Wanchese, N.C.*

99   He (my father) didn' take nothin' offa nobody.—*Henry Gr., 60, E. Atlanta, Ga.*

In all such dialects negative concord is optional. Mrs. Gratton's husband used negative concord more than she did—17 times—but did not use it 12 times in the face-to-face interview. In group sessions within the family, the percentage of negative concord rises, but never predominates to the exclusion of the *any* forms. This confirms our view that *any* with the negative does not contain the feature [+NEG] as some linguists have suggested, since it always contrasts with NEG + *any*.

7.1. Negative Concord in Black English Vernacular

The first thing that we note in BEV is the extraordinary proliferation of the negative.

100   Once you get an even break, don't fuck it up, cause you might not never get no time see 'im again.—*Larry H., 15, Jets*

101   I ain't never had no trouble with none of 'em.—*William T., 25, Fla.*

102   You better *not* never steal nothin' from me.—*Jesse H., 16, Jets*

103   He ain't not no Jenkins.—*Speedy J., 15, Cobras*

The expansion of the negative goes beyond the two environments *Indet* and *Vb*, since we have in 103 two negatives associated with the verb. *Not* can occur in foregrounded position without the attraction of an indeterminate:

104   I can walk through this wall, but not my physical structure can't walk through this wall.—*Stanley K., 15, Cobras*

This development can be related to elliptical *not*, which negates constituents without verb phrases, as in standard *Not exactly.*

105   Not no more. They don't fly no more.—*Lawrence W., 15, Jets*

106   Not none—Not none o'our friends, but *big* people.—*David H., 13, Thunderbirds*

This negative is realized from the sentence modality without going through the morphophonemics of preverbal location. The fact that it can do so means that we cannot allow negative concord to be dependent upon a preverbal transformation. There is also a meta-linguistic *not*, which is used to edit texts and correct mistakes. This too can generate negative concord:

107   I went to some f—not no friends of mine, but a friend of *my* friend.—*Pauline J., 37, S.C.*

Another aspect of the exuberant use of the negative in BEV is negative concord referring to a negative not contained in the sentence at all, but contained in a presupposition or implication of the sentence. This "neg from nowhere" shows up in a toast, "The Letter." A whore who left the hero to rot in jail asks him for a dime:

108   Bitch, before you get the price o' *nothin'*,
A grape got to grow as large as a pumpkin.

All dialects normally have *anything* in clauses introduced by *before* or *unless*. The implication of 108 and all that follows is that she won't get any money ever. We also observe this abstract negative concord in

109   She always gets kids in trouble for nothin' they didn'
             do.—*Vineland, N.J.*

Here the standard equivalent is not immediately obvious: 'She
always gets kids in trouble for things they didn't do.' The fact that
those things are *nothing* from the standpoint of the kids seems to
influence the negative concord.[32]

The most relevant fact about negative concord in BEV is that it
is *not* optional; in the major environment, within the same clause,
negative concord to indeterminates is obligatory. Before we examine
the evidence for this statement, the relevant environments must be
strictly defined and a number of distinctions made.

a. Negative concord is never obligatory to the preverbal position.
We can easily locate BEV sentences where the negative is not transferred to preverbal position:

110   Nobody was after 'im.—*Lawrence W., 15, Jets*
111   Nobody fights fair.—*Henry N., 29, Bronx*

b. The indefinite article *a* is not an indeterminate and is not
involved in negative concord.

112a   I ain't never lost a fight. I ain't never lost a fight.—*Robert,
             13, South Carolina*
112b   Ain't nobody a man.—*Stanley K., 15, Cobras*
112c   You ain't got a funny bone.—*Michael, 13, W. Philadelphia*

From evidence given in various sections of this chapter, we conclude
that the underlying form of *no* is NEG + *any*, not NEG + *a*, which
is realized as *not a*.

113   I'm not a baby.—*Pam, 13, W. Philadelphia*

c. Forms appended as sentence modifiers like *either* or *anything*
are not to be considered within the same clause and are to be classed
with negative concord outside the sentence with NEG. Some of these
show concord:

114   I didn't know nothin' about the people; or nothin'.—
             Pauline J., 37, South Carolina
115   I might can't get no more fines, neither.—*Thomas H., 11,
             New York City*

32. This example is not from BEV, but from a Puerto Rican family in Vineland,
N.J., who had minimal contact with the black English vernacular of New York City
and Philadelphia.

But very often we find no negative concord to such positions among speakers of BEV.

116   They're not too hip, or anything.—*James T., 13, Jets*

d. The obligatory character of negative concord within the clause is not at all similar to the obligatory nature of negative attraction. Any speaker is potentially capable of omitting the rule and producing sentences with *any*. He hears the standard form and can interpret it, and in his careful speech he usually shifts away from 100 percent use of negative concord. Even in casual speech many adults have shifted away from BEV and lost consistency in negative concord. And most importantly, consistent use of negative concord is the characteristic of core speakers of BEV in their peer-group interaction. Marginal members of the peer-group culture and isolated individuals ("lames") do not show consistent negative concord.

Table 4.4 illustrates the four restrictions just outlined on the obliga-

TABLE 4.4.
USE OF THE NEGATIVE CONCORD RULE BY SPEAKERS OF
THE BLACK ENGLISH VERNACULAR AND OTHERS

		Negative concord within the clause			Outside clause
		to indeterminates		to verb	to indeterminates
Group	*Style*	*frequencies*	*no.* 100%*	*frequencies*	*frequencies*
T-Birds	Group	62/62	5/5	2/13	
(9–13 yrs)	Ind'l	94/96	11/13	12/34	1/11
Cobras	Group	70/70	11/11	12/35	0/1
(12–17 yrs)	Ind'l	186/188	14/16	7/18	0/5
Jets	Group	149/151	13/15	10/38	1/3
(12–16 yrs)	Ind'l	360/370	25/30	39/97	2/7
Oscar Bros	Group	53/55	4/5	10/21	5/5
(15–18 yrs)	Ind'l	79/81	3/4	6/12	0/2
Danger Girls					
(13–17 yrs)	Group	48/48		4/13	
Lames	Ind'l	73/81	10/12	1/6	0/3
Inwood (white)	Group	25/32	2/7	0/36	0/2
(11–16 yrs)	Ind'l	34/42	2/8	0/35	0/1

*Number of subjects who used 100 percent negative concord.

tory character of negative concord with evidence gathered from a large body of natural speech.

The table shows five peer groups of BEV speakers. The first four groups show figures on negative concord in two styles: group and individual. The individual interviews were often lively, carried on with interaction from other members of the group present; the interviewer (John Lewis) was a member of the vernacular culture himself. Nevertheless, the individual interviews cannot be taken as fully representative of the most casual style of speech, where the minimum attention is given to speech (*Sociolinguistic Patterns*, chapter 8). As long as questions are being asked and answered, we consider that the style used is not the basic vernacular as just defined. The group sessions provide the context which defines the vernacular—where speech is controlled by the same factors that are operating in every day life (see Introduction).

The first row of Table 4.4 shows that in group sessions five members of the Thunderbirds spoke 62 sentences in which negative concord might have been used and all speakers always did so. But in only 2 out of 13 cases was the negative transferred to the verb in the same clause. In individual sessions, concord was used in 94 out of 96 possible cases. Eleven of the 13 members used it 100 percent of the time, but two members each used the standard form once. Again, transfer to the verb took place at a much lower frequency—12 out of 34 cases—and in only one out of 11 cases was the negative transferred to an indeterminate in a following clause.

The older groups show essentially the same pattern. The Cobras again show 100 percent negative concord in group sessions to indeterminates within the clause. In the case of the Jets, there are two cases in group sessions where one individual used a standard form once. The Oscar Brothers, who are beginning to move out of the BEV culture, show a slightly greater tendency in this direction. In all cases, the frequency of transfer to the verb is much lower then to indeterminates, and transfer outside the sentence is irregular.

The lames are isolated individuals interviewed in Vacation Day Camps and on the streets of the Jet and Cobra areas, where it was known that they were not members of the central peer groups. Their use of negative concord is slightly less than that of the peer groups, though the difference is by no means as striking as in other indices of BEV (chapter 7). The two white Inwood groups are markedly different from the black groups. Even with the small numbers of instances, we find that only two of the speakers used negative concord all the time, and of course there was no transfer of the negative to the verb. Other studies of negative concord among white speakers in New York City confirm this pattern (*Social Stratification*).

If we now turn to the evidence of repetition tests with speakers of BEV, we find a pattern of response which reverses the pattern seen with violations of negative attraction. Sentences with or without negative concord are understood immediately and repeated back usually with negative concord.

117   *Nobody ever took an airplane, and none of us took a bus, either.*

       Boot: N-N-Nobody never took a airplane, none of us took a bus, neither.

       Money: None of us never took an airplane, and none of—take—none of us never take a bus, either.

Among the adolescent Jets, eight of 16 sentences with negative plus *ever* were repeated back with *never,* though a much smaller percentage of sentences with *any* were corrected to *none.* On the other hand, the majority of all BEV negative concord forms were repeated without change. Sentences modified with *anyhow* or *nohow* were usually repeated back without negative concord about 75 percent of the time.

Information from the Detroit study of Shuy, Wolfram, and Riley (1967) fits in with this pattern. The Detroit study was limited to individual interviews, like our 1963 Lower East Side study. The interviewers did not have as much success in identifying and separating casual speech from careful speech within these interviews, so that all of the conversational parts are taken as single style. Wolfram (1969) analyzed the data for 48 black speakers in the Detroit study and included negative concord in his data. In each social class, he selected four preadolescents 10 to 12 and four adolescents 14 to 17 years old. In the Lower Working Class, four out of eight showed 100 percent negative concord and in the Upper Working Class three out of eight. If we compare these figures for the individual interviews in Detroit with our individual interviews by a black participant observer, the Detroit study shows a similar semicategorical use of negative concord in black English vernacular. The Detroit study also agreed with our findings in the restrictions on negative concord. None of the adults showed 100 percent use of this rule. There was much less use of the rule with indefinites outside of the clause or in preverbal position, and if indefinite article *a* was included in the analysis, the percentage of negative concord dropped sharply. Other data support the notion that the indefinite article is not to be included as a site for negative concord.

For a further body of independently gathered data, we can turn to a series of recent observations made of preadolescent black children in West Philadelphia by Marjorie Goodwin.[33] The groups were recorded after long-term participant observation, and the language recorded is that used in the course of everyday activities—making sling shots, jumping rope, gossiping—with members of the vernacular culture actively controlling each other's language. In both form and content, these samples of Philadelphia speech match the vernacular culture recorded in the group sessions in south Harlem. The use of negative concord is shown in Table 4.5.

Both groups come close to consistent negative concord. Among the girls, there was only one use of a standard form. At one point it is suggested that fortune-telling can be the cause of a death in somebody's family. Pam, the leader of the group says

118   No. I don't want anybody to die in my family.

The use of a standard form in a solemn context is a common form

TABLE 4.5.
USE OF NEGATIVE CONCORD BY PREADOLESCENT
BEV SPEAKERS IN WEST PHILADELPHIA

| | Negative concord within the clause | | | Outside clause |
| | to indeterminates | | to verb | indeterminates |
	frequencies	*no. 100%**	*frequencies*	*frequencies*
Girls (9–13 yrs)	75/76	9/10	0/1	5/7
Boys (9–14 yrs)	70/74	7/10	1/4	3/9

*Number of subjects who used 100 percent negative concord.

33. I am much indebted to Marjorie Goodwin for the use of these materials, which were gathered and transcribed by her in the course of research for the Center for Urban Ethnography at the University of Pennsylvania. The analyses of personal interaction being carried out by Goodwin have also provided the insight necessary for a correct semantic interpretation of the sentences cited. In some cases only isolated sentences are quoted, but the interpretation is derived from the extended context of group interaction.

of code switching and supports the view that *NEG* + *any* is in another system as far as Pam is concerned.[34] A little later she says

119   They ain't nobody died in my family.

Among the boys, there are a few more instances of the use of stand-ard forms, mostly by older members of the group. The majority however use consistent negative concord to indeterminates within the sentence.

The use of negative concord outside of the original sentence is less regular, but we do not have adequate data to distinguish various cases. In the Philadelphia group, the negative is consistently trans-ferred to indeterminates in lower sentences commanded by the original negative.

120   Y'all ain't gonna be able to make no slings till we get all
             these sling shots.—*Pouchie, 13*
121   She didn't mean that to do nothin' to you.—*Maria, 13*
122   I ain't know I could do none of that.—*Pouchie, 13*

At the same time, the negative is less often transferred to reduced clauses or sentence modifiers.

123   You can roll your eyes all you want to 'cause I'm tellin'
             you—tellin', I'm not—not askin' you. And I ain't say no
             please, either.—*Pam, 13*
124   They ain't hardly even gonna be able to load 'em that fast
             either.—*Tokay, 13*

This extra-sentence *either* can contrast with the indeterminate *either* within the original sentence.

125   We don't want neither one of y'all.—*Michael, 13*

We thus find that the use of the negative concord rule for the West Philadelphia group is identical with that in Harlem and coin-cides with additional data from exploratory interviews in Detroit, Cleveland, Chicago, and Los Angeles. Since negative concord is practically obligatory in the most important case, we must raise the question: in what way can it be said to be an emphatic trans-formation?

---

34. There is a close parallel here with the form of code switching used in Hawaiian Creole in solemn narrations. The *-ed* past does not appear in the Creole but is imported for solemn effects in such utterances as *He died* (Labov 1971b).

7.2. The Expansion of Emphatic Negation in BEV

We have observed that the standard use of *any + NEG* is available for most BEV speakers, but primarily as an importation from an outside system. Since negative concord is practically automatic within the original sentence it cannot add any emphasis as it did in the case of Mrs. Gratton. It is simply an automatic adjustment of the grammar. For Mrs. Gratton, *I don't measure nothin'* contrasts with *I don't measure anythin'* by the addition of an optional [+NEG] to the final lexical item. If such an addition is obligatory, it cannot contrast with its absence. How then do BEV speakers convey the equivalent of the emphatic contrast registered by Mrs. Gratton?

There are a number of answers to this question which we can illustrate with quotations from the West Philadelphia group. First of all, we can note that black English vernacular often adds negatives beyond the provisions of the negative concord rule. Even within the rule, it provides for negatives in preverbal as well as in subject position. But indeterminate subjects are relatively rare. In most cases negative concord operates from the verb rightward to an object indeterminate or to an indeterminate noun-phrase modifier. Both cases appear in

126   I ain't write nothin' in no street.—*Pam, 13, Philadelphia*

Sometimes an indeterminate modifier is added when there is really only one semantic object to focus on. Thus

127   She ain't in no seventh grade. She in eleventh grade.—
           Maria, 13, Philadelphia

The *NEG + any* which modifies *seventh grade* can only be understood as adding emphasis since there is only one seventh grade to be considered here. That is, Maria is not reviewing all of the possible seventh grades that the girl could be in, but rejecting the notion that she is in the seventh grade at all. Thus *She ain't in no seventh grade* contrasts with *She ain't in the seventh grade* as a more emphatic denial. Similarly, we can observe a contrast of the indefinite article *a* with the *NEG + any* quantifier in

128   I don't want a piece. I want a whole one. I don't want
           no piece.—*Poochie, 13, W. Philadelphia*

Here Poochie strengthens his first negation with the insertion of the underlying quantifier *any* which automatically attracts the negative.

Emphasis is accomplished by substituting the universal [−PARTI-TIVE] quantifier *any* for the existential [+PARTITIVE] pronoun *a*. The negative concord rule heightens the effect in that it automatically adds [+NEGATIVE] to reinforce the contrast.

Such postposed negatives can be heard as emphatic even when negative concord is obligatory, if they are moved further rightward. Flo of West Philadelphia follows up Pam's denial of 126 with a more emphatic form:

129   We ain't write over no streets nothing.

Here the extraposition of *nothing* to the end of the sentence has the same general effect as standard negative postposing

129′   We wrote nothing over any streets.

Even though negative concord is automatic in BEV, we see that there are a number of resources for reinforcing negation in the original sentence: the introduction of extra quantifiers, postposing negatives, transfer to preverbal position, and reduplication of free *not*.

In addition to these devices, BEV has also extended the standard rule of negative inversion to give additional emphasis to sentences with indeterminate subjects. The standard rule as used by black and white speakers preposes *neither, not,* or adverbs containing a negative feature.

130   The Negro doesn't know about the Negro, and neither does
               the white know about the Negro.—*Byrne C., 26, Ohio*
131   Not until he came into United States did—uh—they decide
               to get married.—*Charles I., 31, Bronx*

In many southern dialects, and in black English vernacular, the tense marker and negative can be inverted with an indeterminate subject—the pattern we have called negative inversion (chapter 2).

132   Doesn't nobody really know that it's a God, you know.—
               Larry H., 15, Jets
133   Don't no average motherfucker make no fifty dollars a
               day.—*Vaughn R., 16, Jets*
134   Don't nobody break up a fight.—*Willie J., 15, Chicago*

Along with the tense marker, the first member of the auxiliary can also be moved, just as in the flip-flop rule for questions. Thus negative inversion can involve *can't, wasn't, won't,* and *ain't*. An examination of negative inversion would require a separate discussion; the most important feature for us to note here is the strongly emphatic character of this transformation.

135   Didn't nobody see it, didn't nobody hear it!—*Benjamin S., 45, N.Y.C.*

136   Ain't no white cop gonna put his hands on me!—*Jesse H., 16, Jets*

137   Ain't nobody in my family Negro!—*Boot B., 12, Thunderbirds*

138   I know a way that can't nobody start a fight.—*Willie J., Chicago*

139   Won't nobody catch us!—*Willie J., 15, Chicago*

Negative inversion plainly depends upon and follows negative transfer from subject indefinite to the verb, i.e. *Nobody will catch us* → *Nobody won't catch us* → *Won't nobody catch us*. Six cases of negative inversion in West Philadelphia should accordingly be added to the figures on negative transfer to the verb by rule 53 in Table 4.5, giving $\frac{3}{4}$ for girls and $\frac{4}{7}$ for boys. One could argue that the movement of the negative to the left of the indefinite is a continuation of the negative attraction rule and is reinforced by the factors outlined in section 6. However, negative inversion is always optional, and it can be seen in these examples to have the same emphatic force as the negative concord rules.

When negative inversion moves an auxiliary like *won't* as in 139, it must be derived from an underlying sentence with only one tense marker (*nobody will catch us*). But when *ain't* precedes the subject, there is often the possibility that it originated in a clause of its own with deleted dummy *it*.

140   Ain't nobody know about no club.—*William T., 25, Florida*

This could be based on either of the following:

140'   (It) ain't nobody (that) know about no club.
140"   Nobody ain't know about no club.

This is a possible route for 136 and 137 as well. Note that these cases require deletion of relative pronoun *that* in subject position; such deletion seems to be more common in BEV and other southern dialects than elsewhere.[35] On the other hand, 141 can only be based on 141' and not on 141":

141   Ain't nothin' you can do about it.
141'   (It) ain't nothin' (that) you can do about it.
141"   *Nothin' ain't that you can do about it.

We occasionally have sentences that are syntactically ambiguous like 140 and that also contain a negative in the second clause. Then one interpretation of such sentences is that they are not derived by negative inversion but by *it* deletion and therefore show negative concord to a verb in a following clause:

142   Ain't no cop never beat me in my head.—*Jesse H., 16, Jets*

7.3. Expansion of Negative Concord to Other Quantifiers

There is one final way in which the use of emphatic negation has expanded in BEV. Transformations which were originally limited to indeterminates *any, ever,* and *either* can occasionally apply in the presence of other quantifiers like *many* and *much.* In 1, 47, and 48, we see that the rule which extends negative concord to the verb in following clauses requires an indeterminate in the first clause; but in 50, this rule operates with a subject *much.* This extension should not be entirely unexpected, since as Baker (1970) has pointed out, *much* has negative polarity: *He didn't say much* but **He said much.* The same cannot be said of *many,* however. In 143 and 144 we see negative inversion operating with subjects containing this adverb.

143   It's against the rule; that's why don't so many people do
           it.—*Willie J., 15, Chicago*
144   Don't many of them live around here.—*Hough area,*
           Cleveland

And in the citation from "The Fall" 49, the extension of negative concord to a following clause is triggered by an indefinite with *a,* which is not a part of the usual negative concord rule and does not incorporate the negative in the way that *any* does: *For there wasn't*

---

35. For example, *There is a lot of women wanna make you do more than just hit 'em* (Weldon S., 46, N.C., #665); *An tha's the rules mean* (Boot, 12, T-Birds); *I got a man to come out here Saturday is gon' paint* (Henry G., 60, E. Atlanta); *We have very few go to college* (Monnie O., 35, North Carolina).

a son of a gun who this whore couldn't shun. We therefore see
speakers of BEV extending the scope of the negative transfer rules
to environments beyond any formal rule that we can now write since
there is no reason to believe that these are productive patterns.

8. An Overall View of Negative Transfer Rules

We now have an understanding of the operation of negative attraction, negative postposing, and negative concord in four different
dialects: Standard English (SE); the nonstandard white vernacular
which does not transfer the negative to preverbal position, of which
New York City may be taken as an example (WNS$_1$); the nonstandard
white vernacular which does show negative concord to the verb, of
which Atlanta may be taken as an example (WNS$_2$); and black
English vernacular (BEV), which is relatively uniform throughout
the United States.

In section 5, we considered the possibility of combining these rules
into a single negative transfer rule. But sections 6, 7, and 8 showed
that there are two radically different kinds of rules involved with
different conditions, directions, functions, and frequencies. Rather
than use a single negative distribution rule like 16, we will first place
the negative in its preverbal position with the tense marker, by the
normal cyclical rule 145:

145   NEGPLACEMENT: categorical

$$W - [+\text{NEG}] - NP - \begin{cases} \emptyset & -V \\ \begin{cases} M \\ be \\ have \end{cases} & -X \end{cases}$$

$$1 \qquad 2 \qquad 3 \qquad 4 \qquad 5 \rightarrow 1 \ 3 \ 4+2 \ 5$$

Negative attraction follows as a categorical leftward movement to
a subject indeterminate with the single condition that was summarized in section 5. The abbreviation *Indet* now stands for the
complex of features [+QUANTIFIER, −DEFINITE, −PARTITIVE,
+DISTRIBUTIVE, −FACT → ⟨PRED⟩]. The general condition on
146 still appears as a set of three superficially unconnected conditions which must all hold if the transformation is to be obligatory.
In section 6 we put forward an explanation of this conjunction,
depending upon the fact that the net result of this conjunction was
that only surface structures corresponding to the logical configuration $(\forall x) \sim Fx$ were categorically prohibited. But in terms of current

workable syntactic apparatus, the condition on 146 must still reflect the syntactic constraints of the output condition 28.

146   NEGATTRAC
         W — Indet — [+NEG][36]
         1   2   3   →   1   3 + 2
         Condition: Obligatory if 1 ∼[+NEG] or [−FACT] com-
                    manding 2 and 4 and 2 is [−STRESS]

It should now be possible to combine negative postposing and negative concord into a single rightward transformation. There is a great deal to be learned yet about the conditions governing negative postposing; on the whole, it is in complementary social distribution with negative concord, but there seem to be some cases where a speaker of any dialect will use negative postposing instead of negative concord. Since we do not know the conditions under which speakers will exercise this option, we will show the two transformations as separate rules pending further investigation.

147   NEGPOSTPOSING: variable
         W — [+NEG] — X — Indet
         1   2   3   4   →   1   3   2 + 4
         Conditions: a. X ∼[Indet
                     b. 4 cannot be dominated by an S dominated
                        by a lexical NP which does not domi-
                        nate 2.
                     c. 4 cannot be dominated by an S adjoined
                        to THAT and commanded by 2.

148   NEGCONCORD: variable
         $$W - [+NEG] - X - \begin{Bmatrix} \text{Indet} \\ \text{Vb} \end{Bmatrix}$$
         1   2   3   4   →   1   2   3   2 + 4
         Conditions: a. 4 cannot be directly dominated by a VP
                        which is dominated by an S_i dominated
                        by a lexical NP which does not domi-
                        nate 2.
                     b. 4 = Vb in WNS_2 and BEV only; in WNS_2
                        2 and 4 must be clause mates.

36. The presumption in showing *Indet* directly before NEG in (146) is that the features of Indeterminate are assigned to the entire noun phrase of the subject. Similarly, we see the plural feature in English assigned to the entire noun phrase which contains the plural head noun. Thus *Indet* in 146 extends over such phrases as *any red-blooded American who wants to do his duty*.

The three negative transfer rules are now stated in reasonably simple forms. There would follow the negative inversion rule which might be combined with other flip-flop rules. Negative raising also follows,[37] so that we have

149   I don't think the other guy had no chance either.—*Danny W., 16, Oscar Brothers*
150   I told you, I *don't* believe there's no God.—*Vaughn R., 16, Jets*

We will not explore further the conditions for negative inversion and negative raising since our main concern is with negative concord. Of all the negative transfer rules, this shows the widest range of environment and dialect differentiation. Condition *b* of 148 does not provide us with all the information we need to characterize the uses of NEGCONCORD: this is best displayed in the matrix of Table 4.6, which then replaces that condition.[38]

This matrix shows the gradual expansion of negative concord through four environments and four dialects as we move from the standard language to black English vernacular. The symbol "0" indicates that the rule is not used at all; "X" that it is used variably; and "1" that it is used regularly, that is, semicategorically. Since negative concord is not used at all in SE, there is a row of zeros across the top. In WNS_1 it is used in only two environments, in WNS_2 in three, and in BEV, in all four. In BEV, we observe the semicategorical use of negative concord to indeterminates within the sentence and a variable use in all three other environments.

37. Either ordering of negative raising can be made to work here. If negative raising occurs before negative concord, then the subcase of NEGCONCORD governing transfer outside the clause will apply, otherwise the major case within the clause. Since NEGCONCORD seems to co-occur with negative raising with great consistency, the latter seems preferable, but the issue is still open.

38. As we explore the relevant details of rules used by the speech community, it becomes apparent that many rules will require a matrix of two or more dimensions to describe the use of the rule. One dimension will be the order of environment, the various syntagmatic environments, the other will be the range of dialects or idiolects which differ in their assignment of categorical, variable, or prohibited status to a given environment. The ordering of the columns and rows of this matrix for maximum scalability on a Guttman scale of implications is of considerable significance in explaining the semantic, syntactic, or phonological motivation of the rule as it develops in more or less favorable environments. The ordering of the linguistic environments shows which linguistic features favor the rule, and the ordering of the nonlinguistic features shows either the point of origin of the rule for change in progress or the social significance of the rule for well-established variables.

TABLE 4.6.
USE OF NEGATIVE CONCORD IN FOUR
ENGLISH DIALECTS

4 (in Rule 148) = 2 and 4 clause mates?	Indeterminate		Verb	
	Yes	No	Yes	No
SE	0	0	0	0
WNS$_1$	X	X	0	0
WNS$_2$	X	X	X	0
BEV·	1	X	X	X

Note: $0 < X < 1$

Table 4.6 gives us the answer to the question asked in section 1: how can it come about that a sentence means X in dialect A and not-X in dialect B? What process of dialect divergence can lead to completely opposing interpretations of

1   It ain't no cat can't get in no coop.

In this matrix we see the coupling of two changes: (1) that negative concord has lost its emphatic character in BEV in the major environment, and (2) negative concord has spread into a new environment. We have seen the reinforcement of emphatic negation through a variety of grammatical devices: the introduction of more quantifiers (*She ain't in no seventh grade*), free floating negatives (*but not my physical structure can't walk through that wall*), negative inversion (*ain't nobody in the block go to school*), and involvement of concord with new quantifiers (*don't so many people do it*).

This pattern is the most striking example of the interrelation of BEV rules which makes this dialect a distinct system in itself (chapter 2). But the answer to our initial problem is in the pattern of Table 4.6: *it is the extension of negative concord to verbs in following clauses which brings about the dialect conflict in interpretation.* White speakers are surprised by 1 because they cannot envisage such a possibility. With the understanding provided by Table 4.6, our intuitions as speakers of other dialects begin to extend to an appreciation of the logic of 1.[39] There is no inherent reason why *can't* in 1 must refer to a separate deep structure negative of its own; it is

39. Recent empirical work on the outer limits of a grammar has confirmed and extended our expectation that speakers of English who have never heard the BEV extension can adapt to it, following the logic of Table 4.6 (Labov 1972d).

simply the arbitrary convention of the dialects we know that negative concord does not operate there.

The extension of negative concord in 1 does not lead to any serious misunderstanding in ordinary conversation. Speakers of English are not unaccustomed to sudden inversions of positive and negative. *I couldn't care less* seems to mean the same as *I could care less*. In Maine and surrounding eastern New England, young people say *So don't I* to mean the same thing as their parents' *So do I*. Even without negative concord, we have learned that not every negative means what it might.

On the other hand, there is no reason to fear that BEV speakers have lost their grip on the distinction between positive and negative. The underlying semantic features of quantifiers and negatives seem to be the same in all dialects of English, which tend to differ in just the ways indicated here—by slight extensions and adjustments of conditions on the same set of rules. Speakers of BEV are just as able as others to multiply or to cancel negatives and just as able to operate with two or more negatives in their deep structure. Consider the following discussion from West Philadelphia:

151   *Huey:* And he said, "Nobody talks about my mother."
           Michael: Well I'm not nobody; I'm somebody. That's what
           he said, "I'm not nobody; I'm somebody."

Games that play on the ambiguity of negatives, originating in deep or surface structure, are popular among speakers of all dialects. In the same way, speakers of BEV play games with indefinites:

152   *Poochie:* Hold it, Tokay. Somebody shot.
           Michael: That's tough. 'Cause ain't nobody down here
           name somebody.
           Robby: You name somebody.

It is a reasonable assumption that speakers of all dialects of English have the same range of linguistic and metalinguistic abilities and that the most striking differences in the surface forms of language represent the differential operation of principles found in all dialects: different ordering of the same rules, specifications and generalizations of conditions on a single rule, and different weightings of conditions within the rule. A careful consideration of the obligatory and variable properties of the rules involved will often throw a great deal of light upon their function. We do not say that transformational rules have "meaning" in the strict sense of the term. But operations which shift, combine, delete, and multiply have the effect of focusing, emphasizing, subfocusing, and eliminating information. In the long run, most people find it necessary to emphasize, focus on, conceal, or mitigate the same kinds of things. It is reasonable to assume that speakers of any language will have a need for a wide range of more emphatic and less emphatic negatives; if the range is constricted in one area it must be expanded in another, and it is this kind of economy which we have been studying in negative concord.

Though Table 4.6 has answered our initial question, we have not exhausted its possibilities by any means. It is merely a bare schema for negative concord, suggesting how this rule may actually be located in time and space. This table provides a grammatical model of the kind of matrices which C.-J. Bailey has been exploring in phonological rules (1971). The matrix is a realization of weightings assigned to the variable constraint on the rule. Such weights indicate the internal linguistic constraints which govern the rule and predict in what environments it will first become active. As the rule develops, we frequently find that it becomes categorical in the original environments before it operates variably in more extended, less favorable environments. It is also possible for reweighting of the environments to take place.[40] As Tables 4.4 and 4.5 indicate, the variable symbol "X" in Table 4.6 actually stands for relations of "greater than" and "less than" in which each cell is greater than that above it and greater than that to the right. We have only begun a detailed examination of the use of negative concord, with the exploration of one dialect—BEV. More detailed studies of the use of negative concord in a range of English dialects will allow us to organize the parameters of Table 4.6 with greater confidence and deepen our understanding of the semantic factors which underlie the organization of grammars.

The most general implication of our investigation is in the contrast between the categorical rule of negative attraction and the variable rules of negative concord. While other studies of dialect differences in rule systems have concentrated upon variability (chapter 3, Carden 1970, Bailey 1971), here our primary focus has been upon

---

40. That is, the relative order of the variable constraints can be altered. The direction of each constraint is constant across dialects and age levels, but their relative strength can shift in the course of time or age. See C.-J. Bailey 1971.

the categorical character of negative attraction, as opposed to the variable or semicategorical treatment of negative concord in black English vernacular.

Rules such as NEGATTRAC which are uniform and invariant in all dialects of a language appear as resolutions of conflicts among abstract conceptual features of language. Whereas violations of many grammatical rules become more acceptable as they are repeated, violations constructed for such rules become if anything less acceptable. They are truly uninterpretable: the listener finds himself unable to construct a logical, social, or aesthetic rationale for the anomaly. We seem to encounter more than a contradiction in meaning; there is also a contradiction of intent. The listener is led down the path and then perceives that the intention of the speaker led in an entirely different direction.

When a speaker begins with *Anyone,* we confidently expect some positive general prediction; when he continues with *doesn't* we are faced with an unaccountable reversal of polarity.[41] There are practical jokes and puns which rely on this mechanism of leading the listeners up (or is it down?) the garden path. But a sentence like *Anyone doesn't sit there anymore* is not practical, it is not sensible, it is not even in good taste; and if there is a joke, it is not on anyone at all.

If we have correctly understood this phenomenon, our investigation of negative attraction and negative concord will have added considerably to our grasp of the nature of linguistic rules.

41. This effect of leading in two directions at once can be observed in some other constructed violations of categorical rules of discourse. Some of the same uninterpretable character clings to such violations as *Hello, I'm Bill Labov. How do you get to the Empire State Building?* Introductions are anomalous if the speech event is "asking for directions." But as Erving Goffman has pointed out (pers. comm.) this violation is more striking than *Joan of Arc is dead. How do you get to the Empire State Building?* The latter is simply uninterpretable nonsense. The strong reaction against the introduction is that it begins with an appropriate series of moves for one type of speech event, then suddenly switches to another.

Part II

THE VERNACULAR

IN ITS

SOCIAL SETTING

5 | The Logic of
Nonstandard English

IN the past decade, a great deal of federally sponsored research has been devoted to the educational problems of children in ghetto schools.[1] In order to account for the poor performance of children in these schools, educational psychologists have attempted to discover what kind of disadvantage or defect they are suffering from. The viewpoint that has been widely accepted and used as the basis for large-scale intervention programs is that the children show a cultural deficit as a result of an impoverished environment in their early years. Considerable attention has been given to language. In this area the deficit theory appears as the concept of verbal deprivation. Black children from the ghetto area are said to receive little verbal stimulation, to hear very little well-formed language, and as a result are impoverished in their means of verbal expression. They cannot speak complete sentences, do not know the names of common objects, cannot form concepts or convey logical thoughts.

Unfortunately, these notions are based upon the work of educational psychologists who know very little about language and even less about black children. The concept of verbal deprivation has no basis in social reality. In fact, black children in the urban ghettos receive a great deal of verbal stimulation, hear more well-formed sentences than middle-class children, and participate fully in a highly verbal culture. They have the same basic vocabulary, possess the same capacity for conceptual learning, and use the same logic as anyone else who learns to speak and understand English.

The notion of verbal deprivation is a part of the modern mythology

---

1. This chapter first appeared in *Georgetown Monographs in Languages and Linguistics No. 22* (1969).

of educational psychology, typical of the unfounded notions which tend to expand rapidly in our educational system. In past decades linguists have been as guilty as others in promoting such intellectual fashions at the expense of both teachers and children. But the myth of verbal deprivation is particularly dangerous, because it diverts attention from real defects of our educational system to imaginary defects of the child. As we shall see, it leads its sponsors inevitably to the hypothesis of the genetic inferiority of black children that it was originally designed to avoid.

The most useful service which linguists can perform today is to clear away the illusion of verbal deprivation and to provide a more adequate notion of the relations between standard and nonstandard dialects. In the writings of many prominent educational psychologists, we find very poor understanding of the nature of language. Children are treated as if they have no language of their own in the preschool programs put forward by Bereiter and Engelmann (1966). The linguistic behavior of ghetto children in test situations is the principal evidence of genetic inferiority in the view of Jensen (1969). In this paper, we will examine critically both of these approaches to the language and intelligence of the populations labeled "verbally deprived" and "culturally deprived,"[2] and attempt to explain how the myth of verbal deprivation has arisen, bringing to bear the methodological findings of sociolinguistic work and some substantive facts about language which are known to all linguists. Of particular concern is the relation between concept formation on the one hand, and dialect differences on the other, since it is in this area that the most dangerous misunderstandings are to be found.

Verbality

The general setting in which the deficit theory arises consists of a number of facts which are known to all of us. One is that black children in the central urban ghettos do badly in all school subjects, including arithmetic and reading. In reading, they average more than two years behind the national norm (see *New York Times*, December

2. I am indebted to Rosalind Weiner of the Early Childhood Education group of Operation Head Start in New York City and to Joan Baratz of the Education Study Center, Washington, D.C., for pointing out to me the scope and seriousness of the educational issues involved here and the ways in which the cultural deprivation theory has affected federal intervention programs in recent years.

3, 1968). Furthermore, this lag is cumulative, so that they do worse comparatively in the fifth grade than in the first grade. Reports in the literature show that this poor performance is correlated most closely with socioeconomic status. Segregated ethnic groups seem to do worse than others—in particular, Indian, Mexican-American, and black children. Our own work in New York City confirms that most black children read very poorly; however, studies in the speech community show that the situation is even worse than has been reported. If one separates the isolated and peripheral individuals from members of central peer groups, the peer-group members show even worse reading records and to all intents and purposes are not learning to read at all during the time they spend in school (chapter 6).

In speaking of children in the urban ghetto areas, the term *lower class* frequently is used, as opposed to *middle class*. In the several sociolinguistic studies we have carried out, and in many parallel studies, it has been useful to distinguish a lower-class group from a working-class one. Lower-class families are typically female-based, or matrifocal, with no father present to provide steady economic support, whereas for the working-class there is typically an intact nuclear family with the father holding a semiskilled or skilled job. The educational problems of ghetto areas run across this important class distinction. There is no evidence, for example, that the father's presence or absence is closely correlated with educational achievement (e.g., Coleman et al. 1966). The peer groups we have studied in south-central Harlem, representing the basic vernacular culture, include members from both family types. The attack against cultural deprivation in the ghetto is overtly directed at family structures typical of lower-class families, but the educational failure we have been discussing is characteristic of both working-class and lower-class children.

This paper, therefore, will refer to children from urban ghetto areas rather than lower-class children. The population we are concerned with comprises those who participate fully in the vernacular culture of the street and who have been alienated from the school system.[3] We are obviously dealing with the effects of the caste system

3. The concept of the black English vernacular (BEV) and the culture in which it is embedded is presented in detail in CRR 3288; sections 1.2.3 and 4.1. See chapter 7 for the linguistic traits which distinguish speakers who participate fully in the BEV culture from marginal and isolated individuals.

of American society—essentially a color-marking system. Everyone recognizes this. The question is: By what mechanism does the color bar prevent children from learning to read? One answer is the notion of cultural deprivation put forward by Martin Deutsch and others (Deutsch and associates 1967; Deutsch, Katz, and Jensen 1968). Black children are said to lack the favorable factors in their home environment which enable middle-class children to do well in school (Deutsch and assoc. 1967; Deutsch, Katz, and Jensen 1968). These factors involve the development of various cognitive skills through verbal interaction with adults, including the ability to reason abstractly, speak fluently, and focus upon long-range goals. In their publications, these psychologists also recognize broader social factors.[4] However, the deficit theory does not focus upon the interaction of the black child with white society so much as on his failure to interact with his mother at home. In the literature we find very little direct observation of verbal interaction in the black home; most typically, the investigators ask the child if he has dinner with his parents, and if he engages in dinner-table conversation with them. He is also asked whether his family takes him on trips to museums and other cultural activities. This slender thread of evidence is used to explain and interpret the large body of tests carried out in the laboratory and in the school.

The most extreme view which proceeds from this orientation—and one that is now being widely accepted—is that lower-class black children have no language at all. The notion is first drawn from Basil Bernstein's writings that "much of lower-class language consists of a kind of incidental 'emotional' accompaniment to action here and now." (Jensen 1968:118). Bernstein's views are filtered through a strong bias against all forms of working-class behavior, so that middle-class language is seen as superior in every respect—as "more abstract, and necessarily somewhat more flexible, detailed and subtle." One can proceed through a range of such views until one comes to the practical program of Carl Bereiter, Siegfried Engelmann and their associates (Bereiter et al. 1966: Bereiter and Engelmann 1966). Bereiter's program for an academically oriented preschool is based

---

4. For example, in Deutsch, Katz and Jensen 1968 there is a section on "Social and Psychological Perspectives" which includes a chapter by Proshansky and Newton on "The Nature and Meaning of Negro Self-Identity" and one by Rosenthal and Jacobson on "Self-Fulfilling Prophecies in the Classroom."

upon their premise that black children must have a language with which they can learn, and their empirical finding that these children come to school without such a language. In his work with four-year-old black children from Urbana, Bereiter reports that their communication was by gestures, "single words," and "a series of badly connected words or phrases," such as *They mine* and *Me got juice.* He reports that black children could not ask questions, that "without exaggerating . . . these four-year-olds could make no statements of any kind." Furthermore, when these children were asked "Where is the book?", they did not know enough to look at the table where the book was lying in order to answer. Thus Bereiter concludes that the children's speech forms are nothing more than a series of emotional cries, and he decides to treat them "as if the children had no language at all." He identifies their speech with his interpretation of Bernstein's restricted code: "the language of culturally deprived children . . . is not merely an underdeveloped version of standard English, but is a basically nonlogical mode of expressive behavior" (Bereiter et al. 1966:112–13). The basic program of his preschool is to teach them a new language devised by Engelmann, which consists of a limited series of questions and answers such as *Where is the squirrel? The squirrel is in the tree.* The children will not be punished if they use their vernacular speech on the playground, but they will not be allowed to use it in the schoolroom. If they should answer the question *Where is the squirrel?* with the illogical vernacular form *In the tree* they will be reprehended by various means and made to say, *The squirrel is in the tree.*

Linguists and psycholinguists who have worked with black children are apt to dismiss this view of their language as utter nonsense. Yet there is no reason to reject Bereiter's observations as spurious. They were certainly not made up. On the contrary, they give us a very clear view of the behavior of student and teacher which can be duplicated in any classroom. In our own work outside of adult-dominated environments of school and home, we have not observed black children behaving like this. However, on many occasions we have been asked to help analyze the results of research into verbal deprivation conducted in such test situations.

Here, for example, is a complete interview with a black child, one of hundreds carried out in a New York City school. The boy enters a room where there is a large, friendly, white interviewer, who puts on the table in front of him a toy and says: "Tell me everything you

can about this." (The interviewer's further remarks are in parentheses.)

> (12 seconds of silence)
>
> (What would you say it looks like?)
>
> (8 seconds of silence)
>
> A space ship.
>
> (Hmmmm.)
>
> (13 seconds of silence)
>
> Like a je-et.
>
> (12 seconds of silence)
>
> Like a plane.
>
> (20 seconds of silence)
>
> (What color is it?)
>
> Orange. (2 seconds) An' whi-ite. (2 seconds) An' green.
>
> (6 seconds of silence)
>
> (An' what could you use it for?)
>
> (8 seconds of silence)
>
> A je-et.
>
> (6 seconds of silence)
>
> (If you had two of them, what would you do with them?)
>
> (6 seconds of silence)
>
> Give one to some-body.
>
> (Hmmm. Who do you think would like to have it?)
>
> (10 seconds of silence)
>
> Cla-rence.
>
> (Mm. Where do you think we could get another one of
> these?)
>
> At the store.
>
> (Oh ka-ay!)

We have here the same kind of defensive, monosyllabic behavior
which is reported in Bereiter's work. What is the situation that
produces it? The child is in an asymmetrical situation where anything he says can literally be held against him. He has learned a
number of devices to avoid saying anything in this situation, and
he works very hard to achieve this end. One may observe the intonation patterns of

$$_2a\ ^{3}o'\ _2know$$

and

$$a\ ^2space\ ^2sh\ ^{3}ip$$

which black children often use when they are asked a question to which the answer is obvious. The answer may be read as: "Will this satisfy you?"

If one takes this interview as a measure of the verbal capacity of the child, it must be as his capacity to defend himself in a hostile and threatening situation. But unfortunately, thousands of such interviews are used as evidence of the child's total verbal capacity, or more simply his verbality. It is argued that this lack of verbality explains his poor performance in school. Operation Head Start and other intervention programs have largely been based upon the deficit theory—the notions that such interviews give us a measure of the child's verbal capacity and that the verbal stimulation which he has been missing can be supplied in a preschool environment.

The verbal behavior which is shown by the child in the situation quoted above is not the result of the ineptness of the interviewer. It is rather the result of regular sociolinguistic factors operating upon adult and child in this asymmetrical situation. In our work in urban ghetto areas, we have often encountered such behavior. Ordinarily we worked with boys 10 to 17 years old, and whenever we extended our approach downward to eight- or nine-year-olds, we began to see the need for different techniques to explore the verbal capacity of the child. At one point we began a series of interviews with younger brothers of the Thunderbirds. Clarence Robins interviewed eight-year-old Leon L., who showed the following minimal response to topics which arouse intense interest in other interviews with older boys.

> CR: What if you saw somebody kickin' somebody else on the ground, or was using a stick, what would you do if you saw that?
> Leon: Mmmm.
> CR: If it was supposed to be a fair fight—
> Leon: I don' know.
> CR: You don' know? Would you do anything? . . . huh? I can't hear you.
> Leon: No.
> CR: Did you ever see somebody got beat up real bad?
> Leon: . . . Nope . . .
> CR: Well—uh—did you ever get into a fight with a guy?
> Leon: Nope.
> CR: That was bigger than you?
> Leon: Nope . . .

> CR: You never been in a fight?
> Leon: Nope.
> CR: Nobody ever pick on you?
> Leon: Nope.
> CR: Nobody ever hit you?
> Leon: Nope.
> CR: How come?
> Leon: Ah 'o' know.
> CR: Didn't you ever hit somebody?
> Leon: Nope.
> CR: (incredulously) You never hit nobody?
> Leon: Mhm.
> CR: Aww, ba-a-a-be, you ain't gonna tell me that!

It may be that Leon is here defending himself against accusations of wrongdoing, since Clarence knows that Leon has been in fights, that he has been taking pencils away from little boys, and so on. But if we turn to a more neutral subject, we find the same pattern:

> CR: You watch—you like to watch television? . . . Hey, Leon . . . you like to watch television? (Leon nods) What's your favorite program?
> Leon: Uhhmmmm . . . I look at cartoons.
> CR: Well, what's your favorite one? What's your favorite program?
> Leon: Superman . . .
> CR: Yeah? Did you see Superman—ah—yesterday, or day before yesterday? When's the last time you saw Superman?
> Leon: Sa-aturday . . .
> CR: You rem—you saw it Saturday? What was the story all about? You remember the story?
> Leon: M-m.
> CR: You don't remember the story of what—that you saw of Superman?
> Leon: Nope.
> CR: You don't remember what happened, huh?
> Leon: Hm-m.
> CR: I see—ah—what other stories do you like to watch on TV?
> Leon: Mmmm? . . . umm . . . (glottalization)

> CR: Hmm? (four seconds)
> Leon: Hh?
> CR: What's th' other stories that you like to watch?
> Leon: Mi-ighty Mouse . . .
> CR: And what else?
> Leon: Ummmm . . . ahm . . .

This nonverbal behavior occurs in a relatively favorable context for adult-child interaction. The adult is a black man raised in Harlem, who knows this particular neighborhood and these boys very well. He is a skilled interviewer who has obtained a very high level of verbal response with techniques developed for a different age level, and he has an extraordinary advantage over most teachers or experimenters in these respects. But even his skills and personality are ineffective in breaking down the social constraints that prevail here.

When we reviewed the record of this interview with Leon, we decided to use it as a test of our own knowledge of the sociolinguistic factors which control speech. In the next interview with Leon we made the following changes in the social situation:

1. Clarence brought along a supply of potato chips, changing the interview into something more in the nature of a party.

2. He brought along Leon's best friend, eight-year-old Gregory.

3. We reduced the height imbalance by having Clarence get down on the floor of Leon's room; he dropped from six feet, two inches to three feet, six inches.

4. Clarence introduced taboo words and taboo topics, and proved, to Leon's surprise, that one can say anything into our microphone without any fear of retaliation. The result of these changes is a striking difference in the volume and style of speech. (The tape is punctuated throughout by the sound of potato chips.)

> CR: Is there anybody who says *your momma drink pee?*
> {Leon: (rapidly and breathlessly) Yee-ah!
> {Greg: Yup!\
> Leon: And *your father eat doo-doo for breakfas'!*
> CR: Ohhh! ! (laughs)
> Leon: And they say your father—*your father eat doo-doo for dinner!*
> Greg: When they sound on me, I say *C.B.S. C.B.M.*
> CR: What that mean?
> {Leon: Congo booger-snatch! (laughs)
> {Greg: Congo booger-snatcher! (laughs)

Greg: And sometimes I'll curse with *B.B.*

CR: What that?

Greg: Black boy! (Leon crunching on potato chips) Oh that's a *M.B.B.*

CR: *M.B.B.* What's that?

Greg: 'Merican Black Boy.

CR: Ohh . . .

Greg: Anyway, 'Mericans is same like white people, right?

Leon: And they talk about Allah.

CR: Oh yeah?

Greg: Yeah.

CR: What they say about Allah?

{ Leon: Allah—Allah is God.

{ Greg: Allah—

CR: And what else?

Leon: I don' know the res'.

Greg: Allah i—Allah is God, Allah is the only God, Allah . . .

Leon: Allah is the *son* of God.

Greg: But can he make magic?

Leon: Nope.

Greg: I know who can make magic.

CR: Who can?

Leon: The God, the *real* one.

CR: Who can make magic?

Greg: The son of po'—(CR: Hm?) I'm sayin' the po'k chop God![5] He only a po'k chop God! (Leon chuckles).

(The "nonverbal" Leon is now competing actively for the floor; Gregory and Leon talk to each other as much as they do to the interviewer.)

We can make a more direct comparison of the two interviews by examining the section on fighting. Leon persists in denying that he

---

5. The reference to the *pork chop God* condenses several concepts of black nationalism current in the Harlem community. A *pork chop* is a black who has not lost the traditional subservient ideology of the South, who has no knowledge of himself in Muslim terms, and the *pork chop God* would be the traditional God of Southern Baptists. He and His followers may be pork chops, but He still holds the power in Leon and Gregory's world.

fights, but he can no longer use monosyllabic answers, and Gregory cuts through his facade in a way that Clarence alone was unable to do.

> CR: Now, you said you had this fight now; but I wanted you to tell me about the fight that you had.
>
> Leon: I ain't had no fight.
>
> ⎰ Greg: Yes you did! He said Barry . . .
> ⎱ CR: You said you had one! you had a fight with Butchie,
>
> ⎰ Greg: An he say Garland! . . . an' Michael!
> ⎱ CR: an 'Barry . . .
>
> ⎰ Leon: I di'n'; you said that, Gregory!
> ⎱ Greg: You did!
>
> ⎰ Leon: You know you said that!
> ⎱ Greg: You said Garland, remember that?
>
> ⎰ Greg: You said Garland! Yes you did!
> ⎱ CR: You said Garland, that's right.
>
> Greg: He said Mich—an' I say Michael.
>
> ⎰ CR: Did you have a fight with Garland?
> ⎱ Leon: Uh-Uh.
>
> CR: You had one, and he beat you up, too!
>
> Greg: Yes he did!
>
> Leon: No, I di—I never had a fight with Butch! . . .

The same pattern can be seen on other local topics, where the interviewer brings neighborhood gossip to bear on Leon, and Gregory acts as a witness.

> CR: . . . Hey Gregory! I heard that around here . . . and I'm 'on' tell you who said it, too . . .
>
> Leon: Who?
>
> CR: about you . . .
>
> ⎰ Leon: Who?
> ⎱ Greg: I'd say it!
>
> CR: They said that—they say that the only person you play with is David Gilbert.
>
> ⎰ Leon: Yee-ah! yee-ah! yee-ah! . . .
> ⎱ Greg: That's who you play with!
>
> ⎰ Leon: I 'on' play with him no more!
> ⎱ Greg: Yes you do!
>
> Leon: I 'on' play with him no more!

> *Greg:* But remember, about me and Robbie?
> *Leon:* So that's not—
> *Greg:* and you went to Petey and Gilbert's house, 'member? *Ah haaah!!*
> *Leon:* So that's—so—but I would—I had came back out, an' I ain't go to his house no more . . . .

The observer must now draw a very different conclusion about the verbal capacity of Leon. The monosyllabic speaker who had nothing to say about anything and cannot remember what he did yesterday has disappeared. Instead, we have two boys who have so much to say they keep interrupting each other and who seem to have no difficulty in using the English language to express themselves. In turn we obtain the volume of speech and the rich array of grammatical devices which we need for analyzing the structure of black English vernacular; for example: negative concord ("I 'on' play with him no more"), the pluperfect ("had came back out"), negative perfect ("I ain't had"), the negative preterite ("I ain't go"), and so on.

We can now transfer this demonstration of the sociolinguistic control of speech to other test situations, including IQ and reading tests in school. It should be immediately apparent that none of the standard tests will come anywhere near measuring Leon's verbal capacity. On these tests he will show up as very much the monosyllabic, inept, ignorant, bumbling child of our first interview. The teacher has far less ability than Clarence Robins to elicit speech from this child. Clarence knows the community, the things that Leon has been doing, and the things that Leon would like to talk about. But the power relationships in a one-to-one confrontation between adult and child are too asymmetrical. This does not mean that some black children will not talk a great deal when alone with an adult, or that an adult cannot get close to any child. It means that the social situation is the most powerful determinant of verbal behavior and that an adult must enter into the right social relation with a child if he wants to find out what a child can do. This is just what many teachers cannot do.

The view of the black speech community which we obtain from our work in the ghetto areas is precisely the opposite from that reported by Deutsch or by Bereiter and Engelmann. We see a child bathed in verbal stimulation from morning to night. We see many speech events which depend upon the competitive exhibition of verbal skills—sounding, singing, toasts, rifting, louding—a whole range of activities in which the individual gains status through his use of language (chapters 8 and 9). We see the younger child trying to acquire these skills from older children, hanging around on the outskirts of older peer groups, and imitating this behavior to the best of his ability. We see no connection between verbal skill in the speech events characteristic of the street culture and success in the schoolroom.

Verbosity

There are undoubtedly many verbal skills which children from ghetto areas must learn in order to do well in the school situation, and some of these are indeed characteristic of middle-class verbal behavior. Precision in spelling, practice in handling abstract symbols, the ability to state explicitly the meaning of words, and a richer knowledge of the Latinate vocabulary, may all be useful acquisitions. But is it true that all of the middle-class verbal habits are functional and desirable in the school situation? Before we impose middle-class verbal style upon children from other cultural groups, we should find out how much of this is useful for the main work of analyzing and generalizing, and how much is merely stylistic—or even dysfunctional. In high school and college, middle-class children spontaneously complicate their syntax to the point that instructors despair of getting them to make their language simpler and clearer. In every learned journal one can find examples of jargon and empty elaboration, as well as complaints about it. Is the elaborated code of Bernstein really so "flexible, detailed and subtle" as some psychologists believe (e.g., Jensen 1969:119)? Isn't it also turgid, redundant, bombastic, and empty? Is it not simply an elaborated style, rather than a superior code or system?[6]

Our work in the speech community makes it painfully obvious that in many ways working-class speakers are more effective narrators, reasoners, and debaters than many middle-class speakers who

6. The term *code* is central in Bernstein's (1966) description of the differences between working-class and middle-class styles of speech. The restrictions and elaborations of speech observed are labeled as codes to indicate the principles governing selection from the range of possible English sentences. No rules or detailed description of the operation of such codes are provided as yet, so that this central concept remains to be specified.

temporize, qualify, and lose their argument in a mass of irrelevant detail. Many academic writers try to rid themselves of that part of middle-class style that is empty pretension and keep that part that is needed for precision. But the average middle-class speaker that we encounter makes no such effort; he is enmeshed in verbiage, the victim of sociolinguistic factors beyond his control.

I will not attempt to support this argument here with systematic quantitative evidence, although it is possible to develop measures which show how far middle-class speakers can wander from the point. I would like to contrast two speakers dealing with roughly the same topic—matters of belief. The first is Larry H., a fifteen-year-old core member of the Jets, being interviewed by John Lewis. Larry is one of the loudest and roughest members of the Jets, one who gives the least recognition to the conventional rules of politeness.[7] For most readers of this book, first contact with Larry would produce some fairly negative reactions on both sides. It is probable that you would not like him any more than his teachers do. Larry causes trouble in and out of school. He was put back from the eleventh grade to the ninth, and has been threatened with further action by the school authorities.

> *JL:* What happens to you after you die? Do you know?
> *Larry:* Yeah, I know. (What?) After they put you in the ground, your body turns into—ah—bones, an' shit.
> *JL:* What happens to your spirit?
> *Larry:* Your spirit—soon as you die, your spirit leaves you. (And where does the spirit go?) Well, it all depends . . . (On what?) You know, like some people say if you're good an' shit, your spirit goin' t'heaven . . . 'n' if you bad, your spirit goin' to hell. Well, bullshit! Your spirit goin' to hell anyway, good or bad.
> *JL:* Why?
> *Larry:* Why? I'll tell you why. 'Cause, you see, doesn' nobody really know that it's a God, y'know, 'cause I mean I have seen black gods, pink gods, white gods,

7. A direct view of Larry's verbal style in a hostile encounter is given in CRR 3288 Vol. 2:39–43. Gray's Oral Reading Test was being given to a group of Jets on the steps of a brownstone house in Harlem, and the landlord tried unsuccessfully to make the Jets move. Larry's verbal style in this encounter matches the reports he gives of himself in a number of narratives cited in section 4.8 of the report.

all color gods, and don't nobody know it's really a God.
An' when they be sayin' if you good, you goin' t'heaven,
tha's bullshit, 'cause you ain't goin' to no heaven, 'cause
it ain't no heaven for you to go to.

Larry is a paradigmatic speaker of black English vernacular as
opposed to standard English. His grammar shows a high concentration of such characteristic BEV forms as negative inversion ("don't
nobody know"), negative concord ("you ain't goin' to no heaven"),
invariant *be* ("when they be sayin'"), dummy *it* for standard *there*
("it ain't no heaven"), optional copula deletion ("if you're good . . .
if you bad") and full forms of auxiliaries ("I have seen"). The only
standard English influence in this passage is the one case of "doesn't"
instead of the invariant "don't" of BEV. Larry also provides a paradigmatic example of the rhetorical style of BEV: he can sum up a
complex argument in a few words, and the full force of his opinions comes through without qualification or reservation. He is
eminently quotable, and his interviews give us many concise statements of the BEV point of view. One can almost say that Larry speaks
the BEV culture (see CRR 3288, vol. 2: 38, 71–73, 291–92).

It is the logical form of this passage which is of particular interest
here. Larry presents a complex set of interdependent propositions
which can be explicated by setting out the standard English equivalents in linear order. The basic argument is to deny the twin propositions:

(A) If you are good, (B) then your spirit will go to
    heaven.
(~A) If you are bad, (C) then your spirit will go to hell.

Larry denies *B* and asserts that if *A* or ~ *A*, then *C*. His argument
may be outlined as follows:

1. Everyone has a different idea of what God is like.
2. Therefore nobody really knows that God exists.
3. If there is a heaven, it was made by God.
4. If God doesn't exist, he couldn't have made heaven.
5. Therefore heaven does not exist.
6. You can't go somewhere that doesn't exist.
(~B) Therefore you can't go to heaven.
(C) Therefore you are going to hell.

The argument is presented in the order: C, because 2 because 1, therefore 2, therefore ~B because 5 and 6. Part of the argument is implicit: the connection 2 therefore ~B leaves unstated the connecting links 3 and 4, and in this interval Larry strengthens the propositions from the form 2 "Nobody knows if there is . . ." to 5 "There is no . . . ." Otherwise, the case is presented explicitly as well as economically. The complex argument is summed up in Larry's last sentence, which shows formally the dependence of ~B on 5 and 6:

> An' when they be sayin' if you good, you goin' t'heaven,
> (The proposition if A, then B)
> tha's bullshit, (is absurd)
> 'cause you ain't goin' to no heaven (because B)
> 'cause it ain't no heaven for you to go to (because 5 and 6).

This hypothetical argument is not carried on at a high level of seriousness. It is a game played with ideas as counters, in which opponents use a wide variety of verbal devices to win. There is no personal commitment to any of these propositions, and no reluctance to strengthen one's argument by bending the rules of logic as in the 2-5 sequence. But if the opponent invokes the rules of logic, they hold. In John Lewis's interviews, he often makes this move, and the force of his argument is always acknowledged and countered within the rules of logic. In this case, he pointed out the fallacy that the argument 2-3-4-5-6 leads to ~C as well as ~B, so it cannot be used to support Larry's assertion C:

> JL: Well, if there's no heaven, how could there be a hell?
> Larry: I mean—ye-eah. Well, let me tell you, it ain't no hell, 'cause this is hell right here, y'know! (This is hell?) Yeah, this is hell right here!

Larry's answer is quick, ingenious, and decisive. The application of the 3-4-5 argument to hell is denied, since hell is here, and therefore conclusion C stands. These are not ready-made or preconceived opinions, but new propositions devised to win the logical argument in the game being played. The reader will note the speed and precision of Larry's mental operations. He does not wander, or insert meaningless verbiage. The only repetition is 2, placed before and after 1 in his original statement. It is often said that the nonstandard vernacular is not suited for dealing with abstract or hypothetical questions, but in fact speakers from the BEV community take great delight in exercising their wit and logic on the most improbable and problematical matters. Despite the fact that Larry does not believe in God and has just denied all knowledge of him, John Lewis advances the following hypothetical question:

> JL: . . . but, just say that there is a God, what color is he? White or black?
>
> Larry: Well, if it is a God . . . I wouldn' know what color, I couldn' say,—couldn' nobody say what color he is or really *would* be.
>
> JL: But now, jus' suppose there was a God—
>
> Larry: Unless'n they say . . .
>
> JL: No, I was jus' sayin' jus' suppose there is a God, would he be white or black?
>
> Larry: . . . He'd be white, man.
>
> JL: Why?
>
> Larry: Why? I'll tell you why. 'Cause the average whitey out here got everything, you dig? And the nigger ain't got shit, y'know? Y'unnerstan'? So—um—for—in order for *that* to happen, you know it ain't no black God that's doin' that bullshit.

No one can hear Larry's answer to this question without being convinced that they are in the presence of a skilled speaker with great "verbal presence of mind," who can use the English language expertly for many purposes. Larry's answer to John Lewis is again a complex argument. The formulation is not standard English, but it is clear and effective even for those not familiar with the vernacular. The nearest standard English equivalent might be: "So you know that God isn't black, because if he were, he wouldn't have arranged things like that."

The reader will have noted that this analysis is being carried out in standard English, and the inevitable challenge is: why not write in BEV, then, or in your own nonstandard dialect? The fundamental reason is, of course, one of firmly fixed social conventions. All communities agree that standard English is the proper medium for formal writing and public communication. Furthermore, it seems likely that standard English has an advantage over BEV in explicit analysis of surface forms, which is what we are doing here. We will return to this opposition between explicitness and logical statement in subsequent sections on grammaticality and logic. First, however, it will be helpful to examine standard English in its primary natural setting, as the medium for informal spoken communication of middle-class speakers.

Let us now turn to the second speaker, an upper-middle-class, college-educated black adult (Charles M.) being interviewed by Clarence Robins in our survey of adults in central Harlem.

> CR: Do you know of anything that someone can do, to have someone who has passed on visit him in a dream?
> Charles: Well, I even heard my parents say that there is such a thing as something in dreams, some things like that, and sometimes dreams do come true. I have personally never had a dream come true. I've never dreamt that somebody was dying and they actually died, (Mhm) or that I was going to have ten dollars the next day and somehow I got ten dollars in my pocket. (Mhm). I don't particularly believe in that, I don't think it's true. I do feel, though, that there is such a thing as—ah—witchcraft. I do feel that in certain cultures there is such a thing as witchcraft, or some sort of *science* of witchcraft; I don't think that it's just a matter of believing hard enough that there is such a thing as witchcraft. I do believe that there is such a thing that a person can put himself in a state of *mind* (Mhm), or that—er—something could be given them to intoxicate them in a certain—to a certain frame of mind—that—that could actually be considered witchcraft.

Charles M. is obviously a good speaker who strikes the listener as well-educated, intelligent, and sincere. He is a likeable and attractive person, the kind of person that middle-class listeners rate very high on a scale of job suitability and equally high as a potential friend.[8] His language is more moderate and tempered than Larry's; he makes every effort to qualify his opinions and seems anxious to avoid any misstatements or overstatements. From these qualities

---

8. For a description of subjective reaction tests which utilize these evaluative dimensions see CRR 3288:4.6.

emerge the primary characteristic of this passage—its verbosity. Words multiply, some modifying and qualifying, others repeating or padding the main argument. The first half of this extract is a response to the initial question on dreams, basically:

1. Some people say that dreams sometimes come true.
2. I have never had a dream come true.
3. Therefore I don't believe 1.

Some characteristic filler phrases appear here: *such a thing as, some things like that,* and *particularly.* Two examples of dreams given after 2 are afterthoughts that might have been given after 1. Proposition 3 is stated twice for no obvious reason. Nevertheless, this much of Charles M.'s response is well-directed to the point of the question. He then volunteers a statement of his beliefs about witchcraft which shows the difficulty of middle-class speakers who (a) want to express a belief in something but (b) want to show themselves as judicious, rational, and free from superstitions. The basic proposition can be stated simply in five words: *But I believe in witchcraft.* However, the idea is enlarged to exactly 100 words and it is difficult to see what else is being said. In the following quotations, padding which can be removed without change in meaning is shown in parentheses.

1. "I (do) feel, though, that there is (such a thing as) witchcraft." *Feel* seems to be a euphemism for 'believe'.
2. "(I do feel that) in certain cultures (there is such a thing as witchcraft)." This repetition seems designed only to introduce the word *culture,* which lets us know that the speaker knows about anthropology. Does *certain cultures* mean 'not in ours' or 'not in all'?
3. "(or some sort of *science* of witchcraft.)" This addition seems to have no clear meaning at all. What is a "science" of witchcraft as opposed to just plain witchcraft?[9] The main function is to introduce the word *science,* though it seems to have no connection to what follows.
4. "I don't think that it's just (a matter of) believing hard enough that (there is such a thing as) witchcraft." The speaker argues that witchcraft is not merely a belief; there is more to it.

9. Several middle-class readers of this passage have suggested that *science* here refers to some form of control as opposed to belief. The science of witchcraft would then be a kind of engineering of mental states. Other interpretations can of course be provided. The fact remains that no such difficulties of interpretation are needed to understand Larry's remarks.

5. "I (do) believe that (there is such a thing that) a person can put himself in a state of mind . . . that (could actually be considered) witchcraft." Is witchcraft as a state of mind different from the state of belief, denied in 4?
6. "or that something could be given them to intoxicate them (to a certain frame of mind) . . ." The third learned word, *intoxicate*, is introduced by this addition. The vacuity of this passage becomes more evident if we remove repetitions, fashionable words and stylistic decorations:

> But I believe in witchcraft.
> I don't think witchcraft is just a belief.

> A person can put himself or be put in a state of mind that is witchcraft.

Without the extra verbiage and the "OK" words like *science, culture,* and *intoxicate,* Charles M. appears as something less than a first-rate thinker. The initial impression of him as a good speaker is simply our long-conditioned reaction to middle-class verbosity. We know that people who use these stylistic devices are educated people, and we are inclined to credit them with saying something intelligent. Our reactions are accurate in one sense. Charles M. is more educated than Larry. But is he more rational, more logical, more intelligent? Is he any better at thinking out a problem to its solution? Does he deal more easily with abstractions? There is no reason to think so. Charles M. succeeds in letting us know that he is educated, but in the end we do not know what he is trying to say, and neither does he.

In the previous section I have attempted to explain the origin of the myth that lower-class black children are nonverbal. The examples just given may help to account for the corresponding myth that middle-class language is in itself better suited for dealing with abstract, logically complex, or hypothetical questions. These examples are intended to have a certain negative force. They are not controlled experiments. On the contrary, this and the preceding section are designed to convince the reader that the controlled experiments that have been offered in evidence are misleading. The only thing that is controlled is the superficial form of the stimulus. All children are asked "What do you think of capital punishment?" or "Tell me everything you can about this." But the speaker's interpretation of these requests and the action he believes is appropriate in response is completely uncontrolled. One can view these test stimuli as requests for information, commands for action, threats of punishment, or meaningless sequences of words. They are probably intended as something altogether different—as requests for display,[10] but in any case the experimenter is normally unaware of the problem of interpretation. The methods of educational psychologists used by Deutsch, Jensen, and Bereiter follow the pattern designed for animal experiments where motivation is controlled by simple methods as withholding food until a certain weight reduction is reached. With human subjects, it is absurd to believe that identical stimuli are obtained by asking everyone the same question.

Since the crucial intervening variables of interpretation and motivation are uncontrolled, most of the literature on verbal deprivation tells us nothing about the capacities of children. They are only the trappings of science, approaches that substitute the formal procedures of the scientific method for the activity itself. With our present limited grasp of these problems, the best we can do to understand the verbal capacities of children is to study them within the cultural context in which they were developed.

It is not only the black English vernacular which should be studied in this way, but also the language of middle-class children. The explicitness and precision which we hope to gain from copying middle-class forms are often the product of the test situation, and limited to it. For example, it was stated in the first part of this paper that working-class children hear more well-formed sentences than middle-class children. This statement may seem extraordinary in the light of the current belief of many linguists that most people do not speak in well-formed sentences, and that their actual speech production, or performance, is ungrammatical.[11] But those who have

---

10. The concept of a request for verbal display is here drawn from a treatment of the therapeutic interview given by Alan Blum.

11. In several presentations, Chomsky has asserted that the great majority (95 percent) of the sentences which a child hears are ungrammatical. Chomsky (1965:58) presents this notion as one of the arguments in his general statement of the nativist position: "A consideration of the character of the grammar that is acquired, *the degenerate quality and narrowly limited extent of the available data* [my emphasis], the striking uniformity of the resulting grammars, and their independence of intelligence, motivation, and emotional state, over wide ranges of variation, leave little hope that much of the structure of the language can be learned . . ."

worked with any body of natural speech know that this is not the case. Our own studies (Labov 1966b) of the grammaticality of everyday speech show that the great majority of utterances in all contexts are complete sentences, and most of the rest can be reduced to grammatical form by a small set of editing rules. The proportions of grammatical sentences vary with class backgrounds and styles. The highest percentage of well-formed sentences are found in casual speech, and working-class speakers use more well-formed sentences than middle-class speakers. The widespread myth that most speech is ungrammatical is no doubt based upon tapes made at learned conferences, where we obtain the maximum number of irreducibly ungrammatical sequences.

It is true that technical and scientific books are written in a style which is markedly middle-class. But unfortunately, we often fail to achieve the explicitness and precision which we look for in such writing, and the speech of many middle-class people departs maximally from this target. All too often, standard English is represented by a style that is simultaneously overparticular and vague. The accumulating flow of words buries rather than strikes the target. It is this verbosity which is most easily taught and most easily learned, so that words take the place of thoughts, and nothing can be found behind them.

When Bernstein (e.g., 1966) describes his elaborated code in general terms, it emerges as a subtle and sophisticated mode of planning utterances, where the speaker is achieving structural variety, taking the other person's knowledge into account, and so on. But when it comes to describing the actual difference between middle-class and working-class speakers (Bernstein 1966), we are presented with a proliferation of *I think*, of the passive, of modals and auxiliaries, of the first-person pronoun, of uncommon words, and so on. But these are the bench marks of hemming and hawing, backing and filling, that are used by Charles M., the devices that so often obscure whatever positive contribution education can make to our use of language. When we have discovered how much of middle-class style is a matter of fashion and how much actually helps us express ideas clearly, we will have done ourselves a great service. We will then be in a position to say what standard grammatical rules must be taught to nonstandard speakers in the early grades.

Grammaticality

Let us now examine Bereiter's own data on the verbal behavior of the children he dealt with. The expressions *They mine* and *Me got juice* are cited as examples of a language which lacks the means for expressing logical relations, in this case characterized as "a series of badly connected words" (Bereiter, et al. 1966:113). In the case of *They mine*, it is apparent that Bereiter confuses the notions of logic and explicitness. We know that there are many languages of the world which do not have a present copula and which conjoin subject and predicate complement without a verb. Russian, Hungarian, and Arabic may be foreign, but they are not by that same token illogical. In the case of BEV we are not dealing with even this superficial grammatical difference, but rather with a low-level rule which carries contraction one step farther to delete single consonants representing the verbs *is, have* or *will* (see chapter 3). We have yet to find any children who do not sometimes use the full forms of *is* and *will*, even though they may frequently delete them. Our recent studies with black children four to seven years old indicate that they use the full form of the copula more often than preadolescents 10 to 12 years old or the adolescents 14 to 17 years old.[12]

Furthermore, the deletion of the *is* or *are* in BEV is not the result of erratic or illogical behavior; it follows the same regular rules as standard English contraction, as we showed in chapter 3. The appropriate use of the deletion rule, like the contraction rule, requires a deep and intimate knowledge of English grammar and phonology. Such knowledge is not available for conscious inspection by native speakers. The rules worked out for standard contraction in chapter 3 have never appeared in any grammar and are certainly not a part of the conscious knowledge of any standard English speakers. Nevertheless, the adult or child who uses these rules must have formed at some level of psychological organization, clear concepts of tense marker, verb phrase, rule ordering, sentence embedding, pronoun, and many other grammatical categories which are essential parts of any logical system.

12. This is from work on the grammars and comprehension of black children, four to eight years old, carried out by Prof. Jane Torrey of Connecticut College 1972 in extension of the research cited above in Labov, et al. (1968).

Bereiter's reaction to the sentence *Me got juice* is even more puzzling. If Bereiter believes that *Me got juice* is not a logical expression, it can only be that he interprets the use of the objective pronoun *me* as representing a difference in logical relationship to the verb— that the child is in fact saying 'the juice got him' rather than 'he got the juice'! If on the other hand, the child means 'I got juice' then this sentence shows only that he has not learned the formal rules for the use of the subjective form *I* and oblique form *me*. We have in fact encountered many children who do not have these formal rules in order at the ages of four, five, six, or even eight. It is extremely difficult to construct a minimal pair to show that the difference between *he* and *him* or *she* and *her* carries cognitive meaning. In almost every case, it is the context that tells us who is the agent and who is acted upon. We must then ask: What differences in cognitive, structural orientation are signalled by the fact that the child has not learned this formal rule? In the tests carried out by Jane Torrey it is evident that the children concerned do understand the difference in meaning between *she* and *her* when another person uses the forms; all that remains is that the children themselves do not use the two forms. Our knowledge of the cognitive correlates of grammatical differences is certainly in its infancy; for this is one of very many questions which we simply cannot answer. At the moment we do not know how to construct any kind of experiment which would lead to an answer; we do not even know what type of cognitive correlate we would be looking for.

Bereiter shows even more profound ignorance of the rules of discourse and of syntax when he rejects *In the tree* as an illogical or badly-formed answer to *Where is the squirrel?* Such elliptical answers are of course used by everyone; they show the appropriate deletion of subject and main verb, leaving the locative which is questioned by *WH + there.* The reply *In the tree* demonstrates that the listener has been attentive to and apprehended the syntax of the speaker.[13] Whatever formal structure we wish to write for expressions such as *Yes* or *Home* or *In the tree,* it is obvious that they cannot be interpreted without knowing the structure of the question which preceded them and that they presuppose an understanding of the syntax of the question. Thus if you ask me "Where is the squirrel?"

13. The attention to the speaker's syntax required of the listener is analyzed in detail in a series of unpublished lectures by Prof. Harvey Sacks, Department of Sociology, University of California–Irvine.

it is necessary for me to understand the processes of *WH*-attachment, *WH*-attraction to the front of the sentence, and flip-flop of auxiliary and subject to produce this sentence from an underlying form which would otherwise have produced *The squirrel is there.* If the child had answered *The tree,* or *Squirrel the tree,* or *The in tree,* we would then assume that he did not understand the syntax of the full form, *The squirrel is in the tree.* Given the data that Bereiter presents, we cannot conclude that the child has no grammar, but only that the investigator does not understand the rules of grammar. It does not necessarily do any harm to use the full form *The squirrel is in the tree,* if one wants to make fully explicit the rules of grammar which the child has internalized. Much of logical analysis consists of making explicit just that kind of internalized rule. But it is hard to believe that any good can come from a program which begins with so many misconceptions about the input data. Bereiter and Engelmann believe that in teaching the child to say *The squirrel is in the tree* or *This is a box* and *This is not a box* they are teaching him an entirely new language, whereas in fact they are only teaching him to produce slightly different forms of the language he already has.

Logic

For many generations, American school teachers have devoted themselves to correcting a small number of nonstandard English rules to their standard equivalents, under the impression that they were teaching logic. This view has been reinforced and given theoretical justification by the claim that BEV lacks the means for the expression of logical thought.

Let us consider for a moment the possibility that black children do not operate with the same logic that middle-class adults display. This would inevitably mean that sentences of a certain grammatical form would have different truth values for the two types of speakers. One of the most obvious places to look for such a difference is in the handling of the negative, and here we encounter one of the nonstandard items which has been stigmatized as illogical by schoolteachers—the double negative, or as we term it, *negative concord.* A child who says *He don't know nothing* is often said to be making an illogical statement without knowing it. According to the teacher, the child wants to say 'He knows nothing' but puts in an extra negative without realizing it, and so conveys the opposite meaning, 'He does not know nothing', which reduces to 'He knows something.' I need not emphasize that this is an absurd interpretation. If a nonstandard speaker wishes to say 'He does not know *nothing*', he does so by simply placing contrastive stress on both negatives as I have done here (He <u>don't</u> *know* <u>nothing</u>) indicating that they are derived from two underlying negatives in the deep structure. But note that the middle-class speaker does exactly the same thing when he wants to signal the existence of two underlying negatives: *He doesn't know nothing.* In the standard form with one underlying negative (He *doesn't know anything*), the indefinite *anything* contains the same superficial reference to a preceding negative in the surface structure as the nonstandard *nothing* does. In the corresponding positive sentences, the indefinite *something* is used. The dialect difference, like most of the differences between the standard and nonstandard forms, is one of surface form, and has nothing to do with the underlying logic of the sentence.

We can summarize the ways in which the two dialects differ:

	SE	BEV
Positive:	He knows something.	He know something.
Negative:	He doesn't know anything.	He don't know nothing.
Double Negative:	He *doesn't* know *nothing*.	He *don't* know *nothing*.

This array makes it plain that the only difference between the two dialects is in superficial form. When a single negative is found in the deep structure, standard English converts *something* to the indefinite *anything*, BEV converts it to *nothing*. When speakers want to signal the presence of two negatives, they do it in the same way. No one would have any difficulty constructing the same table of truth values for both dialects. English is a rare language in its insistence that the negative particle be incorporated in the first indefinite only. The Anglo-Saxon authors of the Peterborough Chronicle were surely not illogical when they wrote *For ne wæren nan martyrs swa pined alse he wæron,* literally, 'For never weren't no martyrs so tortured as these were'. The "logical" forms of current standard English are simply the accepted conventions of our present-day formal style. Russian, Spanish, French, and Hungarian show the same negative concord as nonstandard English, and they are surely not illogical in this. What is termed "logical" in standard English is of course the conventions which are habitual. The distribution of negative concord in English dialects developed in the last chapter can be summarized as follows:

1. In all dialects of English, the negative is attracted to a lone indefinite before the verb: *Nobody knows anything*, not **Anybody doesn't know anything*.

2. In some nonstandard white dialects, the negative also combines optionally with all other indefinites: *Nobody knows nothing, He never took none of them*.

3. In other white nonstandard dialects, the negative may also appear in preverbal position in the same clause: *Nobody doesn't know nothing*.

4. In black English vernacular, negative concord is obligatory to all indefinites within the clause, and it may even be added to preverbal position in following clauses: *Nobody didn't know he didn't* (meaning, 'Nobody knew he did').

Thus all dialects of English share a categorical rule which attracts the negative to an indefinite subject, and they merely differ in the extent to which the negative particle is also distributed to other indefinites in preverbal position. It would have been impossible for us to arrive at this analysis if we did not know that black speakers are using the same underlying logic as everyone else.

Negative concord is more firmly established in black English vernacular than in other nonstandard dialects. The white nonstandard speaker shows variation in this rule, saying one time *Nobody ever goes there* and the next *Nobody never goes there*. Core speakers of BEV consistently use the latter form. In repetition tests which we conducted with black adolescent boys (CRR 3288: section 3.9), standard forms were repeated with negative concord. Consider again three trials by two 13-year-olds, Boot and David, Thunderbirds:

> *Model by interviewer:* Nobody ever sat at any of those desks, anyhow.
>
> *Boot:*
>   1. Nobody never sa—No [whitey] never sat at any o' tho' dess, anyhow.
>   2. Nobody never sat any any o' tho' dess, anyhow.
>   3. Nobody as ever sat at no desses, anyhow.
> *David:*
>   1. Nobody ever sat in-in-in-in- none o'—say it again?
>   2. Nobody never sat in none o' tho' desses anyhow.
>   3. Nobody—aww! Nobody never ex—Dawg!

It can certainly be said that Boot and David fail the test; they have not repeated the sentence back correctly—that is, word for word. But have they failed because they could not grasp the meaning of the sentence? The situation is in fact just the opposite: they failed because they perceived only the meaning and not the superficial form. Boot and David are typical of many speakers who do not perceive the surface details of the utterance so much as the underlying semantic structure, which they unhesitatingly translate into the vernacular form. Thus they have the asymmetrical system we saw in chapter 2 in responses to embedded questions.

> *Model:* I asked Alvin if he knows how to play basketball.
> *Boot:* I ax Alvin do he know how to play basketball.
> *Money:* I ax Alvin if—do he know how to play basketball.

Here the difference between the words used in the model sentence and in the repetition is striking. Again, there is a failure to pass the test. But it is also true that these boys understand the standard sentence, and translate it with extraordinary speed into the BEV form—which is here the regular southern colloquial form. This form retains the inverted order to signal the underlying meaning of the question, instead of the complementizer *if* or *whether* which standard English uses for this purpose. Thus Boot and Money perceive the deep structure of the model sentence in the diagram below.

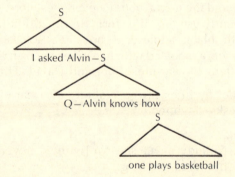

The complementizers *if* or *whether* are not required to express this underlying meaning; they are merely two of the formal options which one dialect selects to signal the embedded question. The colloquial southern form utilizes a different device—preserving the order of the direct question. To say that this dialect lacks the means for logical expression is to confuse logic with surface detail.

To pass the repetition test, Boot and the others have to learn to listen to surface detail. They do not need a new logic; they need practice in paying attention to the explicit form of an utterance rather than its meaning. Careful attention to surface features is a temporary skill needed for language learning—and neglected thereafter by competent speakers. Nothing more than this is involved in the language training in the Bereiter and Engelmann program, or in most methods of "teaching English." There is of course nothing wrong with learning to be explicit—as we have seen, that is one of the main advantages of standard English at its best—but it is important that we recognize what is actually taking place, and what teachers are in fact trying to do.

I doubt if we can teach people to be logical, though we can teach them to recognize the logic that they use. Piaget has shown us that in middle-class children logic develops much more slowly than grammar, and that we cannot expect four-year-olds to have mastered the conservation of quantity, let alone syllogistic reasoning. The problems working-class children may have in handling logical operations are not to be blamed on the structure of their language. There is nothing in the vernacular which will interfere with the development of logical thought, for the logic of standard English cannot be distinguished from the logic of any other dialect of English by any test that we can find.

What's Wrong with Being Wrong?

If there is a failure of logic involved here, it is surely in the approach of the verbal deprivation theorists, rather than in the mental abilities of the children concerned. We can isolate six distinct steps in the reasoning which has led to positions such as those of Deutsch or Bereiter and Engelmann:

1. The lower-class child's verbal response to a formal and threatening situation is used to demonstrate his lack of verbal capacity, or verbal deficit.

2. This verbal deficit is declared to be a major cause of the lower-class child's poor performance in school.

3. Since middle-class children do better in school, middle-class speech habits are seen to be necessary for learning.

4. Class and ethnic differences in grammatical form are equated with differences in the capacity for logical analysis.

5. Teaching the child to mimic certain formal speech patterns used by middle-class teachers is seen as teaching him to think logically.

6. Children who learn these formal speech patterns are then said to be thinking logically and it is predicted that they will do much better in reading and arithmetic in the years to follow.

In the preceding sections of this paper I have tried to show that the above propositions are wrong, concentrating on 1, 4, and 5. Proposition 3 is the primary logical fallacy which illicitly identifies a form of speech as the cause of middle-class achievement in school. Proposition 6 is the one which is most easily shown to be wrong in fact, as we will note below.

However, it is not too naive to ask: What is wrong with being wrong? There is no competing educational theory which is being dismantled by this program, and there does not seem to be any great harm in having children repeat "This is not a box" for twenty minutes a day. We have already conceded that BEV children need help in analyzing language into its surface components and in being more explicit. But there are serious and damaging consequences of the verbal deprivation theory which may be considered under two headings: theoretical bias and consequences of failure.

Theoretical Bias

It is widely recognized that the teacher's attitude toward the child is an important factor in his success or failure. The work of Rosenthal and Jacobson (1968) on self-fulfilling prophecies shows that the progress of children in the early grades can be dramatically affected by a single random labeling of certain children as "intellectual bloomers." When the everyday language of black children is stigmatized as "not a language at all" and "not possessing the means for logical thought," the effect of such a labeling is repeated many times during each day of the school year. Every time that a child uses a form of BEV without the copula or with negative concord, he will be labeling himself for the teacher's benefit as "illogical," as a "non-conceptual thinker." Bereiter and Engelmann, Deutsch, and Jensen are giving teachers a ready-made, theoretical basis for the prejudice they already feel against the lower-class black child and his language (for example, see Williams 1970). When teachers hear him say *I don't want none* or *They mine*, they will be hearing through the bias provided by the verbal deprivation theory—not an English dialect different from theirs, but the "primitive mentality of the savage mind."

But what if the teacher succeeds in training the child to use the new language consistently? The verbal deprivation theory holds that this will lead to a whole chain of successes in school and that the child will be drawn away from the vernacular culture into the middle-class world. Undoubtedly this will happen with a few isolated individuals, just as it happens for a few children in every school system today. But we are concerned not with the few but the many, and for the majority of black children the distance between them and the school is bound to widen under this approach.

Proponents of the deficit theory have a strange view of social organization outside of the classroom. They see the attraction of the peer group as a substitute for success and gratification normally provided by the school. For example, Whiteman and Deutsch (1968:86–87) introduce their account of the deprivation hypothesis with an eyewitness account of a child who accidentally dropped his school notebook into a puddle of water and walked away without picking it up: "A policeman who had been standing nearby walked over to the puddle and stared at the notebook with some degree of disbelief." The child's alienation from school is explained as the result of his coming to school without the "verbal, conceptual, attentional, and learning skills requisite to school success." The authors see the child as "suffering from feelings of inferiority because he is failing; he withdraws or becomes hostile, finding gratification elsewhere, such as in his peer group."

To view the peer group as a mere substitute for school shows an extraordinary lack of knowledge of adolescent culture. In our studies in south-central Harlem we have seen the reverse situation—the children who are rejected by the peer group are most likely to succeed in school. Although in middle-class suburban areas, many children do fail in school because of their personal deficiencies, in ghetto areas it is the healthy, vigorous, popular child with normal intelligence who cannot read and fails all along the line. It is not necessary to document here the influence of the peer group upon the behavior of youth in our society, but we may note that somewhere between the time that children first learn to talk and puberty, their language is restructured to fit the rules used by their peer group. From a linguistic viewpoint, the peer group is certainly a more powerful influence than the family (e.g., Gans 1962). Less directly, the pressures of peer-group activity are also felt within the school. Many children, particularly those who are not doing well in school, show a sudden sharp downward turn in the fourth and fifth grades, and children in the ghetto schools are no exception. It is at the same age, at nine or ten years old, that the influence of the vernacular peer group becomes predominant (see Wilmott 1966). Instead of dealing with isolated individuals, the school is then dealing with children who are integrated into groups of their own, with rewards and value systems which oppose those of the school. Those who know the sociolinguistic situation cannot doubt that reaction against the Bereiter-Engelmann approach in later years will be even more violent on the part of the students involved, and their rejection of the school system will be even more categorical.

The essential fallacy of the verbal deprivation theory lies in tracing the educational failure of the child to his personal deficiencies. At present, these deficiencies are said to be caused by his home environment. It is traditional to explain a child's failure in school by his inadequacy. But when failure reaches such massive proportions, it seems to us necessary to look at the social and cultural obstacles to learning and the inability of the school to adjust to the social situation. Operation Head Start is designed to repair the child, rather than the school; to the extent that it is based upon this inverted logic, it is bound to fail.

Consequences of Failure

The second area in which the verbal deprivation theory is doing serious harm to our educational system is in the consequences of this failure and the reaction to it. As failures are reported of Operation Head Start, the interpretations which we receive will be from the same educational psychologists who designed this program. The fault will be found not in the data, the theory, nor in the methods used, but rather in the children who have failed to respond to the opportunities offered to them. When black children fail to show the significant advance which the deprivation theory predicts, it will be taken as further proof of the profound gulf which separates their mental processes from those of "civilized," middle-class mankind.

A sense of the "failure" of Head Start is already in the air. Some prominent figures in the program have reacted to this situation by saying that intervention did not take place early enough. Caldwell (1967:16) notes that:

... the research literature of the last decade dealing with social-class differences has made abundantly clear that all parents are not qualified to provide even the basic essentials of physical and psychological care to their children.

The deficit theory now begins to focus on the "long-standing patterns of parental deficit" which fill the literature. "There is, perhaps unfortunately," writes Caldwell (1967:17), "no literacy test for motherhood." Failing such eugenic measures, she has proposed "educationally oriented day care for culturally deprived children between six months and three years of age." The children are returned home each evening to "maintain primary emotional relationships with their own families," but during the day they are removed to "hopefully prevent the deceleration in rate of development which seems to occur in many deprived children around the age of two to three years."

There are others who feel that even the best of the intervention programs, such as those of Bereiter and Engelmann, will not help the black child no matter when such programs are applied—that we are faced once again with the "inevitable hypothesis" of the genetic inferiority of the black people. Many readers of this chapter may be familiar with the paper of Arthur Jensen in the *Harvard Educational Review* (1969), which received immediate and widespread publicity. Jensen (p. 3) begins with the following quotation from the United States Commission on Civil Rights as evidence of the failure of compensatory education:

The fact remains, however, that none of the programs appear to have raised significantly the achievement of participating pupils, as a group, within the period evaluated by the Commission (U.S. Commission on Civil Rights 1967, p. 138).

Jensen believes that the verbal-deprivation theorists with whom he had been associated—Deutsch, Whiteman, Katz, Bereiter—have been given every opportunity to prove their case, and have failed. This opinion is part of the argument which leads him to the overall conclusion (p. 82) that "the preponderance of the evidence is . . . less consistent with a strictly environmental hypothesis than with the genetic hypothesis." In other words, racism—the belief in the genetic inferiority of blacks—is the most correct view in the light of the present evidence.

Jensen argues that the middle-class white population is differentiated from the working-class white and black population in the ability for "cognitive or conceptual learning," which Jensen calls Level II intelligence as against mere "associative learning" or Level I intelligence:

. . . certain neural structures must also be available for Level II abilities to develop, and these are conceived of as being different from the neural structures underlying Level I. The genetic factors involved in each of these types of ability are presumed to have become differentially distributed in the population as a function of social class, since Level II has been most important for scholastic performance under the traditional methods of instruction. (Jensen 1969:114)

Jensen found, for example, that one group of middle-class children were helped by their concept-forming ability to recall 20 familiar objects that could be classified into four categories: animals, furniture, clothing, or foods. Lower-class black children did just as well as middle-class children with a miscellaneous set, but showed no improvement with objects that could be so categorized.

The research of the educational psychologists cited here is presented by them in formal and objective style and is widely received as impartial scientific evidence. Jensen's paper has been reported by Joseph Alsop and William F. Buckley, Jr. (*New York Post*, March 20, 1969) as "massive, apparently authoritative . . ." It is not my intention to examine these materials in detail, but it is important to realize that we are dealing with special pleading by those who have a strong personal commitment. Jensen is concerned with class differences in cognitive style and verbal learning. His earlier papers incorporated the cultural deprivation theory which he now rejects as a basic explanation.[14] Jensen (1968:167) classified the black children who fail in school as "slow learners" and "mentally retarded" and urged that we find out how much their retardation is due to environmental factors and how much is due to "more basic biological factors." His conviction that the problem must be located in the child leads him

---

14. In Deutsch et al. (1968), Jensen expounds the verbal deprivation theory in considerable detail, for example (p. 119): "During this 'labeling' period . . . some very important social-class differences may exert their effects on verbal learning. Lower-class parents engage in relatively little of this naming or 'labeling' play with their children . . . That words are discrete labels for things seems to be better known by the middle-class child entering first grade than by the lower-class child. Much of this knowledge is gained in the parent-child interaction, as when the parent looks at a picture book with the child . . ."

to accept and reprint some truly extraordinary data. To support the genetic hypothesis Jensen (1969:83) cites the following percentage estimates by Heber (1968) of the racial distribution of mental retardation (based upon IQs below 75) in the general population:[15]

Socioeconomic status	Percent of whites	Percent of blacks
1 (highest)	0.5	3.1
2	0.8	14.5
3	2.1	22.8
4	3.1	37.8
5 (lowest)	7.8	42.9

These estimates, that almost half of lower-class black children are mentally retarded, could be accepted only by someone who has no knowledge of the children or the community. If he had wished to, Jensen could easily have checked this against the records of any school in any urban ghetto area. Taking IQ tests at their face value, there is no correspondence between these figures and the communities we know. For example, among 75 boys we worked with in central Harlem who would fall into status categories 4 or 5 above, there were only three with IQs below 75. One spoke very little English; one could barely see; the third was emotionally disturbed. When the second was retested, he scored 91, and the third retested at 87.[16] There are of course hundreds of realistic reports available to Jensen. He simply selected one which would strengthen his case for the genetic inferiority of black children.

The frequent use of tables and statistics by educational psychologists serves to give outside readers the impression that this field is a science and that the opinions of the authors should be given the same attention and respect that we give to the conclusions of physi-

15. Heber's (esp. 1968) studies of 88 black mothers in Milwaukee are cited frequently throughout Jensen's paper. The estimates in this table are not given in relation to a particular Milwaukee sample, but for the general United States population. Heber's study was specifically designed to cover an area of Milwaukee which was known to contain a large concentration of retarded children, black and white, and he has stated that his findings were "grossly misinterpreted" by Jensen (*Milwaukee Sentinel,* June 11, 1969).

16. The IQ scores given here are from group rather than individual tests and must therefore not be weighed heavily; the scores are from the Pintner-Cunningham test, usually given the first grade in New York City schools in the 1950's.

cists or chemists. But careful examination of the input data will often show that there is no direct relationship between the conclusions and the evidence (in Jensen's case between I.Q. Tests in a specially selected district of Milwaukee and intelligence of lower-class black children). Furthermore, the operations performed upon the data frequently carry us very far from the common-sense experience which is our only safeguard against conclusions heavily weighted by the author's theory. As another example, we may take some of the evidence presented by Whiteman and Deutsch for the cultural deprivation hypothesis. The core of Deutsch's environmental explanation of poor performance in school is the Deprivation Index, a numerical scale based on six dichotomized variables. One variable is "the educational aspirational level of the parent for the child." Most people would agree that a parent who did not care if a child finished high-school would be a disadvantageous factor in the child's educational career. In dichotomizing this variable Deutsch was faced with the fact that the educational aspiration of black parents is in fact very high, higher than for the white population, as he shows in other papers.[17] In order to fit this data into the Deprivation Index work, he therefore set the cutting point for the deprived group as "college or less." (see Whiteman and Deutsch 1968:100). Thus if a black child's father says that he wants his son to go all the way through college, the child will fall into the "deprived" class on this variable. In order to receive the two points given to the "less deprived" on the index, it would be necessary for the child's parent to insist on graduate school or medical school! This decision is not discussed by the author; it simply stands as a *fait accompli* in the tables. Readers of this literature who are not committed to one point

17. In Table 15.1 in Deutsch and associates (1967:312), section C shows that some degree of college training was desired by 96, 97 and 100 percent of black parents in class levels I, II, and III, respectively. The corresponding figures for whites were 79, 95, and 97 percent. In an earlier version of this chapter, this discussion could be interpreted as implying that Whiteman and Deutsch had used data in the same way as Jensen: to rate the black group as low as possible. As they point out (pers. comm.), the inclusion of this item in the Deprivation Index had the opposite effect, and it could easily have been omitted if that had been their intention. They also argue that they had sound statistical grounds for dichotomizing as they did. The criticism which I intended to make is that there is something drastically wrong with operations which produce definitions of deprivation such as the one cited here. It should of course be noted that Whiteman and Deutsch have strongly opposed Jensen's genetic hypothesis and vigorously criticized his logic and data.

of view would be wise to look as carefully as possible at the original data which lies behind each statement and check the conclusions against their own knowledge of the people and community being described.

No one can doubt that the reported inadequacy of Operation Head Start and of the verbal deprivation hypothesis has now become a crucial issue in our society.[18] The controversy which arose over Jensen's article typically assumed that programs such as Bereiter and Engelmann's have tested and measured the verbal capacity of the ghetto child. The cultural sociolinguistic obstacles to this intervention program are not considered, and the argument proceeds upon the data provided by the large, friendly interviewers whom we have seen at work in the extracts given above.

The Linguistic View

Linguists are in an excellent position to demonstrate the fallacies of the verbal deprivation theory. All linguists agree that nonstandard dialects are highly structured systems. They do not see these dialects as accumulations of errors caused by the failure of their speakers to master standard English. When linguists hear black children saying *He crazy* or *Her my friend,* they do not hear a primitive language. Nor do they believe that the speech of working-class people is merely a form of emotional expression, incapable of expressing logical thought.

All linguists who work with BEV recognize that it is a separate system, closely related to standard English but set apart from the surrounding white dialects by a number of persistent and systematic differences. Differences in analysis by various linguists in recent years are the inevitable products of differing theoretical approaches

18. The negative report of the Westinghouse Learning Corporation and Ohio University on Operation Head Start was published in the *New York Times* (April 13, 1969). The evidence of the failure of the program is accepted by many, and it seems likely that the report's discouraging conclusions will be used by conservative Congressmen as a weapon against any kind of expenditure for disadvantaged children, especially black children. The two hypotheses mentioned to account for this failure are that the impact of Head Start is lost through poor teaching later on, and more recently, that poor children have been so badly damaged in infancy by their lower-class environment that Head Start cannot make much difference. The third "inevitable" hypothesis of Jensen is not reported there.

and perspectives as we explore these dialect patterns by different routes—differences which are rapidly diminishing as we exchange our findings. For example, Stewart (1970) differs with me on how deeply the invariant *be* of *She be always messin' around* is integrated into the semantics of the copula system with *am, is, are,* and so on. The position and meaning of *have . . . ed* in BEV is very unclear, and there are a variety of positions on this point. But the grammatical features involved are not the fundamental predicators of the logical system. They are optional ways of contrasting, foregrounding, emphasizing, or deleting elements of the underlying sentence. There are a few semantic features of BEV grammar which may be unique to this system. But the semantic features we are talking about here are items such as "habitual," "general," "intensive." These linguistic markers are essentially *points of view*—different ways of looking at the same events, and they do not determine the truth values of propositions upon which all speakers of English agree.

The great majority of the differences between BEV and standard English do not even represent such subtle semantic features as those, but rather extensions and restrictions of certain formal rules and different choices of redundant elements. For example, standard English uses two signals to express the progressive, *be* and *-ing*, while BEV often drops the former. Standard English signals the third person in the present by the subject noun phrase and by a third singular *-s;* BEV does not have this second redundant feature. On the other hand, BEV uses redundant negative elements in negative concord, in possessives like *mines,* uses *or either* where standard English uses a simple *or,* and so on.

When linguists say that BEV is a system, we mean that it differs from other dialects in regular and rule-governed ways, so that it has equivalent ways of expressing the same logical content. When we say that it is a separate subsystem, we mean that there are compensating sets of rules which combine in different ways to preserve the distinctions found in other dialects. Thus as noted above BEV does not use the *if* or *whether* complementizer in embedded questions, but the meaning is preserved by the formal device of reversing the order of subject and auxiliary. Linguists therefore speak with a single voice in condemning Bereiter's view that the vernacular can be disregarded. The exact nature and relative importance of the structural differences between BEV and standard English are not in question here. It is agreed that the teacher must approach the teaching of the standard through a knowledge of the child's own system. The methods used in teaching English as a foreign language are recommended, not to declare that BEV is a foreign language, but to underline the importance of studying the native dialect as a coherent system for communication. This is in fact the method that should be applied in any English class.

Linguists are also in an excellent position to assess Jensen's claim that the middle-class white population is superior to the working-class and black populations in the distribution of Level II, or conceptual, intelligence. The notion that large numbers of children have no capacity for conceptual thinking would inevitably mean that they speak a primitive language, for even the simplest linguistic rules we discussed above involve conceptual operations more complex than those used in the experiment Jensen cites. Let us consider what is involved in the use of the general English rule that incorporates the negative with the first indefinite. To learn and use the rule we worked out in chapter 4, one must first identify the class of indefinites involved—*any, one, ever,* which are formally quite diverse. How is this done? These indefinites share a number of common properties which can be expressed as the concepts 'indefinite,' 'hypothetical,' and 'nonpartitive.' One might argue that these indefinites are learned as a simple list, by association learning. But this is only one of the many syntactic rules involving indefinites—rules known to every speaker of English, which could not be learned except by an understanding of their common, abstract properties.

What are we then to make of Jensen's contention that Level I thinkers cannot make use of the concept "animal" to group together a miscellaneous set of toy animals? It is one thing to say that someone is not in the habit of using a certain skill. But to say that his failure to use it is genetically determined implies dramatic consequences for other forms of behavior, which are not found in experience. The knowledge of what people must do in order to learn language makes Jensen's theories seem more and more distant from the realities of human behavior. Like Bereiter and Engelmann, Jensen is handicapped by his ignorance of the most basic facts about human language and the people who speak it.

There is no reason to believe that any nonstandard vernacular is in iself an obstacle to learning. The chief problem is ignorance of language on the part of all concerned. Our job as linguists is to remedy this ignorance; but Bereiter and Engelmann want to reinforce it and justify it. Teachers are now being told to ignore the language of black children as unworthy of attention and useless for learning. They are being taught to hear every natural utterance of the child as evidence of his mental inferiority. As linguists we are unanimous in condemning this view as bad observation, bad theory, and bad practice.

That educational psychology should be strongly influenced by a theory so false to the facts of language is unfortunate; but that children should be the victims of this ignorance is intolerable. It may seem that the fallacies of the verbal deprivation theory are so obvious that they are hardly worth exposing. I have tried to show that such exposure is an important job for us to undertake. If linguists can contribute some of their available knowledge and energy toward this end, we will have done a great deal to justify the support that society has given to basic research in our field.

6 | The Relation of Reading Failure to Peer-group Status

THE first four chapters of this book dealt with the structures of the black English vernacular—the rules which govern it, the relations between these rules, and the relation between them and those of other dialects.[1] We have been particularly concerned with the relation between BEV and the standard English of the classroom, because the conflict between these two dialects of English must be resolved to achieve the educational goals of our society. Both black and white sections of the community strongly endorse the proposition that schools should teach standard English to all children.

Just how and where the two dialects should alternate in the school situation is an open question for educators to resolve. The first part of our work is designed to give them the information they need to cope with, overcome, and perhaps utilize the structural differences between BEV and SE. Some writers seem to believe that the major problem causing reading failure is structural interference between these two forms of English. Our research points in the opposite direction. The structural differences between SE and BEV outlined in chapters 1–4 are largely modifications and extensions of rules found in other dialects. The number of structures unique to BEV are small, and it seems unlikely that they could be responsible for the disastrous record of reading failure in the inner city schools.

That failure is hard to overstate. In our first research in 1965, we interviewed 75 black youth, ages 10 to 12, in a geographically random sample of "Vacation Day Camps" in Harlem. Boys had to be enrolled

---

1. This chapter is a revised version of "A Note on the Relation of Reading Failure to Peer-Group Status in Urban Ghettos," by William Labov and Clarence Robins, which appeared in *The Teachers College Record* 70: No. 5 (Feb. 1969).

by their parents in these recreational programs, held in schoolyards and playgrounds, so that there was a bias of selection for children from intact families with support for educational goals. Nevertheless, we found that the majority of these 10–12 year olds had serious difficulty in reading aloud such second- and third-grade sentences as

> Now I read and write better than Alfred does.
> When I passed by, I read the sign.

At that time, we felt that the central problems behind reading failure were not being attacked by educators. There was a proliferation of educational programs designed to solve the problem, such as "Higher Horizons," but we came to believe that the reading situation would get worse instead of better. This proved to be the case. Year after year, the reports of reading achievement from the Board of Education showed poorer and poorer results for the inner city schools. Three years later, a report of average reading comprehension scores published in the *New York Times* on December 3, 1968, showed the following scores for the schools attended by the black youth we had come to know:

School	Grade	Reading score	National norm
J.H.S. 13	7	5.6	7.7
	9	7.6	9.7
J.H.S. 120	7	5.6	7.7
	9	7.0	9.7
I. S. 88	6	5.3	6.7
	8	7.2	8.7

The average is then more than two full years behind grade in the ninth grade. But as we will see, these reports do not show the worst side of the picture. They give results for each grade as a whole. But school grades are not homogeneous groups, even in the centers of the ghetto areas with 100 percent black and Puerto Rican youth. In any class there are a certain percentage of youth who are members of the vernacular culture, who hang out and participate fully in the social organization of the street. There are also a good percentage who are detached from that culture for a number of reasons. To understand the nature of reading failure, we must distinguish between the records of these two groups. Teachers and educational psychologists do not have the information to do this; they see the population of the classroom as a series of individuals differentiated by IQ, Iowa tests, and disciplinary records, and lack the insight into social organization which work outside institutional settings can give.

The conclusion from our research was that the major cause of reading failure is cultural and political conflict in the classroom. This chapter will give evidence for that finding, examining the relation between reading failure and peer-group status. The next chapter will show in greater detail how the relation of a given individual to the vernacular culture is reflected in the structure of his language.

After we completed our work with isolated black youth in 1965, we turned to our major concern: the study of peer groups in their natural setting. The introduction to this volume gives some idea of the techniques of participant-observation that we used.

Our normal method of work was to interview a few individuals, locate their peer group and become acquainted with it; we then studied the language of the peer group in spontaneous interaction and recorded the remaining individuals in face-to-face interviews. We used this approach first in studying two preadolescent groups in a low-income project, the Thunderbirds and the Aces, against the general population of the project. We then began the study of the major adolescent groups that dominated the tenement areas from 110th Street to 118th Street between Sixth and Eighth Avenues, and followed two groups each composed of many subgroups, for two years. These groups were known as the Cobras and the Jets.[2]

Our knowledge of the social structure, history, activities, and value systems of these groups is an essential aspect of the findings presented in this chapter. We traced the history of group relations and explored the value systems through individual face-to-face interviews, meetings with small groups of two or three close friends, and group sessions with 6 to 12 boys. Our participant-observer John Lewis saw the boys every day on the streets and met with them in their hang-outs and our "club-house." He was present at several moments of crisis when fighting was about to break out between the two major groups.

2. The names "Cobras" and "Jets" are here used as cover symbols for a complex of formal groups which changes over time. The Cobras, in particular, was originally a group formed by mergers of several groups which in turn underwent mergers with other groups under successive changes in nationalist orientation.

We also interviewed a number of isolated individuals in the same tenement areas, who were definitely not members of these groups, but who often knew about them. We are able then to assert that we reached all the major "named" groups in the area, although we did not have a representative sample of all adolescent boys. In the same areas we completed a stratified random sample of 100 adults, but only in the low-income projects did we relate our groups quantitatively to the total population.[3]

The Street Groups

The larger associations, which bear the names Jets and Cobras, are known to the boys as "clubs." They are not to be confused with the groups which are organized within recreation centers by adults, which are also called "clubs" and sometimes overlap in membership. The groups we studied are initiated by the boys themselves and are disapproved of by the adults in the neighborhood.[4]

The structure and value systems of these groups are partly inherited from the period of gang violence of the 1940's and 1950's. The frequency of group fighting, however, is comparatively low. These are not "gangs" in the sense of groups which frequently fight as a unit. Nevertheless, a major source of prestige for the leaders is skill in fighting, and individual fights are very common. The intergroup conflicts which do occur are the most important sources of group cohesion; they become a fixed part of the mythology and ideology of the group, and the obligation to support one's fellow members in a group fight is strongly felt by many members.

The general value systems of these groups conform to the lower-class value pattern which has been described by Walter B. Miller (1958). The focal concerns of the groups are *toughness, smartness, trouble, excitement, autonomy,* and *fate.* Intelligence or smartness is used and valued as a means of manipulating others, rather than a means of obtaining information or solving abstract problems. The specific values of the black nationalist movement are reflected in some groups more than others. The members of the Cobras, within the period that we worked with them, moved from a moderately

3. See below p. 261 for relative sizes of street groups and isolated population in one project.

4. The Thunderbirds are a partial exception here, since the club was formed in a recreation center (and was successively reformed with different names); however, the identity of the group was not confined to the center, and it contained members who had been banned from the center.

nationalist position to deep involvement with the militant Muslim religion and its complex ideology.[5] This ideology involved the members in a strong interest in learning and abstract knowledge; but the general value systems of all the groups were such that school learning was seen as hostile, distant, and essentially irrelevant.

The groups have a formal structure which may include four officers: president, vice-president, prime minister, and war-lord. Junior organizations are often formed by the appointment of a younger brother of an officer to a leading position among the 10- to 13-year-olds. However, this formal structure can be misleading. The day-to-day activities of the boys[6] are in smaller, informal hang-out groups, determined by geography and age; an individual's association with the larger group is often a matter of formal definition of his identity more than anything else. Yet the ultimate sanction of the larger group and its fighting role is often referred to.

Sources of prestige within the group are physical size, toughness, courage and skill in fighting; skill with language in ritual insults, verbal routines with girls, singing, jokes and story-telling; knowledge of nationalist lore; skill and boldness in stealing; experience in reform schools; and connections with family members or others which provide reputation, money, hang-outs, marijuana, or other material goods. Success in school is irrelevant to prestige within the group, and reading is rarely if ever used outside of school.[7]

Group Membership

Full participation in the group consists of *endorsement* of this set of values, and *acceptance* of a set of personal obligations to others within the same environment and value system. The criterion of formal membership ("you are a Jet" or "you are not a Jet") is often disputed. A few individuals want to be members and are rejected; others could easily be members but do not care to. Full membership,

5. As noted above, the Cobras underwent a number of organizational transformations, with new officers, and merged with other groups as nationalist orientation increased.

6. Major activities are flying pigeons, playing basketball, playing cards, petty theft, playing pool, smoking marijuana, and hanging out, although not all members participate in all of these activities. The groups as formal wholes have relatively few activities.

7. As one indication of the importance of reading in the group, we may consider one pair of boys who were best friends and saw each other every day. One read extremely well, the other not at all: the other's performance was a total surprise to each.

as we define it, means that the individual is thoroughly involved with the values and activities of the group and is defined as a member both by himself and by others. If some but not all of these criteria are fulfilled, we term the individual a "marginal member." The clearest evidence for full membership as against marginal status is provided by the symmetrical and asymmetrical relations in a sociometric diagram. The diagram maps responses to the question, "Who are the guys you hang out with?" The network of symmetrical namings shows the main structure of the group, and the categories of membership are revealed most accurately in the relation of names given to names received. Details of this network for the Jets are given in the next chapter and a complete account in CRR 3288. If an individual on the outskirts of the group wants to be a member, yet is prevented by the influence of other environments (family, school) and other value systems, he is classed with other nonmembers. In each area there are "social groups" which are strongly influenced by adult organizations: we do not include membership in such groups in the category of membership which we are studying.

It has been shown in many similar situations that group membership is a function of age.[8] Boys 8 to 9 years old are definitely outsiders for the groups we are studying, and they have only a vague knowledge of group activities. Membership is strongest in the 13-to-15-year-old range, and falls off rapidly in the later teens. A few 18-or-19-year-old boys act as seniors, especially if younger brothers are serving as officers, but as a rule older boys drift off into different activities.

It is difficult to estimate the percentage of boys who are full participants in the street culture. In the next chapter, we report our enumeration of the population of the low-income project in which the Thunderbirds lived: they represented slightly less than half of the boys in the 9-to-13-year-old range in that apartment house. Our general experience would indicate that 50 to 60 percent of the boys in the age range 10 to 16 are full participants in the street culture we are studying here.

Reading Records

In all of our individual interviews, we used a number of special reading tests developed to yield specific information on the ver-

8. Cf. Peter Wilmott 1966:35. In answer to a question on main companions in spare time, 57 percent of those 14–15 years old indicated a group of other males; 44 percent of those 16–18 years old; and only 32 percent of those 19–20 years old.

nacular phonology and grammar.[9] However, the most direct evidence for reading performance in schools is obtained from the Metropolitan Achievement Test given every year in the New York City schools. With the help of the New York City Board of Education, we were able to examine the academic records of 75 preadolescent and adolescent boys with whom we had worked in the years 1965 to 1967. The substance of our findings is the correlation between the Metropolitan Achievement Reading Test and group membership.

Figure 6.1 shows the correlation between grade level and reading achievement for 32 boys we interviewed in the 110th–120th Street area who are not members of the street culture, or whose group status is unknown (from the Vacation Day Camp series). The horizontal axis is grade level at the time of the test; the vertical axis the Metropolitan Achievement Test score. Each individual's score and grade are indicated by a symbol. The diagonal lines group together those who are reading on grade level (0), one to three years above grade level ($+3$ to $+1$), or one to six years behind grade level (-1 to -6). As one would expect, there are a good many boys who are two years behind grade, which is average in New York City, but there are also quite a few on grade and some ahead of grade level. Eleven of the 32 boys are on grade or above. The general direction of the pattern is upward, indicating that learning is taking place.

Figure 6.2 shows the same relationships for 46 boys who are members or marginal members of street groups in south-central Harlem. The overall pattern is entirely different from Fig. 6.1: no one is reading above grade, only one boy reading on grade, and the great majority are three or more years behind. Moreover, there are no boys who are reading above the fifth grade level, no matter what grade they are in. At each grade, the reading achievement for these boys forms a lower, more compact group than for the same grade in Fig. 6.1. The close concentration of boys in the eighth grade below the fifth grade level shows a limitation on achievement which is quite striking. On the whole, Fig. 6.2 shows very little learning as compared to Fig. 6.1.[10]

The lower achievement of group members does not indicate over-

9. Gray's Oral Reading Test was also given to a section of the population for further calibration on school approaches to reading.

10. There is a close correlation between reading achievement and the Pinter-Cunningham IQ test (given in the early grades in New York City in former years) in Fig. 6.1, and less markedly in Fig. 6.2.

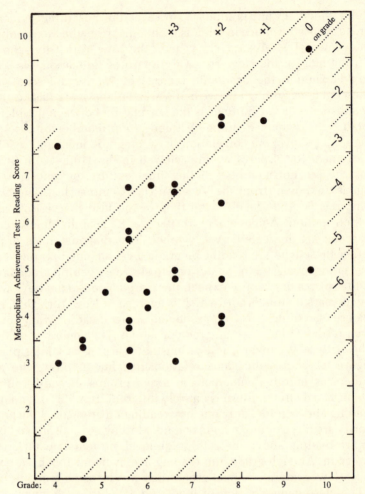

Fig. 6.1. Grade and reading achievement for 32 nonmembers of
street groups in south-central Harlem. From "Blacks" by
William Labov in *Reading for the Disadvantaged*, edited by
Thomas D. Horn, © 1970 by Harcourt Brace Jovanovitch, Inc.,
and reproduced with their permission.

all deficiency in verbal skills. Many of these boys are proficient at
a wide range of verbal skills appropriate for group activity: the verbal
leaders are indicated in Fig. 6.2. While several are clustered near
the highest point of achievement, there are other verbal leaders near
the bottom of the diagram.

To understand the situation of group members, we have to see the confrontation with the school system through their eyes. In the last chapter, we cited the views of Deutsch and his associates who see peer-group membership as a substitute for success in school: members of such groups accept the lesser gratification from social inter-

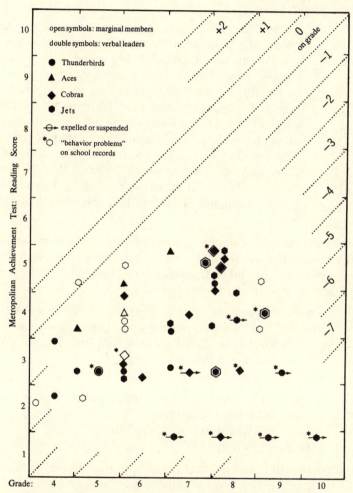

Fig. 6.2. Grade and reading achievement for 46 members of street groups in south-central Harlem. From "Blacks" by William Labov in *Reading for the Disadvantaged* edited by Thomas D. Horn, © 1970 by Harcourt Brace Jovanovitch, Inc., and reproduced with their permission.

action because they have failed to achieve the greater satisfaction
that school achievement can bring. In contrast, we can quote the
statement of Vaughn R., a member of the Jets who moved into the
Jet area from Washington Heights the year before. Vaughn had
already demonstrated that he had all the scholastic ability he needed
to succeed in school, but he turned his back on the school culture
in favor of the Jets.

> *Vaughn:* These men have taught me everything I know
> about all this bullshit, because I'm uptown, that's like
> a different world an' shit. My mind was poisoned,
> y'know, when I moved down here niggers started, you
> know, hipping me to little things an' shit, so you know,
> I figure I'm learning from it, so why *not*, y'understand,
> why not? . . . . (John Lewis: Now dig, like, what sort of
> things have they taught you?) Well, they learned me
> about reefer an' shit. I'm not saying that tha's good . . .
> They hip me to the whitey's *bull*shit, they hip me to
> that. Now I don't—I'm not saying that that's good, either,
> y'understand, but I'm just telling you what they *did* for
> me.

Another verbal leader of the Jets was Junior D., a member of the
younger subgroup in the "200's block" (see next chapter). The following quotations are taken from a conversation between Junior, his
best friend Ronald F., and John Lewis.

> *Junior:* Like I'ma tell you the truth. They jus' want every-
> thin' taken away from us. . . . Who do we work for?
> Whities! Who do we go to school for? Whities! Who's
> our teachers? Whities!
>
> . . . .
>
> *Interviewer:* If the whitey's not different from you, how
> come he has everything?
> *Ronald:* They don't have everything.
> *Junior:* Yes they do!

It is important to note here that Junior and Ronald are members of
the Jets, a group which is quite indifferent and even hostile to black
nationalism and the Muslim religion. Junior has not been taught to
be militant; the resentment expressed here is a product of Junior's
own thinking—the result of his own experience. Despite his antago-

nism towards the dominant white society, he has retained a strong sense of realism in his evaluation of it. An argument with Ronald as to whether high school diplomas are necessary:

> *Ronald:* And I'm 'onna tell you; I'm 'onna say *why* what they say you have to have a high school diploma. Some whitey's probably ain't got a high school diploma, and he still go out to work. My father ain't got a high school diploma.
>
> *Junior:* Your father ain't no whitey, is he?
>
> *Ronald:* No, but he has no high school diploma, but he go out there and work, right?
>
> *Junior:* O.K.! . . . But . . . I'ma tell you, you're wrong in a way—cause ev'ry whitey—ev'ry whitey, if they out o' school, they went through *high* school. If they didn't go to college they went through *high* school. If the whities didn't go through high school, how come they got everything? . . . 'Cause they had the *knowledge*.

It seems clear that Junior is a much better speaker than Ronald. In complex arguments of this sort, Ronald's syntax gets him into problems like the double *but* clauses or the unsolved labyrinth of his first sentence quoted above. Junior has no such difficulty expressing his ideas. Furthermore, he has the ability to put one argument on top of another which is characteristic of those who win verbal contests.

> *Junior:* If you—if you was in a high school—right? Why do people graduate?
>
> *Ronald:* 'Cause they try hard to grad—'cause they *want* to graduate.
>
> *Junior:* 'Cause they *learn* . . . 'cause they *learn*. If they didn't learn, and they just stood around, they wouldn't have everything. 'Cause you got to *work* to get to high school, you got to *work* to get from elementary to junior high . . .

In this dialogue, Junior seems to express very well the values of middle-class society. He shows a full cognitive awareness of the importance of education. It comes as something of a shock then to learn that at the time of this interview he was in the eighth grade and his reading score was 4.6—more than three years behind grade.

On Fig. 6.2 he appears as the highest outlined hexagon in the upper right hand cluster. It is obvious to us from long contact with Junior that he has, like Vaughn, all the ability he needs to succeed in school. The history of his failure in school is best seen most clearly in his disciplinary record, rather than his scholastic record. Over the course of his years in school we find a regular progression of entries which reflect the conflict between Junior and the school system.

Nov. '63. Frequently comes to school without a tie . . . He frequently calls out answer. When told not to call out he made an expression of disgust. He then refused to accept the rexographed sheet the teacher gave to the class.

Nov. '63. When asked to rewrite a composition he adamantly refused. He said, "I will not." He doesn't practice any self control.

Dec. '63. Was fighting with another boy in class today . . .

Sept. '66. F in citizenship.

May '67. Mother has been in touch with school regarding son's truancy.

From the teacher's point of view, Junior is just another discipline problem who cannot compete with the intelligent student and finds a way out in being "bad". But seeing Junior's whole record and knowing his extraordinary verbal and reasoning abilities outside of school, we consider it clear that his record documents the cultural and political conflict between the Jets and the school system. Junior expresses the Protestant ethnic with great clarity: he sees that success comes from hard work and learning. But the principle applies to *them*: "If *they* didn't learn and *they* just stood around, *they* wouldn't have everything." It is also clear to Junior that he and his friends have been defined as outsiders from the beginning and that no one in the school system has seriously considered that this principle is to apply to them.

What Is to Be Done?

The overall view given by Fig. 6.2 strongly reinforces our view that the major problem responsible for reading failure is a cultural conflict. The school environment and school values are plainly not influencing the boys firmly grounded in street culture. The group which does show learning contains a large percentage of boys who do not fit in with street culture—who reject it or are rejected by it. For the majority, Fig. 6.2 confirms indirect evidence that teachers in the city schools have little ability to reward or punish members of the street culture or to motivate learning by any means.

The usual statistics on reading achievement in urban ghettos are alarming, but they do not reveal the full extent of reading failure. Research inside the schools cannot discriminate membership in the street culture from nonmembership, and educators are therefore not aware of the full extent of the cultural barrier between them and their students.

It will be recalled from chapter 5 that the educational goals of the adult black community are the same as that of our society as a whole. Our subjective evaluation tests, for example, show that adults in Harlem are almost unanimous in their norms of correct speech and the goals for language teaching in school (CRR 3288:4.6). Many of the members of the street culture gradually break away and acquire these adult norms in their twenties. However, the norms are of little value for those who do not have the skills to put them into effect.

The reading failure that we have documented here is typical of other performance on the academic records. The pattern of failure is so widespread, in many urban areas, that one cannot hold responsible any one system, school or teacher. The majority of these boys have not learned to read well enough to use reading as a tool for further learning. For many of them, there is no realistic possibility of graduating from high school and acquiring the skills needed for the job market.

The absolute ceiling of Fig. 6.2 is of course an artifact of the limited sample. We know from our own tests that there are group members who read very well, whose school records are not presently available. But even these rare individuals view the educational system with a profound cynicism. The majority of those who learn from the system are located in Fig. 6.1.

We do not believe that the present college-educated teaching staff, black or white, has the specific knowledge of the street culture to solve this problem alone. Black teachers raised in ghetto areas are not members of the *current* street culture. With a few rare exceptions, we find that success in education removes the individual from his culture so effectively that his knowledge of it becomes quite marginal. The specific knowledge of the street culture which is needed is only available to those who are in constant interaction with the peer groups on the streets. Part of the reason is that the value system, though quite general, is intensely *local* in focus. The factors that control language behavior are often local and immediate: what happened last year, last month, or yesterday to that particular subgroup is the best stimulus for evoking spontaneous speech. And the general configurations of the culture change rapidly even though the value system remains intact: a teacher raised in Harlem in the 1950's, returning to the streets today, would find it difficult to understand how and why gang fighting is no longer in style.

We propose that a cultural intermediary be introduced into the classroom in the person of a young black man,[11] 16 to 25 years old, with high-school-level reading skills, but not a college graduate. We propose the creation of a special license to allow this young man to carry out the following functions:

1. To acquaint the teacher with the specific interests of members of the class and help design reading materials centering on these interests.

2. To provide effective rewards and punishments that will motivate members of street culture for whom normal school sanctions are irrelevant.

3. To lead group discussion on topics of immediate concern to members of the class.

4. To lead boys in sports and other recreational activities in school time.

5. To maintain contact with boys outside of school, on the streets, and help organize extracurricular activities.

We are well aware of the difficulties that any school system will have in absorbing such outside elements. The situation in most ghetto schools is plainly desperate enough so that many educators will be willing to endorse a proposal that may create such difficulties. Our proposal is not equivalent to the usual program for para-professionals, who are usually parents or upward-bound youth already removed from the vernacular culture. The difference between such isolated individuals and members is the main topic of the next chapter. Part III of this volume will describe some of the skills and understandings that make up the vernacular culture. These chapters will document the distance between the socialized adult and the members who are now effectively shut out of the educational system.

---

11. We specifically designate a male for this role, in contrast to a number of proposals for para-professionals in the schools which utilize women from the community or from college training courses. We cannot elaborate on the importance of sex differentiation here, except to indicate that we believe it is a matter of prime importance.

7 | The Linguistic Consequences of Being a Lame

Who's the lame who says he knows the game,
And where did he learn to play?
—"The Fall"

THIS chapter studies the grammars of isolated individuals, known as *lames* in the black English vernacular. They are the typical informants made available to investigators who study nonstandard language in schools, recreation centers, and homes with the help of adults who control these institutions. The form of black English vernacular used by lames will be compared with that used by members of the dominant social groups of the vernacular culture. The findings will be of considerable sociological interest, since it appears that the consistency of certain grammatical rules is a fine-grained index of membership in the street culture. The data should also be of interest to theoretical linguistics, since it appears that patterns of social interaction may influence grammar in subtle and unsuspected ways. Finally, we will consider the serious methodological problem which these findings pose for linguists in general. It is in fact the same methodological problem with which this study begins: locating the most consistent and reliable data for describing the grammar of the speech community.

1. Locating the Vernacular

The largest part of our recent research of the speech community has focused upon the language used by primary peer groups in natural, face-to-face interaction. The most important data used in

255

this volume for grammatical analysis were obtained from this setting; in recent work on Hawaiian Creole this was also the major focus (Labov 1971b, Day to appear). We have followed the same policy in exploratory work on sound change in various regions of the United States, England, Ireland, and France (Labov, Yaeger, and Steiner 1972). As we enter any city we look for preadolescent and adolescent peer groups engaged in sports or hanging-out; we encounter family groups at tea or after dinner; we join groups of old men at bowls, in pubs, or sitting at pensioner's benches.

In this approach we are departing more and more from the earlier tradition of sociolinguistic studies which depended upon face-to-face interviews with single individuals drawn from judgment samples (Kurath 1949; *Sociolinguistic Patterns,* chapter 1) or from random samples (*Social Stratification;* Shuy, Wolfram and Riley 1967; Levine and Crockett 1966; Anshen 1969; Trudgill 1971); and we are following the more ethnographic approach that was first outlined by Gumperz in his work in Norway (1964). Random sampling is of course an essential procedure if we want to describe the overall sociolinguistic structure of the community, and our work in south-central Harlem relied heavily on a stratified random sample of 100 adults. But severe problems of explanation and interpretation are created when we extract single speakers from their social network and limit ourselves to records of their speech in one-to-one interaction with the interviewer. It seems most likely that a random sample will be used in future sociolinguistic studies to select individuals for study in the context of the social groups in which they normally operate.

We focus upon natural groups as the best possible solution to the *observer's paradox:* the problem of observing how people speak when they are not being observed (*Sociolinguistic Patterns,* chapter 8). The natural interaction of peers can overshadow the effects of observation and helps us approach the goal of capturing the vernacular of everyday life in which the minimum amount of attention is paid to speech: this is the most systematic level of linguistic behavior and of greatest interest to the linguist who wants to explain the structure and evolution of language.

But there is a second even more compelling reason for us to select natural groups of speakers rather than isolated individuals. The vernacular is the property of the group, not the individual. Its consistency and well-formed, systematic character is the result of a vast number of interactions; the group exerts its control over the vernacular in a supervision so close that a single slip may be condemned and remembered for years.[1] The overt norms of the dominant social class can operate to produce a consistent superordinate dialect, if class is reasonably cohesive and protected from large-scale invasions from below. Thus the Received Pronunciation described by H. C. Wyld was a class dialect rigorously controlled in the British public (private) schools (1936:3). At the other end of the social spectrum, the covert norms of the street culture operate to produce the consistent vernacular of the urban working class. The lower-class culture differs from upper-class culture in that its base in the population becomes progressively narrower with age. In the early adolescent years, the focal concerns of lower-class culture (Miller 1958) involve all but the upper-middle and upper class in America. But individuals are gradually split away from involvement in these concerns, so that only a small percentage of "lower-lower-class" adults retain this orientation wholeheartedly as they grow older.[2]

We usually find that the most consistent vernacular is spoken by those between the ages of 9 and 18. It is well known that in most cities peer-group membership reaches a peak at the ages of 15 to 16 (Wilmott 1966); as the young adult is detached from the teenage hang-out group he inevitably acquires a greater ability to shift towards the standard language and more occasions to do so. In some sharply differentiated subsystems, a consistent vernacular can be obtained only from children and adolescents: the grammars of adults seem to be permanently changed by their use of standard rules. This is the case with both Hawaiian Creole English ("Hawaiian Pidgin") and black vernacular. In general, working adults will use a sharper degree of style shifting than adolescents in their careful speech with outside observers, and only under the most favorable circumstances

1. A classic case, reported in Whyte 1955, is that of the Cornerville group known as the Cream Puffs for many years, because someone had heard one member say "Aw shucks!" when a store was out of something he wanted to buy.

2. In any survey, we run across a few lower-class subjects who openly and defiantly endorse lower-class values. A woman of 55 answered all of the questions in the Lower East Side survey (Labov 1966a) in this style. She told me that when asked by a previous interviewer about her job aspirations, she had answered, "To be a prostitute!", and claimed that she would curse and swear to anyone, it didn't matter who. But one of her married daughters disagreed. "Not when you answer the phone, Ma!"

will their vernacular system emerge. In old age, much of this superposed variation disappears. But it is still an open question how much the basic vernacular system changes in the course of a life-time.[3]

2. Members and Lames

In our work on sound change, we are concerned with the working-class vernacular rather than an upper-class dialect because it forms the main stream in the history of the language. The vernacular affects a much larger number of speakers in a more intimate way than the standard and the transmission of linguistic tradition through successive peer groups takes place in the subculture dominated by the vernacular (which we refer to as the *vernacular culture*). But even in the most solid working-class areas, there are many isolated children who grow up without being members of any vernacular peer group and a steadily increasing number of individuals split away from the vernacular culture in their adolescent years.

The black English vernacular currently refers to such isolated individuals as *lames*. They are not *hip,* since they do not hang out. It is only by virtue of being available and on the street every day that anyone can acquire the deep familiarity with local doings and the sure command of local slang that are needed to participate in vernacular culture. To be *lame* means to be outside of the central group and its culture; it is a negative characterization and does not imply any single set of social characteristics. Some lames can't or won't fight—they are cowards or weaklings; some are "good" in that they do not steal, smoke, shoot up dope, or make out, but others may be just as tough or just as "bad" as peer-group members; they may

---

3. This is a crucial question for the interpretation of standard dialectological materials and even more important for our current work in tracing sound changes in progress through distribution through age levels ("apparent time"). Earlier reports in real time are of course essential supports for any argument about change in progress, no matter how fragmentary they may be. But it is also possible to show from internal distribution what changes have been occurring later in life, since these superposed rules do not have the regular character of the earlier vernacular. Responses to formal questions, like minimal pair tests, will often show a newly acquired norm, quite distinct from the pattern of speech. An 80-year-old man from central Pennsylvania, for example, made a clear distinction between *hock* and *hawk, Don* and *dawn* in his connected speech, but reported them as the same and merged them in his production of minimal pairs—at a completely different point in phonological space.

merely be distant, going their own way with their own concerns. What all lames have in common is that they lack the knowledge which is necessary to run any kind of a game in the vernacular culture. The term *lame* can carry a great deal of contempt especially where someone pretends to knowledge he doesn't have. One of the epic statements of vernacular culture, "The Fall", begins on this note as shown in the epigraph to this chapter. Again we find that in "Mexicali Rose", the protagonist puts down his main man, Smitty, because he hit on a girl and failed.

Smitty dipped easy and from behind
"Lame, you think your game is stronger than mine?"
Sam said, "Not only is my game stronger, but my spiel is tougher,
So move over, Jake, and watch me work."[4]

There are many reasons for someone to be lame. Separation from the peer group may take place under the influence of parents, or of school, or of the individual's own perception of the advantages of the dominant culture for him; on the other hand, he may be too sick or too weak to participate in the peer-group vernacular activities, or he may be rejected by the peer-groups as mentally or morally defective (a *punk*). In our work in south-central Harlem, we encountered many examples of all these factors; one of the most important is the active intervention of parents. For example, a swimming team at Milbank recreation center is said to have been broken up when the mother of Ricky S. objected to his "hanging around with Stanley an' 'em."

A high concentration of lames will be found in any selective social institution or activity which requires the active participation of parents, such as the Vacation Day Camps mentioned in the previous chapter.[5] Since parents had to enroll boys in the program, and it was run in schools by adults, this "VDC" series contrasts as a whole with data provided by the Thunderbirds, Jet, and Cobra peer groups, formed apart from and in spite of the influence of parents and schools.

4. From the version of Big Brown, recorded in New York City in 1965.
5. Although the selection of Vacation Day Camps was done on a geographically random basis, the individual subjects in the camps were not chosen randomly. They were boys who were not engaged in sports or any other social activity at the time, and the bias of the VDC selection was therefore increased in the direction of isolates or lames.

Social institutions like the early grades of the public schools will of course include both lames and members of the vernacular culture (hereafter referred to as *members*). Teachers, testers, educational psychologists, and linguists who work or hang out only in schools have no way of distinguishing these categories. Only by working outside of these institutions can we obtain an overall view of students' status and estimate the relative size of the vernacular component. The importance of this knowledge for an analysis of educational problems cannot be overstated. Chapter 6 showed that lames in Harlem schools read only one or two grades behind the national norms and generally follow an upward curve of reading achievement; but the large body of peer-group members show a very much lower pattern with a ceiling at the fourth grade reading level. The ability to distinguish lames from members is even more important for linguists trying to study the vernacular, for as we shall see, lames and members differ systematically in their grammars as well as in their school performance.

What are the percentages of members and lames in any inner city population? One answer to this question appears in our study of the peer groups located in a 13-story apartment building in a low-income project, 1390 Fifth Avenue. With help from the boys themselves, we carried out an enumeration of all youth living in this building. Table 7.1 shows the population of boys from 6 to 19 years old. The 17 Thunderbirds range from 9 to 13 years, and make up 45 percent of the 38 boys in this range. The 7 Oscar Brothers, a related older group, make up 33 percent of the boys in the 16-to-18 age range.[6] Table 7.1 also indicates some of the reasons that boys are not members. Some have different family backgrounds—West Indian or Puerto Rican. At least one is kept at home by his parents. Some go to Catholic schools. In any case, it is evident that the Thunderbirds are the only self-organized peer-group in their age range, and the rest are isolated individuals, who are lames by definition. We interviewed four of

6. The Oscar Brothers are not in fact a named group like the Thunderbirds. They are an informal hang-out group of older boys, including several older brothers of the Thunderbirds, who have helped them out once or twice in fights with other groups in the neighborhood. No one is sure how the name "Oscar Brothers" originated; it probably refers to the Big O (Oscar Robertson). The Oscar Brothers themselves say the name is used only by the younger boys. In accounts of great fights in the history of the Thunderbirds, the leader Boot is quoted as saying, "Go get the Oscar Brothers!"

TABLE 7.1.
RELATION OF CENTRAL PEER GROUPS TO ALL BOYS
6 TO 19 IN 1390 FIFTH AVENUE

Boy's age	Floor												Total
	2	3	4	5	6	7	8	9	10	11	12	13	
6	n	n								n			4
7	n				nn						n		4
8						n		n	nn	n			5
9		n				n	T		ñ	TT	n	nn	9
10		n	ñ		ñ		TT			T	nñ		8
11				n	TT	T				T	ñ	T	7
12						T	T				ñ		3
13	nññ	T		n		n	Th	T̄		n		T	11
14	n	n	n	n	n		n		n	n	nn	nn	12
15	nn	n			n	n	n		nn			nn	10
16	n	nn			0			n	nñ	0		n0	10
17					0			n0	0	ñ		n	6
18				n	0				n	nñ			5
19													0
													94

T = Thunderbird   ñ̄ = Puerto Rican
O = Oscar Brother   ñ = West Indian
n = nonmember   h = kept at home

these boys individually; we will refer to them as the "1390 Lames".

Membership is demonstrated by actual participation in group activities, but it appears quite clearly in answers to the hang-out question in individual interviews. We can plot answers to "Who are all the cats you hang out with?" on sociometric diagrams such as Fig. 7.1, which shows members of the Thunderbirds from 10 to 13.[7] The double lines show symmetrical naming; the lighter lines with arrow heads indicate a naming by someone who is not named in return. The leaders Boot and Roger and central members Money, David, Ricky, Junior, Calvin are bound by a network of mutual namings. A younger subgroup is formed by Billy, Gary, and Robbie. The isolated position of lames Del, Lesley, and Curtis is apparent.

7. There are several nine-year-olds involved who were not interviewed. The verbal leader Boot has a great many connections with outsiders, while the nonverbal leader, Roger, is located entirely within the Thunderbirds.

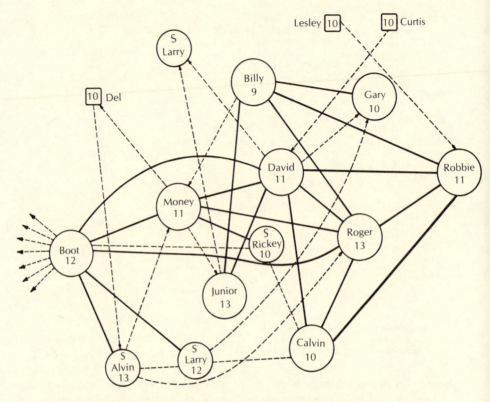

Fig. 7.1. Hang-out pattern of the Thunderbirds.

3. Linguistic Differentiation of
Preadolescent Members and Lames

We can make the most precise comparison of lames and peer-group members by pairing the 1390 Lames with the Thunderbirds. The Aces, who were located in the neighboring project building, are a peer group which we can expect to match the Thunderbirds. On the other hand, the Vacation Day Camp series should be intermediate, since it includes some local boys we know as members as well as a good many lames. The VDC series also covers a much wider area than the Jet, Cobra, and Thunderbird territory, and some boys reported membership in named groups that we were not familiar with.

In the following analysis we will then present four groups of preadolescent speakers: The Thunderbirds, the Aces, 10 boys from the VDC series, and the 1390 Lames. It must be remembered that all of these boys appear to speak the black vernacular at first hearing. None of them are middle-class or standard speakers who would stand out from the others as obviously speaking a different dialect; the linguistic differences we will show here emerge only on close analysis. All groups use the same linguistic variables and the differences in the system are internal variations in the organization of similar rules: differential weightings of variable constraints.

To illustrate this general point, consider the following fight story from Lesley C., one of the 1390 Lames:

> See, Book pushed the door and Calvin pushed it back on him an' then they start pushing each other an' then they started to fight . . . Book was holding Calvin by the neck and Calvin had his han' up at his face . . . Book was almost crying and then Book got a cut right down his nose. (Who won that fight?) I say it was Calvin 'cause he ain't cry or bleed.

There are no grammatical items here which distinguish Lesley's speech from BEV; it has the characteristic syntax of a BEV fight narrative and ends with one of the most marked BEV forms, *ain't* for *didn't*. But Lesley is a lame,[8] and his language reflects this fact. To see how it does so, we will have to look more closely at the Lame use of BEV variable rules.

Table 7.2 shows some of the phonological indices that differentiate these four groups. The variables presented here are the same as those which operate in the white community and have been extensively studied in New York City (*Social Stratification*) and in Detroit (Shuy, Wolfram, and Riley 1967). A detailed description of the first four variables in the adult white community is given in chapter 3 of *Sociolinguistic Patterns*. For a description of the variables of Table 7.2 in the black community see CRR 3288: Vol. 1 and chapters 1–4 of this volume.

The comparisons of Table 7.2 do not give data on Style A, the

---

8. Lesley is far enough outside of the group that he has gotten Boot's name wrong. It is usually pronounced without any final consonant [bu], and for a long time we ourselves thought his name was Boo, but one day he visited us with sneakers labelled across the toes BOOT. Lesley has reconstructed a [k] for the final consonant, a common form of hypercorrection in a dialect where *den* has become *dent*.

TABLE 7.2.
LINGUISTIC CORRELATES OF PEER-GROUP STATUS:
PHONOLOGICAL VARIABLES FOR PREADOLESCENTS

Variable	Style	Aces	T-Birds	VDC Series	1390 Lames
1a. (r##V)	B	06	04	07	21
b. (r)	B	00	00	01	06
	C	03	10	17	31
	D	26	23	20	51
2. (dh) /	B	144	114	140	84
	C	92	57	20	38
	D	108	70	77	44
	All	115	81	79	55
3. (ing)	B	00	04	24	(22)
4a. (KD$_{MM}$) __K	B	98	94	99	93
b. __V	B	64	59	35	61
c. (KD$_P$) __K	B	81	74	81	19
d. __V	B	24	24	24	16
4b-4c		−17	−15	−46	+42
No. of speakers		4	8	10	4

speech used in group sessions, since the lames were recorded only in individual interviews; they include three progressively more formal styles where an increasing amount of attention is paid to speech. Style B is the main body of conversation, Style C is reading style, and Style D includes word lists and minimal pairs where the maximum amount of attention is concentrated on the variable.

The first two variables deal with postvocalic r, which yields fine-grained stylistic and social stratification in many areas where the vernacular is or has been r-less—New England, the upper and lower South, Hawaii, and New York City. As we saw in chapter 2, the black community generally shows a higher degree of r-lessness than the white community and a sharper slope of style shifting between conversational and reading styles. In general, it can be said that the r variables are more important in the black community than any-where else as indicators of formal, educated speech. This is even more true in black communities in r-pronouncing areas, such as Philadelphia or Los Angeles.

The first index is (r##V)—the percentage of constricted [r] used in final position when the next word begins with a vowel, as in four o'clock. This variable operates at a very high level in the white community, but in connected speech the Aces, T-Birds, and VDC groups all show a low figure from 4 to 7 percent. Only the 1390 Lames use a sizeable percentage of constricted [r], at (r# #v)-21.

The general r variable is (r), the percentage of constricted [r] in postvocalic position where the next word does not begin with a vowel; in *car, card, fear, beard*. This always operates at lower levels than (r# #V), and in Table 7.2 the peer groups are at 00, just as in BEV. Only the Lames show any sign of [r] in speech. But in more formal styles, we see a regular slope of upward shifting. Figure 7.2 shows that the slope of style shifting for the 1390 Lames is twice that of the other groups, so that in Style D, the Lames use [r] half of the time.

The (dh) index represents a stigmatized feature, the frequency of stops and affricates for the initial consonant of /ð/ in *this* and *then*. (Unlike the other indices, it does not run from 0–100, but 0–200.) It does not form as regular a pattern as the r variables among adolescents, but Table 7.2 clearly shows that the 1390 Lames are lower than the Aces and T-Birds in their use of this feature. The VDC series is lower than the others only in reading style, but as a whole resembles the peer groups more than the Lames.

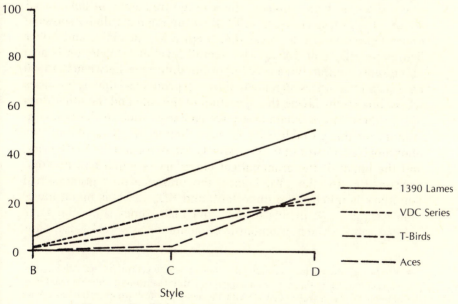

Fig. 7.2. Use of the variable (r) by preadolescent groups.

Perhaps the most sensitive sociolinguistic variable for BEV groups
is (ing)—the percentage of [ɪn] variants for unstressed /ing/. It is
typical of BEV speakers to go from (ing)-00 in causal speech to
(ing)-100 in reading. All of these preadolescent speakers show an (ing)
index of 100 or close to it in their reading styles C and D, and Table
7.2 therefore shows only Style B. The T-Birds and Aces adhere
closely to the vernacular level, but the VDC speakers and the 1390
Lames use the prestige variant almost one quarter of the time.

The last five lines of Table 7.2 concern the deletion of -t,d in final
consonant clusters. As we saw in chapter 2, this (KD) variable is
subdivided into four subvariables, depending on the values of two
environmental features: the absence or presence of a grammatical
boundary before the final /t/ or /d/ (passed vs. past) and the absence
or presence of a following vowel (passed me vs. passed over). The
combination of these gives us the four subcategories shown in Table
7.2:

$$(KD_{MM})\underline{\quad}K \qquad \text{past me}$$
$$(KD_{MM})\underline{\quad}V \qquad \text{past us}$$
$$(KD_{P})\underline{\quad}K \qquad \text{passed me}$$
$$(KD_{P})\underline{\quad}V \qquad \text{passed us}$$

The index numbers represent the average frequency of deletion of
/t/ or /d/ in these contexts. All follow the regular rule by showing
lower figures before a vowel than before a consonant, and lower
figures for KD_P than KD_{MM}. The overall level of t,d deletion is also
remarkably similar. But a very important difference between the 1390
Lames and the others appears in the crossproducts—that is, the cases
where one factor favors the operation of the rule and the other does
not. In these intermediate cases, we can see which of the two constraints on the variable rule is more important. It is plainly the
phonological constraint for the T-Birds, the Aces, and the VDC series,
and the effect of the grammatical boundary is much less by comparison. But for the 1390 Lames, the presence of a grammatical
boundary is much more important, and $KD_P\underline{\quad}K$ is much lower
than $KD_{MM}\underline{\quad}V$. In this respect, the 1390 Lames show the same
pattern as the white nonstandard vernacular of New York City.[9] Thus

9. Studies of other white nonstandard dialects (south-central Texas, Atlanta, Co-
lumbus, Detroit) show that the grammatical constraint is regularly predominant over
the phonological constraint, just as with the white control group in the New York
City studies.

we see a characteristic difference in the weighting of the variable constraints on the *t,d* deletion rule:

1   BEV rule of Aces, Thunderbirds and VDC:

$$\text{t,d} \rightarrow \langle \emptyset \rangle / [+\text{cons}]\ ^{\beta}\langle \emptyset \rangle \underline{\qquad} {}^{\alpha}\langle -\text{syl} \rangle$$

2   General rule of 1390 Lames, adults, and white groups

$$\text{t,d} \rightarrow \langle \emptyset \rangle / [+\text{cons}]\ ^{\alpha}\langle \emptyset \rangle \underline{\qquad} {}^{\beta}\langle -\text{syl} \rangle$$

This qualitative difference in the organization of the deletion rule emerges from a quantitative study of natural speech. It represents a regular development with age as well as a difference among social groups, since even the peer-group members shift to rule 2 when they become adults. The predominant standard English pattern is heavily against deletion in past tense forms, and its influence is thus felt in the internal reorganization of the vernacular rule; since the 1390 Lames are isolated from the black vernacular and are most sensitive to SE influence, they are aligned in the SE direction from the outset.[10]

In the overall pattern of Table 7.2, the VDC series is closer to the BEV peer groups than to the 1390 Lames. There are, however, four measures where the VDC subjects are shifted in the direction of the Lames and away from the peer groups. For all these variables, the T-Birds and the Aces are remarkably similar.

We next consider a more complex phenomenon: the operation of rules for contraction and deletion of *is* as a realization of the copula and auxiliary *be*. Here the comparison will be confined to two groups—the Thunderbirds and the 1390 Lames, who are directly opposed in their relation to the BEV subculture. The upper half of Table 7.3 shows the actual number of full forms (F), contracted forms (C), and deleted forms (D) for both the Thunderbirds and 1390 Lames, subclassified in a variety of grammatical environments. We follow the analysis of chapter 3 in subdividing the cases into those which begin with a full noun phrase (NP__) and those which begin with a pronoun (pro__). Within each of these, we consider three possibilities: that the following element is a noun phrase or sentence (__NP, S), a predicate adjective or locative (__PA, Loc), or a verb

---

10. The influence on the 1390 Lames may come from several directions: parents, the mass media, teachers, or other adolescents outside of the BEV influence. The fact that their pattern matches that of the white nonstandard speakers in many details does not necessarily show any direct influence, since they are moving towards SE along the same axes from a greater distance.

with -*ing* or *gonna* (__Vŋ, gn). Our general study of contraction and deletion of the copula in chapter 3 showed that there is progressively more contraction and deletion in these three environments, and more after pronouns than after full noun phrases. The form of the rule in the analysis of contraction and deletion presented in chapter 3 shows that the rule which deletes *is* is dependent upon the contraction rule and operates only upon auxiliaries with single consonants produced by contraction. The contraction rule is essentially the same as that which operates in the white dialects; the deletion rule is found only in BEV[11] and appears to be uniform throughout the various vernacular communities. The differences which we will now examine have to do with the level of use of the two rules, rather than their specific forms.

The probabilities which govern the use of variable rules can be expressed by the quantity φ, ranging between 0 and 1; the lower half of Table 7.3 gives overall values of φ for the contraction rule, operating upon F to give C, and for the deletion rule, operating upon C to give D.

The data on contraction for the 1390 Lames is limited, but it is sufficient to show that they use this rule in the same way as the Thunderbirds. The overall probability of contraction rule for the Thunderbirds is .73, and for the Lames .65; furthermore, they follow the same pattern throughout the six subcases.[12] But the Thunderbirds and Lames are diametrically opposed in their use of the deletion rule: .52 for the Thunderbirds and only .12 for the Lames. And where the Thunderbirds follow the regular pattern of variable constraints that we find in all other BEV speakers, the 1390 Lames do not. Figure 7.3 contrasts the use of the deletion rule for the Lames and T-Birds

11. The few systematic studies of syntax in southern white communities show that *is* is not deleted in any regular pattern, but that *are* is absent quite regularly. The deletion of *are* may be the result of an extension of the contraction rule, or the contraction rule following on the rule for deletion of postvocalic schwa (chapter 3). Contraction may also be responsible for the reported absence of *is* after *this* in some speakers (James Sledd, pers. comm.). Contraction is normally constrained in this position, but when it does happen, voicing assimilation and the simplification of geminates would remove the resulting sibilant. We would expect, of course that some white speakers will be influenced by blacks in this respect, and that the deletion of *is* will be found in the South. But on current evidence, it is a black pattern.

12. As we can see here, contraction and deletion are similar rules and respond to the same general grammatical constraints—a preceding pronoun and a following verb both favor the rule.

TABLE 7.3.
USE OF CONTRACTION AND DELETION RULES
BY THUNDERBIRDS AND 1390 LAMES

| | Number of forms | | | | | | | |
| | Thunderbirds | | | | 1390 Lames | | | |
	F	C	D	N	F	C	D	N
is	68	100	110	278	18	30	4	52
NP__								
—NP, S	43	16	3	62	9	3	1	13
—PA, Loc	10	9	6	25	5	2	0	7
—Vŋ, gn	0	0	4	4	0	1	0	1
Pro__								
—NP, S	4	46	29	79	1	8	1	10
—PA, Loc	11	21	29	61	3	9	1	13
—Vŋ, gn	0	8	39	47	0	7	1	8

| | Use of the contraction and deletion rules | | | |
	φ_C $(C + D)/N$	φ_D $D/(C + D)$	φ_C $(C + D)/N$	φ_D $D/(C + D)$
is	.73	.52	.65	.12
NP__				
—NP, S	.31	.16	.31	.25
—PA, Loc	.40	.39	.29	(.00)
—Vŋ, gn	1.00	1.00	(1.00)	(.00)
Pro__				
—NP, S	.95	.39	.90	.11
—PA, Loc	.82	.58	.77	.10
—Vŋ, gn	1.00	.83	1.00	.12

F: full form
C: contracted form
D: deleted form
N: total numbers of instances for each group

for the six subcases and adds a comparison on the absence of *are*. The Lames' use of the rule is minimal: they delete the copula often enough so that it is evident that the rule is present in their system, but it is plainly being suppressed. In this respect, as in the case of -t,d deletion, the 1390 Lames have brought their rule system into alignment with that of the dominant white society.

There are also a number of grammatical features of BEV which demonstrate the linguistic differentiation of the Lames. For these

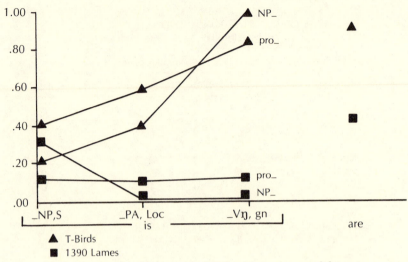

Fig. 7.3. Use of deletion rule for *is* and *are* by preadolescent
Thunderbirds and 1390 Lames.

grammatical variables we can contrast 12 of the Thunderbirds with
four 1390 Lames.

1. BEV uses the dummy subject *it* where standard English uses
there, as in *It's a difference* or *It's a policeman at the door.* This
is not a categorical rule, but it rises to a very high frequency in the
vernacular. The T-Birds use 79 percent *it* and only 21 percent *there;*
the 1390 Lames use 91 percent *there* and only 9 percent *it.*

2. In BEV, the rule of negative concord operates regularly to
indefinites *any* and *ever* within the clause, so that *Nobody knows
nothing about it* is expected in place of *Nobody knows anything*
(chapter 4). In all white nonstandard dialects, this is an optional rule.
The T-Birds apply the negative concord rule in 98 percent of these
cases, the 1390 Lames only 76 percent of the time. We have here a
qualitative contrast between a semicategorical use of the rule and
a variable one.

3. One of the characteristic features of informal southern syntax
is the use of inverted word order in embedded questions: *I asked
him could he do it* instead of the northern form *I asked him if he
could do it.* This is the normal use in BEV but is heard only rarely
in northern white dialects. The Thunderbirds use the inverted order

without *if* 80 percent of the time, the 1390 Lames only 20 percent. We saw in chapter 2 that this feature was quite compelling for many members, but it is not so for Lames.

There are many more such indicators which we might select from our grammatical studies of BEV, but by now the overall pattern should be apparent. Categorical or semicategorical rules of BEV are weakened to variable rules by the Lames; rules that are in strong use in BEV are reduced to a low level by the Lames. Whenever there is a contrast between SE and BEV, the language of the Lames is shifted dramatically towards SE. In many cases, this leads to a close alignment between the Lames and white nonstandard vernaculars. This does not necessarily imply that the Lames are modeling their behavior directly on the white nonstandard speakers, but rather that their interaction with SE patterns brings them from a point farther away from SE to roughly the same distance as members of the white vernacular culture.

If we now return to the speech of Lesley C. on page 263, his distance from the vernacular becomes more apparent. Lesley uses the [ɪŋ] version three times in a row in connected speech, which is simply not done by members. He preserves consonant clusters in the second *pushed* (the first is neutralized), and in *almost crying*, though he deletes the *-d* in *and* and *hand*. The use of the preterit *ain't* shows that Lesley is within the BEV system, but his use of that system is lame.

4. Verbal Agreement and Disagreement for Members and Lames

For a broader view of the contrast between the language of members and lames, we can turn to a series of measures which are very sensitive to distance from the vernacular culture. In general, we can say that the black vernacular has no agreement between subject and verb. There is one exception: some agreement is clearly registered in the finite forms of *be*. Here the 1st person singular regularly has contracted *'m*, 3rd person singular has *is* or *'s* when realized, and other persons when realized mostly have *are*, sometimes *is*. Aside from this, we have invariant verb forms with no relation to the person and number of the subject. Forms in *-s* are rarely found for *have*, *do*, *don't*, *want*, or *say*. The invariant form for *be* in the past is *was*, not *were*. These facts are illustrated by Tables 7.4 and 7.5,

TABLE 7.4.
PERSON-NUMBER AGREEMENT OF *HAVE, DO, WANT, SAY*
FOR BEV PEER-GROUP MEMBERS AND OTHER GROUPS

Group		Have $+3s$	Have $-3s$	Do $+3s$	Do $-3s$	Don't $+3s$	Don't $-3s$	Want $+3s$	Say $+3s$
Club members (31)	−s:	5	0	0	0	2	0	2	1
	∅:	21	44	20	44	61	163	16	26
Oscar Brothers (3)	−s:	6	0	2	1	7	0	3	3
	∅:	10	41	4	20	11	83	0	9
Lames (10)	−s:	6	0	1	0	10	0	7	0
	∅:	4	29	8	8	18	107	4	12
Inwood (8)	−s:	26	0	13	0	8	0	6	19
	∅:	0	23	0	40	17	74	2	0

$+3s$ = third singular subjects
$-3s$ = other subjects

which show the actual forms used by 31 club members, including
T-Birds, Aces, Jets, and Cobras. A total of 10 -s forms are found for
all 31 club members for the five verbs, as against 395 zero forms—
hardly enough to indicate any basis for subject-verb agreement. The
ratios of zero to -s forms for the five successive verbs are 21/5, 20/0,
61/2, 16/2, and 26/1. In Table 7.5, *was* predominates and *were* is
used occasionally in all environments.

The second line of Tables 7.4 and 7.5 shows the figures for three
Oscar Brothers. As an older, informal peer group they are already

TABLE 7.5.
PERSON-NUMBER AGREEMENT FOR *WAS* AND *WERE*
FOR BEV PEER-GROUP MEMBERS AND OTHER GROUPS

		1st Sing. Aux	1st Sing. Verb	3rd Sing. Aux	3rd Sing. Verb	Elsewhere Aux	Elsewhere Verb
Club members (31)	was:	40	54	54	117	54	51
	were:	2	2	13	5	9	8
Oscar Brothers (3)	was:	11	13	8	32	2	3
	were:	0	0	0	0	7	6
Lames (10)	was:	13	19	28	20	3	5
	were:	1	0	0	0	15	4
Inwood (8)	was:	11	24	25	76	0	4
	were:	0	0	0	0	21	8

beginning to modify their speech in the direction characteristic of adults. They show 22 -s forms altogether in Table 7.4, though the predominant use is still the zero form in all cases except *want*. In Table 7.5, they show a clear tendency towards the use of *were* with the plural and 2nd person singular.

The third line of Tables 7.4 and 7.5 shows the figures for 10 lames, drawn from the T-Bird, Cobra, and Jet areas. There is a clear reversal of the BEV pattern for *have* and *want*, where *has* and *wants* are preferred in 3rd person singular contexts. There is also a pronounced shift towards *doesn't*. In Table 7.4, only *do* and *say* keep their vernacular forms. In Table 7.5, the Lames have clearly adopted subject-verb agreement. They show almost no *were* with 1st and 3rd person singular and use mainly *were* forms elsewhere.

The last line of Tables 7.4 and 7.5 gives us a comparison with the white Inwood groups, speakers of the nonstandard New York City vernacular. There is no deviation from the standard pattern of agreement for *have*, *do*, or *say*. A few anomalies appear for *want* and *was/were*. The only place where there is any sizeable lack of agreement is with the predominant use of *don't* for *doesn't* with third person singular subjects. Note that the Lames match the Inwood group closely on this verb and differ from the Inwood group only on *do* and *say*.

The pattern of agreement and disagreement can be summed up in Table 7.6, which shows the use of the standard marker of agreement for the five auxiliaries studied in Tables 7.4 and 7.5. The club

TABLE 7.6.
USE OF STANDARD VERB FORMS
BY CLUB MEMBERS, LAMES, AND WHITES

Present tense forms of verb	Percent		
	Club members	Lames	Inwood
has (3rd sg.)	19	60	100
doesn't (3rd sg.)	03	36	32
were (2nd sg., pl.)	14	83	100
does (3rd sg.)	00	13	100
says (3rd sg.)	04	00	100
No. of subjects:	31	10	8

members use these forms with very low frequency. The Lames use *has* and *were* and show some use of *doesn't*. The white Inwood group uses all of them except *doesn't*, where its use is about that of the Lames.

We can therefore conclude that the use of *has, were,* and *doesn't* is a clear sign of shifting away from the black vernacular which distinguishes lames from members.

5. Analysis of the Jet Membership

Having determined that the lames are indeed marked linguistically by their distance from the vernacular culture, we can ask whether the same principle may not operate within the central peer groups as well. If peer-group pressures are important in maintaining the vernacular in its present uniform state and in resisting the pressures of other dialects, then those who are most bound by the norms of the group should show the most consistent form of the vernacular. It is the leaders of vernacular peer groups who are most closely governed by group norms, as Whyte (1955) and others have shown. We might therefore ask what linguistic consequences follow if we decompose the group into leaders and followers, core and periphery, and see if peer-group pressures can make such fine discriminations.

The largest of the groups that we studied in south-central Harlem was the Jets, the adolescent club which dominated West 112th Street between Eighth Avenue and St. Nicholas Avenue.[13] Figure 7.4 shows the distribution of the Jet membership in that area; altogether, 36 persons were interviewed. There are plainly two centers from a geographic point of view: one is concentrated on the short block between Seventh and St. Nicholas Avenues—the 100's block—and the other at the far end of the 200's block, near Eighth Avenue.[14] These areas also represent two separate subgroups in social organization.

13. The analyses of the social structure of the Jets and the conceptual framework used here are the work of Teresa Labov, to whom I am greatly indebted. For further analysis of peer terminology, club names, the associative plural *and 'em,* and the relations of hang-out groups to the club, see T. Labov 1969.

14. There are also one or two scattered members to the north, including the president, Stanley, but this is a result of recent relocation by his family. The apartment rented by John Lewis (club house) is located in the middle of the 100's block.

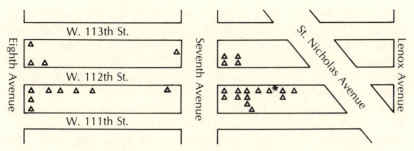

Fig. 7.4. Location of the Jets in south-central Harlem. * = John Lewis' club house.

The Jets are a street club, organized by the members, without adult initiation, supervision, or guidance. As a named club, the Jets have the following features:

1. Leaders: a president, vice-president, war-lord, and prime minister.
2. Members.
3. A name.
4. A history and mythology.
5. A song.
6. Initiation ceremonies.
7. An associated junior club.

The history of the Jets goes back to 1958. It was formed as a junior club to the Red Devils, which was then headed by Mickey Collins. Mickey's younger brother Stanley became the president of the junior club and has continued to be the number one man in all the various changes that the group has been through. The Little Red Devils, with about 16 members, were renamed the Little Diamonds in 1960; in 1962 became in rapid succession the Jets, the Cobrastetas, the Horsemen, and again the Jets.[15] Shortly before we contacted them in 1965, the numbers of the Jets were doubled by the joining up of the 200's block, giving a total membership of 35 to 40.

The internal structure of the Jets is much more complex than we first realized: it is a product of geography, local interests, and primary group alliances. The club is actually a superordinate organization, the largest unit of social structure in the vernacular culture, called

15. The Cobras, located on 115th–116th Streets, was at one time a brother club but at the time of the study was in conflict with the Jets. In 1962, the Cobras were known as the Jets for a time, which explains the rapid shifting of names.

into existence only on ritual occasions or at moments of crisis in conflict with another group. Members normally associate in hang-out groups, smaller aggregates who are involved in a range of daily transactions quite distinct from the Jet activities. As we will see below, the primary influence and major control on linguistic behavior is exercised by these hang-out groups.

Our most systematic information on the structure of the hang-out groups is derived from two questions: "Is there a bunch of cats you hang out with?" and "Of all the cats you hang with, who's the leader?" These data yield sociometric diagrams such as Fig. 7.5, which shows the hang-out groups in the 100's block. Again, the main social links are the reciprocal namings, shown as heavy dark lines. Connections with the 200's block are quite weak: there are no such reciprocal namings between the 100's and 200's. Fig. 7.5 shows that the leader, Stanley, is a pivotal member of two distinct hang-out groups of core members. One is the "six best fighters:" Deuce, Vaughn, Larry, Jesse, Ronald, and Stanley. The other is a group of five that owns and flies pigeons on the roof-tops: Stanley, Hop, Rednall, Doug, and Rel. At the lower end of Fig. 7.5 is a group of younger members, from 12 to 14; the core members at the upper end are 15 to 16 years old. The complete pattern of namings is shown in Table 7.7, in which the Jets are broken down into *core, secondary,* and *peripheral* members. Core members are clearly marked in the number of reciprocal namings, with at least two, and as many as eight; secondary and peripheral members have only one or two. The secondary members of the Jets are located entirely within the structure where they hold an inferior status; this is their primary "social address." Peripheral members, on the other hand, are partially detached from the group because they are older, live at a distance, or have other interests, but not because they have lower status.[16] They are less under the control of the group, and we may therefore expect them to be less dominated by it in their linguistic patterns.

On the outer edge of the networks in Fig. 7.5 we see a few lames who name some Jets in the hang-out question, but are not normally mentioned in turn by anyone (with one exception, by a peripheral member). These are definitely not considered members by anyone,

---

16. Senior members such as Deuce are actually peripheral in this sense. Other members of the Jet age range who are under pressure from parents to break away, but resist this pressure, may also hold a respected position, as with Ricky S.

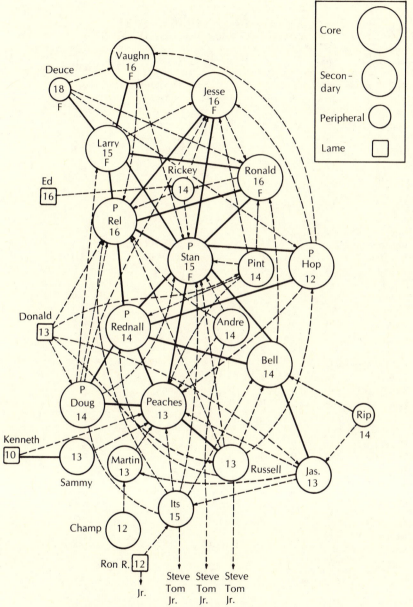

Fig. 7.5. Hang-out pattern for the Jets: 100's block. F = six best fighters. P = pigeon flyers.

TABLE 7.7.
NAMES GIVEN AND RECEIVED BY JETS
IN ANSWERS TO THE HANG-OUT QUESTION

Name	Age	G	R	Rp	Name	Age	G	R	Rp
100's Core					*200's Core*				
Stanley	15	8	15	8	Junior D.	15	2	12	2
Jesse H.	16	6	9	3	Ronald F.	14	8	6	2
Vaughn	16	4	4	2	Tommy	13	5	13	3
Ronald W.	16	4	7	3	Stevie W.	13	4	14	4
Larry H.	15	16	5	4	Tinker	13	6	7	3
Rel	16	6	15	5					
Rednall	14	6	10	6					
Doug	14	6	4	2					
Bell	14	7	10	3					
Peaches	13	4	16	4					
Hop	12	8	5	2					
100's Secondary					*200's Secondary*				
Martin B.	13	1	2	0	Ulysses	13	8	0	0
Russell	13	9	4	1	Poochie	13	8	0	0
James T.	13	7	4	1	Turkey	13	7	3	0
Champ	12	3	0	0	Laundro	13	8	2	0
Sammy	12	2	1	1					
Pint	14	6	1	0					
Its	15	9	1	0					
Andre	14	13	2	0					
100's Peripheral					*200's Peripheral*				
Deuce	18	8	2	1	Ray	14	5	1	1
Rickey S.	16	3	2	0	Leon	13	10	3	1
Rip	14	9	0	0	William G.	12	10	2	0
					Alfred	12	8	0	0
Jet Area Lames									
David D.	17	0	0	0					
Steve Y.	17	0	0	0					
Ed S.	16	1	0	0					
Larry W.	15	10	1	1					
John McN.	14	3	0	0					
Donald G.	13	11	0	0					
Ronald R.	12	5	0	0					
Kenneth A.	10	6	1	1					

G: no. of names given
R: no. of times named
Rp: reciprocal namings

do not fight with the Jets, do not participate in any of the hang-out groups, and are plainly not members of the vernacular culture.[17] In addition, we interviewed a number of lames in the Jet area who do not appear in Fig. 7.5 at all and have no connection with the Jets though they knew of them. We thus have eight lames in the Jet area to contrast linguistically with the members.

We can dispense with a diagram of the sociometric diagram for the 200's block, whose naming pattern is included in Table 7.7. The same principles apply to the division of the 200's membership.

In section 3, we found that the frequencies of the contraction and deletion of is were among the most sensitive indicators of the speaker's relation to the vernacular and the vernacular subculture. The use of the contraction rules was similar for members and lames, but there was a qualitative difference in the use of the deletion rule. We are now in a position to use that index to look for finer linguistic correlates of peer-group membership.

Table 7.8 shows the use of contraction and deletion by the six subcategories of Jet membership developed in Table 7.7. Again, we note no significant differences in the use of the contraction rule, which is the common property of all dialects. But the deletion rule is tightly correlated with subdivisions of Jet membership. The leaders

TABLE 7.8.
USE OF CONTRACTION AND
DELETION RULES FOR IS BY
SUBDIVISIONS OF THE JETS AND LAMES

Group	No. of forms	φ_C	φ_D
100's Core	259	.66	.70
200's Core	81	.63	.63
100's Secondary	75	.75	.61
200's Secondary	148	.72	.56
Peripheral	82	.80	.33
Lame	127	.57	.36

17. Ed and Donald are connected with the pattern only in that they name others but are not named by anyone in return. Kenneth, 10, forms one of two exceptions, since he hangs out with the secondary member Sammy. It should be emphasized that these sociometric patterns are not the only defining characteristics of the members; more substantive accounts of their activity are essential elements in this assignment.

of the group in the 100's core show the highest use of this rule, the 200's core slightly lower, and both sets of secondary members again considerably lower use. The most striking fact is that the peripheral members and lames use the deletion rule less than half as much as core members.

If we now compare Table 7.8 with Tables 7.4 and 7.5, it is evident that the Oscar Brothers and the peripheral members of the Jets are in the same relative position. These are older, somewhat wiser members who have begun to emerge from their total immersion in the vernacular culture. They are not lames—they have not lost their knowledge of local ways and doings; but they have begun to show the effects of a greater awareness of the larger cultural matrix in which the black English vernacular is embedded. They would normally be considered "bidialectal," and they would give outside observers the strong impression that they were capable of switching abruptly between the vernacular and a more standard dialect. But even the most casual style in group sessions among these older members shows a distinct shift away from the vernacular. In general, we do not find bidialectalism in this simple sense of switching from a new to an older dialect. Learning a new set of closely related rules inevitably influences the form of the old rules. Turning to the lames, we observe the same kind of shift away from the vernacular—but at a younger age, with different consequences. The lames have not passed through the same period of adolescent immersion in the vernacular culture. Though they arrive at a similar grammatical stance, the lames do not have the deep experience of the subculture which peripheral members have absorbed. How much of this early knowledge can be retrieved from older members who have shifted away from the vernacular in their own personal use of the BEV rules? We will return to this important question in section 6.

Not all of the features of the vernacular show a regular gradation from the core members of the Jets outward. Some vernacular rules are intact for everyone. One such case is negative concord within the clause, which operates categorically in BEV to yield *Nobody never saw nothin' like that* instead of *Nobody ever saw anything like that* (see chapter 4 in this volume). Thirty-one of the 37 individuals interviewed in the Jet area showed 100 percent use of this rule; the remaining six are all individual cases and do not show any kind of pattern.

There are also some markers of BEV which are common to all

members, but their use differentiates the lames sharply, giving the kind of pattern that we saw in section 3. For example, all members of the Jets use dummy *it* much more often than dummy *there* in such sentences as *It's a difference.* The members range from 60 to 84 percent use of dummy *it;* but the lames use *it* only 23 percent of the time.

If the primary mechanism of social control is the hang-out group, we should find local differentiation of clubs and of units within the club. It is not difficult to locate examples of specific linguistic features which are generalized throughout a primary group. The Cobras, for example, may be differentiated from the Jets in their tendency to use *skr-* for *str-* (as in *skreet*)—a coastal South Carolina feature which has been adopted by members, including those with no family background in that area. In general, we find no correlation between linguistic features used by members and the geographic background of their family; whatever regional influence appears is quickly generalized throughout the group.

A more specific highly localized feature is the pronunciation *an'shi-it* [ænʃiːt] for the common tag *an'shit.* A small tightly-knit subgroup within the six best fighters of the Jets core members uses this form regularly—Larry, Jesse, and Vaughn.[18] There are also a number of intonational features and vocabulary items which differentiate the two major groups and subgroups within them. Such small tokens of group identification bear witness to the powerful group pressures exerted on language.

The social organization known as the Jets has persisted for many years with extraordinary stability, in spite of opposition from all of the other social groups in the community. The adults in the Jet area consider them "hoodlums"; the schools have suspended their leading members; the courts have sent several to correctional institutions; and the neighboring groups of their own age are even more hostile. What then explains the success of the Jets as a stable social institution?

First of all, it is clear that there are socioeconomic factors, not analyzed here, which operate upon inner-city communities to produce similar patterns of social organization. Table 7.9 shows some of the social characteristics of the Jets and Cobras. They are remark-

18. Larry and Jesse are brothers; a third brother is Peaches, a central figure among the younger members of the 100's block.

TABLE 7.9.
SOCIAL CHARACTERISTICS OF
JET AND COBRA CLUBS

Characteristics	Cobras	Jets
Persons interviewed	19	36
Average age	14.1	14.2
Families on welfare	27%	11%
Mother and father living home	41%	40%
Father not living home	47%	50%
Average number of persons in hang-out list	7.5	6.6
Total different persons named	54	82
Average namings per person	2.5	3
only those interviewed	4.7	5.1
those not interviewed	1.5	1.1
Club members said to be		
suspended from school	0	2
"upstate" (in correctional institution)	9	3

ably similar in family structure, in the average number of persons
named in the hang-out group, and both show a record of conflicts
with the law. These figures are similar to those for comparable
vernacular groups in New York and other cities. The Jets provide
a group answer to certain social needs which are not met by the
surrounding society. Groups of Jets can take over empty apartments,
commandeer rooftops to fly pigeons, steal clothes and other loose
goods, and get high together. They also support each other's view
of their individual worth through a system of shared attitudes.

The linguistic forms which differentiate the Jets from the surrounding adults and lames are symbolic representations of the value
system which distinguishes the group and draws new members.
Members can seldom make these values explicit; a quotation from
Champ, a younger secondary member of the Jets, shows some of the
difficulty in formulating covert values.

> John Lewis: I want to ask you, man. How come you join
> the Jets? Do you know?
>
> Champ: First reason I joined 'em, 'cause I like to fight;
> you know, gang fight, and the second reason I joined
> was while they—while we was 'round there and they
> have nothing' to do—play against fightin' each other.
> And the third reason I f—joined, 'cause I lived around
> the neighborhood.

Champ's answer illustrates the Jet values of mutual support and gain of status in fighting and the sense of belonging to a neighborhood. There are also gains in support against the perceived oppression of the surrounding society, the prestige of close association, and the inside knowledge proceeding from that association. In chapter 6, Vaughn R. gives us the clearest view of what the Jets can provide for someone who could follow the upward path of social mobility through education, but refuses. Vaughn moved into the area from Washington Heights the year before. He had demonstrated the ability to use the school culture for his personal advantage, but he deliberately selected the Jets' culture instead. In Vaughn's statement (page 250), we saw that the inside knowledge proceeding from the association with the peer group is a major factor in supporting the group. For Vaughn, the covert values of the vernacular culture have become overt: he sees the Jets as a force directly opposed to the dominant white value system which claimed his allegiance but which he has rejected.

We have already seen that Vaughn is an integral member of the "six best fighters" and has some superficial linguistic markers in common with Larry and Jessie H. But since Vaughn has come into the Jet orbit only in the past year, one would not expect him to have absorbed the whole range of grammatical and phonological patterns of the Jets. Vaughn implies that he was more or less a lame in Washington Heights and it is inevitable that his grammar will reflect this. Whereas other Jets show the usual 100 percent negative concord within the clause, Vaughn is variable: he shows only 30 out of 35 cases of transfer of the negative to a following indefinite. He uses dummy *it* for *there* in only two out of seven cases. Whereas other Jets show 17 out of 18 or 21 out of 22 monomorphemic clusters simplified before a consonant (as in *just me*) Vaughn simplifies only 4 out of 17. We would therefore be justified in removing Vaughn's records from the mean values for the Jets, which would explain some of the slight irregularities noted in the tables above. Vaughn is able to give us an excellent and explicit statement of the value of belonging to the Jets; but his linguistic system cannot adjust as quickly as his value system or his style of life. The remarkably consistent grammar of the Jets is the result of ten years of their continuous interaction with each other and with other groups in the BEV system.

If we see the primary group as the main agent in the social control of language, we then have to explain the great uniformity of the black English vernacular throughout the major cities of the North and

South and even in most rural areas. It has now been well-established that the grammar we are dealing with is essentially the same in New York, Detroit, Washington, Philadelphia, and San Francisco, and such uniformity may very well reflect the presence of a wide-spread Creole grammar used throughout the southern United States in the 18th and 19th centuries. Yet if the primary group can exert such influence on language, what prevents various subgroups from drifting off in different directions? This is a question which cannot be settled in the light of our present knowledge. But it should be noted that it is not merely the grammar which is uniform. The vernacular culture itself is equally constant from one urban area to another; the grammar is just one of the many elements of the social pattern which is transmitted. This uniformity cannot be maintained by adolescents, since the great majority of the members who travel from one city to another are adults. We should therefore be hesitant in saying that the late teens are the upper limit for the consistent use of the black English vernacular. It is true that the adults recorded in interviews with Clarence Robins have as a whole shifted away from the vernacular on all the variables that discriminate members and lames. In their use of (r), (dh), and (ing), working-class adults resemble the lames rather than members. Negative concord is variable in adults and in lames, but obligatory for members. In consonant cluster simplification, adults show the grammatical constraint as more important than the phonological one, again resembling lames more than members. The most sensitive index of the black English vernacular is the use of the deletion rule for *is*: working-class adults are at an even lower level than the lames, $\varphi = .21$ as against .60–.70 for members and .36 for lames. We also find that adults show subject-verb agreement with 3rd person singular -s; while this inflection is present only zero to 40 percent of the time among members, it is found from 70 to 100 percent of the time among adults; furthermore, the adults show a phonological rule operating in that they show more -s before a following vowel, while members show the inflection *less* often in this context. Adults rarely use dummy *it* for *there*, seldom use *ain't* for *didn't*, and rarely use the habitual be_2.

But before we conclude that the entire adult population is lame, it must be remembered that we did not record adults in social interaction with their own friends and neighbors. Even in casual speech, adults fall short of the mark set by the group sessions with members; but the sections of casual speech which we drew from the interview are less valid approximations to the vernacular than the group sessions of the Jets and Cobras. Instead of concluding that the basic grammar of adults has shifted we might say that adults have greater practice in shifting their use of the variables towards the standard in semiformal contexts. Until we have carried out long-term participant observation with adult groups, it is impossible to make any firm statements about adult grammars. If we do finally conclude that adult grammars have shifted away from the vernacular, the problem of explaining the uniformity of the BEV grammar throughout the country will become formidable. If adults are not the ultimate model upon which the vernacular is based, what would prevent the adolescent peer groups from gradually dispersing in 100 different directions?

6. The Prevalence of Lames

The term *lame* carries the negative connotation that was originally intended by the members of the BEV culture who applied it to the isolated individuals around them. But it is evident that the lames are *better* off than members in many ways. They are more open to the influence of the standard culture, and they can take advantage of the path of upward mobility through education, if they are so inclined or so driven (see chapter 6). They are less open to social pressures to fight, to steal, or take drugs. Of course some lames steal, shoot up, and drop out; but as a group, they have a better record. In a study of 37 addict and nonaddict sibling pairs, Glaser et al. 1971 found that 22 of the addicts said that they had hung out in gangs as kids, and only seven of the nonaddicts. In 16 of the cases, it was agreed that the nonaddict had stayed home most as a teenager, and in only seven was this said of the addict. There are any number of positive terms that I might have applied to lames which would reflect this side of the matter, contrasting them with the members of the lower-class peer groups: *nondelinquents* as against *delinquents, culture-free* as against *culture-bound, upwardly mobile* as against *downwardly mobile.* Even a neutral term such as *isolates* would have avoided the pejorative sense of *lame* which must inevitably irritate readers who realize that lames are better individuals from the standpoint of middle-class society—and even more importantly, that it is to the personal advantage of any individual to be a lame. Even if he does not go to college, he has a better chance of making money, staying out of jail and off of drugs, and raising children in an intact family. Given hindsight or a little foresight, who would not rather be a lame?

The term *lame* serves to remind us that it is the normal, intelligent, well-coordinated youth who is a member of the BEV culture and who is suffering from the social and educational depression of the ghetto. The lames are exceptional in one way or another. Some unusually intelligent and some unusually stupid boys are lames; some lames are courageous and self-reliant individuals who go their own way with no need of group support, and some are weak or fearful types who are protected from the street culture by their mothers, their teachers, and their television set. Some lames gain safety or success through isolation, but in exchange they give up the satisfaction of a full social life and any first-hand knowledge of the vernacular culture. Other lames have gained nothing through their isolation: they are the victims of a disorganized and demoralized subsection of the community. Many descriptions of the poor and disadvantaged are explicitly about lame areas and lame children. The study by Pavenstedt et al. of deprived children in the North Point Project of Boston was concerned with disorganized families exhibiting "social and/or psychological pathology":

They do not belong to a "culture," having neither traditions nor institutions. No ethnic ties nor active religious affiliations hold them together. In fact we speak of them as a group only because of certain common patterns of family life and a form of peripheral social existence (Pavenstedt 1967:10).

The descriptions of the language of these children matches the picture of "verbal deprivation" which we find in educational psychologists who have developed the "deficit hypothesis" (*Sociolinguistic Patterns*, chapter 8; Ginsburg 1971). We have not studied children of this type, but many of the apparently unrealistic descriptions of the language behavior of lower-class black children may be based on such specially selected populations.[19] It should also be noted that "verbal deprivation" may occur in isolated upper-working-class families where both parents work, and preschool children are kept at home, forbidden to play with others on the street.

19. Note that some such projects explicitly concentrate on subjects with histories of psychological pathology or work in areas with high concentrations of mental retardation. This was the case with the study of Heber, Dever, and Conry 1968, discussed in chapter 5.

In other discussions of the vernacular we have indicated that the lames have suffered a loss of some magnitude in their isolation from its rich verbal culture.[20] The members themselves, who have responded to the definition of man as a social animal, see most clearly the overwhelming disadvantages of being a lame. For those who are trying to understand the structure and evolution of social behavior, the disadvantages of dealing with lames will eventually appear just as clearly. At first glance, lames appear to be members of the community; they are much more accessible to the outsider than members are; and the limitations of their knowledge are not immediately evident. But the result as we have seen may be an inaccurate or misleading account of the vernacular culture. Many of the informants used by linguists and anthropologists are lames—marginal men who are detached from their own society far enough to be interested and accessible to the language, the problems and preoccupations of the investigator.[21] It is even more common for the linguist to work with captive populations—classes of students who are tested as a whole without regard to their group membership or participation in the culture being studied. Subjects selected with the assitance of teachers, psychologists, or parents are even more heavily biased towards the lame population and unfortunately, the number of studies of black English vernacular made in schools far outnumbers the studies done by direct contact with members in a vernacular context.[22] If

20. See Abrahams (1964), chapters 7 and 8 in this volume and section 4.2 of CRR 3288 for evidence that BEV culture is the most verbal subculture within the United States. As a whole, the lames have lost out on this, although many have managed to transfer their verbal skills into a superbly elaborated version of the Bernsteinian elaborated code.

21. The classic case is the work of Loflin (1967) whose descriptions of the grammar of black English vernacular are explicitly based on data obtained over a period of approximately a year from one 14-year-old boy. Data supplied by an isolated individual in response to direct questions may be skewed from the vernacular in the direction of the standard, as in the data given above. But if the informant understands that the linguist is interested primarily in those features which are most different from the standard he will produce a stereotyped version in the opposite direction. A comparison of Loflin's descriptions with the spontaneous group data from the same community collected in Loman 1967 shows that this kind of distortion is most common: as for example, reporting that there is no preterit −ed or have +en in the dialect.

22. For school-based studies see Loban 1966, Henrie 1969, Entwisle and Greenberger 1969, Baratz 1968, Cazden 1968, Garvey and McFarlane 1968 and many others. For secular studies, see Wolfram 1969, Mitchell 1969, those cited in this study, and not many others.

the vernacular culture is the main stream of linguistic and social evolution as we have argued elsewhere then this is a serious matter. Let us consider for a moment some of the ways in which lames fall short as informants.

We have already seen in section 2 that Lesley and the other 1390 Lames used a kind of black vernacular that was much closer to some of the other nonstandard vernaculars than to BEV. They show subject-verb agreement, variable negative concord, contraction of *is* but very little deletion, and so on. If we begin to explore broader aspects of the vernacular culture, the data are even more skewed. One of the most important regulations in peer-group society are the rules for fair fighting and the violations of those rules that make up street fighting. The information we can get from Curtis is only hearsay. He has been in no major fights of his own, and his accounts of T-Bird fights are those of a bystander who never understands how they started. One of our basic questions in the "Fight" section of our interview schedule is, "What was the best fight you ever saw?" To get the same message across to lames, we have to translate this into "What was the worst fight you ever saw?" A great many lames actually deny the fights they were in—partly because they lost, and partly because they have been trained to think of fighting as a bad thing to do. As a result, lame narratives of personal experience are lame, too.

If we are interested in toasts, jokes, sounds, the dozens, riffing, or capping, we cannot turn to the lames. They have heard sounding from a distance, but proficiency at these verbal skills is achieved only by daily practice and constant immersion in the flow of speech. Lames do not know "Signifying Monkey," "Shine," "The Fall," or any of the other great toasts of the oral literature. But away from home, some lames look back on the vernacular culture and try to claim it as their own; the result can be a very confused report for the outsider who relies on such data.

At recent scholarly meetings on black studies, there have been violent objections from black students and professionals to the use of the term *black English*, with repeated demands for a definition which could not be satisfied. Some educated black speakers argue that *black English* should be used for the language that they themselves use, since they are black, and deny that they use many of the words or grammatical forms quoted by the linguist as "black English." This objection seems to be valid. It seems much more appro-

priate to use the term *black English vernacular, BE vernacular,* or
BEV to identify the consistent grammar of the peer group members
that has been analyzed by linguists. We will then avoid the improper
opposition of "Standard English" to "black English," implying that
this is the major axis dividing the English language. Instead, we
should oppose the standard language to all nonstandard dialects or
vernaculars. One of these is the black English vernacular.

Most of the black professors and students that I have met in the
universities are intent on absorbing whatever the "high culture" of
Western literature, European literature, art, and scholarship has to
offer, but without losing what they feel are the essential values of
their own background. But at the same time, many condemn "ghetto
English" as an inferior means of communication and claim that
black people can improve their social and economic position only
if they acquire the formal means of expression used by this high
culture. There is a division of opinion on the place for the vernacular,
usually referred to as "our own language," "home language" or "soul
language." Most college students will claim to have a deep and
intimate knowledge of it and insert into their basically standard
grammar quotations from the "language of the street". But very few
are willing to examine the grammar of this dialect.

But the findings presented here indicate that unless these speakers
were raised within the majority peer group culture and broke away
from their group only in late adolescence, their grammar will be
peripheral to the black English vernacular. They may be at a greater
disadvantage than they realize in dealing with complex rules such
as those involved in negative concord since their own grammars may
be influenced by other dialects in a number of subtle and indirect
ways. In any case, black students are not yet making the major
contribution to linguistics and the investigation of the black English
vernacular that we hope for.[23] This is a serious problem, for it is
hard to imagine the study of the BE vernacular making good progress
without black linguists carrying the major share of the field work
and analysis. Given our present social situations, most black graduate
students will be lames; but even with the limitations shown here,

---

23. There are a number of graduate students from black communities in the U.S.
who are now working on problems of black English in various research groups throughout the country; there is a good possibility that the statement made here will be obso-
lete by the time this book appears.

it should be clear that they are much closer to the black vernacular than any white student will be. More importantly, they have the background and credentials to become as close as they want to. To do this it is only necessary that they achieve a firm understanding of what the vernacular is, who speaks it, and how they stand in relation to it.

The position of the black graduate student in linguistics is no different from that of any linguist in his removal from the vernacular. If a black student should take seriously Chomsky's claim that the primary data of linguistics is the intuition of the theorist and begin to write an introspective BEV grammar, the results would be bad—but no worse than other grammars now being written on the same basis. The problem we are dealing with here is one of the greatest generality, for it must be realized that most linguists are lames.

7. The Linguist as Lame

There are communities where the basic vernacular is a prestige dialect which is preserved without radical changes as the adolescent becomes an adult. The class dialect used in British public schools had that well-formed character, and presumably a British linguist raised as a speaker of Received Pronunciation can serve as an accurate informant on it.[24] There are middle-class French and Spanish children who may be in the same favorable position in relation to their prestige dialect. To a lesser extent, this may be said about a few Americans who grow up in upper middle-class communities where 90 percent of the high-school graduates go on to college. On the surface, they seem to continue using the dialect that was the main vehicle of communication by peer groups in their preadolescent years and are able to represent that group in speech as well as intuition.

The great majority of linguists are probably not in that position. They were already detached from the main peer group activity in early adolescence as they pursued their own interests, and by the

24. The social controls exerted on that dialect have been discussed at some length and are well known, and deviations from the standard penalized by members looking for linguistic evidence of an inadequate background. If it is true that Received Pronunciation cannot be mastered by someone who has been to the wrong school, this would stand as additional confirmation of the fact that the regular rules of the vernacular must be formed in the preadolescent years.

time they enter graduate studies in linguistics are at some distance from the majority of vernacular speakers in their community. I was a lame myself in my adolescent years; my knowledge of the non-standard vernacular of the working-class majority in Fort Lee, New Jersey, is as indirect as the lames' knowledge of black vernacular described above. The knowledge I now have of how to deal with the vernacular culture of adolescent and adult groups was gained in contacts since then—in factories, in the service, and in many field trips to urban and rural areas—always with a full recognition of this initial distance. Fortunately for linguists interested in the study of language in its social context, the problem of gaining access to peer groups and of observing natural interaction does not require that the full distance be crossed in each encounter. The linguist can learn principles of social organization which are very much the same in regions as distant as Hawaii, Chicago, Kingston, Glasgow, and Paris.

Even if the linguist is raised in a community of peers, fully immersed in the main stream of social life in his high school years, he inevitably broadens his horizon when he pursues college and graduate training and weakens his command of the vernacular. Our studies of sound change in progress in cities throughout England and America shows that college students are in general a very poor source of data. The sharp, clear patterns shown in the working-class speakers are blurred, limited, and mixed in the speech of the college student. The principle seems to hold that learning closely-related dialect rules affects the form of the original ones. The linguist who is alert to the widest range of dialect differences, who may construct the broadest pan-dialectal grammar, is often the worst informant on his own local dialect. There are of course exceptions—some speakers show an extraordinarily tenacious hold on their original dialect. But we do not know who the exceptions are until we have studied the vernacular in the intact speech community itself.

I do not believe that it is natural or inevitable that the linguist be a lame, or that only lames go to college. I am not convinced that linguistic analysis—or a future linguistic science—must be carried out in the grammar of the high culture. Nor is it inevitable that black students who go to college and graduate school be lames. In our present social system, the best way for a lower-class youth to achieve upward social mobility, money and security is by breaking away from his group. The social and psychological price for this move is well-known. But there is some reason to think that the group can move as a whole, and a few signs that this might indeed happen in our society. If this should happen, the gains would be very great for everyone concerned, including the linguist who has more to learn from members than lames.

When we now hear linguists speaking at every hand about "my dialect" and "dialect variation" we are bound to wonder what basis they have for their claims. The only data usually provided is that some other linguist has disagreed with their intuitive judgments on certain sentences, and it is therefore decided that the critic is speaking a different dialect. "My dialect" turns out to be characterized by all the sentence types that have been objected to by others. Although it has been claimed that some speakers differ from each other repeatedly and reliably, no correlation is claimed with geography, peer group, family, or fraternity. Such idiolectal variations are said to be correlated with the systematic development of syntactic rules in particular directions, a product of the language-learning faculty in its most subtle and efficient form. If so, it will undoubtedly appear that no two linguists have the same dialect, unless they are colleagues jointly responsible for the same theory. These are lame dialects, and it is appropriate that they be conceived, developed and analyzed in isolation.

It is difficult for us, caught up in current linguistic practice, to evaluate the overwhelming reliance of our field on the theorist's own intuitions as data. Scholars of the future who must eventually review and explain our behavior may find it hard to understand our casual acceptance of confused and questionable data, the proliferation of ad hoc dialects, and the abandonment of the search for intersubjective agreement. They may point out that most scholars will do whatever they have been told is right and proper by other scholars. But their analysis may also indicate that our current trend is supported by more than local ideology; a theoretical stance can become a congenial way of life. To refine the intricate structure of one's own thoughts, to ask oneself what one would say in an imaginary world where one's own dialect is the only reality, to dispute only with those few colleagues who share the greatest part of this private world— these academic pleasures will not easily be abandoned by those who were early detached from the secular life. The student of his own intuitions, producing both data and theory in a language abstracted from every social context, is the ultimate lame.

Part III

THE USES OF THE
BLACK ENGLISH VERNACULAR

8 | Rules for Ritual Insults

WE now turn to the uses of the black English vernacular and begin to document the claim made in earlier chapters that members of the vernacular culture are in command of great verbal skills.[1] We could consider a wide range of speech events in which these skills are displayed: *shucking, rifting, toasting, sweet-talking* (CRR 3288, Kochman 1970, Abrahams 1970). But instead this chapter will analyze in detail one particular speech event: the system of ritual insults known variously as *sounding, signifying, woofing, cutting,* etc. In this pursuit there will be ample opportunity to demonstrate the verbal resources of peer-group members, their command of complex syntax, and their creative powers. In the following chapter we will take up narratives of personal experience and examine the syntactic devices used to transform that experience so that others can understand it. Here too we will have ample evidence of the great development of verbal resources within the black English vernacular. To explore these uses of language, we will necessarily be engaged in the study of discourse, going beyond the sentence grammar of chapters 1–4.

Linguists have not made very much progress in the study of discourse: by and large, they are still confined to the boundaries of the sentence. If *discourse analysis* is not a virgin field, it is at least technically so in that no serious penetration of the fundamental areas has yet been made. There is of course a well-known publication of Harris entitled *Discourse Analysis Reprints* (1963), but it is concerned with rearrangements of sentence structure which are not related to

---

1. This chapter is reprinted with permission of The Macmillan Company from *Studies in Social Interaction,* edited by David Sudnow. Copyright © 1972 by The Free Press, a division of The Macmillan Company. It has been slightly revised.

the general questions to be raised here.[2] Although many linguists who are beginning to make contributions to the study of discourse—it is somewhat startling for linguists to discover that the major steps have been taken by sociologists. Sacks (1972) and Schegloff (1972) have isolated a number of fundamental problems and made some progress toward solution: the selection of speakers, the identification of persons and places, and the isolation of that social competence which allows members of a society to engage in talk. The influence of their work on this chapter will be apparent in the focus on sequencing in ritual insults and the social knowledge required for their interpretation.

Linguists should be able to contribute their skill and practice in formalization to this study. It would not be too much to say that the concepts of invariance and rule-governed behavior are more fully developed in linguistics than in any other field of social study. Yet there may be such a thing as premature formalization, which Garfinckel, Goffman, Sacks, and Schegloff are anxious to avoid: the categorical model of linguistic behavior may indeed lead linguists to set up paradigms of discrete features, mutually defined by their oppositions, in fields where only open sets are to be found in reality. But formalization is a fruitful procedure even when it is wrong: it sharpens our questions and promotes the search for answers.

Some General Principles of Discourse Analysis

The first and most important step in the formalization of discourse analysis is to distinguish what is *said* from what is *done*. From a grammatical viewpoint, there are only a small number of sentence types: principally *statements*, *questions*, and *imperatives*, and these must be related by discourse rules to the much larger set of actions

---

2. The definition of discourse analysis with which Harris begins his "Discourse Analysis Manual" shows no direct relation to the problems to be raised in this paper. For Harris, "discourse analysis is a method of seeking in any connected discrete linear material . . . some global structure characteristic of the whole discourse . . ." This global structure is "a pattern of occurence . . . of segments of the discourse relative to each other". Harris points out that this is the only type of structure that can be investigated "without bringing into account other types of data, such as relations of meanings throughout the discourse." This pursuit therefore forms part of Harris's previous interest in analyzing the phonology and grammar of a language without reference to meaning.

done with words. It is commonplace to use these terms inter-
changeably with the names of certain actions: *assertions, requests
for information,* and *commands* respectively. But there is no such
simple one-to-one relationship: it is easy to demonstrate, for example,
that requests for information can be made with statements, questions,
or imperatives:

> I would like to know your name.
> What is your name?
> Tell me your name!

Furthermore, there are a great many other actions which are done
with words and which must be related by rule to the utterance:
refusals, challenges, retreats, insults, promises, threats, etc. The rules
which connect what is said to the actions being performed with
words are complex; the major task of discourse analysis is to analyze
them and thus to show that one sentence follows another in a coherent way. If we hear the dialogue:

> *A:* Are you going to work tomorrow?
> *B:* I'm on jury duty.

we know intuitively that we are listening to coherent discourse. Yet
there is no formal basis in sentence-grammar to explicate our reaction to this well-formed sequence. A *statement* follows a *question;*
the question is a *request for information,* but in what way does the
statement form an *answer* to that request? Some fear that linguists
will never be able to answer such questions, because one would have
to enter into our grammars every known relation between persons
and objects: in this case, that people on jury duty are not able to
work.[3] However, the form of discourse rules is independent of such
detail. In answering A's request for information Q-S_1 with a superficially unrelated statement S_2, B is in fact asserting that there is a
proposition known to both A and B that connects this with S_1. When

---

3. It was an unpublished draft by Bever and Ross on "Underlying Structures in
Discourse" (1966) which put the issue most directly. In order to show coherence in
a discourse such as *Everyone should read the Bible. Deuteronomy is one of the great
books of the world,* Bever and Ross thought that it would be necessary to include
in the grammar that Deuteronomy is one of the books of the Bible and that discourse
analysis therefore lay outside of linguistics. The rules of discourse developed here
are not subject to this problem; they would typically show that some such relation
is being asserted by the sequence itself, as listeners unfamiliar with the Bible would
infer without difficulty.

A hears B say "I'm on jury duty," he searches for the proposition which B is asserting; in this case, he locates, 'If someone is on jury duty, he cannot go to work'. B's answer is then heard as 'I'm not going to go to work tomorrow'.

The rule of discourse which we can then formulate will read as follows:

> If A makes a request for information Q-S_1, and B makes a statement S_2 in response which cannot be expanded by rules of ellipsis to the form X S_1 Y, then S_2 is heard as an assertion that there exists a proposition P known to both A and B:

$$\text{If } S_2 \text{, then (E) } S_1$$

> where (E) is an existential operator, and from this proposition there is inferred an answer to A's request: (E) S_1.

This is a rule of interpretation which relates what is said (S_2) to what is done (the assertion of P) and to the answer to Q-S_1. Note that there is no direct connection between the two utterances Q-S_1 and S_2, and it would be fruitless to search for one.

The overall relation of discourse rules to utterances shows several levels of abstraction. Consider a conversation of the following superficial form:

A: Are you going to work tomorrow?   (U_1)
B: I'm on jury duty.   (U_2)
A: Couldn't you get out of it?   ·   (U_3)
B: We tried everything.   (U_4)

To understand the connections between these four utterances, they must be expanded to a scheme such as the following:

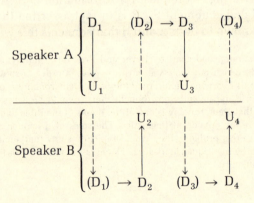

Speaker A begins with the intention of performing the action D_1; by a production rule, he does so with the utterance U_1. Speaker B uses the inverse interpretation rule to interpret U_1 as A's action D_1 and then applies a sequencing rule to decide his response D_2. He then codes D_2 into the utterance U_2 by a production rule, and Speaker A interprets this—in this case, by the rule cited which tells him that the statement *I'm on jury duty* is a response to D_1 to be interpreted as 'I'm not going to work because I'm on jury duty'. The other sequences follow in the same manner.

There are two types of discourse rules here: rules of interpretation UD (with their inverse rules of production DU), and sequencing rules DD which connect actions. There are of course other rules which connect actions at higher levels of abstraction. The diagram may actually show such structures as exhibited below, where D_5, D_6 and D_7 may be considered exchanges, encounters, inquiries, or even challenges and defenses depending on the larger context of interaction and higher level rules.

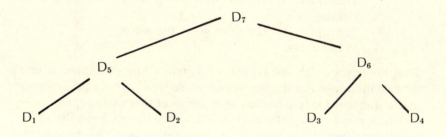

Any statement S_2 will not do in these sequences. If B had replied, "De Gaulle just lost the election," A could reasonably complain "What has that to do with your going to work tomorrow?" The rule tells A to search for a proposition P which will make the connection: if he fails to find it, he will reject B's response. But the operation of the rule is invariant. A must inspect S_2 as a possible element in a proposition *if S_2 then $(E)S_1$* before he can react. Failure to locate such a proposition may reflect a real incompetence; younger members of a social group may not be able to find the proposition being asserted. Thus Linus knocks at Violet's front door and says:[4]

> *Linus:* Do you want to play with me, Violet?
> *Violet:* You're younger than me. (Shuts the door)
> *Linus:* (puzzled) She didn't answer my question.

The unstated proposition being asserted here by Violet is presumed to be part of the communal *shared knowledge,* but it has not in fact reached Linus yet. This concept of "shared knowledge" is an essential element in discourse analysis; to illustrate its importance further, we may consider examples in which statements are heard as *requests for confirmation.* The following exchanges are taken from a therapeutic interview.[5]

> *Therapist:* Oh, so she *told* you.
> *Patient:* Yes.
> *Therapist:* She didn't say for *you* . . .
> *Patient:* No.
> *Therapist:* And it never occurred to her to prepare dinner.
> *Patient:* No.
> *Therapist:* But she does go to the store.
> *Patient:* Yes.

These four instances are typical of a great many examples, where the first utterance is a statement and the second is *yes* or *no.* It seems that a statement is functioning as equivalent to a yes-no question— that is, a request for information. These statements have the same compelling force as requests made in question form: we frequently see that the patient is not allowed to continue until a yes or no answer is given.

A great many speakers habitually use statements to ask for confirmation. How is it that we regularly and reliably recognize these

---

4. Charles M. Schulz, *Peanuts à Vendre* (J. Dupuis, Marcinelle-Charleroi-Belgíque, 1968), p. 64. I happen to have seen this in a French translation, but I am sure that the English original reflects many parallel cases in real life.

5. From current studies of therapeutic interviews being carried out by David Fanshel of the Columbia School of Social Work and myself.

as requests and not as assertions? There is a simple and invariant rule of discourse involved here; it depends upon the concept of shared knowledge, which I will introduce into the rules by classifying all reported events as A-events, B-events, or AB-events. Given any two-party conversation, there exists an understanding that there are events which A knows about, but B does not; and events which B knows about but A does not; and AB-events which are known to both. We can then state simply the rules of interpretation:

> If A makes a statement about a B-event, it is heard as a request for confirmation.

If A makes a statement about an A-event ("I'm sleepy"), it is not heard as such a request. But if he utters a statement about a B-event, ("You were up late last night") it is heard as requesting a confirmation, "Is it true that . . ."[6]

In addition to these concepts of shared and unshared knowledge, there are other elements of discourse which are based on sociological concepts: notions of role, rights, duties, and obligations associated with social rules. Now consider the following exchange from a narrative of the patient, Rhoda, in the therapeutic sessions cited above.

> *Rhoda:* Well, when are you planning to come home?
> *Rhoda's mother:* Oh, why-y?

In the face of such a sequence, it is common to say that "a question is answered with a question." But questions do not answer questions, any more than statements do. Answers are given to requests; they may occasionally take the form of questions. Closer examination of this sequence shows that Rhoda's question is a request for action, not information, and her mother's question is a refusal of that request. But what are the rules which allow us to make this interpretation?

A parallel case can be observed in the following extract from one of our group sessions with the Jets.[7] The speakers involved here are Stanley, the president of the Jets, and Rel, a Puerto Rican member

---

6. There are cases where A makes a statement about an AB-event which requires an answer, but these seem to be equivalent to rhetorical questions which are not requests for information and should probably be covered by a different rule.

7. This particular session was the subject of considerable study: it was recorded on video-tape as well as on multiple audio tracks.

who is also one of the officers (prime minister). At one point Rel
called for quiet:

> Rel: Shut up please!
> Stanley: . . . . 'ey, you tellin' me?
> Rel: Yes. Your mother's a duck.

Rel's first remark—an imperative—is clearly a command or request
for action. Stanley's response is formally a question, but it is certainly
not a request for information; again, we intuitively recognize that
Stanley is refusing but by what regular rule of interpretation do we
recognize this?[8] The general form of the answer may be outlined
as follows. The underlying rules for requests for action appear to
have the form: A requests B to do X for the purpose Y under conditions Z. For this to be heard as a valid command, it is necessary
for the following additional preconditions to hold. B must believe
that A believes that:

1. X needs to be done.
2. B has the ability to do X.
3. B has the obligation to do X.
4. A has the right to tell B to do X.

There are many ways to perform this request and many ways of
aggravating or mitigating the force of the command. One device
involves making statements or asking questions which refer to any
of the four preconditions. The same mechanism can be used to refuse
the request. In both of the examples just given, B refuses by asking
a question concerning the relation of A, B, and X which is heard
as a question about (and a challenge to) precondition 4.

These brief illustrations from current work on discourse analysis
show that the form of discourse rules is independent of the particular
propositions being asserted, challenged, or denied. These rules have
to do with invariant relations between the linguistic units and actions
intended or interpreted. Discourse rules also contain references to
unstated assumptions about social relations, which we are only
beginning to work out. These involve the concepts of shared or social

---

8. At a higher level of analysis, this is a challenge to Rel (see CRR 3288: sec. 4.2.4).
However the rules presented here are aimed at the lowest level of abstraction, closest
to the linguistic material.

knowledge, the roles of speaker, addressee and audiences, their rights and obligations, and other constraints which have not appeared before in the array of linguistic primitives. Some linguists who are currently analyzing the deep structure of sentences have come to realize that one must posit elaborate presuppositions to explain syntactic data, but they have not yet attempted to incorporate such presuppositions into their formal rules.

The questions we have posed so far have been based upon examples relatively transparent to our intuitive sense of what was being done (especially when larger sections of the text are taken into account). But the last example is not at all clear in this sense. Why did Rel tell Stanley that his mother was a duck? Does this have any cognitive meaning, and if so, what rules of interpretation are operating? Rel's remark performed some kind of work, because Stanley then retired from his threatening posture and he apparently considered the incident closed. Stanley regularly insists on his status as president of the Jets; he never backs down from a challenge or backs away from a fight. There are a number of times in this group session when sequences such as these led to fights—semiserious, but none the less real. If Rel had just said "Yes," there would certainly have been some punches traded. But his last remark was accepted as appropriate, coherent discourse, which established some kind of closure to the incident. To those outside this subculture, Rel's utterance (and the action intended) are as opaque as the previous examples were transparent. Those who have some knowledge of urban ghetto culture will recognize Rel's remark *Your mother's a duck* as a ritual insult, and they will connect it with the institution of *the dozens, sounding,* or *signifying. Sounding* is a well-organized speech event which occurs with great frequency in the verbal interaction of black adolescents we have studied and occupies long stretches of their time. This speech event is worth describing as part of the general program of "the ethnography of speaking" outlined by Hymes 1962. Here we have an opportunity to go further, and hope to establish the fundamental rules which govern sounding and use this investigation to achieve some deeper understanding of discourse analysis. If the rules for sounding are appropriate and well constructed, it should be possible to throw light on the particular problem cited here: why does Stanley retire when Rel says to him "Your mother's a duck"?

The following pages will present a large body of information about this speech event.[9] There should be very little difficulty in under-standing the literal meaning of the sounds as English sentences: the grammar used (BEV) presents no particular difficulty to most Amer-icans; the vocabulary is not especially hip or esoteric; the trade names and personalities mentioned are a part of the general Ameri-can scene. But the activity itself is not well known: the point of the whole proceeding will escape many readers. The ways in which sounds are delivered and the evaluation of them by the group follow a well-established ritual pattern which reflects many assumptions and much social knowledge not shared by members of other sub-cultures. To understand the significance of sounds and the function of this activity for members of the vernacular culture, it will be necessary to write explicit rules of discourse for producing, inter-preting, and answering sounds. In our original investigation of sounding, we were much concerned with the syntactic structures involved: much of this material is preserved here, since it adds considerable depth to our understanding of the abstract operations involved.

Terms for the Speech Event

A great variety of terms describe this activity: the dozens, sound-ing, and signifying are three of the most common. The activity itself is remarkably similar throughout the various black communities, both in the form and content of the insults themselves and in the rules of verbal interaction which operate. In this section we will refer to the institution by the most common term in Harlem—sounding.

Sounding, or playing the dozens, has been described briefly in a number of other sources, particularly Dollard 1939 and Abrahams 1962. Kochman (1968) has dealt with sounding in Chicago in his general treatment of speech events in the black community. The oldest term for the game of exchanging ritualized insults is the dozens. Various possibilities for the origin of this term are given in Abrahams (1962: fn. 1), but none are very persuasive. One speaks of the dozens, playing the dozens, or putting someone in the dozens. The term sounding is by far the most common in New York and is

---

9. I am particularly indebted to Benji Wald for suggestions incorporated in the present version of the analysis of sounding. Much of the following material on sounding is adapted from CRR 3288 Vol. 2: section 4.2.3.

reported as the favored term in Philadelphia by Abrahams. *Woofing* is common in Philadelphia and elsewhere, *joning* in Washington, *signifying* in Chicago, *screaming* in Harrisburg, and on the West Coast, such general terms as *cutting, capping,* or *chopping.* The great number of terms available suggests that there will be inevitably some specialization and shift of meaning in a particular area. Kochman suggests that *sounding* is used in Chicago for the initial exchanges, *signifying* for personal insults, and *the dozens* for insults on relatives. In New York, *the dozens* seems to be even more specialized, referring to rhymed couplets of the form

> I don't play the dozens, the dozens ain't my game
> But the way I fucked your mama is a god damn shame.

But *playing the dozens* also refers to any ritualized insult directed against a relative. *Sounding* is also used to include such insults and includes personal insults of a simpler form. Somebody can "sound on" somebody else by referring to a ritualized attribute of that person.

It seems to be the case everywhere that the superordinate terms which describe a verbal activity are quite variable and take on a wide range of meanings, while the verbal behavior itself does not change very much from place to place. People talk much more than they talk about talk, and as a result there is more agreement in the activity than in the ways of describing it. A member of the BEV subculture may have idiosyncratic notions about the general terms for sounding and the dozens without realizing it. He can be an expert on sounds and be quite untrustworthy on 'sounding'.

The Shape of Sounds

As noted above, some of the most elaborate and traditional sounds are dozens in the form of rhymed couplets. A typical opening dozen is cited above. Another favorite opening is:

> I hate to talk about your mother, she's a good old soul
> She got a ten-ton pussy and a rubber asshole.

Both of these initiating dozens have "disclaiming" or retiring first lines, with second lines which contradict them. They are in this sense typical of the usage of young adults, who often back away from the dozens, saying "I don't play that game," or quoting the proverb, "I laugh, joke and smoke, but I don't play" (Abrahams 1962:210). There is a general impression that sounding is gradually moving down in the age range—it is now primarily an adolescent and preadolescent activity and not practiced as much by young men 20 to 30 years old; but we have no exact information to support this notion. The rhymed dozens were used by adolescents in New York City 20 years ago. In any case, most young adolescents do not know many of the older rhymed dozens and are very much impressed by them. To show the general style, we can cite a few others which have impressed the Jets and Cobras (and were not included in the 20 examples given by Abrahams):

I fucked your mother on top of the piano
When she came out she was singin' the Star Spangled Banner.

Fucked your mother in the ear,
And when I came out she said, "Buy me a beer."

The couplet which had the greatest effect was probably

Iron is iron, and steel don't rust,
But your momma got a pussy like a Greyhound Bus.

The winner in a contest of this sort is the man with the largest store of couplets on hand, the best memory, and perhaps the best delivery. But there is no question of improvisation, or creativity when playing, or judgment in fitting one dozens into another. These couplets can follow each other in any succession: one is as appropriate as the other. The originators certainly show great skill, and C. Robins remembers long hours spent by his group in the 1940's trying to invent new rhymes, but no one is expected to manufacture them in the heat of the contest. The Jets know a few rhymed dozens, such as "Fucked his mother on a red-hot heater/I missed her cunt 'n' burned my peter," but most of the traditional rhymes are no longer well known. One must be quite careful in using the rhymed dozens with younger boys: if they cannot top them, they feel beaten from the start, and the verbal flow is choked off. To initiate sounding in a single interview, or a group session, we used instead such primitive sequences as "What would you say if someone said to you, 'Your momma drink pee?'" The answer is well known to most peer-group members: "Your father eat shit." This standard reply allows the exchange to begin along conventional lines, with room for elaboration and invention.

For our present purposes, the basic formulas can be described in terms of the types of syntactic structures, especially with an eye to the mode of sentence embedding. I will draw most of the examples from two extended sounding sessions in which sounds were *used* rather than simply *quoted*. One was on a return trip from an outing with the Jets: 13 members were crowded in a microbus; 180 sounds were deciphered from the recording made in a 35-minute ride. The other was a group session with five Thunderbirds in which Boot, Money, David, and Roger sounded against each other at great length. For those 60 sounds the record is complete and exact identification is possible.

There are of course many other sessions where sounds are cited or used; included in the examples given below are some from a trip with the Cobras where 35 sounds were deciphered from one short section of a recording. Where the quotations are actual sequences, speakers are indicated by names or initials.

a. *Your mother is (like)* ——. Perhaps the simplest of all sounds is the comparison or identification of the mother with something old, ugly, or bizarre: a simple equative prediction. The Jets use great numbers of such simple sounds:

> Your mother look like Flipper . . . like *Hoppity* Hooper . . . Your mother's a Milk Dud . . . A Holloway Black Cow . . . a rubber dick . . . They say your mother was a Gravy Train . . . Your mother's a bookworm . . . a ass, period. Your mother James Bond, K.C. . . . Your mother Pussy Galore.

The Cobras use a number of sounds of this type:

> Your mama's a weight-lifter . . . a butcher . . . a peanut man . . . a iceman . . . a Boston Indian. Your mother look like Crooked-Mile Hank! . . . like that piece called King Kong! . . . Quahab's mother look like who did it and don't want to do it no more!

Note that the mass media and commercial culture provide a rich body of images. Such sounds were particularly appropriate on the Jet outing because every odd or old person that passed on the way would be a stimulus for another sound.

Your mother look like that taxi driver . . . Your mother
a applejack-eater . . . a flea-bag . . . the Abominable
Snowman . . . Your mother is a Phil D. Basket (calypso
accent) . . . Your mother's a diesel . . . a taxicab driver.

Another passer-by sets off a train of simple identifications at the very
end of the Jet outing:

J1: There go Willie mother right there.
J2: Your mother *is* a lizard.
J3: Your mother smell like a roach.
J4: Your mother name is Benedict Arnold.

One passing lady is the focus of a whole series of sounds. One can
sound on someone simply by saying, "There go your mother."

J1: Hey-ey (whistle) . . . That's your mother over there!
J2: I know that lady.
J1: That's your mother.
J3: Hell, look the way that lady walk.
J4: . . . she sick in the head.
J3: Walk like she got a lizard-neck.

b. *Your mother got* ——. Equally simple, from a syntactic point
of view, is the series of sounds with the form *Your mother got so
and so.* The Thunderbirds use long sequences of this type.

Boot: Your mother got a putty chest.
Boot: Your mother got hair growin'out her dunkie hole.
Roger: Your mother got a .45 in her left titty.
Money: Your mother got a 45-degree titty.
Boot: Your mother got titties behind her neck.

The Jets use simple sounds of this sort as well. (The first statement
here is not a sound: it simply provides the base on which the sound
is built, in this case the verb *got*.)

J1: You got the nerve to talk.
J2: Your mother got funky drawers.
J3: Your mother got braces between her legs.

Again,

Your mother got boobies that shake . . . hangdown lips
Bell mother got a old beat-up boot . . .
Her mother got a face like a rubber ass . . .
Junior got a face like a clown . . .

From an adolescent Chicago group:

> Your momma got three titties: chocolate milk, white milk,
> and one half-and-half.

The Cobras show the same style; note that *wear* does as well as
got where clothes are concerned:

> Your mother got on sneakers!
> Your mother wear high-heeled sneakers to church!
> Your mother wear a jock-strap.
> Your mother got polka-dot drawers!
> Your mother wear the seat of her drawers on the top of
> her head!

The Cobra sounds on clothes gradually drift away from the basic
sounding pattern to a more complex structure that plays on the
names of New York City Department stores:

> Your momma got shit on . . .
> Bel's mother bought her clothes from Ohrbach's. All front
> and no back.
> You got your suit from Woolworth! All wool but it ain't
> worth shit!
> You get your shoes from Buster Brown—brown on the top
> and all busted on the bottom!

Note that one of the Jets or Cobras can appear as the subject of a
sound, though the majority are directed against someone's mother.
In some ways, sounds of the X *got* . . . type are more complex when
directed against a member, possibly because the comparisons are
not as ritualized. Some of these are original and/or complex similies:

> He got a head like a water-hydrant, and shit . . .
> He got a head like a water-pump . . . a mailbox.
> . . . like the front of a bus.
> You got a nose like a car fender!

The Thunderbirds say:

> *Boot:* Money got a head like a tornado mixed with a horse.
> *Money:* You got a head of a motor.

c. *Your mother so —— she ——.* More complex comparisons are
done with a quantifier, an adjective, and an embedded sentence of
the type *b* or other predication.

> *David:* Your mother so old she got spider webs under her
> arms.
> *Boot:* Your mother so old she can stretch her head and
> lick out her ass.

Such sounds can be made freely against a member of the group.

> *Roger:* Hey Davy, you so fat you could slide down the
> razor blade without gettin' cut.
> ... an' he so thin that he can dodge rain drops.

These are traditional "fat" and "thin" similes; they take on a particular value here because David *is* fat (a ritualized attribute for him).
Boot continues with ritual sounds along these lines:

> *Boot:* Eh, eh, your mother so skinny she could split
> through a needle's eye.
> *Boot:* Your mother's so skinny, about that skinny, she can
> get in a Cheerioat and say, "Hula hoop! hula hoop!"

This last variant is one step more complex; it has two subordinate
clauses and two commerical products conjoined into one rhetorical
figure. The same simile appears with a different breakfast cereal
in a Jet sound:

> *Stanley:* Your mother so skinny, she do the hula hoop in
> a Applejack.

Other Jet similes show a wide range of attributes sounded on:

> Bell grandmother so-so-so ugly, her rag is showin'.
> Bell mother was so small, she bust her lip on the curve
> (curb).
> Your mother so white she hafta use Mighty White.
> Your mother so skinny, she ice-skate on a razor blade.
> ... so skinny she can reach under the doorknob ...
> ... so low she c'play Chinese handball on the curve.
> ... so low, got to look down to look up.
> ... so black, she sweat chocolate.
> ... so black that she hafta steal to get her clothes.
> ... so black that she has to suck my dick to get home.

The syntax of these similes can become very complex and involve a second subordination: "your mother is so ____ that when she ____ she can ____." It is not easy to get all of this into one proposition in the heat of the moment.

> Your mother's so small, you play hide-and-go-seek, y'all
> c'slip under a penny.

In this version, the conjunction *when* is omitted (not uncommon in the speech of children), but in addition the *y'all* seems out of place; the syntax of this sound is just beyond the range of performance available to the speaker. Boot of the Thunderbirds can handle constructions of this complexity, but he is the only one who can. The following sound of Boot is even more complex, since the *when* clause conjoins two other clauses:

> *Boot:* His mother was so dirty, when she get the rag take
> a bath, the water went back down the drain.

Here the only flaw in the surface structure is perhaps the absence of *and* before *take a bath*. The underlying structure of this sentence might be shown as in the diagram below.

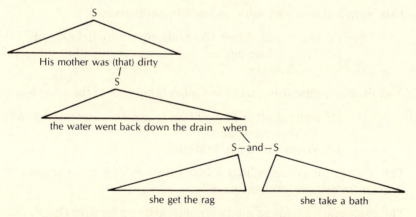

The structure of the sound makes it necessary to foreground the *when*-clauses, so that, rather than end with a condition, the action which makes the insult is last. This means that two clauses interpose between the quantifier and the predication *went down*—a type of left-hand embedding in the surface which is indeed rare in colloquial speech. Boot uses a similar construction without the initial

so clause in the following sound, which again is well beyond the
syntactic competence of most members.

> Boot: Your mother, when she go to work and she had—
> those, you know—open-toe shoes, well, her stockings
> reach her—be sweeping the ground.

Notice that the following sound is much simpler, since the main point
is made by a subordinated clause which can therefore appear in final
position.

> Boot: His mother go to work without any drawers on, so
> that she c'd get a good breeze.

Some of the Jets use constructions of a complexity equal to those
of Boot just given. The most complex syntax occurs in sounds of
the type Your X has Y with attributive quantifiers dominating several
sentences.

> J1: Who father wear raggedy drawers?
> J2: Yeh, the ones with so many holes in them when-a-you
> walk, they whistle?

This sound is received with immediate enthusiasm.

> J3: Oh, shi-it! When you walk they whistle! Oh shit!
> J4: Tha's all he got lef' . . . He never buys but one pair
> o'drawers.

And shortly afterwards, this sound models another of the same form:

> J1: Ronald got so many holes in his socks, when he walks
> them shoes hum!
> J2: Them shoes say MMMM!

The abstract structure which underlies sounds of this complexity
is diagrammed on the next page.

The comparative node so many is contained in a relative clause, and
in turn it dominates a sentence which dominates a time clause. It
cannot be accidental that all of these complex structures are positively evaluated by the group: we can argue that only an idea of
exceptional merit would justify for the originator the effort of using
such syntax and that the evaluation refers to the idea; or we can
argue that the complexity of the structure itself is impressive for the
listener.

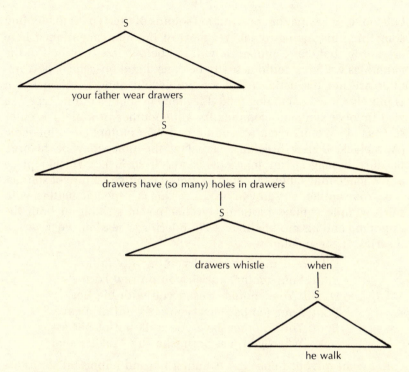

d. *Your mother eat* _____. We now return to a different type of sound which does not involve similes or metaphors, but portrays direct action with simple verbs. The power of these sounds seems to reside in the incongruity or absurdity of the elements juxtaposed—which may be only another way of saying that we do not really understand them.

> *Boot:* I heard your mother eat rice crispies without any milk.
> *Roger:* Eat 'em raw!
> *Boot:* Money eat shit without puttin' any cornflakes on.

The Jets use such constructions freely as well.

> His mother eat Dog Yummies.
> They say your mother eat Gainesburgers.
> Your mother eat coke-a-roaches.
> Your mother eat rat heads.
> Your mother eat Bosco.
> Your mother a applejack-eater.

One obvious recipe for constructing sounds of this type is to mention something disgusting to eat. Yet most of the items mentioned here are not in that class, and as we will see below, less than half of the examples we have could actually be considered obscene. Dog Yummies are not disgusting (they are edible but not palatable) but it is plainly "low" to eat dog food. Elegance in sounds of this type can also involve syntactic complexity. *Your mother a applejack eater* seems to be a more effective sound then *Your mother eat applejack*. (Applejack, a new breakfast cereal at the time, may be favored because it suggests applejack whiskey). If so, it is a further piece of evidence that syntactic complexity is a positive feature of sounds.

   e. *Your mother raised you on* ____. This is a specific pattern with fairly simple syntax, particularly effective in striking at both the opponent and his mother. In one Thunderbirds' session, we triggered a series of these sounds:

> *WL:* Your mother raised you on ugly milk.
> *Boot:* Your mother raised you on raw corn.
> *David:* Your mother raised you with big lips.
> *Boot:* Your mother gave you milk out of a cave.
> *Boot:* Your mother gave you milk out of her ass.
> . . . when you just born, she say "Take a shot."

   f. *I went to your house* . . . A numerous and important series are sounds directed against the household and the state of poverty that exists there. Some of these are complex rhymes, quite parallel to the rhymed dozens:

> *Boot:* I went to your house to ask for a piece of cheese.
> The rat jumped up and say "Heggies, please."

(*Heggies* is the claiming word parallel to *dibbs, halfsies, allies, checks,* etc. which was standard in New York City some twenty years ago. Today *heggies* is a minor variant, though it is still recognized, having given way to *thumbs up*.)

   Most sounds of this type are in prose and are disguised as anecdotes. Cockroaches are a favorite theme:

> *Boot:* Hey! I went up Money house and I walked in Money house, I say, I wanted to sit down, and then, you know a roach jumped up and said, "Sorry, this seat is taken."
> *Roger:* I went to David house, I saw the roaches walkin' round in *combat* boots.

Several sounds from a session with the Aces may be quoted here in which the members noted where they had learned various sounds.

> *Tony:* A boy named Richard learned me this one: When I came across your house, a rat gave me a jay-walkin' ticket.
>
> *Renard:* When I came to your house, seven roaches jumped me and one search me.
>
> *Ted:* And I made this one up: I was come in your house; I got hit on the back of my head with a Yoohoo bottle.

Ted's original sound seems weak; it leans upon the humor of the Yoohoo bottle but it departs from the rats-and-roaches theme without connecting up with any of the major topics of sounding. One such topic is the bathroom, or the lack of one:

> *Boot:* I went to your house and ask your mother, could I go to the bathroom. She said, "The submarine jus' lef'."
>
> *Roger:* I went to his house—I wanted to go to the bathroom, and her mother—his mother gave me a pitchfork and a flashlight.
>
> *Roger:* I ringed his bell and the toilet stool flushed.

Remarks about somebody's house are apt to become quite personal as we will see below. The Jets did not produce many of these sounds, but the following occurred in quick succession:

> *J1:* I went in Junior house 'n' sat in a chair that caved in.
>
> *J2:* You's a damn liar, 'n' you was eatin' in my house, right?
>
> *J3:* I went to Bell's house 'n' a Chinese roach said, "Come and git it."
>
> *J1:* I brought my uncle—I brought my uncle up Junior house—I didn't trust them guys.

The tendency to take "house" sounds personally shows up in the second line of this series. As we will see below, the charge that "You was eatin' in my house" returns the accusation of hunger against the originator, and this can have a solid basis in real life.

g. *Other anecdotal forms.* There are many other anecdotal sounds which do not fall into a single mold. Some are quite long and include the kind of extra detail which can give the illusion, at the outset, that an actual story is being told. From the Jets' session we find:

> I ran over Park Avenue—you know, I was ridin' on my
> bike—and—uh—I seen somebody fightin'; I said lemme
> get on this now. I ran up there and Bell and his mother,
> fallin' all over: I was there first x x x gettin' it—gettin'
> that Welfare food x x

The incoherent sections are filled with slurping noises which are an
important part of such food sounds—indicating that those involved
were so desperately hungry and so uncivilized that they behaved
like animals.

One can also deliver an anecdote with the same theme as the
rhymed dozens quoted above:

> Boot: I'm not gonna say who it was, boy. But I fucked
> somebody's mother on this bridge one night, Whooh!
> That shit was so good, she jumped overboard in the
> river.

There are any number of miscellaneous sounds that can be disguised as pseudoanecdotes.

> Roger: One day, Money's mother's ass was stuck up and
> she called Roto-Rooter.

On the other hand, there are anecdotes which take the form of
rhymes:

> Boot: I went down south to buy a piece of butter
> I saw yo' mother layin' in the gutter.
> I took a piece of glass and stuck it up her ass
> I never saw a motherfucker run so fas'.

Such narratives typically use the simplest type of syntax, with
minimal subjects and preterit verb heads. The anecdotal type of
sound appears to be most effective when it is delivered with hesita-
tions and false starts, rather than with the smooth delivery of the
other type of sounds. The technique is therefore closely associated
with certain types of narrative styles in which the point is delayed
to the final clause, where the evaluation is fused with result and coda,
as in a joke (see chapter 9). It is generally true that all sounds have
this structure: the evaluative point must be at the very end.

h. *Portraits.* Just as narrative calls for simple syntax, sounds which
present elaborate portraits demand syntactic complexity. The most

common are those which place someone's mother on the street as a whore.

> J1: Willie mother stink; she be over here on 128 St. between Seventh 'n' Eighth, waving her white handkerchief: [falsetto] "C'mon, baby, only a nickel."
>
> J2: Hey Willie mother be up there, standin' the corner, be pullin' up her-her dress, be runnin' her ass over 'n' see those skinny, little legs.

i. *Absurd and bizarre forms.* The formal typology of sounds presented so far actually covers the great majority of sounds used. But there are a number of striking examples which are not part of any obvious pattern, sounds which locate some profoundly absurd or memorable point by a mechanism not easy to analyze. There is the darkly poetic sound used by Eddie of the Cobras:

> Your mother play dice with the midnight mice.

Rhyme also plays an essential part in this uncommon sound:

> Ricky got shot with his own fart.

We might also cite the following exchange; which develops its own deep complication:

> J1: Your mother take a swim in the gutter.
>
> J2: Your mother live in a garbage can.
>
> J1: Least I don't live on 1122 Boogie Woogie Avenue, two garbage cans to the right.

The attraction of trade names like *Right Guard* or *Applejacks* may be their bizarre and whimsical character. In charging somebody's mother with unfeminine behavior we can also observe comical effects:

> J1: Willie mother make a living' playin' basketball.
>
> J2: I saw Tommy mother wearing' high-heel sneakers to church.

j. *Response forms: puns and metaphors.* Sounds are usually answered by other sounds, and the ways in which they follow each other will be discussed below. But there is one formal feature of a sound which is essentially made for responses: "At least my mother ain't . . ." Although these forms cannot be used to initiate sounding,

several can succeed each other, as in these sequences from the Aces
session:

> A1: At least I don't wear bubblegum drawers.
> A2: At least his drawers ain't bubblegum, it's not sticky
>   like yours.
> A1: At least my mother don't work in the sewer.
> A2: At least my mother don't live in the water-crack, like
>   yours.

There are a series of traditional responses of this form which incorporate complex puns. Abrahams cites a dozen from South Philadelphia, including five common in Harlem. Perhaps the best known
is:

> At least my mother ain't no railroad track, laid all over
> the country.

Such forms frequently occur as simple similes, such as:

> Your mother's like a police station—dicks going in and
> out all the time.

Although puns such as these seem to have been part of the original
dozens tradition, they are no longer common among adolescents in
Harlem. They seem to have been adopted by white groups in the city,
where they are quite well known. When our white interviewers used
some of these in sounding sessions, they were admired, but they did
not initiate a series of other sounds as in the case of "Your momma
drink pee" or "Your mother raised you on ugly milk."

This presentation of the "shape" of sounds has also given the
reader some idea of the range of topics which are sounded on. Our
own exploratory interviews in other parts of the country show that
this scheme applies quite well to other cities and other black communities. Kochman and his students (1968) have provided descriptions of the Chicago patterns which are very similar to those of
Harlem. O. C. Wortham in San Francisco has collected a large body
of preadolescent sounds, many of which might have been quoted
directly from the Thunderbirds, Jets, or Cobras. "Your mama got a
cast on her right titty"; "Your mama wears a jocky strap"; "Your
mother wears holy drawers"; "Ricky's mama eat shit"; "Your mother
named Mike"; "Your mother wears tennis shoes to work"; "He say
his mama plays Batman"; "Hey, it's so cold in your house the

roaches walk around with fur coats on"; "Man I done busted you so low, you can walk up under that piece of paper with a top hat on".

Ritual Insults Among White Peer Groups

While some elements of the dozens and other black ritual insults have appeared among white peer groups in the urban centers, the typical forms used among whites are quite different from those of blacks. The personal experience of several of our own investigators (Paul Cohen and Benji Wald) drawn from different areas of New York City, shows firm agreement on ritual insults. Whereas the BEV practice of sounding ranges over a wide variety of forms and topics which are combined with great flexibility, the white forms are essentially a limited set of routines. Two of the most common begin with "Eat shit":

> A: Eat shit.
> B: What should I do with the bones?
> A: Build a cage for your mother.
> B: At least I got one.
> A: She *is* the least.

> A: Eat shit.
> B: Hop on the spoon.
> A: Move over.
> B: I can't, your mother's already there.

These are indeed ritual and impersonal insults, directed in part against the opponent's mother. But the sequencing occurs in a fixed form, and there is little room for individual choice. These are essentially "snappy answers" which show how knowledgeable rather than how competent the speaker is. It is the aptness of the rejoinder which is looked for:

> A: Kiss my ass.
> B: Move your nose.

> A: Fuck you.
> B: Yeh, that would be the best one you ever had.

> A: You motherfucker.
> B: Your mother told.

> *A*: Got a match?
> *B*: My ass against your face.

These are trick responses. The first speaker may say something aggressive (but not particularly clever) or he may be tricked into a routine such as:

> *A*: How tall are you?
> *B*: Five foot seven.
> *A*: I didn't think shit piled that high.

The white groups also use a certain number of comparisons of the "You are so X that Y" type: "You're so full of shit your eyes are brown." Furthermore, there are similes directed against one's mother that overlap those cited under *b*: "Your mother so low she could play handball on the curb . . . walk under a pregnant cockroach without stooping."

The white material is limited in content as well as form and quantity. *Shit* is the most common topic, and in general the insults are based on the taboo words rather than taboo activities. We do not find the proliferation of odd and bizarre elements and the wide range of choice characteristic of the BEV forms. Furthermore, this activity does not occupy any considerable time for the white groups—in a word, it is not a speech event for white groups in the sense that sounding is a speech event for the black groups. There is some evidence that southern whites (e.g. Mississippi Delta area) show the same range of ritual insults as northern whites and that the rich development of sounding described here is indeed a characteristic of the black speech community.

Attributes and Persons Sounded On

A review of the content of the sounds given above under *a–j* will show that a wide but fairly well-defined range of attributes is sounded on. A mother (grandmother, etc.) may be cited for her age, weight (fat or skinny), ugliness, blackness, smell, the food she eats, the clothes she wears, her poverty, and of course her sexual activity. As far as persons are concerned, sounding is always thought of as talking about someone's mother. But other relatives are also mentioned—as part of the speech for variety in switching, or for their particular attributes. In order of importance, one can list the opponent's relatives as: mother, father, uncle, grandmother, aunt. As far as number of sounds is concerned, the opponent himself might be included as second most important to his mother, but proverbially sounds are thought of as primarily against relatives.

One of the long epic poems of the BEV community called "Signifying Monkey" gives us some insight into the ordering of relatives. Signifying Monkey stirs up trouble ("signifies") by telling the lion that the elephant had sounded on him:

> "Mr. Lion, Mr. Lion, there's a big burly motherfucker comin' your way,
> Talks shit about you from day to day."

The monkey successively reports that the elephant had talked about the lion's sister, brother, father and mother, wife, and grandmother.

> The monkey said, "Wait a minute, Mr. Lion", said, "That ain't all,
> he said your grandmother, said she was a lady playin' in the old backyard.
> Said ever'time he seen her, made his dick get on the hard."

Even more relatives are brought in, which brings the monkey to the inevitable conclusion:

> He said, "Yeah he talked about your aunt, your uncle, and your cousins,
> Right then and there I knew the bad motherfucker was playin' the dozens."

What is said about someone's mother's age, weight, or clothes can be a general or traditional insult, or it can be local and particular. The presence of commercial trade names in the sounds is very striking; Bosco, Applejacks, Wonder Bread, Dog Yummies, Gainesburgers, Gravy Train, as well as the names of the popular figures in the mass media: James Bond, Pussy Galore, Flipper. The street culture is highly local, and local humor is a very large part of sounds. As noted before, one of the best ways to start a loud discussion is to associate someone with a local character who is an "ultra-rich" source of humor. Trade names have this local character—and part of the effect is the superimposing of this overspecific label on the general, impersonal figure of "your mother" as in "Your mother look like Flipper." Local humor is omnipresent and overpowering in every peer group—it is difficult to explain in any case, but its importance cannot be ignored.

The odd or whimsical use of particular names can be illustrated by a sequence that occurred when John Lewis left the microbus at an early stop. As a parting shot, he leaned back in the window and shouted genially "Faggots! Motherfuckers!" This set up a chain of responses including a simple "Your mother!" from Rel, "You razor-blade bastard!" from someone else, and finally an anonymous "Winnie the Pooh!"

Obscenity does not play as large a part as one would expect from the character of the original dozens. Many sounds are obscene in the full sense of the word. The speaker uses as many "bad" words and images as possible—that is, subject to taboo and moral reprimand in adult middle-class society. The originator will search for images that would be considered as disgusting as possible: "Your mother eat fried dick-heads." With long familiarity the vividness of this image disappears, and one might say that it is not disgusting or obscene to the sounders. But the meaning of the sound and the activity would be entirely lost without reference to these middle-class norms. Many sounds are "good" because they are "bad"— because the speakers know that they would arouse disgust and revulsion among those committed to the "good" standards of middle-class society. Like the toasts, sounds derive their meaning from the opposition between two major sets of values: *their* way of being "good" and *our* way of being "bad".

The rhymed dozens are all uniformly sexual in character; they aim at the sexual degradation of the object sounded on. But the body of sounds cited above depart widely from this model: less than half of them could be considered obscene, in any sense. At one point in the Jet session, there is a sequence of three sounds concerning fried dick-heads; this is immediately followed by

> J1: Your mother eat rat heads.
> J2: Your mother eat Bosco.
> J3: Your mother look that taxi driver.
> J4: Your mother stinks.
> J5: Hey Willie got a talkin' hat.
> J4: Your mother a applejack-eater.
> J5: Willie got on a talkin' hat.
> J4: So, Bell, your mother stink like a bear.
> J5: Willie mother . . . she walk like a penguin.

This sequence of nine remarks contains no sexual references; the strongest word is *stink*. Many sounds depend upon the whimsical juxtaposition of a variety of images, upon original and unpredictable humor which is for the moment quite beyond our analysis. But it can be noted that the content has departed very far from the original model of uniform sexual insult.

Only someone very unfamiliar with the BEV subculture could think that the current generation is "nicer" and less concerned with sex than previous generations. The cry of "Winnie the Pooh!" does not mean that the Jets are absorbing refined, middle-class wit and culture. Its significance can only be understood by a deeper study of the nature of this ritual activity.

Evaluation of Sounds

One of the most important differences between sounding and other speech events is that most sounds are evaluated overtly and immediately by the audience. In well-structured situations, like the Thunderbird sounding session, this is true of every sound. In wilder sessions with a great many participants, like the Jet session in the microbus, a certain number of sounds will follow each other rapidly without each one being evaluated.

The primary mark of positive evaluation is laughter. We can rate the effectiveness of a sound in a group session by the number of members of the audience who laugh. In the Thunderbird session, there were five members; if one sounded against the other successfully, the other three would laugh; a less successful sound would show only one or two laughs. (The value of having a separate recording track for each speaker is very great.)

A really successful sound will be evaluated by overt comments: in the Jet session the most common forms are: "Oh!", "Oh shit!" "God damn!", or "Oh lord!" By far the most common is "Oh shit!" The intonation is important; when approval is to be signalled the vowel of each word is quite long, with a high sustained initial pitch, and a slow-falling pitch contour. The same words can be used to express negative reaction, or disgust, but then the pitch is low and sustained. The implication of the positive exclamations is 'That is too much' or 'That leaves me helpless.'

Another, even more forceful mode of approving sounds is to repeat the striking part of the sound oneself.

> *John L:* Who father wear raggedy drawers?
> *Willie:* Yeh the ones with so many holes in them when-
> a-you walk they whistle?
> *Others:* Oh . . . shi-it! When you walk they whistle! Oh
> shit!

Negative reactions to sounds are common and equally overt. The most frequent is "Tha's phony!" or "Phony shit!", but sounds are also disapproved as *corny, weak,* or *lame.* Stanley elaborates his negative comments quite freely:

> *Junior:* Aww, Nigger Bell, you smell like B.O. Plenty.
> *Bell:* Aww, nigger, you look like—you look like Jimmy
> Durante's grandfather.
> *Stan:* Aw, tha's phony [bullshit] . . . Eh, you woke me up
> with that phony one, man . . .
> *Bell:* Junior look like Howdy Doody.
> *Stan:* That's phony too, Bell. Daag, boy! . . . Tonight ain't
> your night, Bell.

At another point, Stanley denounces a sound with a more compli-cated technique: "Don't tell 'im those phony jokes, they're so phony, you *got* to laugh."

The difference between these negative terms is not clear. For our present purposes, we may consider them equivalent, although they are probably used in slightly different ways by different speakers. The Cobras do not use the same negative terms as the Jets. They will say "You fake!" "Take that shit outa here!" or most often, "That ain't where it's at."

These evaluative remarks are ways of responding to the overall effect of a sound. There is also considerable explicit discussion of sounds themselves. In the case of a traditional sound, like a rhymed dozen, one can object to an imperfect rendition. For example, Stevie answers one of our versions with "Tha's wrong! You said it wrong! Mistake!" Members are also very clear on who the best sounders are. Among the Thunderbirds, it is generally recognized that "Boot one of the best sounders . . . he's one of the best sounders of all." This very reputation will interfere with the chances of getting other members to initiate sounding—they know in advance that they will be outdone. In general, sounding is an activity very much in the forefront of social consciousness: members talk a great deal about it, try to make up new sounds themselves, and talk about each other's success. Sounding practices are open to intuitive inspection. It is possible to ask a good sounder, "What would you say if somebody said to you . . ." and he will be glad to construct an answer. Members will also make metacomments on the course of a sounding session: "Now he's sounding on you, Money!" or announce their intentions, as Roger does: "Aw, tha's all right. Now I'm gonna sound on you pitiful."

Furthermore, members take very sharp notice of the end result of a sounding contest, as noted below. In a sounding session, everything is public—nothing significant happens without drawing comment. The rules and patterning of this particular speech event are therefore open for our inspection.

The Activity of Sounding

We can distinguish two very different uses of sounds: (1) ritual sounding and (2) applied sounding. The quotations given above are taken from sounding sessions which are examples of the first: rituals in which the sounding is done for its own sake. Applied sounding involves the use of sounds for particular purposes in the midst of other verbal encounters and follows a very different set of rules. We will consider ritual sounding first, beginning with the general rules which apply, and then the operation of these rules in the two sessions which have been cited.

There are three participants in this speech event: antagonist A, antagonist B, and the audience. A sounds against B; the audience evaluates; B sounds against A; his sound is evaluated. The general structure is then more complex than most ABABAB exchanges: it is

$$A\text{-}1 \ e \ B\text{-}1 \ e \ A\text{-}2 \ e \ B\text{-}2 \ e \ . \ . \ .$$

A-1 almost always contains a reference to B's mother. B-1 should be based on A-1; to the extent that it is an original or well-delivered transformation of A-1, B may be said to have won. A-2 may be an entirely new sound. But if A-2 is a further transformation of B-1, it is usually evaluated even more highly. Whereas we may say that A-2 "tops" B-1 if it is intrinsically better, A may be said to "get" B most often if A-2 is a variant or clearly related to B-1. This is what is meant by "topping" B—the exchange is held open. A skillful sounder can hold an exchange of variants open beyond the point where it would normally be considered ended by conventional estimates. The series may be terminated by one antagonist clearly winning over the other. Thus in that part of the Thunderbirds' session following Ricky's collapse, Boot clearly beats Money. The exchange starts with Boot's long story of how Money was tricked into thinking that a jar of urine was ice tea, and he drank it. Money objects, rather incoherently: "I know you love thuh—ice tea . . . I know you love to pee—i—ice cream tea." Boot then begins sounding.

> A-1   *Boot:* His mother go to work without any draws on so that she c'd get a good breeze.
> B-1   *Money:* Your mother go, your mother go work without anything on, just go naked.
> e   *David:* That's a lie.

In the first exchange, Money clearly fails, as evidenced by his hesitation: he simply exaggerates Boot's well-constructed and witty sound without the corresponding wit. David's comment is negative—particularly in that it takes Money's sound to be a factual claim.

> A-2   *Boot:* Your mother, when she go to work and she had—those, you know—open-toe shoes, well her stockings reach her be—sweeping the ground.
> e⎰ *Ricky:* (laughs)
> e⎱ *Roger:* Ho lawd! (laughs)

Boot's A-2 is stretching the limits of the syntax available to him, and he has considerable difficulty in getting it out. It is clearly an extension of A-1 and B-1, of the form "Your mother go to work with . . ." But instead of the conventional wit of A-1, or the reduced variant of B-1, A-2 enters the field of the unconventional and absurd. Boot scores two strong responses from Ricky and Roger.

Money cannot build further on the syntactic model, but he does attempt to respond to the theme of holes in shoes. There is no audience response.

> B-2   *Money:* Your mother have holes—potatoes in her shoes.

Since Boot has won this exchange, he now begins a new sequence:

> A-3   *Boot:* Your mother got a putty chest (laugh).
> B-3   *Money:* Arrgh! Aww—you wish you had a putty chest, right?

Money responds, but he does not sound. Boot continues with another sound of the "got" type; now, however, the pattern is complicated as Roger joins in, sounding specifically against Money. This is a second stage which occurs when one antagonist is clearly losing ground: he becomes the object of group sounding:

A-4   *Boot:* Your mother got hair growin' out her dunkie
          hole.
C-4   *Roger:* Money your mother got a .45 in her left titty.
          Money: Awwww!
e   *Ricky:* (laughter)

Money now responds to Roger's sound with a variant which strikes us as a very able one.

B-4   *Money:* Your mother got a 45-degree titty.

Now it is Roger who answers Money and gets a strong response. Boot then adds a sound which is delivered incoherently and gets no response.

C-5   *Roger:* Your mother got baptised in a whiskey bottle.
e   ⎰ *Money:* (laughs)
e   ⎱ *Ricky:* (laughs)
e   ⎰ *David:* (laughs)
A-5   *Boot:* Yourmothersailthesevenseasinasardine can.
          [laughs]

The situation has become unclear. Sounding is defined for members as one person sounding upon another, but three are involved. Money's laughter indicates that he thinks Roger's sound is not against him, but against Boot. David now explicitly says that the antagonists are Boot and Roger, but Roger denies this: he is still sounding against Money. Boot adds a further dig which recognizes that Roger's *him* means Money, not Boot:

David: Now you and Roger sounding. (laughs)
Roger: I'm sounding on him.
Boot: That half of a motor. (laughs)

Given the sanction of a group attack against Money, David now begins his own. But Money turns to us suddenly and says, "Could we sing now?" (the formal recording of singing was one of the purposes of the session). Money's question is interpreted as a transparent attempt to escape, and a storm of abuse descends on his head from the leaders of the group. He is forced to acknowledge his defeat explicitly.

D-6   *David:* Everytime Money looks at the moon, everytime
       Money: Could we sing now?
       Boot: (laughs)
       Roger: (laughs)
       David: Money look at moon, he say "Ooo, look at the moonshine."
       Roger: He changing the subject!
       Ricky: Awww! Tryin' to change thuh—ih—subject
       Roger: What's the matter, you feeling all right, or you want some more sounding?
       Money: Uh-uh.

The sounding session goes on, with Money saying nothing. When he speaks up later on. Ricky says "Hey Money, you better keep quiet, if you don't want 'em soundin' bad on you." It should be quite clear that there are winners and losers in sounding sessions.

The speech event we call sounding is not isolated from other forms of verbal interaction: it can merge with them or become transformed into a series of personal insults. When ritual insult changes into personal insult, the difference between the two becomes quite clear. We take as an instance the beginning of the sounding session with the Thunderbirds. To save space, evaluative reactions to each sound will be put in parentheses after it.

In this session, we can observe the difficulty that members have in distinguishing between hypothetical and actual sounding. The question "What would you say if . . ." is quickly transformed into actual sounding. The series was initiated by an effort of C. Robins to get Money to sound.

       CR: (to Money) What would you say if Boot said "Your father look like Funjie!"? (Roger: "Oh Lord, oh Money . . . oh . . . ho . . . Funjie . . . oo!" Roger, Boot, Ricky, David: laugh)
       Money: Hunh?
       CR: That's like Funjie's your father. (Roger: Ohh! Boot, Ricky: Laugh)
       Boot: He's sounding on you, Money!
       CR: No, no if *Boot* said it . . .

At this point, other staff members joined in and tried to make it clear that we were only asking what Money would say *if*. Money tried to answer, but Boot took over with the support of the rest of the group.

> *David:* Boot one of the best sounders.
> *Money:* I say, uh—uhm—
> *Boot:* Now if you said that to me . . .
> *CR:* No no no no, you sound him, tell him, say say that
> . . .
> *Money:* He's one of the best sounders of all.
> *CR, WL:* Money sounds good too.
> *Boot:* Now if he said that to me know what I'd say I'd say—

Our efforts to push Money to the fore did not succeed. Money's failure to sound well in the face of Boot's dominant position is the same phenomenon that Whyte (1955) observed in Doc's corner gang. Followers did not bowl as well against the leader of the group as they could by themselves. In other situations we have seen Money sound very well.

We now begin a series of hypothetical sounds—what "would" be said. Boot is *B*; Money is *A*.

> B-1 *Boot:* I'd say, "His father got four lips."
> A-2 *Money:* I'd say, "Your mother got four lips." (Boot: "That ain't nothin'." CR: "What does that mean?")

Boot's first sound hit on the familiar topic of thick lips; part of an older, self-derogatory pattern in BEV. (For instance, Jets: "Your father got lips like a—Oldsmobile.") Money's hypothetical A-2 is the weakest kind of switch: substitution of one relative for another, and it is properly and immediately downgraded. Money has failed again. The part of second antagonist was then taken up by David: he is a small fat boy who is continually being pushed aside by Boot and is the constant butt of jokes. On the other hand, he has a great deal of courage, and unlike others in the group, never gives up in the struggle to establish his position, and never allows Boot to dominate the situation entirely. In the following sounding session, Boot applied his verbal skill with ruthless force to crush David, but David's verbal resources were greater than one would have predicted.

> C-3 *David:* So your . . . so then I say, "Your father got
> buck teeth."
> B-3 *Boot:* Aw your father got teeth growing out of his
> behind! (Money, Ricky, Roger laugh).

Boot's response is a winning effort. He takes David's hypothetical
A-3 and adds to it elements of absurdity and obscenity; B-3 gets
positive evaluation from all three members of the audience. Note
that Boot's sound is no longer hypothetical: it is the first "real sound"
of the series. David now attempts to top this by staying with the
behind theme, but he fails to get a coherent thought out. He is not
fluent in this area, at least not in the face of Boot's ability:

> C-3 *David:* Yeah, your father, y—got, your father grow,
> uh, uh, grow hair from, from between his, y'know.
> (Money laughs)
> B-4 *Boot:* Your father got calluses growin' up through
> his ass, and comin' through his mouth. (Boot,
> Money, and Ricky laugh)

With B-4 Boot builds further on the original model and crushes David
with a display of virtuosity that leaves him with nothing to say. Boot
is not willing to leave it there; like many a good sounder, he can
seize his advantage by piling one sound on another. He switches
abruptly to B-5:

> B-5 *Boot:* Your father look like a *grown pig.* (Boot,
> Money, and Ricky laugh).

David now reaches out for a sound which breaks the rules. It is not
a ritual insult at all, but a personal remark that hits on a real failing
of Boot's step-father.

> C-5 *David:* Least my—at least my father don't be up
> there talking uh-uh-uh-uh-uh-uh!

The fact that this is a personal insult and not a ritual insult is shown
by the fact that Boot now answers it. Since ritual insults are not
intended as factual statements, they are not to be denied. But Boot
does respond to David and Roger acknowledges that Boot has been
hit. (A denial of an insult A-x will be marked B-x′).

> B-5′ *Boot:* Uh—so my father talks stutter talk what it
> mean? (Roger: He talk the same way a little bit.)

Next Boot responds to David's insult with an insult related to A-5 in exactly the way that one sound is related to another. Boot's father stutters; David's father is old and has gray hair.

> B-6   *Boot:* At least my father ain't got a gray head! His father got a big bald spot with a gray head right down there, and one long string . . .

David is hurt, and he denies the personal insult as best he can. But Boot doesn't stop: he picks up the point of "one long string" and grinds it in to the amusement of Roger and Money.

> C-6′   *David:* Because he' old he's old, that's why! He's old, that's why! . . .
>
> B-7   *Boot:* . . . and one long string, that covers his whole head, one, one long string, about that high, covers his whole head. (Roger: Ho Lord, one string! Money, Boot laugh).

Boot brings tears to David's eyes. Boot's side-kick Money does not mind, but Ricky objects.

> C-7′   *David:* You lyin' Boo! . . . You know 'cause he old, tha's why!
>
> *Ricky:* Aw man, cut it out.

Boot has won the day, but he has no sense of restraint. What follows now is no longer the controlled counterpoint of sounding, of the form A e B a, but rather an excited argument, in which both parties are in strident overlap most of the time. It is mostly David against Boot now: Boot's insults do not draw much response from the others, and one can sense the group support ebbing from him.

> B-8   *Boot:* Your father look like this—with his butt coming out, and he go (slurp) he look like . . .
>
> C-8′   *David:* You a liar!
>
> B-9   *Boot:* You know one time I came over his house, I saw some slop in the garbage, you know, and then, and I left it there, and David say (slurp, chomp, chomp, chomp) (Money laughs).

David is now ready to take up any weapon at hand. He seizes on the poverty theme, and he makes a personal charge that hits home. It takes some time for David to be heard; but finally Boot does hear him, and he stops his chomping to issue a vigorous (but ineffective) denial.

> C-9 *David:* So! and you always come over my house and say, yeah, Boot always come over my house and say, Boot always coming over my house to eat. He ask for food, and Ohhh lawww . . .
>
> B-9′ *Boot:* I don't come over your house—I don't come nuttin! I only come over your house on school days and from now on I do.

David senses his advantage and pursues it.

> C-10 *David:* . . . and when we go swimmin', we go, you ask for food, and ever ti—and you come over my house—

Boot can no longer deny the factual truth of David's charge, but he tries to mitigate the facts: foolishly perhaps, because David is now ready with a crushing response.

> B-10′ *Boot:* Yeah, I only be playin', I only be playin'!
>
> C-11 *David: Yeah, but you sure be eatin'!*

Not every story ends with the underdog showing as well as David. David's momentary success is all the more striking because Boot is without a doubt in verbal control of the group. Boot continued his triumphant progress in sounding against others, in no way daunted by this reversal. In these extracts, we have the full weight of evidence for the important point that Boot is *the verbal leader* of the Thunderbirds—that he excels at all the verbal skills of the BEV subculture. It is not only that Boot has a larger store of sounds at his disposal and can draw upon them more readily. His syntax is also more complex, and he can deliver sounds that no one else can; all of the more complex examples from the Thunderbirds cited above are his.

The Rules for Ritual Sounding

In the presentation of sounding so far, we have seen that this speech event has a well-articulated structure. These rules can be broken: it is possible to hurl personal insults and it is possible to join in a mass attack on one person. But there is always a cost in stepping out of the expected pattern; in the kind of uncontrolled and angry response which occurs or in the confusion as to who is doing what to who.

As we examine these examples of sounding, the fundamental opposition between ritual insults and personal insults emerges. The appropriate responses are quite different: a personal insult is answered by a denial, excuse, or mitigation, whereas a sound or ritual insult is answered by longer sequences, since a sound and its response are essentially the same kind of thing, and a response calls for a further response. The complexity of sounding follows from this comparatively simple structure, so that our diagram of sounding might be reduced to:

$$\text{S-1 e S-2 s S-3} \ldots$$

On the other hand, personal insults produce dyads of interaction: insult (I) and denial or excuse (D). We observe a chain in this last exchange between Boot and David:

$$\text{I-1 D-1 I-2 D-2 I-3 D-3.} \ldots$$

but there is no inherent, structural reason for chaining as in the case of sounds. A denial can end the series. But the denials that are normal and automatic for a personal insult are unthinkable with sounds. We have the exchanges A: *You come over to my house and ask for something to eat* B: *I do not!* and A: *Your father got grey hair and one long string* . . . B: *That's cause he's old, that's why!* But we do not have such exchanges as A: *Your momma drink pee.* B: * *That's a lie!* Instead the right response is B: *Your father eat shit.* This is an invariant rule: sounds are not denied. If it were merely a semicategorical rule we would expect joking responses with denials, deliberate misinterpretations of the sounds, parallel to those we sometimes hear with requests: *Would you mind opening the window? No. Can you give me the time? Yes.* Since responses to sounds are so automatic and deep-seated, we must presuppose a well-formed competence on the part of members to distinguish ritual insults from personal insults. On the face of it, it does not seem easy to make this distinction. It is a question, among other things, of how serious the antagonist is: does he want to start a fight? Does he mean it? Are people going to believe this is true? What is the internal competence which allows Boot to recognize immediately David's personal insult and to respond with a denial? How can the Jets sound on each other for hours without anyone being insulted?

To answer these questions, it is necessary to specify more precisely the structure of sounds. The superficial taxonomy given above under *a–j* merely charts the differences in the syntactic forms of sounds as they are uttered. If sounds are heard as one kind of utterance, there must be a uniform mode of interpretation which shows all of these forms as derived from a single underlying structure. We propose that this structure is

> T(B) is so X that P

where T is the target of the sound, X is the attribute of T which is focused on, and P is a proposition that is coupled with the attribute by the quantifier *so . . . that* to express the degree to which T has X. The target T(B) is normally B's mother or other relative. (It may seem as if there are more complex targets such as "Your mother's clothes" or "Your mother's face" but these may best be seen as derived from constructions such as "Your mother is so ugly that her face . . .") The attribute X is drawn from the range of features or topics outlined above: age, weight, clothes, etc. It is limited to a specifically *pejorative* value: age is specifically *old*, weight is *skinny* or *fat*, clothing is *ragged* or *dirty*, appearance is *ugly* or *dirty*, sexual behavior is *loose* or *immoral*; smell is *stink*, wealth is *poor*, food is *poor* or *disgusting*. The proposition P may have a wide variety of forms, although there are lower-level sequencing rules and standards of excellence that govern its form. Thus we have a typical sound, *Your mother* [T(B)] *so old* [X], *she fart dust* [P].

It will be observed that there are a great many sounds with simpler forms than this, and some that are more complex. We might consider that the simpler forms such as *Your mother the Abominable Snowman* are derived from a full form *T(B) is so X that P* by rules of deletion parallel to syntactic rules for ellipsis. However, it seems more plausible to write discourse rules for making sounds indirectly, parallel to the rules for making commands or requests. One can make preconditions for such commands. Thus someone can request a glass of water by stating that he is thirsty. A sound may be made by simply stating the proposition P. The deletion of *T(A) is so X that . . .* is recoverable in the interpretation of the listener, who has the competence to know what attribute is being sounded on. For example, *Your mother look like Flipper* must be understood as 'Your mother is so ugly that she looks like Flipper,' whereas *Your mother name the Black Boy* will be interpreted as 'Your mother is so black that she is named "Black Boy"'. *Your father got teeth growing out his ass* is one of many sounds that must refer to an attribute *odd, crazy,* or perhaps most literally, *fucked-up.*

Of the simpler forms listed under *a–d* above, the only types which offer serious difficulty in this interpretation are the equative forms. Type *a, Your mother the Abominable Snowman* can be understood as either 'Your mother is so ugly that she looks like the Abominable Snowman' or '. . . that she is named the Abominable Snowman.' If one takes a more mystical approach—that the speaker is asserting 'Your mother is in fact the Abominable Snowman'—this is equivalent to saying that the insult is directed against the opponent himself, rather than his (ritual) mother. If we hold the notion that the sound is intended to insult or degrade the opponent's mother, rather than to claim he has an altogether different mother, then the interpretations of "like" and "is named" are called for.

Sounds of type *d Your mother eat* . . . are usually interpreted as referring to the attribute "poor" (or "hungry" which may be subsumed under "poor"). Thus *Your mother eat corn flakes without any milk* may be understood as 'Your mother is so hungry that she eats corn flakes without any milk!' or as 'Your mother is so poor that she has to eat corn flakes without any milk.'

On the other hand, the following sequence of sounds must be given a different interpretation:

> J1: His mother eat Dog Yummies . . .
> J2: Somebody said your mother's breath smell funny.
> J3: They say your mother eat Gainesburgers.
> J4: They say your mother was a Gravy Train.

These are plainly based on the traditional mode of insulting someone's mother by calling her a dog. The direct insults *Your mother's a bitch . . . a dog . . . You're a son of a bitch* do not have any weight in sounding today. But the existence of this model makes it plain that the underlying interpretation is not 'Your mother is like a dog' or 'Your mother is named *dog*' but rather 'Your mother is a dog.'. On the other hand, Boot's sound *Your father looks like a grown pig* is not equivalent to saying *Your father is a pig . . . a swine!* but rather must be taken to mean 'Your father is so fat that he looks like a grown pig.'

Type *e, Your mother raised you on ugly milk* is unique in this series, because it must be interpreted as a sound directly against the opponent: 'You are so ugly that your mother [must have] raised you on ugly milk.' But we might add that the mother is also being insulted here, so that the sound adds in effect 'and it's your mother's fault!'

The more complex sounds such as the anecdotal *f, I went to B's house* . . . must be taken as directed against the whole family: B's family is so poor that . . . On the other hand, complex comparisons as *Your father drawers have so many holes in them that when he walk they whistle* can be interpreted as 'Your father is so ragged that his drawers have so many holes in them that when he walks they whistle.'

There are, of course, a certain number of miscellaneous sounds which are difficult to interpret in any scheme: *Your mother play dice with the midnight mice* is many ways ambiguous.

It is clear that the formal definition given does not include the rhymed dozens, which have the underlying structure *I fucked your mother so much that* . . . A number of other sounds, such as *I took your mother* are based upon the model in which the sounder asserts that he sexually insulted or degraded the opponent's mother. This model must be added as an alternative mode of sounding to the one outlined above. But the great majority of sounds used by the Jets, Cobras, and Thunderbirds fit the *T(B) is so X that P* model. We must presuppose that members have the competence to make such interpretations if we are to explain their behavior.

The capacity to interpret sounds frequently depends on the ability to locate the underlying negative adjective X when only the proposition P remains. What does it mean to say *Your mother eat Bosco?* It requires native competence to decide if this is a sound against your mother's blackness (Bosco is a chocolate product; as in *Your mother so black she sweat chocolate*); or her poverty (as in *Your mother eat corn flakes without any milk*); or her decency (as in *Your mother eat scumbag*).

We can now write rules for sounding that will account for the interpretation of a sound and selection of an appropriate response to it. The following rule begins with the listener B's position, as he hears what is said and interprets it to decide what has been done: it is a rule of interpretation UD in the scheme on page 300.

1   If A makes an utterance S in the presence of B and an audience C, which includes reference to a target related to B, T(B), in a proposition P, and

a. B believes that A believes that P is not true and
b. B believes that A believes that B knows that P is not
   true . . .
then S is a *sound,* heard as *T(B) is so X that P* where X
is a pejorative attribute, and A is said to have *sounded
on* B.

This rule can (and must) be abbreviated by identifying conditions
a and *b* as conditions for shared or social knowledge. These are only
the first of an infinite series of recursive conditions which represent
the fact that there is shared knowledge between A and B that P is
not true. In the terminology of discourse analysis now being developed, an A-event is one known to be known only to A (in A's biography) and a B-event is one known to be known only to B, whereas
an AB-event is one known to be known to both. We may summarize
conditions *a* and *b* as *it is an AB-event that P is not true.*

The audience C is an essential ingredient here. It is true that one
person *can* sound against another without a third person being
present, but the presupposition that this is public behavior can easily
be heard in the verbal style. Sounds are not uttered in a direct,
face-to-face conversational mode. The voice is raised and projected,
as if to reach an audience. In a two-person sounding situation, the
antagonists treat each other as representing the audience.

Note that rule 1 does not require the attribute A to be explicitly
mentioned. On the other hand, the proposition P must be present.
We rarely hear sounds of the form *T(B) is (Q) X* where Q is a simple
quantifier, and it is doubtful if they are to be classified as sounds.
Your mother is very fat; your father is real black are not heard as
sounds. Indeed, we can explain the nondeletability of P as we return
to the question of the conditions for recognizing sounds as opposed
to personal insults. Rule 1 is designed to answer the original question:
how does B recognize a ritual insult? First, he recognizes an appropriate target. Secondly, he recognizes the *sounding situation:* a
remark is made by A in a loud voice designed to be heard by the
audience C. Thirdly, he judges the proposition P to be appropriate
to a ritual insult in that everyone present plainly knows that it is
not true. The Jets' mothers do not look like Flipper or Howdy Doody;
they are not the Abominable Snowman; they do not eat Dog Yummies
or fried dick-heads. Futhermore, it is a matter of human competence
to know that everyone knows that these propositions are not true.

On the other hand, the attributes X may justly be attributed to one's mother; she may very well be fat, or skinny, or ugly, or black, or poor, or old. If the proposition P were deleted, the ritual insult would become a personal insult. *Your family is poor!* is not a ritual insult, but a personal one. We have noted that Boot's stepfather does stutter; David's father is old and has gray hair—and all the Thunderbirds know this.

Outsiders would of course be able to recognize ritual propositions P, but without the shared knowledge of members as to whose family was poor, which family was poorest, and which mother was blackest, the outsider could not as readily recognize a personal insult. He would have to suspend judgment. The group does not share all knowledge equally, and sounding is not confined within a single peer group or hang-out group. Therefore sounds must be recognized as ritual insults in themselves, without presupposing any specific knowledge of the sounder's family. For this reason, the propositions P tend to become more and more bizarre and unlikely. *Your mother so low she c'play Chinese handball on a curve* (curb) is a safe sound. Nobody is that low. On the other hand, there is something dangerously personal in *Your mother look like* HIS *father, boy; 'n' you know how* HE *look, boy.*

There are other cases, some noted below, where weak sounds can be interpreted as personal insults; they are then denied, and conflict follows. But if one reviews the sounds quoted above, it will be immediately obvious in almost every case that the propositions P are known to be untrue.

The same argument applies to the rhymed dozens. Among young adults, to say *I fucked your mother* is not to say something obviously untrue. But it is obviously untrue that "I fucked your mother from tree to tree / Your father said, 'Now fuck me!'" The situation can become difficult in some neighborhoods. In the Puerto Rican barrio of East 111th Street, it is common sound to say "Your mother's on Fifth Avenue!" meaning that she is a prostitute. To the question, "What about the kids whose mothers *are* on Fifth Avenue!", members reply, "They don't say much."

First it is worth noting that P *can* be deleted if X is also missing; we then have *Your mother!* This is a very common sound; as cited above,

> *John Lewis:* Faggots!! Motherfuckers!!
> *Rel:* Your *mother!*

Here of course there is unrecoverable deletion—that is, there is no X or P that can be reconstructed. We can interpret *Your mother* as signaling either a generalized insult or as referring to the intention to sound on someone. It may also be used in public places as an elliptical form where behavior is not as free as normally. Observe the following sequence used by two ten-year-olds entering a delicatessen:

> A: Your mother!
> B: Your father!
> A: Your uncle!

The danger of sounds being misinterpreted as personal remarks cannot be overstated. One real incident is worth citing.[10] A group of musicians were returning to New York City on a bus, and they started sounding on the wife of one member of the band who lived in Detroit: she jumps into the hay with the ice man, and so on. When they got to the hotel, they noticed he was missing. Later they found out that he had gone back to Detroit and that he did find his wife in bed with someone. A short while after he committed suicide.

There is no need to compile a great many such incidents to demonstrate the danger of a ritual sounding which is not obviously untrue. In dealing with strangers, it is considerably harder to say what is a safe sound, and there are any number of taboos which can be broken with serious results. Generally speaking, extended ritual sounding is an in-group process, and when sounding occurs across group lines, it is often intended to provoke a fight. One such case has been documented by Swett (1966). A young musician named Young Beartracks killed another young man known as Chicago Eddie outside a poolroom in East Palo Alto. In the court testimony, it was said that there had been an argument between the two preceding the shooting. Swett, who knew the situation quite well, points out that they were engaged in the dozens, and that there was considerable tension already present between the two: Eddie was a member of an urban gang, and Young Beartracks a recent member of a rural gang. The role of the dozens in this situation was plainly relevant to the shooting that followed—actually a case of verbal aggression

---

10. While this incident is necessarily anonymous, it was reported to me through close associates who are related to some of those involved.

by Eddie against Young Beartracks—but the judge and jury did not understand this point:[11]

The first witness for the prosecution, the poolroom attendant and a member of the urban gang, did state in cross-examination that "Eddie put him (Young Beartracks) in the dozens," but the effort of the defense counsel to procure a clarification of the term *dozens* was objected to by the prosecution on the grounds that the witness had not been qualified as an expert in semantics. (Swett, 1966)

We can now give rule 2 for responding to a sound.

2   If A has sounded on B, B sounds on A by asserting a new proposition P' which includes reference to a target related to A, T(A), and such that it is an AB-event that P' is untrue. P' may be embedded in a sentence as a quantification of a pejorative attribute X' of T(A).

This is a production rule in the scheme outlined on page 300. It also contains reference, in the first clause, to the DD sequencing rule which may be stated independently as

3   the response to a sound is a sound.

We have thus filled out the original paradigm for discourse analysis which may be shown as

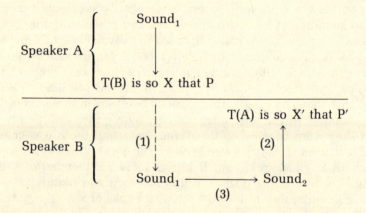

11. I am indebted to Dan Swett of San Francisco State College for further data on this incident; he was directly acquainted with some of the principals in this affair.

There is an interesting condition here on P' which is that *If* X' ≠ X, *then* P' ≠ P. In other words, if A says, *Your mother so old she fart dust,* B cannot say *Your mother so skinny she fart dust,* or *Your mother so black she fart dust.* But if X' = X, then it is possible for P' = P, if the target T is shifted, although this is the weakest kind of response. Among young children who do not sound well, one will hear such sequences as:

> Your mother got funky drawers.
> Your father got funky drawers.

But one does not hear as an answer, "*Your* mother got funky drawers," for this would be equivalent to a denial of the sound. We can now see why denial of ritual sounds is impossible; for to deny a sound is to admit that it is *not* a matter of general knowledge that it is obviously untrue, just as to excuse or mitigate the sound is to admit it as factually true.

The description of P as being obviously untrue—that its untruth is an AB-event—is equivalent to deciding that the sounder is not "serious." This decision must be made in any conversational exchange; whether it is a matter of commands, requests, assertions, or sounds, it is the first act of interpretation which the listener must make. As Harvey Sacks has pointed out (1966) there are important consequences of this decision: if the speaker is judged serious, a suitable response must be constructed to fit the situation. If the speaker is joking, then all that is usually required is a laugh—no matter what was said by the first speaker. In the case of sounding, the judgment is made that the speaker is not serious—the insult is a ritual one—but the answer will be governed to a certain extent by the nature of the proposition P. Excellence in sounding, and the winning of the contest, will depend upon the relation of P' to P.

The following more general formulation of the interactional structure of sounding is based upon the suggestions of Erving Goffman, in response to an earlier presentation of this analysis. Goffman's framework isolates four basic properties of *ritual* sounding, as opposed to other types of insult behavior:

1. A sound opens a *field,* which is meant to be sustained. A sound is presented with the expectation that another sound will be offered in response, and that this second sound may be built

formally upon it. The player who presents an initial sound is thus offering others the opportunity to display their ingenuity at his expense.
2. Besides the initial two players, a third-person role is necessary.
3. Any third person can become a player, especially if there is a failure by one of the two players then engaged.
4. Considerable symbolic distance is maintained and serves to insulate the event from other kinds of verbal interaction.

These properties, illustrated in the previous sections, are the means by which the process of insult becomes socialized and adapted for play. They may eventually be formalized in higher level rules of verbal interaction. In the following discussion, we will see in greater detail how the first principle operates in ritual sounding.

Sequencing in the Content of Sounds

The rules given in the subsection above are all that are needed to generate a series of sounds between two antagonists. There are further complications involved when a third person enters the exchange and when a number of members join in sounding on one antagonist who is falling behind. But sequencing is much more than the fact that speakers take turns and succeed each other: sequencing involves the substance of sounds which succeed each other—how one sound is built on another and how a series of sounds are brought to a conclusion. Above all, we are concerned with the standards of excellence in sounding—what makes one person a better sounder than another and how the group evaluates the performance of an individual. This topic will provide us with the best insight into the factors which control the use of language in the street culture. In settings far removed from the classroom, under standards of performance that are alien to those of the school, peer-group members develop a high level of competence in syntax, semantics, and rhetoric. One part of this competence was seen in the toasts developed by adults; in this discussion of sounding, we will observe the creative use of language by adolescents. We will consider first simple sequences of the type A B, where B builds on A's sound to achieve a greater level of complexity and may be judged in some sense to have surpassed it.

The extensive selections from the Thunderbirds' session show a number of such A B sequences. We cited:

> *David:* Your father got buck teeth.
> *Boot:* Your father got teeth growin' out his behind.

Note that both sounds feature the same attribute: odd or misshapen appearance, and the same target (relative to the speaker). Boot also preserves the same surface form: that is, in neither sound does the *T is so X that . . .* sentence appear. We do not in fact find sequences of the form:

> *A:* Your father got buck teeth.
> ** B:* Your father got such long teeth that they growin' out his behind.

We also note that the most superficial syntax of the proposition P is preserved: *Your father got . . .* Finally, Boot builds his sound on the same specific notion of misshapen teeth that David introduced. But Boot does not limit himself to mere exaggeration, such as *Your father got teeth a mile long.* Instead, he adds a new theme which combines anal interest with absurdity. We will not attempt to explore here the question of how "original" Boot's effort is. Most sounds are repetitions or recombinations of elements that have been used before. But it should be clear that sheer memory will not do the trick here, as it will with rhymed dozens. The reply must be appropriate, well-formed, it must build upon the specific model offered. It was observed before that Boot clearly won this round, judging by the responses of the audience.

Turning to the Jet session, we find that the targets usually shift more rapidly, since more than two members are involved and there is more overt play to the audience. The sequence A B is illustrated by many examples such as:

> *A:* Eh man, Tommy mother so little, look like she got hit by lightning.
> *B:* Your mother so small, you play hide-and-go-seek, y'all c'slip under a penny.

Here the target and attribute are preserved by B, who adds another clause going far beyond A in syntactic complexity (and apparently to the limits of his syntactic competence). The same pattern prevails when two different sounders are sounding on the same third man.

A: Bell grandmother so-so-so ugly, her rag is showin'.

B: Bell grandmother got so many wrinkles in her face, when they walk down the street, her mother would say, "Wrinkles and ruffles."

In the second sound, the attributes of age and ugliness overlap. The proposition is embedded in a more complex way in the *T is so X clause;* the embedded P combines three sentences as against the one sentence of the A model and again shows the left hand embedding which is so rare in colloquial speech. The underlying structure of this sentence, shown below, is certainly as complex as any we have seen.

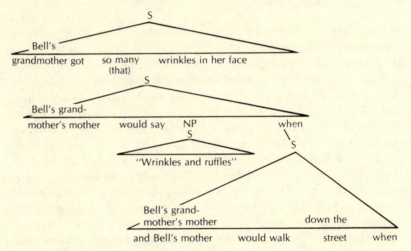

Most of the sequences in the Jet session are not as complex as this, but throughout we see the general pattern that B builds on A. We do not find sequences which reverse this order—in which the same target and attribute are preserved, but in which the proposition P is simpler—as would be the case, for example, if B and A were reversed above.

In the Cobras' sounding, we get many long sequences of comparable structure until someone arrives with a more complex form which ends the series:

C1: Your momma's a peanut man!

C2: Your momma's a ice-man!

C3: Your momma's a fire man!

C4: Your momma's a truck driver!
C5: Your father sell crackerjacks!
C6: Your mother *look* like a crackerjack!

The last sound in this series cannot be topped, and the sounding goes off in a completely different direction: "Your father named Theodore . . ." Here is another example of Cobras' building on each other:

C1: Your mother got on sneakers!
C2: Your mother wear high-heeled sneakers to church!
C3: Your mother wear high-heeled sneakers to come out and play on the basketball court!

The complication which B adds is often a semantic one—an additional pejorative attribute is inserted, as in the following:

A: Your mother name Black—Black Boy.
B: Your mother name the Black Bruiser.

The attribute attributed to the target is now not only blackness, but also masculinity or lack of feminity (as in *Your mother James Bond*). When a sound becomes too ordinary—too possible—we can then observe a sudden switch in the pattern of response to that appropriate for a personal insult. This can happen by accident, when a sound is particularly weak. For example, in the Jet session:

A: I went in Junior house 'n' sat in a chair that caved in.
B: You's a damn liar; 'n' you was eatin' in my house, right?

This is the only instance in the Jet sounding session where a statement is denied, and it is plainly due to the fact that the proposition P is not appropriate for ritual insult. Its untruth is not at all a matter of general knowledge—it is quite possible that a chair in somebody's house would cave in, and that the chair in Junior's house *did* cave in. It is interesting that Junior takes the same line that David took in countering Boot's personal insult. First Junior denies the charge; second, he hits back with another proposition that is again a personal, not a ritual insult: 'You come over to my house to eat (since there was no food in your own), and so what right have you to complain?' Of course, the second part implicitly contradicts the first—if no chair caved in, how does Junior know what occasion is being talked about? Just as Boot was forced to concede the truth of

David's point, so Junior here is plainly speaking of an actual event. There is no immediate response to contradict Junior's last remark. Instead, the theme of sounding is continued, based on A as a first element in the series.

> B: I went to Bell's house 'n' a Chinese roach said, "Come and git it."
>
> A: I brought my uncle—I brought my uncle up Junior house: I didn't trust them guys.

Triads

There are many triads in the Jet session where B tops A, and a third person adds a sound against B. This third sound often has a different target, attribute and/or form of proposition: it is shorter and more pointed, and acts as a coda which terminates the series.

> A: Your mother got funky drawers.
> B: Your mother got braces between her legs.
> C: Looks like your mother did it 'n' ran.

> A: Bell mother got a old beat-up boot.
> B: Her mother got a face like a rubber ass.
> C: Junior got a face like a clown.

In both of these cases, the final sound is contributed with authority by Bell, a senior member of the 100's group. In the second triad, it is Bell who is sounded against by A, and again by B, and Bell who answers as C. A short, firmly-delivered sound of this sort, with heavy stress on the last monosyllable, seems to close off debate effectively. After the first two members of a series, the closing element provided by a third person will usually show formal simplification. Thus we have:

> A: Your mother eat coke-a-roaches.
> B: Your mother eat fried dick-heads.
> A: Your mother suck fried dick-heads.
> C: His mother eat cold dick-heads.

The theme here from the beginning is "so hungry that she eats . . ."; the sounder is engaged in a search for something as disgusting to eat as he can find. B certainly tops A in this respect; note the complex noun phrase with an embedded participle. But A does not lose; he keeps the series open, capitalizing on the sexual element introduced by B. A's reply does not depend upon syntactic complexity. In simply changing the verb, he introduces semantic complexity by introducing the implicit attribute of sexual immorality. Sex takes a higher place on the implicit agenda of relevant topics than hunger or poverty, so that we now have to read the sound as 'Your mother is so hot that . . .' Thus A's reply achieves semantic change with a minimum of formal change. The third man achieves closure by returning to the original verb and shortening the form with a much simpler noun phrase. The absurdity of C's sound is based upon the assertion that the substitution of *cold* for *hot* food can be relevant at this stage in the search for disgusting attributes. This is a very low-ranking item on the agenda of relevance which governs discourse. It is a common source of humor to make such a sudden, incongruous claim to reverse the order of relevance.

We have seen that one way to achieve excellence in sounding is to develop comparisons with a high degree of left-hand embedding which suspends the final proposition. Another is to learn to close-off sequences with short sounds which abruptly change the prevailing form. The third, and perhaps the subtlest method has been illustrated here—bringing about striking semantic shifts with minimal changes of form: a "minimax" solution. This is best illustrated by the following sequence from the very beginning of the Jet session:

> *John L:* I'll take you to the last man.
> *Junior:* I'll take your mother.
> *Rel:* I took your mother.

The initial remark of John Lewis is not a sound; he is simply "louding," or "granning." Junior's counter is a sound of the "dozens" model. The introduction of the target *your mother* also introduces the sexual meaning of *take* so that ambiguity is achieved with a minimum formal change. Rel's final addition seems to us an even more adept example of semantic shift with a minimal effort. By changing from the challenge of the future form to the simply assertion of the past tense, Rel's sound also fits the pattern of a short, decisive closure.

There are other forms of sounding which use the same targets and attributes, but very different formal structure. For example, questions are not common as sounds, but the following series begins with two:

A: Hey didn't I see . . . shit on your mother bed?

B: A shot gun . . .

C: Did you see me under your mother bed when your father came in?

D: No I saw your uncle.

C: Oh my uncle was there too.

This whole series is positively evaluated by the group with great enthusiasm. But we will not explore the formal side of sounding further in this discussion.

Applied Sounding

So far, we have been considering the speech event called sounding as the principal focus of verbal activity. But sounding also occurs as an element in other kinds of interaction. Members with great verbal "presence of mind" are able to use sounds at critical moments to channel the direction of personal interaction in a direction that favors them. We may call such a use of ritual insults "applied sounding." It will be immediately apparent that applied sounds do not follow the rules set forth for ritual sounding—they are embedded in other rule sequences and other higher level structures of verbal interaction. But rule 1 for interpreting utterances as sounds will apply. Of the four more general properties of the ritual sounding situation, set forth on pages 343-4 above, only the fourth property is preserved—that symbolic distance is obligatory. But this property will prove essential to the analysis and ultimately to the solution of the initial problem posed in this chapter.

First it must be understood that verbal interaction among the Jets requires great verbal "presence of mind." Sounding is only one of the many ways of putting someone down. For example, the sounding session in the microbus cited above was initiated when Junior called out:

Junior: Hey what's your name! When are we goin' on the next one, K.C.?

This was out of line in two respects, first, in using *What's your name* with someone whose name was as well known as his own. By adding "K.C." (the usual term of address for John Lewis), the insult was only compounded. Secondly, this remark was out of line in that there had been no promise of a second outing, and Junior was far out of line in demanding it. John Lewis turned around and replied without hesitation:

John L.: Next time you give me some pussy!

There was considerable uproar at this—it was evident to one and all that Junior had been put down decisively.

John Lewis's remark is one of a large class of ritual insults which impute homosexuality to the antagonist by indirection. Here it catches Junior in a double bind. If he wants to refute the ritual charge of homosexuality, then he has to interpret Lewis's reply as meaning 'Never!' But that is his decision—John Lewis has neatly left it up to him. If Lewis had said, "You're not going!" he would have been faced with a roar of injured innocence and fierce denunciation: "You cheap bastard!" etc. He has sidestepped the problem and put Junior down decisively: "Got you Junior—got you that time!"

Among the Jets, Rel is one of the most skilled at using sounds in this way. At one point in the Jets session, 13-year-old Stevie was trying to push his way into a fight developing between Larry and Rel by warning Larry, "He gon' getchyou with 'is legs . . . he got legs—he got leg like—lik—'

Larry gave Stevie no more than a withering look, but Rel said

Aah, your *mother* got legs on 'er *nose!*

This sound crushed Stevie, and he made no effort to reenter the higher status group for some time. Rel's sound was as apt and crushing as Stevie's effort was bumbling and ineffective. Note however that Stevie is ordinarily a verbal leader of his own age group—another instance of the dominance of power relations over verbal skill.

We are now in a position to return to the original problem posed by Rel's sound, "Your mother's a duck." How is this a coherent response to Stanley's challenge? A closer examination of the context will help. First of all, we can note that when Rel first called for quiet, he was talking to the group as a whole, especially the younger, lower-status members at the other end of the table.

Rel: Shut up, please!

It was a deliberate, half-serious decision on Stanley's part to interpret Rel's request for action as being directed at *him.* As president, it was quite in order for him to challenge Rel's right to tell *him* to be quiet.

Stanley: . . . 'ey, you tellin' *me?*

Stanley put his elbow on the middle of the table and stretched out his long forearm towards Rel. His emphasis on *me* indicated that he was choosing to take this request personally. At this point, neither Rel nor Stanley could retreat.

> *Rel:* Yes.
> *Stanley:* Come a li'l closer.

Now Rel applied a simple sound against Stanley:

> *Rel:* Your mother's a duck. Get outa here.
> *Stanley:* Come a li'l closer an' say—
> *Rel:*   Your mother's a duck.

At this point, Stanley withdrew his arm, looked around, and became involved with someone else. Our understanding of why Stanley retreated is based on the definition of a sound as a ritual insult—one that is obviously not true. Though Stanley chooses to say, 'I take this personally,' Rel puts him down by redefining the situation as a ritual one. Informally, the message is 'What are you carrying on for? This is just a game we're playing, and you know it—unless your mother *is* a duck.' If Stanley insisted on taking the situation seriously, then he would be saying that it *could* be true—his mother could be a duck.

The logic of Rel's sound is the same as that of John Lewis's reply to Junior. The skill of the sounder leaves the ultimate decision up to the challenger: if he insists on taking the matter personally, the fight will go on, but he has already condemned himself and will find it very hard to regain his lost ground.

Thus the answer to the original problem we posed lies in the concept of a ritual event as one which is formulated without regard to the persons named. Sounds are directed at targets very close to the opponent (or at himself) but by social convention it is accepted that they do not denote attributes which persons actually possess: in Goffman's formulation, symbolic distance maintained serves to insulate this exchange from further consequences. The rules given above for sounding, and the development of sounds in bizarre and whimsical direction, all have the effect of preserving this ritual status. As we have seen, the ritual convention can break down with younger speakers or in strange situations—and the dangers of such a collapse of ritual safeguards are very great. Rituals are sanctuaries; in ritual we are freed from personal responsibility for the acts we are engaged in. Thus when someone makes a request for action in other subcultures, and he is challenged on the fourth precondition, "What right have you to tell me that?", his reply may follow the same strategy:

> It's not my idea—I just have to get the work done.
> I'm just doing my job.
> I didn't pick on you—somebody has to do it.

Any of these moves to depersonalize the situation may succeed in removing the dangers of a face-to-face confrontation and defiance of authority. Ritual insults are used in the same way to manage challenges within the peer group, and an understanding of ritual behavior must therefore be an important element in constructing a general theory of discourse.

9 | The Transformation of Experience in Narrative Syntax

IN the course of our studies of vernacular language, we have developed a number of devices to overcome the constraints of the face-to-face interview and obtain large bodies of tape-recorded casual speech.[1] The most effective of these techniques produce *narratives of personal experience,* in which the speaker becomes deeply involved in rehearsing or even reliving events of his past. The "Danger of Death" question is the prototype and still the most generally used: at a certain point in the conversation,[2] the interviewer asks, "Were you ever in a situation where you were in serious danger of being killed, where you said to yourself—*'This is it'?''* In the section of our interview schedule that deals with fights, we ask "Were you ever in a fight with a guy bigger than you?" When the subject says "Yes" we pause and then ask simply, "What happened?"[3] The

1. For a review of these techniques and quantitative analysis of their effectiveness, see "The Isolation of Contextual Styles" in *Sociolinguistic Patterns.* The present discussion is based upon the investigation of the structure and function of the language used in south-central Harlem; a preliminary version appears as section 4.8 in CRR 3288.

2. Our techniques do not utilize fixed questionnaires, but a schedule of topics with some transitions and questions specified in exact detail. It should be noted that the placement of the danger-of-death question is an important point. Ludicrous results are obtained when students introduce it in a mechanical way in the style of a conventional interview.

3. Note that the original question calls for only one or two words; this is a "Yes-No" question. The subject first becomes committed to a narrative by a simple 'yes'. He then becomes involved in the more detailed account of what happened as a necessary justification of the claim made by his first response. The initial impetus provided by the Yes-No question is an important element in this procedure. Many formal interviews use questions of the form "Can you tell me something amusing (dangerous, exciting, important) that has happened to you?" Though such questions will produce some response in some listeners, they are quite unsatisfactory as a rule to both speaker and interviewer; the reasons for their inadequacy make a nice topic for discourse analysis.

narratives that we have obtained by such methods form a large body of data on comparative verbal skills, ranging across age levels, classes, and ethnic groups. Because they occur in response to a specific stimulus in the interview situation, they are not free of the interactive effect of the outside observer. The form they take is in fact typical of discourse directed to someone outside of the immediate peer group of the speaker. But because the experience and emotions involved here form an important part of the speakers' biography, he seems to undergo a partial reliving of that experience, and he is no longer free to monitor his own speech as he normally does in face-to-face interviews (*Sociolinguistic Patterns*, chapter 3).

In a previous study we have presented a general framework for the analysis of narrative which shows how verbal skills are used to evaluate experience (Labov and Waletzky 1967). In this chapter we examine the narratives we obtained in our study of south-central Harlem from preadolescents (9 to 13 years old), adolescents (14 to 19), and adults to see what linguistic techniques are used to evaluate experience within the black English vernacular culture. In the earlier analysis we concentrated upon the placement of evaluative clauses in an "evaluation section" which suspended the action of the narrative at a crucial point; this discussion considers a wider range of evaluative elements, including the syntactic elaboration of the clause itself. An unexpected result of the comparison across age levels is that the use of many syntactic devices for evaluation does not develop until late in life, rising geometrically from preadolescents to adolescents to adults.

Before beginning the analysis, it will be helpful for the reader to be acquainted with the general character and impact of narratives in black vernacular style. We will cite here in full three fight narratives from leaders of vernacular peer groups in south-central Harlem who are widely recognized for their verbal skills and refer to these throughout the discussion to illustrate the structural features of narrative. The first is by Boot.[4]

1   (Something Calvin did that was really wild?)
           Yeah.
           a   It was on a Sunday
           b   and we didn't have nothin' to do after I—after we
               came from church

4. Remarks in parentheses are by the interviewer. The initial questions asked by the interviewer are also given to help clarify the evaluative focus of the narrative.

c   Then we ain't had nothin' to do.
d   So I say, "Calvin, let's go get our—out our dirty clothes
      on
        and play in the dirt."
e   And so Calvin say, "Let's have a rock—a rock war."
f   And I say, "All right."
g   So Calvin had a rock.
h   And we as—you know, here go a wall
i   and a far away here go a wall.
j   Calvin th'ew a rock.
k   I was lookin' and—uh—
l   And Calvin th'ew a rock.
m   It oh—it almost hit me.
n   And so I looked down to get another rock;
o   Say "Ssh!"
p   An' it pass me.
q   I say, "Calvin, I'm bust your head for that!"
r   Calvin stuck his head out.
s   I th'ew the rock
t   An' the rock went up,
u   I mean—went up—
v   came down
w   an' say [slap!]
x   an' smacked him in the head
y   an' his head busted.

The second narrative is by Larry H., the core member of the Jets
whose logic was analyzed in chapter 5. This is one of three fight
stories told by Larry which match in verbal skill his outstanding
performance in argument, ritual insults, and other speech events of
the black vernacular culture.[5]

2

a   An' then, three weeks ago I had a fight with this
      other dude outside.
b   He got mad
        'cause I wouldn't give him a cigarette.
c   Ain't that a bitch?
      (Oh yeah?)

5. See chapters 5 and 8 for other quotations from Larry.

d   Yeah, you know, I was sittin' on the corner an' shit,
       smokin' my cigarette, you know
e   I was high, an' shit.
f   He walked over to me,
g   "Can I have a cigarette?"
h   He was a little taller than me,
       but not that much.
i   I said, "I ain't got no more, man,"
j   'cause, you know, all I had was one left.
k   An' I ain't gon' give up my last cigarette unless I
       got some more.
l   So I said, "I don't have no more, man."
m   So he, you know, dug on the pack,
       'cause the pack was in my pocket.
n   So he said, "Eh man, I can't get a cigarette, man?
o   I mean—I mean we supposed to be brothers, an'
       shit."
p   So I say, "Yeah, well, you know, man, all I got is
       one, you dig it?"
q   An' I won't give up my las' one to nobody.
r   So you know, the dude, he looks at me,
s   An' he—I 'on' know—
       he jus' thought he gon' rough that
       motherfucker up.
t   He said, "I can't get a cigarette."
u   I said, "Tha's what I said, my man".
v   You know, so he said, "What you supposed to be
       bad, an' shit?
w   What, you think you *bad* an' shit?"
x   So I said, "Look here, my man,
y   I don't think I'm bad, you understand?
z   But I mean, you know, if I had it,
          you could git it
aa   I like to see you with it, you dig it?
bb   But the sad part about it,
cc   You got to do without it.
dd   That's all, my man."
ee   So the dude, he 'on' to pushin' me, man.
       (Oh he pushed you?)
ff   An' why he do that?

gg   *Everytime somebody fuck with me,*
        why they do it?
hh   I put that cigarette down,
ii   An' boy, let me tell you,
        I beat the shit outa that motherfucker.
jj   I tried to *kill* 'im—over one cigarette!
kk   I tried to *kill* 'im. Square business!
ll   After I got through stompin' him in the face, man,
mm   You know, all of a sudden I went crazy!
nn   I jus' went crazy.
oo   An' I jus' wouldn't stop hittin the motherfucker.
pp   Dig it, I couldn't stop hittin' 'im, man,
        till the teacher pulled me off o' him.
qq   An' guess what? After all that I gave the dude the
        cigarette, after all that.
rr   Ain't that a bitch?
     (How come you gave 'im a cigarette?)
ss   I 'on' know.
tt   I jus' gave it to him.
uu   An' he smoked it, too!

Among the young adults we interviewed in our preliminary exploration of south-central Harlem, John L. struck us immediately as a
gifted story teller; the following is one of many narratives that have
been highly regarded by many listeners.

3   (What was the most important fight that you remember,
              one that sticks in your mind . . .)
     a   Well, one (I think) was with a girl.
     b   Like I was a kid, you know,
     c   And she was the baddest girl, *the baddest girl in*
            the neighborhood.
     d   If you didn't bring her candy to school,
            she would punch you in the mouth;
     e   And you had to kiss her
            when she'd tell you.
     f   This girl was only about 12 years old, man,
     g   but she was a killer.
     h   She didn't take no junk;
     i   She whupped all her brothers.
     j   And I came to school one day
     k   and I didn't have no money.

l   My ma wouldn't give me no money.
m   And I played hookies one day,
n   (She) put something on me.[6]
o   I played hookies, man,
p   so I said, you know, I'm not gonna play hookies no more
    'cause I don't wanna get a whupping.
q   So I go to school
r   and this girl says, "Where's the candy?"
s   I said, "I don't have it."
t   She says, powww!
u   So I says to myself, "There's gonna be times my mother won't give me money
    because (we're) a poor family
v   And I can't take this all, you know, every time she
    don't give me any money."
w   So I say, "Well, I just gotta fight this girl.
x   She gonna hafta whup me.
y   I hope she don't whup me."
z   And I hit the girl: powwww!
aa   and I put something on it.
bb   I win the fight.
cc   That was one of the most important.

This discussion will first review briefly the general definition of narrative (section 1), its overall structure (section 2), types of evaluation and their embedding in narrative structure (section 3); we will then consider the basic syntax of narrative clauses and sources of syntactic complexity (section 4), and finally the use of complex syntactic devices in evaluation and developments with age (section 5). The main body of narratives cited will be from our work in south-central Harlem, but frequent references will be made to materials drawn from other urban and rural areas, from both white and black subjects.

1. Definition of Narrative

We define narrative as one method of recapitulating past experience by matching a verbal sequence of clauses to the sequence of

---

6. To *put something on someone* means to 'hit him hard'. See also aa, *I put something on it* 'I hit hard'.

events which (it is inferred) actually occurred. For example, a preadolescent narrative:

4   a   This boy punched me
           b   and I punched him
           c   and the teacher came in
           d   and stopped the fight.

An adult narrative:

5   a   Well this person had a little too much to drink
           b   and he attacked me
           c   and the friend came in
           d   and she stopped it.

In each case we have four independent clauses which match the
order of the inferred events. It is important to note that other means
of recapitulating these experiences are available which do not follow
the same sequence; syntactic embedding can be used:

6   a   A friend of mine came in just
               in time to stop
               this person who had a little too much
                  to drink
               from attacking me.

Or else the past perfect can be used to reverse the order:

7   a   The teacher stopped the fight.
           b   She had just come in.
           c   I had punched this boy.
           d   He had punched me.

Narrative, then, is only one way of recapitulating this past experience: the clauses are characteristically ordered in temporal sequence;
if narrative clauses are reversed, the inferred temporal sequence of
the original semantic interpretation is altered: *I punched this boy/
and he punched me* instead of *This boy punched me/and I punched
him.*

With this conception of narrative, we can define a *minimal narrative* as a sequence of two clauses which are *temporally ordered*: that
is, a change in their order will result in a change in the temporal
sequence of the original semantic interpretation. In alternative terminology, there is temporal juncture between the two clauses, and

a minimal narrative is defined as one containing a single temporal juncture.

The skeleton of a narrative then consists of a series of temporally ordered clauses which we may call *narrative clauses*. A narrative such as 4 or 5 consists entirely of narrative clauses. Here is a minimal narrative which contains only two:

8   a I know a boy named Harry.
           b Another boy threw a bottle at him right in the head
           c and he had to get seven stitches.

This narrative contains three clauses, but only two are narrative clauses. The first has no temporal juncture, and might be placed after *b* or after *c* without disturbing temporal order. It is equally true at the end and at the beginning that the narrator knows a boy named Harry. Clause *a* may be called a *free clause* since it is not confined by any temporal juncture.

Sometimes a number of clauses will seem to contain a narrative, but closer inspection shows that they contain no narrative juncture, and that they are not in fact narratives in this sense. For example, the following material was given in answer to the Danger of Death question by a member of the Inwood group:

9   (You ever been in a situation where you thought you were
               gonna get killed?)
        Oh, Yeah, lotta time, man.
        (Like, what happened?)
        a Well, like we used to jump off the trestle
        b and the trestle's about six-seven stories high.
        c You know, we used to go swimmin' there . . .
        d We used to jump offa there, you know.
        e An' uh-like, wow! Ya get up there
        f An' ya feel like
           you are gonna die and shit, y'know.
        g Couple a times I almost . . . I thought I was gonna
           drown, you know.

Because all of these clauses refer to general events which have occurred an indefinite number of times, it is not possible to falsify the situation by reversing clauses. Clauses *f* and *g* refer to ordered events on any one occasion, but since they are in the general present they refer to an indefinite number of occasions, so that it *is* the case

that some g followed some f. Clauses containing *used to, would,* and
the *general present* are not narrative clauses and cannot support a
narrative.

It is also the case that subordinate clauses do not serve as narrative
clauses. Once a clause is subordinated to another, it is not possible
to disturb the original semantic interpretation by reversing it. Thus
John L.'s narrative:

3   d   If you didn't bring her candy to school
                      she would punch you in the mouth.
              e   And you had to kiss her
                      when she'd tell you.

contains two sets of events, each of which is in fact temporally
ordered: *first* you didn't bring the candy, *then* she would punch you;
first the girl told you, and *then* you kissed her, not the other way
around. But this is not signalled by the order of the clauses; a reversal
does not disturb this interpretation:

              d' She would punch you in the mouth
                      if you didn't bring her candy to school,
              e' and when she'd tell you
                      you had to kiss her.

It is only independent clauses which can function as narrative
clauses—and as we will see below, only particular kinds of independent clauses. In the representation of narratives in this section,
we will list each clause on a separate line, but letter only the independent clauses. The internal syntax of the individual clauses will
be the focus of sections 4 and 5; for the moment we will consider
the clauses as a whole, classified as narrative and free.[7] The relative
arrangement of these clauses is the aspect of narrative analysis
considered in Labov and Waletzky 1967; we will deal with this only
briefly before proceeding to the internal structure.

2. The Overall Structure of Narrative

Some narratives, like 4, contain only narrative clauses; they are
complete in the sense that they have a beginning, a middle, and an
end. But there are other elements of narrative structure found in

7. There are also *restricted clauses,* which can be displaced over a large part of
the narrative without altering the temporal sequence of the original semantic interpretation, but not over the entire narrative.

more fully developed types. Briefly, a fully-formed narrative may show the following:

10   1. Abstract.
            2. Orientation.
            3. Complicating action.
            4. Evaluation.
            5. Result or resolution.
            6. Coda.

Of course there are complex chainings and embeddings of these elements, but here we are dealing with the simpler forms. Complicating action has been characterized in section 1, and the *result* may be regarded for the moment as the termination of that series of events. We will consider briefly the nature and function of the abstract, orientation, coda, and evaluation.

2.1 The Abstract

It is not uncommon for narrators to begin with one or two clauses summarizing the whole story.

11   (Were you ever in a situation where you thought you were
                in serious danger of being killed?)
            I talked a man out of—Old Doc Simon I talked him out
                of pulling the trigger.

When this story is heard, it can be seen that the abstract does encapsulate the point of the story. In 12 there is a sequence of two such abstracts:

12   (Were you ever in a situation where you were in serious
                danger of being killed?)
            a My brother put a knife in my head.

               (How'd that happen?)
            b Like kids, you get into a fight
            c and I twisted his arm up behind him.
            d This was just a few days after my father died . . .

Here the speaker gives one abstract and follows it with another after the interviewer's question. Then without further prompting, he begins the narrative proper. The narrative might just as well have begun with the free clause *d; b* and *c* in this sense are not absolutely required, since they cover the same ground as the narrative as a

whole. Larry's narrative (2) is the third of a series of three, and there
is no question just before the narrative itself, but there is well-formed
abstract:

2   a An' then, three weeks ago I had a fight with this other
                  dude outside.
               b He got mad
                  'cause I wouldn't give him a cigarette.
               c Ain't that a bitch?

Larry does not give the abstract in *place* of the story; he has no
intention of stopping there, but goes on to give the full account.

   What then is the function of the abstract? It is not an advertisement
or a warning: the narrator does not wait for the listener to say, "I've
heard about that," or "Don't tell me that now." If the abstract covers
the same ground as the story, what does it add? We will consider
this problem further in discussing the evaluation section below.

2.2 Orientation

   At the outset, it is necessary to identify in some way the time,
place, persons, and their activity or the situation. This can be done
in the course of the first several narrative clauses, but more com-
monly there is an orientation section composed of free clauses. In
Boot's narrative (1), clause *a* sets the time (*Sunday*); clause *b* the
persons (*we*), the situation (*nothin' to do*) and further specification
of the time (*after we came from church*); the first narrative clause
follows. In Larry's narrative (2), some information is already available in the abstract (the time—*three weeks ago*; the place—*outside
of school*); and the persons—*this other dude and Larry*). The orientation section then begins with a detailed picture of the situation—
Larry sittin' on the corner, high.

   Many of John L.'s narratives begin with an elaborate portrait of
the main character—in this case, clauses *a–i* are all devoted to *the
baddest girl in the neighborhood,* and the first narrative clause brings
John L. and the girl face to face in the schoolyard.

   The orientation section has some interesting syntactic properties;
it is quite common to find a great many past progressive clauses in
the orientation section—sketching the kind of thing that was going
on before the first event of the narrative occurred or during the entire
episode. But the most interesting thing about orientation is its *placement.* It is theoretically possible for all free orientation clauses to

be placed at the beginning of the narrative, but in practice, we find much of this material is placed at strategic points later on, for reasons to be examined below.

2.3 The Coda

There are also free clauses to be found at the ends of narratives; for example, John L.'s narrative ends:

cc   That was one of the most important.

This clause forms the *coda*. It is one of the many options open to the narrator for signalling that the narrative is finished. We find many similar forms.

13   And that was that.
14   And that—that was it, you know.

Codas may also contain general observations or show the effects of the events on the narrator. At the end of one fight narrative, we have

15   I was given the rest of the day off.
          And ever since then I haven't seen the guy
             'cause I quit,
             I quit, you know.
          No more problems.

Some codas which strike us as particularly skillful are strangely disconnected from the main narrative. One New Jersey woman told a story about how, as a little girl, she thought she was drowning, until a man came along and stood her on her feet—the water was only four feet deep.

16   And you know that man who picked me out of the water?
          He's a detective in Union City
          And I see him every now and again.

These codas (15–16) have the property of bridging the gap between the moment of time at the end of the narrative proper and the present. They bring the narrator and the listener back to the point at which they entered the narrative. There are many ways of doing this: in 16 the other main actor is brought up to the present: in 15, the narrator. But there is a more general function of codas which subsumes both the examples of 15–16 and the simpler forms of 13–14. Codas close off the sequence of complicating actions and indicate that none of the events that followed were important to the narrative. A chain of actions may be thought of as successive answers to the question "Then what happened?"; "And then what happened?" After a coda such as *That was that,* the question "Then what happened?" is properly answered, "Nothing; I just told you what happened." It is even more obvious after the more complex codas of 15 and 16; the time reference of the discourse has been reshifted to the present, so that "what happened then?" can only be interpreted as a question about the present; the answer is "Nothing; here I am." Thus the "disjunctive" codas of 15 and 16 forestall further questions about the narrative itself: the narrative events are pushed away and sealed off.[8]

2.4 *Evaluation*

Beginnings, middles, and ends of narratives have been analyzed in many accounts of folklore or narrative. But there is one important aspect of narrative which has not been discussed—perhaps the most important element in addition to the basic narrative clause. That is what we term the *evaluation* of the narrative: the means used by the narrator to indicate the point of the narrative, its raison d'être: why it was told, and what the narrator is getting at. There are many ways to tell the same story, to make very different points, or to make no point at all. Pointless stories are met (in English) with the withering rejoinder, "So what?" Every good narrator is continually warding off this question; when his narrative is over, it should be unthinkable for a bystander to say, "So what?" Instead, the appropriate remark would be, "He did?" or similar means of registering the reportable character of the events of the narrative.

8. The coda can thus be seen as one means of solving the problem of indicating the end of a "turn" at speaking. As Harvey Sacks has pointed out, a sentence is an optimal unit for the utterance, in that the listener's syntactic competence is employed in a double sense—to let him know when the sentence is complete and also when it is his turn to talk. Narratives require other means for the narrator to signal the fact that he is beginning a long series of sentences which will form one "turn" and to mark the end of that sequence. Many of the devices we have been discussing here are best understood in terms of how the speaker and the listener let each other know whose turn it is to talk. Traditional folk tales and fairy tales have fixed formulas which do this at the beginning and the end, but these are not available for personal narratives. It can also be said that a good coda provides more than a mechanical solution for the sequencing problem: it leaves the listener with a feeling of satisfaction and completeness that matters have been rounded off and accounted for.

The difference between evaluated and unevaluated narrative appears most clearly when we examine narrative of vicarious experience. In our first series of interviews with preadolescents in south-central Harlem, we asked for accounts of favorite television programs; the most popular at the time was "The Man from U.N.C.L.E."

17   a   This kid—Napoleon got shot
         b   and he had to go on a mission.
         c   And so this kid, he went with Solo.
         d   So they went
         e   and this guy—they went through this window,
         f   and they caught him.
         g   And then he beat up them other people.
         h   And they went
         i   and then he said
               that this old lady was his mother
         j   and then he—and at the end he say
               that he was the guy's friend.

This is typical of many such narratives of vicarious experience that we collected. We begin in the middle of things without any orientation section; pronominal reference is many ways ambiguous and obscure throughout. But the meaningless and disoriented effect of 17 has deeper roots. None of the remarkable events that occur is *evaluated*. We may compare 17 with a narrative of personal experience told by Norris W., eleven years old:

18   a   When I was in fourth grade—
             no, it was in third grade—
             This boy he stole my glove.
         c   He took my glove
         d   and said that his father found it downtown on the
             ground.
             (And you fight him?)
         e   I told him that it was impossible for him to find
             downtown
             'cause all those people were walking by
             and just his father was the only one
             that found it?
         f   So he got all (mad).

g   Then I fought him.
h   I knocked him all out in the street.
i   So he say he give.
j   and I kept on hitting him.
k   Then he started crying
l   and ran home to his father.
m   And the father told him
n   that he ain't find no glove.

This narrative is diametrically opposed to 17 in its degree of evaluation. Every line and almost every element of the syntax contributes to the point, and that point is self-aggrandizement. Each element of the narrative is designed to make Norris look good and "this boy" look bad. Norris knew that this boy stole his glove—had the nerve to just walk off with it and then make up a big story to claim that it was his. Norris didn't lose his cool and start swinging; first he destroyed this boy's fabrication by logic, so that everyone could see how phony the kid was. Then this boy lost *his* head and got mad and started fighting. Norris beat him up, and was so outraged at the phony way he had acted that he didn't stop when the kid surrendered—he "went crazy" and kept on hitting him. Then this punk started crying, and ran home to his father like a baby. Then his father—his *very own father* told him that his story wasn't true.

Norris's story follows the characteristic two-part structure of fight narratives in the BE vernacular; each part shows a different side of his ideal character. In the account of the verbal exchange that led up to the fight, Norris is cool, logical, good with his mouth, and strong in insisting on his own right. In the second part, dealing with the action, he appears as the most dangerous kind of fighter, who "just goes crazy" and "doesn't know what he did." On the other hand, his opponent is shown as dishonest, clumsy in argument, unable to control his temper, a punk, a lame, and a coward. Though Norris does not display the same degree of verbal skill that Larry shows in 2, there is an exact point-by-point match in the structure and evaluative features of the two narratives. No one listening to Norris's story within the framework of the vernacular value system will say "So what?" The narrative makes its point and effectively bars this question.

If we were to look for an evaluation section in 18, concentrating upon clause ordering as in Labov and Waletzky 1967, we would have to point to *d–e*, in which the action is suspended while elaborate arguments are developed. This is indeed the major point of the argument, as shown again in the dramatic coda *m–n*. But it would be a mistake to limit the evaluation of 18 to *d–e*, since evaluative devices are distributed throughout the narrative. We must therefore modify the scheme of Labov and Waletzky 1967 by indicating E as the focus of waves of evaluation that penetrate the narrative as in Fig. 9.1.

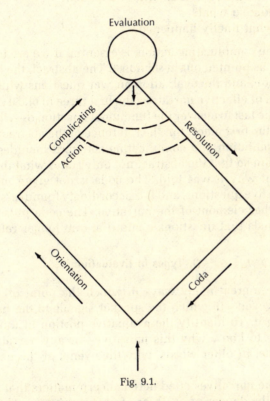

Fig. 9.1.

A complete narrative begins with an orientation, proceeds to the complicating action, is suspended at the focus of evaluation before the resolution, concludes with the resolution, and returns the listener to the present time with the coda. The evaluation of the narrative forms a secondary structure which is concentrated in the evaluation section but may be found in various forms throughout the narrative.

In the following sections we will see how that penetration is accomplished through the internal structure of narrative clauses as well as the ordering of those clauses.

We can also look at narrative as a series of answers to underlying questions:

a. Abstract: what was this about?
b. Orientation: who, when, what, where?
c. Complicating action: then what happened?
d. Evaluation: so what?
e. Result: what finally happened?

Only c, the complicating action, is essential if we are to recognize a narrative, as pointed out in section 1. The abstract, the orientation, the resolution, and the evaluation answer questions which relate to the function of effective narrative: the first three to clarify referential functions, the last to answer the functional question d—why the story was told in the first place. But the reference of the abstract is broader than the orientation and complicating action: it includes these and the evaluation so that the abstract not only states what the narrative is about, but why it was told. The coda is not given in answer to any of these five questions, and it is accordingly found less frequently than any other element of the narrative. The coda *puts off* a question—it signals that questions c and d are no longer relevant.

3. Types of Evaluation

There are a great many ways in which the point of a narrative can be conveyed—in which the speaker signals to the listener why he is telling it. To identify the evaluative portion of a narrative, it is necessary to know why this narrative—or any narrative—is felt to be tellable; in other words, why the events of the narrative are *reportable*.

Most of the narratives cited here concern matters that are always reportable: the danger of death or of physical injury. These matters occupy a high place on an unspoken permanent agenda. Whenever people are speaking, it is relevant to say "I just saw a man killed on the street." No one will answer such a remark with "So what?" If on the other hand someone says, "I skidded on the bridge and nearly went off," someone else can say, "So what? That happens to me every time I cross it." In other words, if the event becomes common enough, it is no longer a violation of an expected rule of behavior, and it is not reportable. The narrators of most of these stories were under social pressure to show that the events involved were truly dangerous and unusual, or that someone else really broke the normal rules in an outrageous and reportable way. Evaluative devices say to us: this was terrifying, dangerous, weird, wild, crazy; or amusing, hilarious, wonderful; more generally, that it was strange, uncommon, or unusual—that is, worth reporting. It was not ordinary, plain, humdrum, everyday, or run-of-the mill.

In this section we will consider briefly some of the large-scale, external mechanisms of evaluation and then turn in section 4 to a more detailed examination of the syntactic devices within the clause which carry out this function.

3.1 External Evaluation

The narrator can stop the narrative, turn to the listener, and tell him what the point is. This is a common trait of middle-class narrators, who frequently interrupt the course of their narrative. For example, a long story told by secretary about a trip from Mexico City in which the plane almost didn't get over the mountains. She frequently interrupted the narrative with such comments as

19   gg and it was the strangest feeling
          because you couldn't tell
            if they were really gonna make it
      hh if they didn't make it,
          it was such a small little plane,
          there was no chance for anybody.

      . . .

      xxx But it was really quite terrific
      yyy it was only a half-hour's ride to Mexico City

      . . .

      aaaa But it was quite an experience.

Other narrators would be content to let the narrative itself convey this information to the listener—to give *them* the experience. But this speaker finds it impossible to remain within the bounds of the narrative. Such external evaluation is common in therapeutic interviews, where it may form the main substance of an hour's discussion. The narratives themselves may serve only as a framework for the evaluation.

There are a number of intermediate steps in providing external evaluation for a narrative which do not overtly break the flow of narrative clauses. The simplest is for the narrator to attribute an evaluative remark to himself at that moment. A black woman raised in North Carolina was telling about a near-accident on the roads on her way to a funeral:

20   j   I just closed my eyes
            k   I said, "O my God, here it is!"

But feeling that the full reason for her fright would escape the listener, she steps out of the narrative to explain what was in her mind with this external evaluation:

            l   Well, 'cause you have heard of people
                    going to a funeral
                and getting killed themselves
                    before they got there
            m   and that is the first thing
                    that came to my mind.

3.2 *Embedding of Evaluation*

The first step in embedding the evaluation into the narrative, and preserving dramatic continuity, is for the narrator to quote the sentiment as something occurring to him at the moment rather than addressing it to the listener outside of the narrative. The paradigmatic form "This is it!" appears in 20 and in our original danger-of-death question. In John L.'s narrative (3), the action is suspended by the evaluation of the reasons he has to fight the baddest girl in the neighborhood, expressed as what he said to himself at the time, in u–y. Of course it is unlikely that all of this internal dialogue took place between the time the girl said *powww!*[9] and the time that he hit her back, but listeners are willing to accept this dramatic fiction.

A second step towards embedding evaluation is for the narrator to quote himself as addressing someone else. Boot expresses his moral indignation at Calvin's wild behavior in 1 as

            q   I say, "Calvin, I'm bust your head for that!"

---

9. In BEV, objects that do not speak but that make noises are not said to go X but to *say* X. In Boot's narrative 1, the *rock say shhh!* and in 3 *the girl says powww!* whereas in white vernacular, people *go powww!* with their fists.

And Larry's most elaborate evaluation of the problem with the last cigarette is expressed as three rhymed couplets, supposedly addressed to the dude in x–dd. Larry's role of provocateur is brilliantly maintained by the use of an apology in the form of rhyme: since sincere apology is supposedly spontaneous, nothing could be less sincere than this elaborate ritual.

The next step inward is to introduce a third person who evaluates the antagonist's actions for the narrator. A 74-year-old man who had worked in carnivals all his life told a story about a man who threatened to kill him because he thought his wife had committed suicide on the narrator's account. He concludes:

21   z   But, however—that settled it for the day.

          aa But that night the manager, Lloyd Burrows, said, "You
                better pack up and get out
                because that son of a bitch never forgives anything
                once he gets it in his head."

          bb And I did.

          cc I packed up and got out.

          dd That was two.

The narrator might just as well have attributed this evaluative comment to himself, but it carries more dramatic force when it comes from a neutral observer. It should be emphasized that this technique is used only by older, highly skilled narrators from traditional working-class backgrounds. Middle-class speakers are less likely to embed their evaluative comments so deeply in the narrative and are in fact most likely to use external evaluation.

3.3 Evaluative Action

A further step in dramatizing the evaluation of a narrative is to tell what people *did* rather than what they said. A lower-class youth from the Lower East Side told what happened at maritime training school when a rope broke and left him hanging on the masthead:

22   I never prayed to God so fast and so hard in my life!
          (What happened?)
          Well, the boys came up
          and they got me.
          I couldn't touch nuttin'.
          I was shakin' like a leaf.

In the story about the airplane flight from Mexico City (19), there are many striking examples of actions that reveal the tension of the actors. Though this speaker uses a great deal of external evaluation, she is also capable of maximal embedding of the evaluation:

z   and we were sitting with our feet—
    just sitting there
    waiting for this thing to start.
    people in the back saying prayers, 'n
    everything . . .

nnn   and when we saw that he was really over
ooo   and then everybody heaved a sigh of relief
ppp   and everybody came to
qqq   and put away their prayer beads

         . . .

sss   and when we realized
      that we were really out of danger
      then we found out
          that we had been so tense
          that our feet were up against the panel, you
          know
          and we were holding on to everything.

3.4 Evaluation by Suspension of the Action

Most of the evaluative devices mentioned so far will have the effect of suspending the action of the narrative. The emotions that are expressed may have been instantaneous or simultaneous with the action at the time, but when they are expressed in separate sentences, the action stops. Stopping the action calls attention to that part of the narrative and indicates to the listener that this has some connection with the evaluative point. When this is done artfully, the listener's attention is also suspended, and the resolution comes with much greater force. Thus as we have noted in John L.'s narrative (3), there is a major suspension of the narrative in between the time the girl hit him and the time he decided to hit back. This suspension can be diagrammed as in Labov and Waletzky 1967 by indicating the displacement sets of all narrative clauses as in Table 9.1. The horizontal axis represents the occurrence of the narrative clauses in narrative sequence; the vertical axis the range of clauses which could

TABLE 9.1.
DISPLACEMENT SETS FOR JOHN L.'s NARRATIVE
ABOUT THE BADDEST GIRL IN THE NEIGHBORHOOD

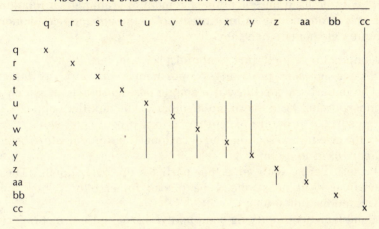

	q	r	s	t	u	v	w	x	y	z	aa	bb	cc
q	x												
r		x											
s			x										
t				x									
u					x								
v						x							
w							x						
x								x					
y									x				
z										x			
aa											x		
bb												x	
cc													x

have been placed before or after any given clause without changing the temporal sequence of the original semantic interpretation. The vertical lines show such *displacement sets* for each clause. This particular narrative begins with a long character sketch of the antagonist, consisting of free or restricted clauses, and then after the first narrative event introduces a flashback. We then return to the first narrative event with q: Table 9.1 shows the main sequence of the narrative q–cc. There are four narrative events in narrative clauses, each of which forms its own displacement set—q, r, s, t. We then have a displacement set of five evaluative clauses, u–y, all one narrative pseudoevent. We then pass to the resolution in z–bb and the coda cc. John L.'s narrative therefore fits the paradigm of Fig. 9.1, with a long orientation section a–p, complicating action q–u, evaluation v–y, resolution z–bb, and coda cc.

4. Departures from Basic Narrative Syntax

The narrative clause itself is one of the simplest grammatical patterns in connected speech. The surface structures are for the most part quite simple and related in a straightforward way to an equally simple deep structure. It will be useful to describe this structure as a series of eight elements, without hierarchical phrase structure; the first of these eight is the sentence adverbial, the second the subject-noun phrase, the third through eighth the verb phrase. The linear display to be used here is not a statement of grammatical relations but only a device for calling attention to the appearance of more complex elements when they do occur.

1. Conjunctions, including temporals: *so, and, but, then.*
2. Simple subjects: pronouns, proper names, *this girl, my father.*
3. The underlying auxiliary is a simple past tense marker which is incorporated in the verb; no member of the auxiliary appears in the surface structure except some past progressive *was . . . ing* in the orientation section, and occasional quasimodals *start, begin, keep, used to, want.*[10]
4. Preterit verbs, with adverbial particles *up, over, down.* (These particles will occasionally be placed under 6 or 7 by transformations not shown.)
5. Complements of varying complexity: direct and indirect objects.
6. Manner or instrumental adverbials.
7. Locative adverbials. Narrative syntax is particularly rich in this area.
8. Temporal adverbials and comitative clauses.[11]

The first preadolescent narrative (4) cited as a paradigm of simplicity may also be seen as an example of this basic syntax:

1	2	3	4	5	6	7	8
a		This boy		punched	me		
b	and	I		punched	him		
c	Then	the teacher		came			in
d	and			stopped	the fight		

10. The quasimodals produce many problems which are not fully resolved. There are some very close to the "true" modals in meaning, like *needs to, ought to;* though they do not flip-flop, they are basically sentence modifiers of the *It ought to be that . . .* type, and they are plainly evaluative. The situation is less clear with *start* and *keep (on).* The inchoative *start* does not seem to function as an evaluative element, but *keep* is almost always so; "I kept on hitting him." But in this sense, *keep* is surely an intensifier, not a comparator.

11. It seems clear that there is a temporal slot before the subject, filled by *then* or *when* clauses. But when a temporal phrase such as *ever since then* is introduced at this point, it seems heavily marked.

Many long preadolescent fight narratives are confined almost entirely to this basic syntactic pattern. We get sequences of narrative clauses such as 23:

23

	1	2	3	4	5	6	7
m		I		hit	him		in the jaw.
n	So	we		went			up on the sidewalk
o	and	we	start	fightin',			
p		I		knocked	him		down
q	and	we	was	rolled over			in the gutter.
r	And	he		took	some doodoo		
s				rubbed	it		in my face
t	and	I		took	some		
u	and			rubbed	it	all	in his mouth.
v		We	was	fightin'			
w	Then	a man		came			
x	and			grabbed	me		by my shirt
y	and			pulled	me		off
z	and	he	hadda	get up			
aa		I		thought *			
*		he	had	kicked	me		in my back
bb	So	I		turned			around
cc	and			kicked	him		in the knee

Each of the columns is filled by a set of simple and regular structures (except the temporal slot 8 which is not represented in this extract). We have occasional right-hand embedding with *that* complements after verbs of saying or infinitive complements after verbs such as *try*. This is indicated here by asterisks; no rearrangement of the linear order is required.

The fundamental simplicity of narrative syntax is not confined to the stories of preadolescents. Large sections of narratives told by adults will show the same pattern. Narrative as a whole contrasts sharply with ordinary conversation, which shows a much more complex structure. The simple auxiliary structure of narratives is the most striking point. In ordinary conversation, we hear a rich variety of modals, negatives, *have*'s and *be*'s before the verb, and a great many transformations and embeddings not found in these narratives. Given the existence of this simple organization of narrative clauses, we can ask: where, when, and with what effect do narratives depart from it? Since syntactic complexity is relatively rare in narrative, it must have a marked effect when it does occur. And in fact, we find that departures from the basic narrative syntax have a marked evaluative force. The perspective of the narrator is frequently expressed by relatively minor syntactic elements in the narrative clause. Investigations along these lines have led us to classify the evaluative elements in narrative under four major headings: *intensifiers, comparators, correlatives,* and *explications.* These four headings each include six to ten subtypes, depending on the syntactic devices used to carry out the functions involved.

4.1 Intensifiers

The major modifications of narrative clauses can best be understood in relation to the following basic scheme:

$$\longrightarrow \quad \longrightarrow \quad \longrightarrow \quad \longrightarrow \quad \longrightarrow$$

This indicates a linear series of events which are organized in the narrative in the same order as they occurred. An *intensifier* selects one of these events and strengthens or intensifies it:

intensifiers: $\longrightarrow \quad \longrightarrow \quad \longrightarrow \quad \Longrightarrow \quad \longrightarrow$

There are many ways in which this intensification can be carried out; most of them involve minimal departures from basic narrative syntax. We will proceed from the simplest to the most complex from the syntactic point of view.

Gestures usually accompany a deictic *this* or *that* in the tape-recorded narrative. From a fight story of Speedy, the leader of the Cobras:

24   g   He swung
            h   and I backed up
            i   and I do like *that*

                 . . .

            q   Then all the guys start hollerin',
                "You bleedin'
                you bleedin'
                Speedy, you bleedin'!"
            r   I say (sound) like that.

Sometimes the gesture is used instead of a sound, as in Boot's narrative (1): *and the rock say (slap!)*

Expressive phonology is superimposed upon other words of the clause. One of the most common modes is to lengthen vowels. In another of Larry's narratives he emphasizes:

25   And we were fightin' for a lo-o-ong ti-i-me, buddy.

Most punches are described with *powww!!* It is long and usually devoiced throughout. Such verbal devices are much more common than simple manual gestures and are usually conventional; but see Boot's way of describing the rock's passage: *it say shhhh!*

Quantifiers are the most common means of intensifying a clause, used by narrators of all age levels. The intensifier *all* is often inserted at a critical point in preadolescent narratives; from a fight narrative of one of the Aces:

26   g   and then, when the man ran in the barber shop
                   he was all wounded
            h   he had cuts all over

In Norris's fight narrative (18) we have a similar use of *all*:

            h   I knocked him all out in the street.

Some operations with quantifiers are fairly mechanical. If two guys jump someone, that is bad; but if six guys jump him, that is an event of another degree of magnitude and calls for a different kind of action.

The device of *repetition* is relatively simple from the syntactic point of view but is effective in narrative in two senses: it intensifies a particular action, and it suspends the action. We have seen above many examples of such repetition. In Boot's story about the rock, he says "The rock went up—I mean went up." In the extract from Speedy's narrative given above, we have an exceptionally effective use of repetition: "You bleedin', you bleedin', Speedy, you bleedin'!" A narrative by a well-known story teller on Martha's Vineyard involves a bird dog who was sent over to bring back a duck that had been shot down. He came back twice without it, and he was sent again with strict instructions to "go over there and git that duck;" the narrator reports

27   Well sir, he went over there a third time.
            And he didn't come back.
            And he didn't come back.

In fight narratives there are many *ritual utterances* which do not contain any overt markers of emphasis—neither taboo words, nor quantifiers, nor expressive phonology. Yet a knowledge of the culture tells us that these apparently unexpressive utterances play an evaluative role: they are conventionally used in that position to mark and evaluate the situation. In an adult narrative from the Harlem series, a black man raised in New York City told about a fight with "a great big guy in the back alley."

28   f   And I went to pieces inside, you know?
                 Before I know it
         g   I picked me up a little rock,
         h   hauled off,
         i   and landed me a David and Goliath.
         j   I hit him up with that rock.
         k   An' he grabbed his head
         l   An' I grabbed *him,*
         m   told him "Come on right back up the back stairs."
         n   And there it was.

Clause *n* is a ritual utterance; it can be read as 'and then the real action started' or 'and the shit was on.'

Intensifiers as a whole do not complicate the basic narrative syntax. But the other three types of internal evaluation are sources of syntactic complexity.

4.2 Comparators

The simplicity of narrative syntax should not be surprising if we take the opposite point of view: why *should* narratives require syntactic complexity? Why should the auxiliary contain anything but simple preterits and quasimodals? If the task of the narrator is to tell what happened, these will serve very well. What use has he for questions, or what reason does he have to speak of the future, since he is dealing with past events? And why should the auxiliary contain negatives? What reason would the narrator have for telling us that something did not happen, since he is in the business of telling us what did happen?

We can approach this problem by re-examining the negative. The use of negatives in accounts of past events is not at all obvious, since negation is not something that happens: rather it expresses the defeat of an expectation that something would happen. Negative sentences draw upon a cognitive background considerably richer than the set of events which were observed. They provide a way of evaluating events by placing them against the background of other events which might have happened, but which did not. *Comparators*, including negatives, compare the events which did occur to those which did not occur. In terms of the narrative scheme:

comparators: $\longrightarrow$ $\longrightarrow$ $\longrightarrow$ $----\rightarrow$ $\longrightarrow$

As we look down the auxiliary column at the various instances of negatives, futures, and modals, it can be seen that they typically occur at the point of evaluation, either in co-occurrence with other evaluative elements or carrying out this function alone.

Instead of considering each of these possibilities separately, let us examine the auxiliaries of some of the narratives already studied in the light of this proposed function of modals, futures, and negatives.

Boot's narrative about the rock war has a few negatives in the orientation, which plainly have a referential function—*we ain't had nothin' to do*, along with the planning imperatives of *Let's go*. Then there is a past progressive *I was lookin'* in the first evaluation section where Boot suspends the narrative for a moment to emphasize what a close call it was. All the rest of the verbs are preterits[12] except one future *I'm bust*. In speaking of an event which has not yet occurred, Boot explicitly marks it as an evaluation of Calvin's wild act: it is for *that* that the head busting will (and eventually did) take place.

The adolescent fight narrative of Larry is much richer in auxiliary structure. The abstract contains a negative question at the outset that is clearly evaluative and is repeated in the coda: *Ain't that a bitch?* It is in fact an abstract of the evaluative component of the narrative. The orientation section contains *d-e* which are progressives and copulas, as we would expect. We then have a series of modals and negatives, which are best shown by isolating the auxiliary column 2 for the narrative clauses alone and neglecting verbs of saying and the tense marker:

---

12. *Say* cannot be considered an historical present form, since it is regularly used for the past in the black English vernacular when no other present tense irregular forms occur.

		Aux	
f	He		walked over to me.
g	"I	can	have a cigarette?"
h	He		was a little taller than me . . .
i	"I	ain't	got no more, man . . .
j	I	ain't gon'	give up my last cigarette . . .
k	"I	don't	have no more."
l	He		dug on the pack.
m	"I	can't	get a cigarette?
	We	supposed to	be brothers . . ."

This series contains a question with a modal, several negatives, a negative future, a negative with a modal, and the quasimodal *supposed to*. We can turn from this highly evaluated narrative to the narrative of vicarious experience that we cited as 17.

		Aux	
a	Napoleon		got shot
b	he	had to	go on a mission
c	this kid		went with Solo.
d	they		went
e	they		went through
f	they		caught him.
g	he		beat up them other people
h	they		went
i	he		said
j	this old lady		was his mother
k	he		say
l	he		was the guy's friend.

The auxiliary column is blank except for a single *had to* in what might pass for the orientation of this narrative. Again, let us contrast this absence of comparators with the highly evaluated narrative of John L. The initial characterization of the baddest girl in the neighborhood is given in terms of things that *would* happen if other things didn't happen.

		Aux	
a	Well	one	was with a girl.
b	Like	I	was a kid . . .
c	And	she	was the baddest girl in the neighborhood . . .

			Aux	
d	If	you	didn't	bring her candy to school*
		she	would	punch you in the mouth
e	And	you	had to	kiss her*
	*when	she	would	tell you.
f		This girl		was only 12 years old
g	but	she	didn't	take no junk.

In rapid succession we have three modals and two negatives in the auxiliary column. The flashback which follows explains the reason why John L. came to school with no money; it is also stated in terms of what was not the case and what he did not want to happen. We then have the narrative proper which was examined in Table 9.1:

		Aux	
q	I		go to school
r	This girl		says*
	* "Where		's the candy?"
s	I		said*
	* "I	don't	have any."
t	She		says: powww!

There are no comparators in the main verbs of the four narrative clauses, but the quotation in s has a negative. How should such embedded comparators be analyzed? In the light of our general discussion of the embedding of evaluation, we must accept it as evaluative in the same sense as those in a–i. The speakers are in fact evaluating the situation: the girl who does not see the candy makes a demand in the form of a request for information about some unseen state of affairs, presupposing the existence of the candy; the boy denies her expectation. They are dealing with a level of expected and unrealized events which go beyond basic narrative sequence. For this sequence of four narrative clauses we have one negative and one intensifier. Let us now examine the evaluation section that follows:

			Aux	
u	So	I		says to myself,*
		* "There	's gonna	be times*
		* my mother	won't	give me money*

			Aux	
	*because	we		're a poor family
v	and	I	can't	take this all, every time*
		she	don't	give me any money."
w	So	I		say,*
	*Well,	I	just gotta	fight this girl.
x		She	gonna hafta	whup me.
y		I		hope*
		*she	don't	whup me."

This set of six clauses are bound together as the remembered evaluation of the situation by the narrator. They contain four futures, four negatives, and three modals—a total of eleven comparators—as well as the intensifier *this all*.[13] Clearly the evaluation section contains a much higher concentration of these evaluative devices. The resolution returns to basic syntax.

z	I	hit the girl: powww!
aa	I	put something on it.
bb	I	win the fight.

Reviewing these three narratives, we have seen some evidence that negatives, futures, and modals are concentrated in the evaluative sections of the narrative. It also seems that when such elements occur, they have an evaluative function as comparators. We can now consider other types of comparators, of a higher degree of syntactic complexity.

The quoted question in *r* of John L.'s narrative suggests that *questions* are also comparators. When the girl asks "Where's the candy?" she is asking about an unseen state of affairs, presupposing the existence of the candy; but on a higher level, she is making a request for action, and in light of previous experience, it is heard as a threat: *hand it over*, or . . . If we consider the compelling character of all questions (*mands* in Skinner's terminology), it is clear that all requests, even the most mitigated, are to be heard against an unrealized

---

13. There is also a complex embedding here which has evaluative force. Though we do not count single right branchings as evaluative, a structure such as that in clause *u* is counted as a correlative below.

possibility of negative consequences if they are not answered. In Larry's narrative there are many examples of such implied threats. Most of these are embedded in the speech of the actors. Questions that are more openly evaluative are posed directly to the listener. These brief considerations show us that the evaluative force of questions cannot be assigned on the basis of their superficial interrogative form. A deeper study would require the analysis of each quoted speech act in terms of the hierarchical series of actions being performed: e.g. *request for information* → *request for action* → *challenge* → *display*. Overt questions that are not embedded in the dramatic action, but asked directly of the listener, have a direct evaluative function. Thus Larry, assuming a false innocence in his role of provocateur, addresses the listener:

> ff   An' why he do that?
> gg   *Everytime somebody fuck with me,*
>   Why they do it?

These questions ask for an evaluation of the dude's actions. He in turn asks for an evaluation of Larry's action when he says, "What you supposed to be, *bad* an' shit?" And Larry in turn asks for an evaluation from the listener at the end:

> qq   An' guess what?
>   After all that, I gave the dude the cigarette,
>   after all that.
>   Ain't that a bitch?

The *imperative* is also a comparator, since the force of the command in narrative is frequently: 'you do this or else . . .' A Lower East Side taxi driver told a long narrative about a passenger that he was sure wanted to hold up the cab and kept giving him directions to out-of-the-way places. Luck was with him, though, and he managed to get out of it. At the end:

29	mm	and	I		said,*
			* "I	can't	run around with you all night.
	nn	Now		let's	put an end to this.
	oo	This			is the fare,
	pp		You		go your way
	qq	and	I	'll	go mine."
	rr	so	I		got out of it that way.

The close connection between the imperative and the future appears in *nn, pp,* and *rr;* both of them involve unrealized events that are weighed in the balance.

The suggestion so far is that negatives, futures, modals, questions, and imperatives are all comparators and all involve comparison. The paradigmatic comparison is of course the *comparative* itself in its various forms: as the grammatical comparative and superlative in clauses with *as,* in prepositional phrases with *like,* in metaphors and similes. Among the various syntactic forms that give younger speakers trouble, the comparative is foremost, and in our "strange syntax" file we have collected a great many odd problems with complex comparative constructions. Of the various comparators, it is the comparative itself which reaches the highest level of syntactic complexity.

There are no comparatives in Boot's rock war narrative. In 2, Larry uses a fairly complex comparative which has great weight in establishing the meaning of everything that follows:

> h   He was a little taller than me, but not that much.

The comparative is used by John L. at the same point in 3 to evaluate the meaning of the following events by characterizing the opponent—in this case in the superlative form:

> c   And she was the baddest girl, *the baddest girl* in the neighborhood.

John L. also uses the superlative in his final evaluation:

> ee   That was one of the most important.

As we examine the narratives of older, highly skilled narrators, we find a proliferation of comparisons which are quite beyond the normal capacity of an adolescent. In the dog story cited above (27), the following evaluation is made when the dog returned without the duck:

> 27   And that was unusual.
>   He'd track a duck same as a hound would take a rabbit track.

To show how exasperated he was with the dog;

> I never come nearer bootin' a dog in my life.

And at the end, he finds that the duck in question wasn't a wild duck at all—it was a tame decoy that had broken loose and the dog was holding him down with his paw.

> By gorry sir, that that dog knew more than I did.
> If I had booted that dog, I'd a felt some bad.

One of the most dramatic danger-of-death stories was told by a retired postman on the Lower East Side: his brother had stabbed him in the head with a knife. He concludes:

30   And the doctor just says, "Just about this much more," he says, "and you'd a been dead."

Comparators then include negatives, futures, modals, quasimodals, questions, imperatives, or-clauses, superlatives, and comparatives, more or less in increasing order of syntactic complexity.

4.3 Correlatives

A comparator moves away from the line of narrative events to consider unrealized possibilities and compare them with the events that did occur; correlatives bring together two events that actually occurred so that they are conjoined in a single independent clause.

Correlatives: ⟶   ⟶   ⟶   ⟹   ⟶

This operation requires complex syntax; it quickly goes beyond the syntactic range of the younger narrators. In order of their increasing syntactic complexity, we can list:

1. *Progressives* in *be . . . ing* which are usually used in narratives to indicate that one event is occurring simultaneously with another, but also may indicate extended or continued action. Most of these occur in orientation sections; some can actually form narrative clauses.[14] But *was . . . ing* clauses also are found suspending the action in an evaluative section, as we have seen in Boot's narrative.

2. *Appended participles:* One or more verbs in *-ing* are aligned, with tense marker and *be* deleted; the action described is heard as occurring simultaneously with the action of the main verb of the

---

14. The past progressive *was . . . ing* cannot be taken as an addition to basic narrative syntax in many cases, since it seems to serve as a narrative clause. While *was . . . ing* is usually simultaneous with other events, it is occasionally only *extended*, and can act as the head of a narrative clause. For example: 'And [we] got back—it was a tent show—she was laying on a cot with an ice bag on her head.'

sentence, which itself may be a progressive. Such doubled progressives are frequently used in orientation sections; in Larry's narrative we find:

> d I was sittin' on the corner an'shit,
>   smokin' my cigarette, you know.

Here the progressives characterize the setting for the narrative as a whole. But more often such devices are used to highlight and evaluate the event of a particular narrative clause. From another narrative of Larry:

31		e So	the dude		got smart.	
			I		know*	
	*		he		got smart	
	'cause	I	was	dancin'		with her, you know,
	'cause	I	was	dancin'		with her, to her, an' shit,
				talkin'		
				whisperin'		in her ear, an' shit,
				tongue kissin'	with her, an' shit.

Such multiple participles serve to suspend the action in an evaluative section; they bring in a wider range of simultaneous events while the listener waits for the other shoe to fall, as in this example from the evaluation section of the airplane flight (19):

	z and we	were sitting	with our feet—
		just sitting there,	
		waiting	for this thing to start
	people in		
	the back	saying	prayers, 'n' everything.

Another type of correlative is the *double appositive,* which is relatively rare; it is used to heighten or deepen the effect of a particular description. From a preadolescent narrative:

32   f and I knocked 'im down
            g and one of them fought for the Boys' Club
            h I beat him.
            i and then, they gave him *a knife, a long one, a dagger,*
            j and I fought,
            k I fought him with that . . .

We find that *double attributives* are as rare as double appositives. One would think that such noun phrases as *big red house* and *cold wet day* would occur often enough but the fact of the matter is that they are uncommon in colloquial style. In subject position, even a single attributive is uncommon (other than demonstratives, articles, and possessives), as inspection of the narratives quoted here will show. Some adults use such complex noun phrases more than others; one working-class man from the Harlem adult sample introduced his narrative with this clause:

33   a You see, a great big guy in the back alley,
              He tried to make them push him on the swing
                 by him pestering them
                 or trying to take advantage of them.

This double attributive is associated with the very complex syntax that follows. Some practised, adult narrators naturally run to such combinations and use other correlatives such as *left-hand participles*. For example, we find the following complex structure in narrative 29 cited above:

        j and suddenly somebody is giving me a destination
        k I look in the back
        l There's *an unsavory-looking passenger* in the
            back of the cab
               who had apparently gotten into the cab
                   while it was parked
               and decided he's gonna wait for the driver.

The phrase *an unsavory-looking passenger in the back of the cab* might be paraphrased as several narrative clauses: I looked into the back of the cab/I saw this character/I didn't care for the way he looked. The left-hand participle then does a great deal of work in characterizing the antagonist in this narrative—more concisely perhaps, than the elaborate descriptions given by John L. in 3. It is not accidental that some of the most complex syntax is used in describing the principal antagonist, who is the chief justification for the claim that the narrative is reportable. Note that one reason for this complex form is that it is coupled with three other propositions about the antagonist so that it is quite helpful to get this descriptive material out of the way in attributive, left-hand position.

The emphasis on *left-hand* vs. *right-hand* is motivated by the fact that the former is far more complex for speaker and listener alike. Absolute right-hand embedding is a simple matter for most children, as we see in "The House that Jack built." It is one thing to add a right-hand participle to qualify an action, as in this example from an adult narrative:

34   But some reason every day after school
            this kid was come
            and slap me side o 'my head,
                impressin' this girl.

It is another to build up participles as attributives before a noun, keeping the syntactic structure open while the equivalent of an entire sentence intervenes between other modifiers and the head:

35   She was a big, burly-looking, dark type sort of girl, a real,
                geechy-lookin' girl

This complex construction with two left-hand participles and multiple attributives is used to enrich and deepen the characterization of the chief antagonist in a fight story.

4.4 Explicatives

Some of the evaluation and explication of a narrative is necessarily done in separate clauses, appended to the main narrative clause or to an explicit evaluative clause. These may be *qualifications* connected with such conjunctions as *while, though;* or *causal,* introduced by *since* or *because.* We further distinguish three types of attachment to the main clause: simple, complex, and compound. By *simple,* we mean that there is only one clause; by *complex,* that a clause is embedded in a clause which is in turn embedded in the main clause; and by *compound,* that two clauses are embedded at the same point in the matrix clause. We do not count here embedding on verbs of saying and knowing, since the use of absolute right-hand embedding with verbs of this type is universal and automatic among all speakers. The diagram below shows one such embedding on *realize* followed by one on *found out* and two deeper explications that are both compound and complex.

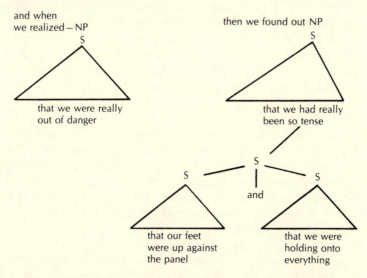

Note that these two last *that* clauses are embedded on the comparative mode *so*. At first glance, it would seem that such embedded finite clauses differ only technically from the nominalizations and participles classified as correlatives. In the correlatives, we have additional transformations which delete the tense markers and combine this material into single clauses, while in the explicatives, complete clauses are added. This is usually treated as a trivial difference; for example, the three complementizers *for-to, possessive + -ing,* and *that* are often considered as a set—three equivalent ways of attaching embedded sentences to the matrix sentence. But for our purposes there is a crucial difference in the deletion of the tense marker after *for-to* and *ing*.[15] No separate time distinction can be made with infinitives and gerunds; they necessarily are considered coextensive with the main verb as far as temporal sequence is concerned. That is not the case with the finite clauses which have *that* complementizers. Here we can explain an event by referring to something

15. For other reasons to discriminate these complementizers, see Kiparsky and Kiparsky 1970 and chapter 4. The dimension which distinguished these three complementizers is essentially three degrees of [FACT].

that happened long before or long after. This is the case with 19, where the tenses of the explicative clauses are overtly realized and refer to points much earlier in the narrative. Thus explicatives do not necessarily serve the evaluative function of bringing several actions together. The action of the narrative is suspended, but the attention of the listener is not maintained at that point in time—it may be transferred backward or forward, or into a realm of abstract speculation wholly unrelated to the narrative. We may represent explicatives in the narrative scheme as

Explicatives: $\longrightarrow$ $\longrightarrow$ $\longrightarrow$ $\underset{}{\overset{\uparrow}{\longrightarrow}}$ $\longrightarrow$

The explication of the various complications inherent in the narrative situation may serve an evaluative function—e.g., to explain why a person was frightened or how big someone was. But explication may itself be required only to describe actions and events that are not entirely familiar to the listener. We would then expect that the distribution of explications would be very different from that of the other sources of syntactic complexity, and in the next section it will appear that that is the case.

In this discussion of the sources of syntactic complexity in narrative, we have set out a classification of the various ways in which the minimal syntactic pattern is developed. There are many other technical devices used in narrative which might have been discussed here: *deletions*, which include claims to ignorance; the use of the *passive*, and *ellipsis*; *reorderings*, which include monologues, flashbacks, and displacement of orientation. There are also dysfunctional aspects of narrations: confusion of persons, anaphora and temporal relations. This discussion has been limited to those evaluative devices which involve the internal structure and syntactic complexity of narrative units.

Some of the syntactic features discussed here occur in clauses which have a purely referential function: they clarify for the listener the simple factual circumstances surrounding the narrative. But most occurrences of these features are closely linked to the evaluation of the narrative: they intensify certain narrative events that are most relevant to the main point; they compare the events that did occur to those which might have but did not occur; they correlate the linear dimension of the narration by superimposing one event upon another; and they explicate the point of the narrative in so many words. The examples we have cited above illustrate, but do not prove, this association between syntactic complexity and evaluation. In the next section, we will present certain quantitative data which will make this association more evident and show the growth of syntactic complexity with age.

5. Development of Evaluative Syntax with Age

It is often said that a child coming to school at the age of five has already learned most of the grammar of his language. This proposition may be a healthy corrective to those who argue that they are teaching the child to speak the English language in the first grade, but it is easy to overstate. In the course of our study of narrative structure and syntactic complexity, we made a comparison of stories told by black preadolescents (age 10–12), adolescents (age 13–16), and adults from the Harlem sample in order to see what development actually takes place in the use of the evaluative devices outlined above. It is clear that every child is in possession of the basic narrative syntax: it is also true that children know how to use gestures, quantifiers, repetition, negatives, futures, modals, and *because* clauses. The question is whether they know how and when to use these devices for specific purposes in the course of telling a story.

Ten fight narratives were chosen for each group: the basic pattern emerges with great clarity from this small set. Table 9.2 shows the use of the four major types of evaluational devices for the three age groups. The first column shows the raw totals; the second column the totals corrected for the average length of the narrative measured as the number of independent clauses. This average length is longest for the adults (Ad)—27.4 clauses—slightly less for adolescents (TA), but much shorter for preadolescents (PA).

TABLE 9.2.
TOTAL USE OF EVALUATIVE CATEGORIES IN NARRATIVE BY AGE

	PA		TA		Ad	
	Tot	Tot/L	Tot	Tot/L	Tot	Tot/L
Intensifiers	12	1.23	51	2.05	88	3.20
Comparators	12	1.23	71	2.85	113	4.10
Correlatives	1	.12	12	.48	23	.84
Explicatives	1	.12	12	.48	20	.73
L:		9.6		24.8		27.4

L = Average number of independent clauses.

The figures for all four evaluative categories show a regular and marked increase from preadolescents to teenagers and another large increase from adolescents to adults. The intensifiers show the shallowest slope, roughly 1 to 2 to 3; the comparators are somewhat steeper in their rate of growth; and the correlatives and explicatives show the sharpest rate of all, about 1 to 4 to 8. Looking at this table, we can assert that the preadolescents still have a great deal of language learning ahead of them. The ability to use negatives, futures, and modals in ordinary conversation is not equivalent to the ability to use them in narrative.

One can ask whether this is a syntactic ability, a question of verbal skill on a broader sense, or a growth of cognitive ability. In any case there is a major aspect of development in narrative itself which takes place long after the basic syntax of the language is learned, and it is quite possible that some of the more complex comparators and correlatives are outside of the linguistic capacities of the preadolescents.

Table 9.3 shows the use of the various subtypes of evaluational

TABLE 9.3.
NUMBER OF NARRATORS USING
EVALUATIVE DEVICES AT LEAST ONCE

Intensifiers	PA	TA	Ad	Comparators	PA	TA	Ad
Gestures	0	1	1	Imperatives	1	3	6
Phonology	0	5	3	Questions	1	4	4
Quantifiers	4	6	10	Negatives	4	7	10
Lexical items	0	5	7	Futures	0	1	2
Foregrounding	1	1	2	Modals	2	4	7
Repetitions	0	5	3	Quasimodals	2	6	7
Ritual	3	1	5	Or-clauses	0	3	2
WH-exclamations	1	3	1	Comparatives	1	6	6
Total	9	27	32	Total	11	34	44

Correlatives				Explicatives			
Be . . . ing	0	3	0	Simple: qual.	0	3	3
Double . . . -ing	0	1	0	Simple: caus.	1	3	5
Double appositive	1	1	2	Complex: qual.	0	0	2
Double attrib've	0	1	2	Complex: caus.	0	1	1
Participle: rt.	0	1	5	Compound: qual.	0	0	0
left	0	1	1	Compound: caus.	0	1	2
Nominalizations	0	1	2	Total	1	8	13
Total	1	9	13				

devices as the number of narrators who used each device at least once. The numbers range from 1 to 10: it appears that the only 100 percent categories are the use of negatives and quantifiers by adults.

As far as intensifiers are concerned, we see that the preadolescents are most apt to use quantifiers; the adolescents show a much richer use of expressive phonology and marked lexical items. Among the comparators, the most striking correlation with age is in the comparative itself. The correlatives as a whole are practically outside of the range of the preadolescents sampled here: the only item used with any degree of frequency by any group is the right-hand participle used by adults. Explicatives show the same distribution by age; the most frequent item is the simple causative clause.

We compared these narratives of black speakers from Harlem with our white working-class control group, Inwood. Six fight narratives told by the Inwood adolescents show the following use of evaluators:

	Total	Tot/L
Intensifiers	29	1.26
Comparators	23	1.00
Correlatives	4	.16
Explications	0	.00

$$L = 23.3$$

The values for this small group of white teenagers are comparable to those of the black preadolescents, rather than to the black adolescents, though the length of the narratives is typical of this age. The profile for the four types of evaluators is approximately the same as for the Harlem preadolescents. It is perhaps too much to assert from this small study that the black speakers are more advanced in narrative skills than the Inwood group, but they are certainly not behind or backward in this respect. On the contrary, there is evidence here to support the proposition we advanced earlier that the highest concentration of verbal skills is to be found in the black English vernacular culture.

The late development in the use of evaluative syntax appears to be general to all subcultures, though we have not yet investigated systematically age levels in white working-class and middle-class groups. It is surprising that this use of complex syntax in narrative should fall so far behind competence in ordinary conversation. The contrast appears most sharply with comparators; there is no question that preadolescents are thoroughly skilled in the use of other devices such as modals, questions, or futures. But they do not call upon these elements as freely as adults in presenting their own experience. The skilled adult complicates his representation of experience, moving back and forth from real to imaginary events. Children complain, question, deny, and worry, but adults are more aware of the significance of this activity and more likely to talk about it.

In reporting their own experience, adults have developed the ability to evaluate their own behavior with more complex linguistic devices. In middle-class speakers, this process often gets out of hand, and many narrators can lose the point of their story entirely in an excess of external evaluation and syntactic elaboration. But when these devices are concentrated and embedded deeply in the dramatic action, they can succeed in making the point. Many of the narratives cited here rise to a very high level of competence; when they are quoted in the exact words of the speaker, they will command the total attention of an audience in a remarkable way, creating a deep and attentive silence that is never found in academic or political discussion. The reaction of listeners to these narratives seems to demonstrate that the most highly evaluated form of language is that which translates our personal experience into dramatic form. The vernacular used by working-class speakers seems to have a distinct advantage over more educated styles. We have not been comparing black and white vernaculars; but in this respect, it should be clear that the black English vernacular is the vehicle of communication used by some of the most talented and effective speakers of the English language.

BIBLIOGRAPHY

Abrahams, Roger. 1962. Playing the dozens. *Journal of American Folklore* 75:209–18.

——. 1964. *Deep down in the jungle: Negro narrative folklore from the streets of Philadelphia.* Chicago: Aldine Publishing Company.

——. 1970. Rapping and capping: black talk as art. In *Black America*, ed. John F. Szwed. New York: Basic Books.

Anshen, Frank. 1969. Speech variation among Negroes in a small southern community. Unpublished New York University dissertation.

Bach, Emmon. 1967. *Have* and *be* in English syntax. *Language* 43:462–85.

Bailey, Beryl. 1966. *Jamaican Creole syntax.* London: Cambridge University Press.

Bailey, Charles-James. 1971. Trying to talk in the new paradigm. *Papers in Linguistics* 4:312–38.

——. 1972. The integration of linguistic theory: internal reconstruction and the comparative method in descriptive analysis. In *Historical linguistics and generative theory*, eds. R. P. Stockwell and R. Macaulay. Bloomington, Ind.: Indiana University Press.

Baker, C. L. 1970. Double negatives. *Linguistic Inquiry* 1:169–86.

Baratz, Joan C. 1969. Teaching reading in an urban Negro school system. In *Teaching black children to read*, eds. Joan Baratz and Roger Shuy. Washington, D.C.: Center for Applied Linguistics.

Bellugi, Ursula. 1967. The acquisition of negation. Unpublished Harvard University dissertation.

Bereiter, Carl, et al. 1966. An academically oriented pre-school for culturally deprived children. In *Pre-school education today*, ed. Fred M. Hechinger. New York: Doubleday.

Bereiter, Carl, and Engelmann, Siegfried. 1966. *Teaching disadvantaged children in the pre-school.* Englewood Cliffs, N.J.: Prentice-Hall.

Bernstein, Basil. 1966. Elaborated and restricted codes: their social origins and some consequences. In *The ethnography of communication,* eds. J. Gumperz and D. Hymes. Special publication. *American Anthropologist* 66 (no. 6, part 2).

Bickerton, Derek. 1971. On the nature of the Creole continuum. Mimeographed.

Bloom, Lois. 1970. *Language development: form and function in emerging grammars.* Cambridge, Mass.: MIT Press.

Caldwell, Bettye M. 1967. What is the optimal learning environment for the young child? *Am. J. of Orthopsychiatry* 37:8–21.

Carden, Guy. 1970. A note on conflicting idiolects. *Linguistic Inquiry* 1:281–90.

————. 1972. Disambiguation, favored readings and variable rules. Mimeographed.

Cazden, Courtney. 1968. The acquisition of noun and verb inflections. *Child Development* 39:433–48.

Cedergren, Henrietta, and Sankoff, D. 1972. Variable rules: performance as a statistical reflection of competence. To appear in *Language.*

Chomsky, Noam. 1955. *Syntactic structures.* The Hague: Mouton.

————. 1965. *Aspects of the theory of syntax.* Cambridge, Mass.: MIT Press.

Chomsky, Noam, and Halle, Morris. 1968. *The sound pattern of English.* New York: Harper and Row.

Cohen, Paul, 1970. The tensing and raising of short *a* in the metropolitan area of New York City. Unpublished Columbia University Master's essay.

Cole, Michael, and Bruner, Jerome S. 1972. Cultural differences and inferences about psychological processes. *American Psychologist* 26:867–76.

Coleman, J. S., et al. 1966. *Equality of educational opportunity.* Washington, D.C.: U.S. Government Printing Office.

Day, R. To appear. Patterns of variation in the use of tense, aspect, and diathesis in the Hawaiian Creole continuum. University of Hawaii dissertation in progress.

Deutsch, Martin, and associates. 1967. *The disadvantaged child.* New York: Basic Books.

Deutsch, Martin; Katz, Irwin; and Jensen, Arthur. 1968. eds. *Social class, race, and psychological development*. New York: Holt, Rinehart and Winston.

Dillard, J. L. 1970. The creolist and the study of nonstandard Negro dialect of the United States. In *Pidginization and creolization of languages*, ed. D. Hymes. London: Cambridge University Press.

Dollard, John. 1939. The dozens: the dialect of insult. *American Image* 1:3–24.

Entwisle, Dorris R., and Greenberger, Ellen. 1969. Racial differences in the language of grade school children. *Sociology of Education* 42: no. 3 (summer).

Fasold, Ralph. 1969. Tense and the form *be* in Black English. *Language* 45:763–76.

Fillmore, Charles J. 1967. On the syntax of preverbs. *Glossa* 1:91–125.

Fries, C. C., and Pike, K. 1949. Co-existent phonemic systems. *Language* 75:25–29.

Gans, Herbert. 1962. *The urban villagers*. New York: The Free Press.

Garfinckel, H. 1967. *Studies in ethnomethodology*. Englewood Cliffs, N.J.: Prentice-Hall.

Garvey, Catherine, and McFarlane, Paul T. 1968. *A preliminary study of standard English speech patterns in the Baltimore City public schools*. Report no. 16. Baltimore: Johns Hopkins University.

Gauchat, Louis. 1905. *L'unité phonétique dans le patois d'une commune*. Halle: Max Niemeyer.

Ginsburg, Herbert. 1971. *The myth of the deprived child*. Englewood Cliffs, N.J.: Prentice-Hall.

Glaser, Daniel; Lander, Bernard; and Abbott, William. 1971. Opiate-addicted and non-addicted siblings in a slum area. *Social Problems* 18:510–21.

Grant, William, and Dixon, J. M. 1921. *Manual of modern Scots*. London: Cambridge University Press.

Gumperz, John. 1964. Linguistic and social interaction in two communities. In *The ethnography of communication*, eds. J. Gumperz and D. Hymes. Special publication. *American Anthropologist* 66 (no. 6, part 2):137–53.

———. 1971. *Language in social groups*. Palo Alto, Calif.: Stanford University Press.

Harris, Zellig S. 1963. *Discourse Analysis Reprints*. The Hague: Mouton.

Heber, R.; Dever, R.; and Conry, J. 1968. The influence of environmental and genetic variables on intellectual development. In *Behavioral research in mental retardation*, eds. J. H. Prehm, L. A. Hamerlynck, and J. E. Crossom. Eugene, Oregon: University of Oregon Press.

Henrie, Samuel N., Jr. 1969. A study of verb phrases used by five-year-old non-standard Negro English speaking children. Unpublished University of California (Berkeley) dissertation.

Homans, George. 1955. *The human group*. New York: Harcourt, Brace and Company, Inc.

House, Arthur S. 1961. On vowel duration in English. *Journal of the Acoustical Society of America* 33:1174–78.

Hymes, Dell. 1962. The ethnography of speaking. In *Anthropology and human behavior*, pp. 13–53. Washington, D.C.: The Anthropological Society of Washington. Reprinted in *Readings in the sociology of language*, ed. Joshua Fishman. The Hague: Mouton, 1968.

Jensen, Arthur. 1969. How much can we boost IQ and scholastic achievement? *Harvard Educational Review:* no. 39.

Jespersen, O. 1924. *Philosophy of grammar*. London: Allen and Unwin.

Karttunen, Lauri. 1971. Some observations of factivity. *Papers in Linguistics* 4:55–70.

Keenan, Edward. 1971. Quantifier structures in English. *Foundations of Linguistics* 7:255–84.

Kiparsky, Paul, and Kiparsky, Carol. 1970. Fact. In *Progress in linguistics*, eds. M. Bierwisch and K. Heidolph, pp. 143–73. The Hague: Mouton.

Klima, Edward S. 1964. Negation in English. In *The structure of language: readings in the philosophy of language*, eds. J. A. Fodor and J. J. Katz. Englewood Cliffs, N.J.: Prentice-Hall.

Kochman, Thomas. 1970. Towards an ethnography of black speech behavior. In *Afro-American anthology*, eds. Norman E. Whitten, Jr. and John F. Szwed. New York: Free Press.

Kökeritz, H. 1953. *Shakespeare's pronunciation*. New Haven, Conn.: Yale University Press.

Kurath, Hans. 1949. *Word geography of the eastern United States*. Ann Arbor, Mich.: University of Michigan Press.

Labov, Teresa. 1969. When is the Jets? Social ambiguity in peer terminology. Unpublished Columbia University Master's essay.

Labov, William. 1964. Stages in the acquisition of standard English. In *Social dialects and language learning*, ed. Roger Shuy, pp. 77–103. Champaign, Ill.: National Council of Teachers of English.

———. 1966a. *The social stratification of English in New York City*. Washington, D.C.: Center for Applied Linguistics.

———. 1966b. The linguistic variable as a structural unit. *Washington Linguistics Review* 3:4–22.

———. 1969. Contraction, Deletion, and Inherent Variability of The English Copula. *Language* 45, No. 4 (Dec. 1969): 715–62.

———. 1971a. The place of linguistic research in American society. In *Linguistics in the 1970's*, pp. 41–70. Washington, D.C.: Center for Applied Linguistics. To be published by the Smithsonian Institution.

———. 1971b. On the adequacy of natural languages I: the development of tense. Mimeographed.

———. 1971c. The reading of the -ed suffix. In *Basic studies on reading*, eds. H. Levin and J. Williams. New York: Basic Books.

———. 1972a. *Sociolinguistic Patterns*. Philadelphia: University of Pennsylvania Press.

———. 1972b. The internal evolution of linguistic rules. In *Historical linguistics and generative theory*, eds. R. Stockwell and R. Macaulay. Bloomington, Ind.: Indiana University Press.

———. 1972c. Methodology. In *A survey of linguistic science*, ed. William Dingwall. College Park, Md.: University of Maryland.

———. 1972d. Where does grammar stop? In *Georgetown Monographs in Languages and Linguistics* No. 25, ed. R. Shuy.

Labov, William; Cohen, Paul; and Robins, Clarence. 1965. *A preliminary study of the structure of English used by Negro and Puerto Rican speakers in New York City*. Co-operative Research Project 3091. Washington, D.C.: Office of Education.

Labov, William; Cohen, Paul; Robins, Clarence; and Lewis, John. 1968. *A study of the non-standard English of Negro and Puerto Rican speakers in New York City*. Report on Co-operative Research Project 3288. New York: Columbia University.

Labov, William, and Waletzky, Joshua. 1967. Narrative analysis. In *Essays on the verbal and visual arts,* ed. June Helm, pp. 12–44. Seattle: University of Washington Press.

Labov, W.; Yaeger, M.; and Steiner, R. 1972. *A quantitative study of sound changes in progress.* Final report on National Science Foundation contract NSF-3287. Philadelphia, Pa.: U.S. Regional Survey, 204 N. 35th St., Philadelphia 19104.

Laffal, Julius. 1965. *Pathological and normal language.* New York: Atherton Press.

Lakoff, George. 1970. *Linguistics and natural logic.* Ann Arbor: University of Michigan Press.

Lakoff, Robin. 1969. Some reasons why there can't be any *some-any* rule. *Language* 45:608–15.

Langacker, R. 1969. On pronominalization and the chain of command. In *Modern studies in English,* eds. S. Schane and D. Reibel. Englewood Cliffs, N.J.: Prentice-Hall.

Legum, Stanley; Pfaff, Carol; Tinnie, Gene; and Nicholas, Michael. 1971. *The speech of young black children in Los Angeles.* Technical report no. 33 (Sept.). Los Angeles: Southwestern Regional Laboratory.

Levine, Lewis, and Crockett, H. J., Jr. 1966. Speech variation in a Piedmont community: *postvocalic r.* In *Explorations in sociolinguistics,* ed. S. Lieberson. Bloomington: Indiana University Research Center for the Language Sciences. Reprinted as publication 44 by *International Journal of American Linguistics,* 1966.

Loban, Walter. 1963. *The language of elementary school children.* Research Monograph no. 1. Champaign, Ill.: National Council of Teachers of English.

———. 1966. *Language ability, grades seven, eight, and nine.* Washington, D.C.: U.S. Government Printing Office.

Loflin, Marvin. 1967a. A note on the deep structure of English in Washington, D.C. *Glossa* 1:1.

———. 1967b. On the structure of the verb in a dialect of American Negro English. Washington, D.C.: Center for Applied Linguistics. Mimeographed.

Loman, Bengt. 1967. *Conversations in a Negro American dialect.* Washington, D.C.: Center for Applied Linguistics.

Miller, Walter B. 1958. Lower class culture as a generating milieu of juvenile delinquency. *The Journal of Social Issues* 14:5–19.

Mitchell-Kernan, Claudia. 1969. *Language behavior in a black urban community.* Working paper no. 23. Berkeley, Calif.: Language Behavior Research Laboratory.

Pavenstedt, Eleanor, ed. 1967. *The drifters: children of disorganized lower-class families.* Boston: Little, Brown.

Plumer, Davenport. 1970. A summary of environmentalist views and some educational implications. In *Language and poverty,* ed. F. Williams. Chicago: Markham.

Postal, Paul. 1968. Cross-over phenomena. In *Specification and utilization of a transformational grammar.* Scientific report no. 3. Yorktown Heights, N.Y.: IBM.

Raubicheck, Letitia; Davis, Estelle; and Carll, Adele L. 1940. *Voice and speech problems.* Rev. ed. New York: Prentice-Hall.

Reichenbach, Hans. 1947. *Elements of symbolic logic.* New York: Macmillan.

Ross, John R. 1967. Constraints on variables in syntax. Unpublished M.I.T. dissertation.

Rosenbaum, Peter. 1968. *Grammar II.* Yorktown Heights, N.Y.: IBM.

Rosenthal, R., and Jacobson, Lenore. 1968. *Pygmalion in the classroom.* New York: Holt, Rinehart and Winston.

Sacks, Harvey. 1969. The search for help. In *Studies in social interaction,* ed. D. Sudnow. New York: Free Press.

Savin, Harris. 1971. Every any means every. To appear in *Proceedings of the conference on current problems in psycholinguistics,* eds. J. Mehler and A. Bresson. Paris: Centre Nationale de la Recherche Scientifique.

Schegloff, E. 1969. Notes on a conversational practice: formulating place. In *Studies in social interaction,* ed. D. Sudnow. New York: Free Press.

Shuy, Roger; Baratz, Joan; and Wolfram, Walter. 1969. *Sociolinguistic factors in speech identification.* Washington, D.C.: Center for Applied Linguistics.

Shuy, Roger; Wolfram, Walter; and Riley, William K. 1967. *A study of social dialects in Detroit.* Report on project 6-1347. Washington, D.C.: Office of Education.

Sivertsen, E. 1960. *Cockney phonology*. New York: Humanities Press.

Solomon, Denis. 1966. The system of predication in the speech of Trinidad: a quantitative study of de-creolization. Unpublished Columbia University dissertation.

Stewart, William. 1966. Social dialect. In *Research planning conference on language development in disadvantaged children*. New York: Yeshiva University.

―――. 1968. Continuity and change in American Negro dialects. *Florida Foreign Language Reporter* 6:1.3 ff.

―――. 1970. Toward a history of Negro dialect. In *Language and poverty*, ed. Frederick Williams. Chicago: Markham.

Stockwell, Robert; Schachter, Paul; and Partee, Barbara Hall. 1968. *Integration of transformational theories of English syntax*. Los Angeles: University of California.

Swett, Daniel. 1966. Cross-cultural communications in the courtroom: applied linguistics in a murder trial. San Francisco: San Francisco State College. Mimeographed.

Torrey, Jane. 1972. *The Language of Black Children in the Early Grades*. New London, Conn: Department of Psychology, Connecticut College.

Trudgill, P. J. 1971. The social differentiation of English in Norwich. Unpublished Edinburgh University dissertation.

Weinreich, Uriel. 1966. Explorations in semantic theory. In *Current trends in linguistics*, vol. 3, ed. Thomas A. Sebeok. The Hague: Mouton.

Whiteman, Martin and Deutsch, Martin. 1968. Social disadvantage as related to intellective and language development. In *Social class, race, and psychological development*, eds. Deutsch, Katz, and Jensen. New York: Holt, Rinehart and Winston.

Whyte, William F. 1955. *Street corner society: the social structure of an Italian slum*. Enlarged ed. Chicago: University of Chicago Press.

Williams, Frederick. 1970. Language, attitude, and social change. In *Language and poverty*, ed. F. Williams. Chicago: Markham.

Wilmott, Peter. 1966. *Adolescent boys of East London*. London: Routledge and Kegan Paul.

Wolfram, Walt. 1969. *A sociolinguistic description of Detroit Negro speech*. Urban Language series, no. 5. Washington, D.C.: Center for Applied Linguistics.

Worthan, O. C. 1966. Negro culture in the Americas. Mimeographed.

Wyld, H. C. 1936. *A history of modern colloquial English.* 3rd ed. Oxford: Basil Blackwell.

Zwicky, Arnold, 1970. Auxiliary reduction in English. *Linguistic Inquiry* 1:323–336.

INDEX

Aces (black peer group): phonological patterns compared, 264–71; *sounding* session, 317; mentioned, xx, 45, 243, 262

Adjectives: and *any,* 163

Adverbs: verb forms as, 59; negative, 60; temporal, 164

Age: and vernacular usage, 52, 257–58, 280; and BEV grammar, 83, 284–85; effect on phonological conditioning, 105n; and peer-group membership, 246; and lower-class culture, 257–58; style shifting, 284–85; and narrative style, 386, 393–96

ain't, 284

am, 70n. *See also* Copula; *I'm*

any: in negative constructions, 132, 133–35, 142, 167–76, 270; in positive sentences, 157–67

"Apparent time," 258n

Appositive, double, 388

are: in BEV, 52, 71–72, 119–20. *See also* Copula; Verb, auxiliary

as, 80

be: in BEV, 48–55, 271; invariant form, 51–53, 284; contraction and deletion rules, 267–68. *See also* Copula

been, 53–55

Bereiter, Carl: on language of black children, 204–5; confuses logic and explicitness, 223–25

Bernstein, Basil: on language of black children, 204; code concept, 213, 222

better, 56

"Black English" (term): criticized, xiii, 288–89; existence of, 6–7, 10

"Black English vernacular" (term): defined, xiii–xiv; justification for use, 289

Black English vernacular (BEV): sources of data, xviii–xxiii, 66; study of, xviii, 10–11, 38, 287, 289–90; compared with white dialects, 8–9, 11–12, 38–44; his-torical origins, 8, 51, 70, 131n; distinct dialect of English, 9, 36–38, 61, 63–64, 130–31, 193–94, 238; phonological patterns, 13–14; in Philadelphia, 14, 53, 54, 184–87, 194, 264, 284; in Chicago, 21n, 185; in New York City, 21n, 36, 53, 128, 185, 284; compared with Standard English, 23, 60–63, 225, 238; *r* in, 38–44; uniformity throughout urban centers of US, 65, 283–84; and age of speaker, 83, 284; in Detroit, 120n, 127–28, 183–84, 284; in Los Angeles, 128, 185, 264, 284; in San Francisco, 128, 284; in Cleveland, 185; verbal skills, 212–13; effective vehicle for logic, 215–16, 225; and educational problems in inner city, 241; peer-group influence on, 276; attitude of black middle class to, 288–89; narrative style in, 355–59. *See also* Peer groups

Black nationalism, 244–45

Can: double modal usage, 58–59; as adverb, 59

Capping. See Sounding

Carelessness: no explanation of dialect difference, 10

Child: and negation, 148; linguistic knowledge, 204–5, 393; theory of cultural deprivation, 204–5; interview techniques for, 206–13; verbal capacities, 221; logic, 229; language development, 231–32. *See also* Deprivation, verbal; Education

Chomsky, Noam: stress rules, 109, 127; on grammaticality, 221n. *See also* Grammar, generative

Chopping. See Sounding

Class, socioeconomic: regional dialect may become marker of, 9–10; lower class/working class distinction, 203; middle-class verbal habits, 204–5,